14.90

To Maria.
With personal regards
B A Santarawia
24. 11. 86.

# Against the Tide

# SANTAMARIA

## Against the Tide

MELBOURNE
OXFORD UNIVERSITY PRESS
OXFORD WELLINGTON NEW YORK

*Oxford University Press*

LONDON GLASGOW NEW YORK TORONTO
DELHI BOMBAY CALCUTTA MADRAS KARACHI
KUALA LUMPUR SINGAPORE HONG KONG TOKYO
NAIROBI DAR ES SALAAM CAPE TOWN
MELBOURNE AUCKLAND
*and associate companies in*
BEIRUT BERLIN IBADAN MEXICO CITY

*First published 1981*
*Reprinted in paperback with corrections 1981*

NATIONAL LIBRARY OF AUSTRALIA CATALOGUING IN
PUBLICATION DATA

Santamaria, Bartholomew Augustine, 1915—
 Against the Tide

 Index
 ISBN 0 19 550593 X (casebound)
 ISBN 0 19 554346 7 (paperback)

 1. Santamaria, Bartholomew Augustine, 1915—.
 2. Politicians—Australia—Biography. I. Title.

324.2'092'4

DESIGNED BY GUY MIRABELLA
TYPESET AND PRINTED IN AUSTRALIA AT GRIFFIN PRESS LIMITED, ADELAIDE
PUBLISHED BY OXFORD UNIVERSITY PRESS, 7 BOWEN CRESCENT MELBOURNE

*For Helen*

# Foreword

When I visited Australia some twenty-five years ago it was in the midst of the tumultuous events associated with the Labor split of the 1950s. The name of Santamaria, previously unknown, was engulfed in controversy. Finding myself in Melbourne, I sought him out, and from the moment of our meeting he became a friend; someone of inexhaustible interest, whose company was always invigorating, and of whom I always thought with affection and admiration.

After that first encounter he took me to meet his hero and mentor, Archbishop Mannix, then approaching his hundredth year. I remember him vividly; despite his great age, very much alive, like some seasoned old tree obstinately going on, year by year, budding and producing green shoots and leaves on its gnarled branches. The love and trust between the two men, one nearly at the end of his days and the other shaping up to the world, was both appealing and beautiful.

The running theme of his autobiography revolves around the decision made by Santamaria quite early in his life to devote himself wholly to organizing and directing a counter-force to the Marxist materialism and atheism he saw as eroding the whole structure of Christendom, or, as we now call it in its final decrepitude, Western Civilization. This involved specifically confronting the growing influence of Communists and Communism in the Australian trade unions, sometimes overtly and sometimes clandestinely exercised. From Santamaria's position, the only possible counter-force available for such a purpose was the Catholic Church and the Christian faith of which it was the custodian. Naturally, his close relationship with Archbishop Mannix fostered the undertaking: nevertheless, in the circumstances of the twentieth century, he was bound to enlist as a Christian soldier, and to find himself in the forefront of the battle.

The manner in which Santamaria succeeded in dislodging actual and pseudo-communists from certain key trade union positions; and later, in ensuring enough representation for the Democratic Labor

Party to prevent Dr Evatt, the leader of the Australian Labor Party, from ever being in a position to form a government, is part of Australian political history. For students in this field his auto-biography will henceforth be required reading.

As it happens I had occasion to meet with Dr Evatt once or twice when the battle was on, and found him in an altogether enraged state of mind. Any mention of Santamaria's name was liable, as I discovered, to produce an explosion.

In the context of Australian politics the two men, so different in every way, represented a worldwide conflict; and though all my sympathies were with Santamaria, Evatt's very vulnerability and distractedness drew one to him as to a sort of New South Wales King Lear. (In the event, I benefited from the inordinate pride generated when power-maniacs like King Lear and Evatt feel themselves to be frustrated. Talking with him on television, I mentioned that the Chinese Communists he so admired seemed not to want Western journalists visiting their country, since my application for a visa to go there had not even been acknowledged. He angrily denied the imputation, and said that he would get me a visa, which in fact he did. When I arrived in Hong Kong one was awaiting me there.) Subsequently, I heard he had been made a judge. It is one of the intimations of an endearing tendency among Australians to hold law and order in derision that in Australia dementia in politicians is often rewarded with a seat on the Bench.

In his autobiography Santamaria describes with great clarity and coolness the hopes and disappointments, the successes and failures of his political campaigning, which inevitably resolved itself into an exercise, fascinating and instructive to follow, in the everlasting dilemma as to what is due to Caesar and what to God. In the event, his most formidable adversaries proved to be not, as might have been supposed, the professed Communists and their fellow-travelling affiliates and liberal dupes, but the ecclesiastical hierarchy themselves—with the exception of Archbishop Mannix and some others—on whose behalf Santamaria was ostensibly operating.

His feelings are kept well under control in this narrative but the irony he found in the situation could be expressed in private conversation. I recall one occasion on a later visit to Australia when I had been telling him about the circumstances in which I resigned the rectorship of Edinburgh University over the insistence of the elected officers of the Student Union that I should support their demand for the free distribution of contraceptives by the university medical unit. 'And who do you think was the first person to lambast me for this?', I asked him. Without a moment's hesitation he replied with a question, 'The Catholic chaplain?' When I asked him how he guessed this, he replied that his own experience made anything possible. Some future Gibbon tracing the decline and fall of

Western Civilization may well derive great amusement from the ix manner in which Church dignitaries turned a complacent eye on the destructive purposes of the Church's enemies, easily tolerating such absurdities as dialogue between Christians and Marxists with a view to future collaboration and liberation movements under Kremlin auspices, while implacably opposing efforts like Santamaria's to ensure that, in the counting of votes and the allotment of positions of authority, account should be taken of the rights and beliefs of those who profess the Christian faith.

My own experience, reinforced by the evidence of Santamaria's first chapters, was that these serious events were lived in an atmosphere greatly lightened by the intimacies of family living.

On all subsequent visits to Australia I managed one way or another to see Santamaria, and got to know his numerous and attractive family, some of whom, to my wife Kitty's and my own great delight, have visited us in Sussex. The Santamarias, indeed, provide an excellent illustration of how poor Italians arriving in Australia as aliens in their traditions, religious faith and temperament, can be absorbed and, through application and hard work, become in due course not just authentic Australians, but eminent in their different spheres and occupations.

All this is well conveyed in Santamaria's autobiography, without any attempt to over-dramatize the story, or any indulgence in megalo- or minimo-mania—opposites that, like self-indulgence and extreme asceticism, amount essentially to the same thing.

Everyone who has had the good fortune to get to know him, or who with seeing eyes surveys his life and career, cannot but recognize that he is a truly remarkable human being in his own right, who would have been seen as such if his family had gone westwards to the United States instead of eastwards to Australia, or, for that matter, if they had stayed in Italy. Chance brought him into contact with Archbishop Mannix. Yet, after all, was it chance? Hidden within his severely realistic temperament and mastery of Machiavellian strategy and tactics, there is a seer, someone who understands, and who, whatever his circumstances, would never have satisfied himself with any purely worldly achievement, whether in politics, scholarship, money-making or whatever.

There have been times when he found himself in a position of great strength. It would have been remarkable if he could not have asked for pretty well anything he wanted. He never did ask; his modest establishment in Melbourne remained unchanged. Nor has that home been irretrievably geared to seriousness. I remember arriving there once, and finding everyone glued to the television-screen. What momentous event, I wondered, was thus holding their attention? It turned out to be a football match, with the master of the house the most deeply absorbed.

x    What makes the writings and the company of Santamaria so invigorating is simply that he thinks and lives in terms of what is really happening in the world, and of what the happenings really signify, instead of being caught up in the fantasies that have always existed, but that in our time have been made outward and visible as never before; given a voice and an image by the media, and even a name—the consensus. Today, Don Quixote would not need to go on his travels; just sitting in front of his television screen, he could go into battle with windmills and set the galley-slaves free. Nor would he need a Sancho Panza; there are plenty available on the campuses, in the pulpits and the television studios.

Because of its bizarre circumstances, the fantasies are particularly in evidence in Australia; so much so that it has sometimes occurred to me that perhaps the country owes its very existence to God's having set it up to be His special theatre of the absurd, or, in Blake's idiom, theatre of fearful symmetry. How otherwise to account for a population roughly the same as that of Greater London, spread thinly round the coast of a huge, rich continent, congratulating themselves on having achieved zero growth? Or for Australians helping to chase away the Americans from their foothold in Southeast Asia, thereby ensuring that Australia is left defenceless amidst a thousand million Asians?

John Douglas Pringle has justly said of Santamaria, *à propos* a collection of his *Point of View* television broadcasts, that he possesses what is so rare among politicians, a 'hard mind' and a lucid, simple forceful style to express it. Such rare attributes are liable to be considered as intimations of authoritarian, if not out-and-out fascist, inclinations in our contemporary consensus world. Hence it has been possible to cast Santamaria in the role of a bogeyman in Australian politics. Rather, he has been a voice of sanity in a scene that has often drifted into confusion and farce and seemed set upon a disaster course. The primrose path to the Gulag Archipelago is paved with benign intentions, and resounds with cries of 'Fascist!' directed against all who point out the dangers of taking it. Santamaria, in any case, can stand on his record, as it is set forth in his autobiography, straightforwardly and unpretentiously.

I consider it a great honour to have been asked by the publishers to write an introduction to Santamaria's autobiography. It will be of deep interest to all who are concerned, or even curious, about what lies ahead for the peoples of the West, especially those who find themselves increasingly on their own in the Antipodes.

*Malcolm Muggeridge*

# Contents

CONTENTS

# Illustrations

# Acknowledgements

The author and publishers would like to thank the following for their permission to reproduce copyright material: *Age*, Melbourne, for the extracts from news reports of 10 and 16 September quoted on pp. 317-18; Angus & Robertson Publishers for permission to reproduce James McAuley's poem 'Nocturnal', quoted on p. 281; Australian Government Publishing Service and Department of Foreign Affairs for the extract from the Approved Defence Projects Act 1947, quoted on pp. 109-10; *Bulletin*, Sydney, for the extracts from the interview by Peter Samuel of Gordon Freeth, 22 August 1969, quoted on pp. 316-17; *Canberra Times* for the extract from a book review by Professor Hedley Bull, 25 April 1970, quoted on p. 302; Professor C. M. H. Clark for the extracts from his Notes for a Talk at Graduate Ceremony, 1974, quoted on pp. 37-8; the Rev. P. J. Duffy, SJ, for the extracts from Catholic Judgements on the Origins and Growth of the A.L.P. Dispute 1954-61, quoted on pp. 88-9, 157, 257 and 261; *Economist*, London, for the extract from a report by Barbara Ward, 7 March 1953, quoted on p. 301; Herald & Weekly Times Ltd for the extracts from C. Sharpley, *I was a Communist Leader*, Melbourne *Herald* publication, 1949, quoted on pp. 102 and 107, and from the *Argus* of 29 May 1939, quoted on pp. 41-2; Mr M. C. Hogan for the extracts from *The Catholic Campaign for State Aid*, 1978, quoted on pp. 265-7; Hughes Massie Ltd. and W. W. Norton & Co for the extracts from Dean Acheson, *Present at the Creation*, 1970, quoted on pp. 60-1; Jacaranda Wiley Ltd for the extracts from P. L. Reynolds, *The Democractic Labor Party*, quoted on pp. 249 and 253; Mr J. T. Kane for the extracts from Kane's Notes, quoted on pp. 189, 204-5 and 218-19; Mr Rupert Lockwood and the Australian Broadcasting Commission for the extracts from 'The Making of an Australian Communist', 1973, quoted on p. 63; Mr T. R. Luscombe for the extracts from *Builders and Crusaders*, 1967, quoted on pp. 48-9; Mrs Norma McAuley, care of Curtis Brown (Aust.) Pty Ltd, for permission to reproduce the following poems of James McAuley, 'Retreat', pp. 282-3, Untitled, pp. 285-6, and the extracts from his letters quoted on pp. 225-6, 274-6, 284, and those from his essay 'Reflections on Poznan', 1956, quoted on p. 279, and from the Newman College Lecture, 1958, quoted on p. 280; Mr Robert Murray and Longman Cheshire Pty Ltd for extracts from *The Split*, 1970, quoted on pp. 143, 145-6, 153, 157, 170 and 303; Mr Alan Reid for the extracts from the *Sun*, Sydney, 5 October 1954.

# Introduction

Autobiographical writing tends to be an essay in self-indulgence. It normally implies one of three things: either that the writer believes that the details of his life have some objective importance other than his own subjective interests, which is true only of a relative few; or that he believes that what he is writing is 'history'; or that it serves some purpose to show that he was generally right, whereas those he opposed or criticized were generally wrong. What follows is written from none of those viewpoints.

Since the Second World War, the central issue confronting Western men and women has been the survival of the philosophies, ideas and institutions which constitute the heart of Western civilization. In relation to that central issue, it is difficult to conceive that anything really important has happened in the remote Australian backwater; and impossible to suggest that a person who has occupied no public position has, in fact, seriously affected the result of anything. As for being right where others were wrong, the narrative reveals too many errors of judgement and mistakes in action. Nor does what is written make any pretence to being 'history'. It can be nothing more than a single historical source, expressing one individual's personal view of the events of a particular period. Together with all the other views, his may be worth considering by the professional historian writing the history of that particular epoch.

So why write at all? The explanation is twofold: the publisher's invitation and a strictly limited purpose. The limited purpose, to which the invitation opened the way, was to explain what lay behind a particular pattern of activity undertaken in Australia by a small group of men from the 1930s to the 1980s.

The members of this small group were possessed of a specific philosophy. It was an idea about man, the family, the economy, the trade union, Marxism, the nation. The idea ran against the fashionable current of the times. Hence the title. Almost everything which has been written about them has been written by those to whom their idea was repugnant. The popular judgement therefore has been generally negative.

I have tried to look at the same events from a different set of assumptions, which are important only because they were the assumptions of the men who acted. That does not prove that either their assumptions or their policies were right. It simply tells the other side of the story.

Not infrequently a well-known name appears in the following pages. I have no wish to delude anyone that these public figures were close associates. With one or two exceptions they were chance acquaintances with whom I had no particular intimacy.

If the flow of the narrative is interrupted, as it is, by frequent and occasionally too long quotations, it is because I have tried to show that while what was undertaken in action may or may not have been defective in judgement, it was not chosen without considerable thought and study.

I owe a debt of gratitude to the colleagues with whom I have worked over many years, who deserve the collective credit for any good which perchance may have been done. To none of them however do I owe the same debt as I owe to my wife and children. They do not intrude into the narrative, yet they were my one indispensable support. They share my philosophy, so they understand what I have tried to do, and why.

Of my colleagues, none has contributed more than my secretary, Mrs Dorothy Jensen. Having worked with me for thirty years she witnessed many of the events which are narrated, and survived the experience to type the manuscript and check the references. I am grateful to her and her helpers.

# PART I

## Foundations

# 1 At the Beginning

It was late in 1937, as I was about to conclude my Articles and before my admission to legal practice in Victoria, that I was asked by Archbishop Mannix to be one of the two members of the National Secretariat of Catholic Action which was to be inaugurated early in the New Year. I had turned 22 during the previous August. The invitation was totally unexpected. As an ordinary member of the Campion Society—a small study group organization made up mostly of Catholic university men—I had known that plans were proceeding for the formation of such a secretariat, to propagate similar group activities throughout the Church. I was not included in the discussions which preceded the formation of the Secretariat, since these discussions were the province of senior members of the society, Frank Maher, Murray McInerney and Kevin Kelly. They were all between five and ten years my senior, and were regarded by Campion Society members both as 'founding fathers' and policy-makers.

My own particular interest had been confined to the production of a small monthly, the *Catholic Worker*, which in a sense I had founded, and in relation to which I was responsible for a good deal of the writing, finance and distribution. I had expected that Frank Maher, the founder of the Campion Society, would be in charge of the new secretariat if and when it was formed, while the second place would go to another senior member. There was never any question about myself. I would go ahead, try to establish a legal practice, continue to edit the *Catholic Worker*, and continue as a member of the Campion Society.

Equally, when the invitation to consider appointment to the Secretariat came, I was under no illusions as to the real reason. I knew that other senior members of the Campion Society had refused the job, which was both temporary and uncertain, so that my position was that of first—and probably last—emergency.

4 Humanly speaking, it was foolish even to consider the Archbishop's invitation. No one who lived in the industrial environment of Brunswick, as I did, could overlook the disastrous consequences of the unemployment which had ravaged the suburb and finally extended to about a third of its population. In 1938 real recovery still seemed a long way off. To put aside a legal or public service career was to risk unemployment, if and when the Secretariat folded up, as I expected that it would. When I went to my father and told him, by way of consolation, that my initial invitation was only for two years, I expected a difficult discussion. For a person who could be strong and obstinate in opposition, he put up surprisingly little. Clearly it was not the work, which he did not understand, but the name of Dr Mannix which mattered. In a sense then, I took on the job with the National Secretariat, like so many other later decisions, not because I had any long-term view of the future, but because it seemed the right thing to do at the time. Perhaps the reason why it seemed so could be found in the influences which had shaped my mind over the first two decades of my life.

The major influences which determine the course of one's human existence are always questionable. Human beings are probably the very worst witnesses about themselves. For the little that personal evaluations are worth in these matters, the major influences on my own life were the following: pre-eminently, my parents' family and the social background from which they came; the religion in which I was raised; the education which I received, whether at Christian Brothers' schools, at Melbourne University, and, during my University years, in the Campion Society. Finally, there was that product of pure chance, my friendship with Archbishop Mannix, whom I believed, and still believe, to have been the greatest Australian of his time, and whose equal I never met inside or outside Australia.

My parents were characteristic members of the small Italian migrant community in Melbourne. Born in the Aeolian Islands north of Sicily, they had been part of the emigration which ultimately depopulated those islands, and which arose from no more spectacular cause than total poverty and backwardness. If the formation of a United Italy in 1870 had meant political and social progress for the upper middle class which had brought it about, the benefits of unity had not percolated to this obscure part of the Kingdom of the Two Sicilies.

Emigration from one's own country always involves great sacrifices, even if the reasons are compelling. My mother's was the greater sacrifice. My father's parents had preceded him to Australia, but my mother simply came out as a young girl to keep house for two brothers in the mining town of Maryborough (Victoria).

Altogether, my father had five years' formal education, my mother one single year. By extraordinarily hard work, probably beyond the capacity of most Australians then and now, my parents, whose own families were peasants and fishermen, had established themselves as small shopkeepers in the industrial suburb of Brunswick. Their overriding ambition was that their children should be spared their own deprivations. The road was through education, primary and secondary school, to be followed by university; but the latter only if they could win their own way through scholarships, since their own financial resources were extremely strained.

The work of a fruit shop was extremely hard. The shop would open at 7 a.m., when my father returned from market, which, three days a week, meant rising at 2 a.m. It would close at 11 p.m., after the emptying picture theatre, a little way up the road, had sent a few home-going customers into the shop. My mother cared for the family. In the afternoons, she would mind the shop for a couple of hours while my father snatched some sleep, to allow him to make next morning's early rise. As the eldest son, I was expected to take my daily turn in the shop. This went on for years, in fact, until well after I began my studies at Melbourne University.

It was then said, in highly derogatory terms, that 'the dagoes lived on the smell of an oil rag'. My mother's carefully handmade spaghetti, each Sunday and occasionally during the week, was probably more nutritious, and certainly much more palatable than fish and chips, and mince, which were all that only too many Brunswick families of that day were able to afford, because of the general poverty. But we learnt to take the appellation 'dagoes' and not to challenge the superiority of our White Anglo-Saxon, Protestant (or Catholic) tormentors. There were too many of them.

Despite this general attitude, my parents seemed to be greatly esteemed as individuals among all those who knew them, while I found no difficulty in making good friends at St Ambrose's Christian Brothers' Primary School.

I was fortunate enough to have four brothers and one sister who—with the exception of one brother who died in December 1974—have remained a close and intimately knit family to the present day. Three of my brothers ultimately went into business. A fourth is director of the Department of Community Medicine at St Vincent's Hospital, Melbourne. My sister, who I suspect could 'lose' us all in academic ability, won the Final Exhibition in Germanic Languages at Melbourne University.

Even after the children married, they continued to enjoy some of the advantages of the Italian extended family. The reason was that this was the way we were brought up. My mother's parents lived in Italy, but my father's were in Australia and lived about a mile away. They were as much part of our lives as if they lived in the same house. It was the same for one uncle and two aunts.

6    My grandfather was a friendly if venerable figure to whom I generally fled in the not-infrequent moments of tribulation at the hands of my father, if my mother's protecting figure was elsewhere. He wore a large moustache, and in his youth, in the latter part of the last century, had been a sailor on a small tramp steamer in the Mediterranean. One of the treasured relics of his nautical experience was a Turkish scimitar, which he claimed to have wrested from a Cossack in Odessa. Since he never explained how a Cossack owned a Turkish scimitar, and since it seemed improbable that a rather wizened five foot four could have overcome any but the most under-sized Cossack, the claim was treated with permanent derision, particularly by his two daughters.

In the very hard Brunswick of the Depression period, we survived, when so many of the parents of my school associates lost everything they had. We survived because of the incredibly hard work of our parents, and because, although family arguments were legion and conducted with a good deal of declamatory vigour, in a manner familiar to those acquainted with Italian opera, it was a matter of 'one for all, and all for one'. Each one of us knew it, and each one of us relied on it.

Our religion was Catholic—but Catholic in the Italian way. My mother taught us our prayers from infancy. Since there was neither radio nor television to fill the empty spaces of the mind, she filled them instead with the legends of her people, some, like the traditional fairy story, completely secular, some religious, but all opening up the imagination as formal school education opened up the intellect.

But there was never any doubt in her mind, and she permitted none in ours, as to what was fairy story and what was religion. They did not shade imperceptibly into each other so that one would never be sure as to where fables ended and religion began. She went to Mass each Sunday and, as we became old enough, took us with her. In this my father was also characteristically Italian. He took his Catholicism seriously, but Sunday Mass—well, that was something different. To be fair, he had a good excuse, if not altogether a good reason. The cleaning up of the stable, the care of the horse and cart, the packing of the fruit-cases—if these tasks were not carried out on Sunday, it would be difficult to work out when they could be done. We understood these necessities, since unlike many of my school friends during the Depression, we were never permitted to go hungry; even when we wished that he would come to Mass with the rest of the family.

As far as I remember, he suddenly decided to go to Sunday Mass in about 1931, and I do not recall his ever being absent after that time. It was about then that an impressive young Irish curate, Fr Patrick Gleeson, was stationed at St Ambrose's. He had a magnificent bass voice, and his rich Irish tones would reverberate through a very large church long before the day of the microphone.

One of the products of the Depression in Brunswick was the creation of a local branch of the Communist Party. Opposite St Ambrose's Church, there was the Mechanics' Institute, with its diminutive strip of lawn which used to serve as a tiny Hyde Park for public meetings. It was only a stone's throw from our shop, so that not infrequently I listened to speakers of the Central Unemployed Committee, most of whom I was later to discover were Party members.

Father Gleeson began a series of Sunday sermons on Marxism, of which he was an extremely competent student. He was determined to be fair to the ideology against which he was warning his flock. Since the few local Party members whom I knew seemed as often as not to be Catholics, I wondered occasionally whether his sermons were not more effective in explaining Marxist theories than whatever Party schools existed. But I suppose that the Catholics in the Party would not be those who went to Mass. As for my father, he was loud in his praise of the abilities of the new curate who, he hoped, would cure his closest Italian friend, Tony Lanassa, of his professed Socialism. Since nobody could drag Tony within a hundred yards of a church, it was difficult to see how, short of a miracle, this could be achieved.

When Tony finally had a son, his wife insisted that the baby should be baptized which, to the child's father, was the ultimate blasphemy against the sacred tenets of Marxism. He compromised by insisting that my father should be the boy's godfather, and then— a safe distance away from his wife—he further insisted that the child's name should be Francis Marx. My father knew what the parish priest's response to this proposal would be. So he double-crossed his friend, who would come no nearer the baptismal font than the back porch of the Church, by affixing on the beleagured child the name Francis Mark. This was close enough to deceive the father, and orthodox enough to please both mother and parish priest.

I was sent to school when I was a little more than four years of age, simply because there was practically no playing room around the shop, while Sydney Road was too busy and dangerous to encourage playing on the streets. This early beginning gave me a couple of years' lead over my contemporaries in the various primary classes, a very useful margin if some important decision as to one's future had to be made.

My six years at St Ambrose's Boys Primary School introduced me to the Christian Brothers. I will not say that it was always a pleasant experience, since some of the Brothers carried discipline to excess, or so it seemed to one who often deserved and received it. There were also those Brothers whose religious and theological formation seemed somewhat narrow and even Jansenist. In more recent times, these have become the butt of ex-Catholic writers seeking to establish themselves in various poor man's versions of James Joyce's *Portrait of the Artist as a Young Man*, simply substituting the Brothers for Joyce's Jesuits. Apart from observing that all of the accounts the writers give of their falls from grace are not as *bona fide* as they might be, and that their personal habits of life might serve to explain their defection from Catholicism, with or without the Christian Brothers, it is extremely easy to make a case against any institution by arguing from the exception and the abuse.

Having experienced both the occasional excesses and the rigidities, particularly in my earlier years at St Ambrose's, I can only say that my experience of the Christian Brothers was quite different.

They imparted a level of secular learning which on the record of results in public examinations was second to none. Through this service, they opened the way to a somewhat better position in society to thousands of children of working-class families who otherwise would have had no alternative but to remain hewers of wood and drawers of water in the society into which they were born, on the bottom rung of the ladder.

More important by far, they inculcated a set of religious and moral values which sustained generations in their belief as Christians. To their lasting credit, they insisted that faith must be validated by reason, placing a high premium on the intellectual foundations of both religion and morality.

After St Ambrose's, I went to St Joseph's, North Melbourne, and then to St Kevin's, East Melbourne. St Kevin's College was naturally critical to my development as an adult, since it was in those years a central matriculation college preparing its students specifically for the universities, the professions and the public service. It had been opened in 1918, in the same year as Newman College, and indeed as part of the same plan.

Dr Mannix was always opposed to the concept of a specifically Catholic university of the type well-known in Europe and the United States. Newman's failure to establish a Catholic university in Ireland had convinced Archbishop Mannix that such an institution would not only add to the 'ghetto' existence of Irish Catholics in Australia, but that inevitably, for lack of resources, it would be of low academic quality as well. A Catholic university college, modelled on the several Protestant denominational colleges established around Melbourne University, was his solution to the problem. Hence Newman College. Recognizing that there were few Catholic religious teachers capable of establishing and maintaining a suitable pre-university standard, and conscious of the increasing competition which would come from the State secondary system after its reformation by Frank Tate, as Director of Education, Archbishop Mannix persuaded the Christian Brothers to concentrate their best manpower in this pre-university college in East Melbourne. Materially poor, St Kevin's was to gain an enviable academic reputation, the number of government university scholarships and free places which it won annually being the equal of the best of the public schools, and very much higher than the general average.

No one could therefore complain at the level of purely academic education. Hence there was nothing unique in the fact that, like so many other St Kevin's students who had preceded me, I should win a Senior Government Scholarship at the end of 1930. The two years' educational advantage meant that I was only a few months over fifteen years when this happened. Hence I had to stay back at St Kevin's for what was a second matriculation year before I could enrol at Melbourne University at the beginning of 1932.

Within the school, there was an enviable spirit of camaraderie, all the more remarkable since we had all come from different Brothers' Colleges, with a high level of sporting rivalry between them, and since we met for the first time at St Kevin's only for the last two or three years of school education. There were two to a desk. My last desk-colleague, so to speak, was Jim McClelland, who was to become Minister for Labour in the Whitlam Government. Even as a schoolboy he showed the outstanding intellectual capacity which developed further in his professional and political life. As adults, our philosophical choices were as different as our political careers.*

What I owed primarily to St Kevin's was not the opportunity to win the scholarship which took me to Melbourne University, which would otherwise have been beyond the financial possibilities of the family. It was that when, as a result of the sufferings which the Depression inflicted on so many of our friends in Brunswick, I felt serious religious doubts for the first time, the religious training imparted by the Christian Brothers gave me the resources to handle my problem, not for ever, but at least for the time being.

Books, on their own, do not answer these problems. If the daily life of our teachers had not been in harmony with the books which they prescribed, their religious teaching would have meant little.

---

* Much later in life, I met him as an able and prosperous Sydney lawyer, when he was acting for Laurie Short, in the latter's case against Ernie Thornton, Communist boss of the Ironworkers' Federation. McClelland was thus closely associated with John Kerr, whom he had briefed to act for Short. It was through McClelland that I met the future Governor-General.

On this occasion, and until the Labor split of 1955, McClelland and I were on the same side, that of the Industrial Groups. In the meantime he had been a member of the University Labor Club and then, as I understand it, a member of a Trotskyite group. In my simplicity, I regarded the fact that we were once again on the same side as a mark of the somewhat ironic workings of Providence. Unfortunately, after the Labor split, we diverged once again.

10

The type of Catholic 'apologetics' which was the strength of religious teaching at St Kevin's prepared my mind for John Henry Newman and later C. S. Lewis, who both provided confirmation of my religious beliefs. To the professional philosopher, Newman and C. S. Lewis may appear no more than popularizers of other men's ideas. Yet I do not despise the popularizer, since it seems that there are few new objections to religious belief. What one normally encounters are new formulations of old objections—except, of course, for those contemporary philosophic systems which, in complete self-contradiction, pretend to prove the uselessness of reason as a mechanism in the search for truth.

Aquinas's proof for the existence of God from contingency, which underlay our 'apologetics', seems to me not coercive but based on a high level of probability, in terms of common-sense in the basic meaning of that word, the 'sense' of ordinary men and women. In the last analysis, the 'apologetics' we absorbed could not lift religion above dependence on an act of faith, but an act of faith sustained by, and consonant with, reason; not an act of faith standing, as it were, unsupported or contrary to reason. Many of the ordinary judgements made by human beings are no more. Of course, the physical scientists, with their black holes, their quasars and what have you, may one day disprove it all. They have not done so yet, nor do I see how they can.

Sheehan's *Apologetics and Christian Doctrine* provided me, as a schoolboy at matriculation standard, with the rational justification for my act of faith in Catholic Christianity. When I examine what so many Catholic students at the same level are offered today, I stand appalled not merely at the intellectual poverty of the offering, but at the ease with which so many so-called teachers of religion dismiss the intellect as a convincing support for religious belief in favour of highly subjective 'religious experience'. I wonder how students believe anything at all: for that which reason does not sustain rests on most unsubstantial foundations when confronted with the challenges of the 'new morality' which, as someone remarked, is only the old immorality writ large.

Religion apart, I am particularly grateful to St Kevin's for giving its pupils both the encouragement and the means to express themselves on whatever they cared to write about. The school had two journals—called 'journals', although they were never printed, but simply read out one afternoon a fortnight during second term. They were the 'Central Critic' and the 'Glendalough Chronicle'. God knows what boredom must have been endured by those students who did not have either literary or social or political interests, and who therefore while contributing to neither, nevertheless had to listen. In my second year matriculation, I was editor of the latter, while the editorship of the 'Central Critic' went to my friend Charles

Sweeney, later to become a judge of the Arbitration Court and now Federal Judge in Bankruptcy.

It was the period of the Depression and of the Premier's Plan. Charles Sweeney was a strong supporter of Joseph Lyons, who had left the Labor Party to lead the United Australia Party, which had replaced the Nationalists as the conservative political party. I was a Labor supporter, emotionally drawn to Prime Minister James Scullin, and intellectually to the financial ideas of Federal Labor Treasurer E. G. Theodore, which in retrospect appear to have been founded on a rudimentary Keynesianism.

The battle between the two journals reached such a level of dialectical bitterness—while the editors remained perfectly friendly—that Brother Duffy, who was in charge of these activities, warned both of us to tone things down. To no avail. Charles Sweeney felt that he had produced a journalistic 'king-hit' when he published an editorial heavily laden with statistics, very much in the style of Professor Giblin, who was then writing for the Melbourne *Herald*. He headed it: 'Figures Can't Lie'. He was studying economics, a discipline from which, for good reason, I had steered clear. I thought it was very unfair of him to clobber me with statistics. So I replied in an editorial headed: 'But Liars Can Figure'. This was too much for Brother Duffy, who thereupon suspended the journals for the rest of the year. He took me aside and said to me: 'You have an execrable English style, but unfortunately for you, a good journalistic style. It will get you into a lot of trouble'.

Melbourne University in the early thirties was an exhilarating experience for one who signed the roll when only a few months over 16. With approximately 3,000 students, its grounds, combined with those of the surrounding colleges, were wide and green. Wilson Hall was a magnificent essay in Gothic. A strongly knit circle of friends and acquaintances from other schools, many of them Jewish, coming from Melbourne High, also included Chester Wilmot, later to win fame as a war correspondent. He seemed to have to wrestle with an ancestral bigotry before we became friends. There was Hugh Brodie, a fine poet, who published little before he was killed while serving in the RAAF. My choice for an Arts degree before I began Law was the School of History and Political Science. History introduced me to Professor Ernest Scott, whose intellectual forbears seemed to have been Macauley, Trevelyan and the Whigs, from whom he had absorbed an ingrained distrust of Catholicism. Yet he was scrupulously fair and friendly, and I recall his memory with affection.

Political Science was in the hands of a senior lecturer (later Professor) William Macmahon Ball. I had at least two reasons for gratitude to my Political Science lecturer. The first was the competence with which he covered the course, raising and sustaining a level of interest which I found in no other subject. The second was

12 | that, although as one strongly influenced by the Fabians he must have found my viewpoint 'backward', 'reactionary', and generally extremely irritating, he took the wind completely out of my sails by awarding me the Exhibition.

Formal studies, however, became increasingly peripheral to the main business of my university years, and the promising results which I had obtained in the first two years of my course shaded downwards to a Law degree at pass standard. Externally, it was a period of immense intellectual challenge. The Soviet Union was the intellectual vogue of this period, a period with which David Caute has dealt so competently in *The Fellow-Travellers*. The vogue conditioned the entire climate of intellectual opinion, with the left-liberal climax at the time of the Abyssinian War, and of the Spanish Civil War which soon followed. The Labor Club, largely but not exclusively composed of Communist Party members of considerable intellectual capacity, profited greatly from the climate of the time.

Externally, that was the new world which I entered from St Kevin's: hostile to my basic assumptions, supremely confident that the future belonged to the Left and that the tide of 'reaction', particularly that based on religion, was ebbing fast.

It was the Depression which had awoken Melbourne University from a period of intellectual lethargy. One aspect of the revival of student thought was the formation of a Conservative Club, which did not have a very long life. The Labor Club was far more vital, attracted far better intellects and gradually developed a fascination for Marxist theory and practice especially for 'the great Soviet experiment'. By the mid-thirties this current had been fed by a series of exciting new books from fellow-travellers like the Webbs, and the Dean of Canterbury, who had visited the Soviet Union and, in the spirit of Lincoln Steffens, 'had seen the future and [discovered that] it worked'.

In April 1930, the Labor Club signified this new interest by supporting the motion 'that the effects of the Russian Revolution were really desirable'—still a long way from the later inflammatory revolutionary rhetoric—in a debate held under the auspices of the University Debating Society. It was significant that the opposition team—Murray McInerney, Gerard Heffey and Ray Triado—were all Catholic resident students of Newman College. The debate took place before my time at the University; but it was said that it was this debate which convinced a number of young Catholics that their intellectual equipment was inadequate to the task of meeting the Marxist challenge, and that they had no access to any means whereby they might fill the gap in their general knowledge. They had discovered that the intellectual foundations of faith which were adequate to the protected enclave of the Catholic school were utterly inadequate in a new and hostile intellectual environment. In one aspect, that environment was grounded in the Whig interpretation of history and in the philosophic liberalism of the Enlightenment still dominated by Voltaire's sentiment '*Écrasez l'Infame*'. This philosophic liberalism was now beginning to discover a new extension in Marxism, with its vision of an earthly paradise this side of the grave, and its categorization of religion as the opiate of the people.

There is no reason to believe that I would have proved more resistant to that environment than many others with my background. It is easy and pleasant to swim with the tide. My membership of the Campion Society changed all that. The future was to be not with, but against, the tide.

The Santamaria Family
*Back Row:* Bob (B.A.), Josephine, Phil
*Front Row:* Bernard, Joseph (Snr), John, Maria, Joseph (Jnr)

# 2 The *Catholic Worker*

The study group formed by this small number of Catholics to repair the gaps in their equipment had its first meeting on 28 January 1931. The founding members were Frank Maher, Denys Jackson, John Merlo, Murray McInerney, Gerard Heffey, William Knowles, Frank Quaine and Arthur Adams. A heated argument between Jackson and Quaine on the neo-scholasticism of Maritain, and the relationship between Latin culture and the Christian Faith monopolized the meeting. With the decision to meet a fortnight later to discuss Hilaire Belloc's *Survivals and New Arrivals*, the new organization could be regarded as established.

It could just as easily have collapsed after a short time. Permanence was given to the new effort, however, by its association with the Central Catholic Library, which for many years was to remain the powerhouse of Melbourne's Catholic intellectual life. The Library was under the direction of a remarkable Jesuit, the Rev. William Hackett, who had left Ireland 'for his country's good', his close association with supporters of Michael Collins during the Civil War making continued residence in Ireland impossible. It was this library which made available to the members of the new group the works of Christopher Dawson, G. K. Chesterton, Hilaire Belloc, and their literary controversies with H. G. Wells and Bernard Shaw; and the works of the French Catholic writers, who paralleled the English Catholic literary revival, Maritain, Mauriac and Bernanos among them. It was a new world at whose existence they had not previously guessed.

It was their discovery of the fact that they were the heirs not merely of a religious apologetic but of a complete intellectual system with a philosophy, a theology, a history, a set of social and political principles, which filled them with enthusiasm and indeed exuberance. It is this spirit which remains the predominant memory of my first meeting with them when I joined them late in 1931.

I had been introduced to the Campion society by one of my teachers at St Kevin's immediately on leaving school. This teacher, whose accidental interest in my work at school was to be so decisive as to my future life, was Frank Maher, who for more than a quarter of a century was senior lecturer and Reader in Law at Melbourne University. He was an exceptionally gifted and personally sympathetic teacher whose professional capacities assisted me to obtain the Senior Scholarship. His moral influence was even more powerful. It could not but impress a 16-year-old that the religious positions which one would regard as normal coming from the Christian Brothers should be explained and defended with such confidence by a layman with a mind deeply grounded in European history and at home with all of the intellectual currents of the day.

By this time the Campion Society had already established itself as a semi-official Catholic society. The name chosen was that of Edmund Campion, the English Jesuit who had been martyred in the days of Elizabeth I. The choice of Campion was meant to indicate a definite break in the Irish monopoly within Australian Catholic life.

The most influential of the new figures in the society, who had preceded my own entry by a few months, was Kevin T. Kelly, who retired some years ago from the Australian diplomatic service, where he had served in several ambassadorial posts. A public servant, who had been precluded from undertaking full-time university studies by economic necessity, he was a part-time Arts/Law student, already an active member of the Labor Party, and a councillor of the Victorian Public Service Association. To an effervescent intellect, always bubbling with new insights, there was added a fine speaking ability, which made him formidable in controversy and in all ways an inspiring figure to his Campion colleagues.

The fate of most discussion groups is to become introverted and then to die. With the Campion Society it was precisely the opposite. It was out-going from the beginning.

The Brisbane Catholic paper *Australia*, various 'Old Boys' magazines, the literary organ of the Catholic Young Men's Society, were all used as outlets for Campion articles. Addresses to various branches of the latter body; lectures to the younger clergy at Corpus Christi College, which had been established as a seminary by the Victorian Bishops to produce a clergy of great openness of mind and sympathy with the laity: these guaranteed the future expansion of the Campion Society. Yet it is doubtful whether those who could be described as fully formed Campions were ever more than forty in number. It was, in fact, impossible to dilute the currency and still maintain the value of the medium of exchange. Living in West Brunswick, with the assistance of my sister, I organized half-a-dozen groups which called themselves 'Campion'. The thirty-odd members could not compare in intellectual capacity with the two or three

16 | central groups meeting in the city. What was important, however, was that the Campion idea, however diluted, exercised a real appeal for a group of young industrial workers whose interests should have been remote from anything as forbidding as a mere discussion group.

The Campion Society was the product of a single decade; and by the end of the decade, it was, to all intents and purposes, dead. But it has influenced the subsequent developments in Australian Catholicism to the present day, although not a few Campions have proved themselves strongly opposed to some of its results.

One direct product of the Campion Society was the Catholic Evidence Guild, which provided a battery of trained speakers on Catholic doctrine and philosophy for Melbourne's Yarra Bank on a Sunday afternoon. It was to become the special responsibility of Brian Harkin and Frank Murphy, although without doubt its most able and challenging speaker was Kevin Kelly.

My own contribution to the expansion of the Campion spirit was in the establishment of a new monthly paper which was called *The Catholic Worker*. The higher flights of philosophy and history in which men like Maher, Kelly and Denys Jackson (later to become editor of the Catholic *Tribune*) were so fully at home, were, in those early years, quite beyond me. I still recall with a sense of shame that I slept through the first two Campion meetings I attended in 1931, at which Jackson gave two papers on the Byzantine Empire. It took a particular level of philistinism to sleep through two papers delivered by so attractive a speaker. Although it was later to be written that I was profoundly influenced by the writings of Belloc and Chesterton, in fact whatever influence there was came from the reading of others, and listening to their discussion. Belloc's *Servile State* was a masterly piece of social analysis of the structures of industrial capitalism and was fifty years before its time. His phrase 'Europe is the Faith, and the Faith is Europe' was otherwise. If taken literally, it seemed to me to destroy the universality of Christianity, to reduce it to little more than the characteristic religious system of a particular civilization, and to circumscribe its validity both as to time and place. Christopher Dawson's *The Age of the Gods* and *The Making of Europe* were founded on far more substantial historical scholarship than several of Belloc's historical biographies.

The proposal to publish a monthly Catholic working-class paper, modelled in part on Dorothy Day's New York *Catholic Worker*, which had been spoken of as a vague possibility, was precisely what I was seeking. It was a project which would enable me to contribute something to the Campion idea; to try to apply that idea to the necessities of those who, like the families I knew so well in Brunswick, were still suffering severely from the Depression; while offering them an approach, if not a solution, to the economic crisis grounded not in totalitarian ideologies, but in the teachings of the great Social Encyclicals: Leo XIII's *Rerum Novarum* (1891), Pius XI's *Quadragesimo Anno* (1931), and his later *Divini Redemptoris* (1937).

The discussions associated with the proposal to establish the new monthly seemed interminable. I became impatient of them, simply because I was too foolish and shallow to understand the difficulties of putting even a monthly four-page tabloid on its feet, writing it, distributing it, administering it, paying for it; and, above all, keeping it going if, by any chance, it caught on; and all of this while somehow keeping a university course alive. Just as the Catholic Evidence Guild had become the particular responsibility of Kelly, Murphy and Harkin, so the projected monthly came to be regarded as my responsibility, together with Gerald McLaughlin, who was to handle circulation with me.

The first issue of the *Catholic Worker* was ultimately published on 1 February 1936.

James Murtagh, in his *Australia: The Catholic Chapter*, evokes the unpromising beginnings which prevailed on the night on which it issued from the primitive press owned by a friend, Laurie O'Brien:

The first issue was printed on an over-worked press in a small, suburban printery of a Melbourne industrial suburb in January 1936. The edition was mailed from a grocery store next door, owned by the father of the editor. The first copy was sent to Pope Pius XI and another to Joseph Stalin, Moscow.[1]

As far as I can recall, I wrote almost the whole of the first issue, as indeed I did a somewhat large proportion of the writing for the next eighteen months. We printed only 3,000 copies of the first issue, believing that number would greatly exceed actual sales. We distributed it using my father's old bull-nosed Fiat. It 'took off'. We had to reprint another 8,000 copies before the following Sunday. By August it had reached a circulation of 27,000. Before my connection with the *Catholic Worker* was terminated during 1941, its circulation had risen to approximately 70,000 copies. The administrative problems, as distinct from the financial, had become enormous. They were solved by the efforts of half-a-dozen other Campions who, after a time, constituted the editorial board; but particularly as a result of the administrative thoroughness and application of two consecutive—honorary—managers, Gerald McLaughlin and Dan Donegan.

The latter months of 1935, when most of the preparatory writing was being done, were in a sense the calm before the storm. The outbreak of the Spanish Civil War, which was so radically to change the international climate leading to the abyss of August 1939, still lay in the future. While the Marxist challenge was clearly important, my own view at that stage was that the heart of the social and political problem of the West lay elsewhere. The balance of emphasis, at least as I saw it, was expressed in the editorial in the first issue, headlined rather melodramatically 'WE FIGHT':

18 | The problem which has to be solved is the social problem, a problem of universal importance, affecting every nation and every individual. . . .
The new Communism is only the old capitalism plus a little missionary fervour. Both are the illegitimate offspring of the same diseased materialism; both insult Man by regarding him as a labor unit rather than as God's noblest creation; both regulate their behaviour by economic expediency rather than by considerations of justice . . .
The taunt to which we reply is the frequent Communist allegation that the Catholic Church is a Church of the bosses . . . How is it possible for us, as Catholics, to have the slightest sympathy for a system which has de-christianised the world by its insistence on secular education; which has sacrificed the Home on the altar of the Machine; which has deprived the ordinary man of property and has destroyed his liberty?[2]

In retrospect, the first editorial was more a call-to-arms than a competent economic analysis. It proposed nothing of the nature of structural change to the economic system. It had to content itself with an appeal to the reform of the individual. I re-read it today, wishing that it had tackled the then urgent problems of economic policy—although in 1981, I see how little most economists and bankers understand about the economic system, and how insoluble is the problem of the contemporary inflation unless the economic theorists encourage Western man to reduce his material expectations. That, of course, fundamentally implies a moral change before any economic reform is possible.

Among the necessary preliminaries to the publication of the first issue of the *Catholic Worker* one event occurred which ultimately changed the direction of my life. Since the paper we proposed to produce carried the Catholic name, the correct procedure seemed naturally to refer the proposal to Archbishop Mannix for his approval.

It was the first occasion on which I had met the Archbishop. I was accompanied by a close Campion friend, Val Adami. Nothing in the interview gave any inkling of the closeness of the relationship which was to grow during the forties and remain until the Archbishop's death in 1963. Face-to-face with one whose name was already a legend to every Australian Catholic, I made my request for permission to publish a new Catholic monthly.

As far as the formalities of the interview were concerned, only two justify recording. The first was that Archbishop Mannix continued the discussion for almost two hours, not once referring to the proposal we had come to discuss, but leading the discussion over the widest variety of subjects—from Edmund Campion to the Campion Society, from the war in Abyssinia to the developing troubles in Spain, from Roosevelt to the follies of the Versailles policy, which, as he said, had given Hitler a totally undeserved opportunity.

As the interview continued without a mention of our proposal, I wondered whether we were being politely brushed-off. So, as he rose to end it, without much confidence, I reminded him of the purpose of the appointment. Did we have his permission to attempt to establish a Catholic paper? His answer: 'You have the right: you need no permission from me'. I thought of the Delphic oracle, so I tried again. Would he appoint a priest as a theological adviser, if we needed one? 'No, there is no need. You have your Campion Society chaplain if you want advice. I do not want a priest taking control of your work.' I reminded him that we were inexperienced and that as the paper would bear the name 'Catholic', our mistakes might damage the Church. He smiled: 'You will have heard that the man who makes no mistakes, makes nothing'. He extended his hand with an unexpectedly firm grasp. The support which it signified was never withdrawn in any enterprise in which I engaged with him in nearly thirty years.

# 3 The Mannix Tradition

The tall, spare figure who seemed to treat my request to establish a new Catholic paper so lightly was by this time deeply established in the affection of the mass of Australian Catholics as their one authentic leader. A considerable section of the non-Catholic community regarded him as a mischievous, malicious prelate, who confused religion and politics, and whose politics, to make it worse, favoured the rebellious Irish and attacked the British Crown and Empire. Since he was to exercise so profound an influence on my own thought in relation to public affairs, it is not irrelevant to attempt to understand Daniel Mannix the man, his background, and his perceived mission.

Dr Mannix, born six years before the unification of Italy by Cavour, Garibaldi and Mazzini, and of Germany by Bismarck, lived until less than three weeks before the assassination of President Kennedy in November 1963.

In a sense, the appointment of Archbishop Mannix to Melbourne was accidental. From approximately 1908 onwards, Archbishop Carr of Melbourne was pressing the Vatican to secure the appointment of the then President of Maynooth as his coadjutor, and therefore successor.

Perhaps the most brilliant, certainly the most controversial, contemporary of Daniel Mannix at Maynooth was the person he—quite mistakenly as it turned out—believed to be one of his close friends in the priesthood, Professor Walter (or 'Watty') MacDonald. Professor MacDonald, in fact, had a deep antipathy for Dr Mannix, a fact which emerges clearly from his autobiography *Reminiscences of a Maynooth Professor*. It arose as a result of the bitter controversy over the dismissal of Professor O'Hickey from the Chair of Gaelic Studies. A colleague of both Mannix and MacDonald, Dr Cornelius Mulcahy, judges that 'the *Reminiscences* are not fair to Dr Mannix; yet I know that Dr MacDonald held his ability and administrative

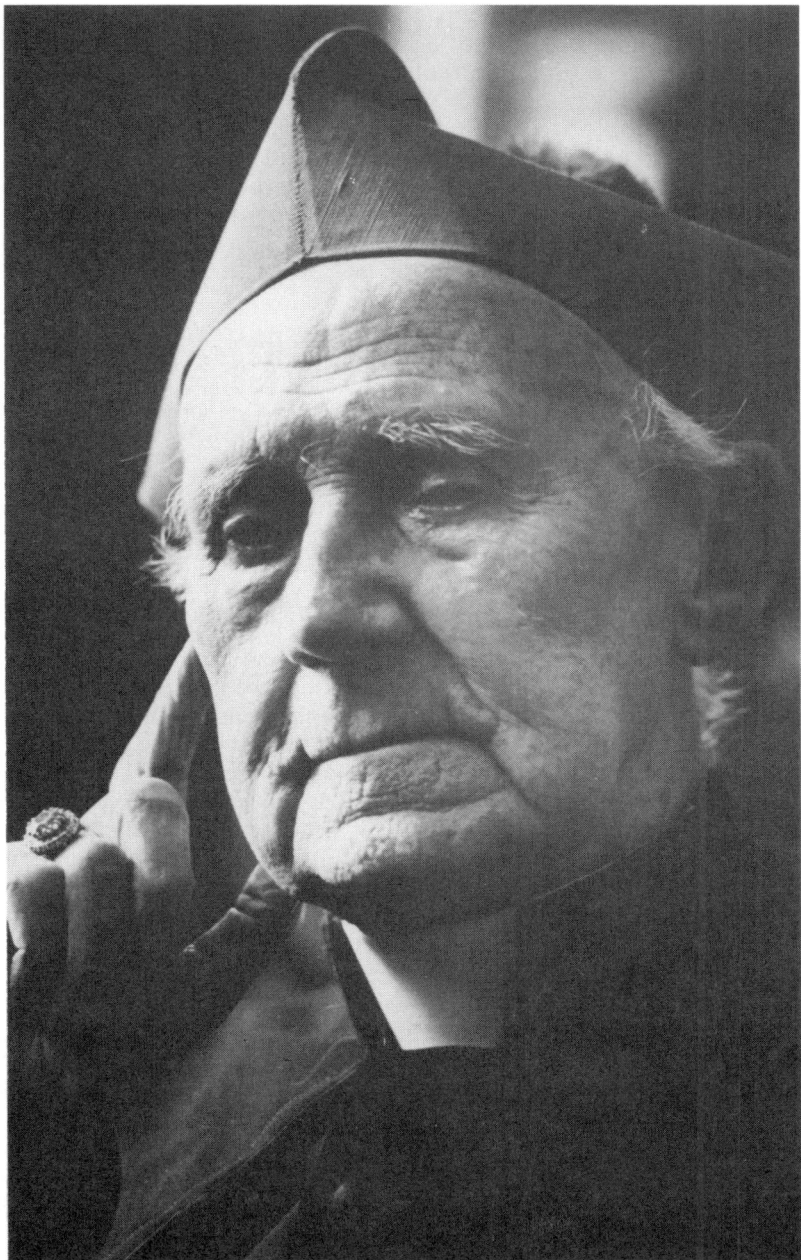

Archbishop Mannix in 1960

capacity in the highest esteem. Frequently I heard him say that he wished Dr Mannix held the see of Dublin which, after Rome, he regarded as the most important office in our day of the Catholic Church'.[1]

But it was not to be Dublin. On 9 July 1912 the Rector of the Irish College in Rome, Monsignor O'Riordan, sent a letter to Dr Mannix in Maynooth, informing him that the Pope had just confirmed his nomination to Melbourne. Monsignor O'Riordan offered his congratulations; and then he added his hope that Dr Mannix would refuse the appointment. Maynooth, he said, was far more important than Melbourne.

Maynooth I hold to be the Ecclesia docens of Ireland. . . I have for long looked on the Presidency of Maynooth as more important than any bishopric or archbishopric in Ireland or Australia except that of Dublin. It is now on the eve, or has entered into, a critical period of its existence; and I believe your presence there, for a few years more, to be, if not necessary exactly, at least of the greatest importance. And when the right occasion came, I should prefer to see your services used for the Church in Ireland, in another sphere of work, than for the Church in Australia.[2]

That other 'occasion' was patently a vacancy in Dublin or Armagh.

Whether it is practically, as distinct from formally, possible for a man who is offered an archbishopric to refuse is beyond my knowledge. Were it possible, a man less inured to duty than Daniel Mannix would have been tempted by that advice. The evidence, contained in a contemporary letter written to his niece, is that his deepest instincts were opposed to the final break with family and country represented by the Melbourne appointment. He accepted it only because it was presented to him as the personal wish of the Pope, as he unquestioningly accepted every decision clearly made by the Pope himself throughout his life. (That is not the same thing as saying that he accepted every piece of advice offered in the name of the Pope by Vatican diplomats, or every theory of Roman, or other, theologians.) It is of course speculative, but highly probable, that if Archbishop Carr had not already settled the Melbourne appointment, Daniel Mannix would have been appointed to Dublin on the death of Archbishop William Walsh in 1921. What his role would have been had he been in Dublin at the time of the Civil War is equally a matter of speculation. That the history of Catholicism in Australia—and of Australia itself—would have been radically different, there can be little doubt.

When Dr Mannix arrived in Australia in March 1913 he was already forty-nine years of age. As president of the most renowned seminary in Ireland, training priests not only for the Irish mission at home, but for the Irish diaspora abroad, for the Irish communities of the United States, Britain and Australia, he had for twelve years occupied the highest post in the Irish Church outside the archbishoprics of either Armagh or Dublin. In his fiftieth year, his personal formation was complete. If one sets aside his own formidable gifts of intellect and character, the influence of parents and family which, in his case, was both intimate and powerful, the primary components of that personal formation were his view of the realities, as distinct from the fictions, of Irish history; and his choice, dictated both by temperament and by judgement, from among the competing models offered by the Irish episcopate.

Between the Irish Bishops and their clergy on the one hand, and the Irish people on the other, there was a relationship which was certainly founded in religion: because religion was the determining element in their culture, however, that relationship extended far beyond religion. They were not, as is sometimes mistakenly asserted, Ireland's political leaders. But they were those to whom the ordinary Irish looked to validate or reject the claims of those who offered themselves for political leadership.

Throughout the nineteenth century, from the days of Daniel O'Connell through those of Parnell, to those of John Redmond at the beginning of the twentieth century, the Irish nation had always had its specifically political leadership. The political leadership had its own social, political and intellectual links, as in the less-developed countries today, with the relatively small group of the educated intelligentsia. Whether this political leadership did or did not enjoy the support of the peasant masses—the condition of its effectiveness—depended, perhaps more than any other single factor, on whether it was legitimized by the support of the Church.

But, who was 'The Church'? To the Irish peasantry, 'The Church' was pre-eminently the parish clergy who lived among them. The sentiment of the parish clergy determined, in turn, which of the episcopal models the people themselves were disposed to follow. Daniel Mannix was never in any doubt that the quality of the parish clergy, who mediated between the people among whom they lived, the Bishops who were their spiritual leaders, and the civil society to which they belonged, was the key to the health of the Church. That was why he regarded the foundation of Corpus Christi College in Victoria, which he believed to be a more successful seminary than Maynooth, as the foundation stone of his episcopate.

There is no need to emphasize the complexity of the problems which such a relationship creates both for Church and State. Yet each nation has its own traditions. There is no universally valid theory of Church and State, whatever some political philosophers may pretend to the contrary.

The models of ecclesiastical leadership which presented themselves to Daniel Manix were far from uniform. They fell into three categories.

The first was the 'Castle Bishop', represented by a Bishop Moriarty and later by a Cardinal McCabe. In essence they believed that it was no part of the role of a bishop to stand publicly beside his people as they challenged a political ascendancy which maintained itself by dint of social oppression. In fairness to these bishops in the Age of Revolutions, it was not unreasonable to hold that revolution would create far greater evils than it cured.

The second category was the open, unabashed nationalist, whose prototypes were Archbishop McHale, the 'Lion of Tuam', and, later, Archbishop Croke of Cashel.

Occupying a place between these utterly opposed positions, there was a third group which sought to canalize the nationalist impetus of the Irish to ecclesiastical and Roman rather than political and Irish purposes. Cardinal Cullen, whose leading role within the Irish hierarchy ranged over the second half of the nineteenth century, was the great protagonist of the third position. That position was simply that the Bishops should concern themselves with the political order, but only so as to preserve the position of the Church and what might be called the ecclesiastical interest.

Dr Mannix saw that the first—those who simply accepted the British Ascendancy—would ultimately destroy the link between the Church and the Irish people. The Ascendancy, through its oppressions, would ensure that the national struggle would continue; but if the 'Castle Bishops' had their way the Church would be visibly absent from what, after simple subsistence, would remain the predominant passion of an intensely Catholic people.

Dr Mannix was equally opposed to the policy of Cardinal Cullen. The latter was in no sense the agent of the British Ascendancy. He was simply interested in the organization and the ecclesiastical interests of the Church. Beyond that, politics as such were of little concern, even when they were an expression of the national cause.

To wean the sentiment of the Irish peasant away from the Fenians and their programme of violent reform, Cardinal Cullen organized his own National Association, so that the political interests of the peasantry could be channelled along lines which he could ultimately direct. Cardinal Cullen had seen the Carbonari in Italy. He did not want them in Ireland. Needless to say, the National Association was totally ineffectual as a weapon of rural reform; but then it is fair to say that it was not seriously intended to be effective.

Dr Mannix opposed Cardinal Cullen's concept of the relationship between Church and State, believing that its terms, objectives and methods were mistaken. His view was that Ireland's evident problems were not religious but political; and that the demands of political and social justice should not simply be subordinated to the ecclesiastical interests of the Church, however legitimate those ecclesiastical interests might be.

There is a complete consistency of principle in Dr Mannix's opposition to Cullen's theory of Church and State and in his opposition to that—rightly or wrongly—epitomized in what came to be known as the 'Sydney policy' at the time of the Labor split in Australia sixty years later.

The model Dr Mannix chose to follow was that of Archbishop Thomas Croke, who succeeded to the see of Cashel in 1875; who supported the Land League against the policy of Cardinal Cullen; and who helped the Land League bring about the conversion of Gladstone to the necessity for progressive rural reform. That was ultimately to transform Ireland from a nation of tenants without security to one of peasants owning their own land. It was the Croke model which Daniel Mannix applied to the situation in which he found himself in Melbourne in 1917, only four years after his arrival in Australia.

By September 1917, Dr Mannix was already in deep conflict with the Australian government of 'Billy' Hughes and faced with the threat of deportation as a result of his participation in the anti-conscription campaigns. These were organized to defeat the Prime Minister's referenda to introduce conscription for overseas service into Australia during the First World War. Dr Mannix was strongly urged—but never commanded—by the Vatican Secretariat of State to modify his public activities. He spoke at Geelong in August 1917 and gave his answer to those who, on the one hand, would deny a Bishop's right to speak on public issues; and to the different group who urged that the interests of the Church would be better served by a policy of silence:

There are people who say that freedom of speech is a valuable thing, but that it should be denied to Catholic Bishops and Archbishops. They should confine themselves to the sacristy, and have no opinions on public questions, or, if they have any, they should not be allowed to speak them above a whisper.

Now I may claim to know something about the Catholic Church, and I know that the countries in which the Church has failed most disastrously are those countries in which ecclesiastics kept within the sacristies and took no interest in the temporal concerns of their people or in public affairs.

I do not accept the theory that the Catholic Church in Australia will best be safeguarded when Bishops retire within the sacristy, keep their opinions to themselves, and so lose touch with the people to whom they should belong.[3]

The words used by Archbishop Mannix in 1917 expressed the same view as that expounded in more colourful language by Archbishop Croke nearly forty years before. His spiritual and intellectual mentor, for that is what Croke effectively was, had said that in those places where the Bishop's voice was silent 'there was moonlighting and murder and the Bishop's word was not worth the weight of a feather'.

It is unnecessary to emphasize that neither Archbishop—neither Thomas Croke nor Daniel Mannix—was unaware of the difficulties

26 inherent in this position. But they both held that, on balance, it did more harm to the Church if a bishop cut himself off from the deepest social interests of his people. Better to be there, to resist the inevitable exaggerations, but nevertheless to be with them, helping to channel and to guide, rather than to abstain because of unsolved theoretical difficulties, more appropriate to other countries and other ages.

It was already clear to Daniel Mannix, long before he left Ireland, that the strongest critics of the political influence of the Church had no principled objection to the involvement of bishops in politics. Whatever they might say in words, they did not, in fact, believe that bishops should keep out. In fact, they believed the opposite: that bishops should intervene, precisely to use their spiritual authority to tame the nationalist passion which threatened the domination of the Ascendancy. Few incidents better illustrate this point than the encounters between the Vatican, the Irish Bishops, and the un-official representative of the British Government at the Vatican, Odo Russell, in 1870.

In 1870 most of the Irish Bishops were in Rome for the First Vatican Council. The Fenian agitation was at its height. It had been condemned by the Irish Bishops nine years before, in 1861, and the parish clergy had generally gone along with their bishops. By 1870, however, while the official condemnation still stood, the attitude of the parish clergy had changed completely as a result of the execution of the Manchester Martyrs in 1867. The British Government, afraid of the likely result, instructed its agent in Rome, Odo Russell, to seek an explicit condemnation of Fenianism from the Pope himself.

As Shane Leslie points out in his life of Cardinal Manning[4], the British Government had done its best to influence the English Catholic Bishops to oppose the declaration of Papal infallibility which took place at that Council, as an affront to the human intellect. Now the British Government wanted the Pope to add his own condemnation of Fenianism to that of the Irish Bishops nine years earlier. The British representative was well up with the theological language of the times. He did not want the Pope to make a purely personal condemnation. He wanted it to be *ex cathedra*. In other words, the condemnation of Fenianism should be pronounced 'infallibly'.

When Cardinal Antonelli, the Vatican Secretary of State, thunder-struck not only at the suggestion, but at its source, attempted to reason with the British agent on the issue, Odo Russell replied that if any Papal declaration succeeded in eliminating revolution from Ireland, he might even come to believe in Papal infallibility himself![5]

It was not cynicism but realism, based on personal knowledge of the difference between the public and private sentiments of politicians, which many years later led Dr Mannix to remark: 'Politicians never really object to Bishops intervening in politics. What they object to is when Bishops intervene on the other side'.

It is impossible to understand Dr Mannix's career in Australia without an understanding of the formative factors which largely created the man who was already almost fifty years of age before he set foot on Australian soil.

The first major conflict between Dr Mannix and what was known in Ireland as 'the Ascendancy', and in Australia 'the Establishment', occurred between 1914 and 1916. Those first three years were decisive. One can generalize that his disillusionment with both began with the repudiation of what were conveniently entitled education claims during the Victorian State election of 1914, and was confirmed by the execution of the leaders of the Easter Rising in 1916. The transformation in the mind of Dr Mannix in those three years was total, resulting from parallel events occurring in Ireland and Australia, but both directly impressing the one mind at the same time.

Before his arrival in Australia, his view of the possibility of accommodation with the Ascendancy in Ireland was different from that of his Archbishop, William Walsh. To Daniel Mannix all the omens had pointed to a different, optimistic, and peaceful conclusion.

While the lessons of seven hundred years of Irish history might have reinforced the conclusion that constitutional methods would not finally avail, when Dr Mannix set sail for Australia at the beginning of 1913, Home Rule appeared to be all but achieved. Asquith's Liberals needed the support of Redmond's Irish Parliamentary Party of eighty-four members who held the balance of power. To obtain their support Asquith promised Home Rule, a kind of Dominion status. The Home Rule Bill was duly passed through the Commons three times. The House of Lords obstructed. But the power of the Lords to veto a Bill passed three times by the Commons had been removed by the British Parliament Act in 1911. By any constitutional criterion, it was all over before Dr Mannix left Ireland for Melbourne early in 1913. Among the new Archbishop's last official acts before leaving Ireland was to dine with the Lord Lieutenant. (It was another mark of the relative optimism of the times that even the redoubtable union leader Jim Larkin was to dine with Lord Aberdeen.)

And yet the whole constitutional process proved a meaningless charade. One whole section of the British military forces, under the political leadership of Sir Edward Carson, and with the active participation of Sir Henry Maitland Wilson, mutinied against the British Crown to prevent an Act passed constitutionally by the British Parliament taking effect as law. Asquith, having passed his law, then weakly acquiesced in the minimum demands of the Curragh mutineers.

28 To any Irish nationalist, indeed to any intelligent man, what further proof was needed that whatever might be the virtues of the English constitutional process elsewhere, where Ireland was concerned nothing had changed and constitutional legality was meaningless? If a further lesson were needed, it was provided when Edward Carson, who had armed the Ulster Volunteers against the authority of Crown and Parliament, was taken into the British Cabinet in 1915, while a year later the Irish leaders of the Easter Rising, whose offence was fundamentally the same, were simply apprehended and shot!

While the Easter Rising was in no sense a broadly based popular movement among the Irish either in Ireland or Australia, the shooting of the rebels, after the endorsement of the Curragh mutineers, transformed the atmosphere both in Ireland and Australia. It finally destroyed in the mind of Dr Mannix, as of most Irish, any belief that the British Constitution meant what its component Acts provided: that if a law were passed constitutionally it would be put into effect. By 1916 the optimistic belief of the Dr Mannix of 1912—that the Constitution would finally provide a peaceful solution to the Irish question—lay buried among the reprisals of the Easter Rising.

By 1916 he also found that his primary concern as an Australian bishop in Australia was equally stalemated. That primary Australian concern was the establishment of a complete system of Catholic education—primary, secondary, tertiary—without which it would be impossible to meet the most pressing problem of his own Catholic community. That problem, as he saw it, was how to enable its most promising sons to lift their feet off the lowest rungs of the economic ladder and to find their places ultimately in the professions, business and the public service. (The last thing which he saw in this process was a means whereby they might feather their own nests.) He saw it as the process whereby a genuine Catholic lay leadership would ultimately develop in Australia.

In 1914 all this was many years ahead. The foundation could not be laid unless admission to the public service was by competitive examination (a principle already established); unless secondary and university scholarships were equally open on the basis of merit to children in State, private and Catholic schools; and unless the burdens of the independent system were alleviated by what came to be known mistakenly as 'State Aid'. All these objectives, realized today, were then apparently out of reach.

If, in addition, Catholics were to make a distinctive contribution to public leadership, it was obvious that, with the exception of those who would find their way through the unions and the Labour Movement, it would be through those who had the advantage of university studies. That was his justification for seizing the chance of the totally unexpected benefaction of £30,000 for a Catholic university college, offered by a Sydney Catholic, Thomas Donovan, on condition that Melbourne's Catholics raised pound for pound. Newman College was established at a time when purely economic arguments might still have counselled delay.*

The massive attempt to redress the educational grievance, through the electoral campaign of the Catholic Federation, failed miserably in Australia over precisely the same period of three years as witnessed the defeat of Home Rule in Ireland. The Australian equivalent of the Irish Ascendancy, whether represented in the press or in Parliament, simply closed ranks. The Establishment took the position that the educational settlement of 1872 was beyond debate. If Catholics wished to enjoy financial equality with the rest of the community, they had first to surrender their schools. If they surrendered their schools they surrendered their identity, for exactly the same reason as the Establishment itself could not retain its own identity without the public schools.

These positions—between Daniel Mannix and the Establishment—were thus already taken when 'Billy' Hughes introduced the conscription issue into a climate already charged with political dynamite. Despite this atmosphere, the truth is that Dr Mannix did not play a major part in the first conscription referendum in 1916, and therefore was not a major factor in its defeat, a fact attested to by Hughes's biographer, Fitzhardinge.

It was otherwise in the campaign leading up to the second conscription referendum, which was held on 20 December 1917. On the conscription issue, Dr Mannix claimed seriously that he had not wished to be involved. Several Anglican—and a number of Catholic—bishops had already come out publicly in support of conscription. He believed that it was proper for him to supply a corrective by stating that, in his belief, Australia was doing as much as it should be called upon to do.

His claim that his involvement was not of his own choosing is in fact supported by Dr Evatt in his book *Australian Labour Leader*, a life of the New South Wales Labor Premier Holman, who sided with Hughes over conscription and left the Labor Party with him. Holman, precisely because he was fighting on the same side as Hughes, understood the Prime Minister's electoral strategy to secure the passage of both referenda. This is how Holman interpreted Hughes's strategy:

---

* It is interesting to note the attitude of the unjustly maligned John Wren to the proposal to establish Newman College and to tertiary education. Archbishop Mannix personally canvassed donations from most of Melbourne's more affluent Catholics. To the Archbishop's personal appeal Wren said that he would not give him a penny. He did not believe in tertiary education. But he would not refuse to give at all. He took out his cheque book and signed a cheque for £100 for the Archbishop's primary schools building fund![6]

30 | Mr Hughes made his fight definitely an anti-Mannix fight, as a matter of tactics. Mannix, said he, is against the British Empire. Very well, then, we are against Mannix. At one time it looked as if the whole organization of the campaign was very much less concerned with the defeat of the Hun than with that of a turbulent Catholic prelate. This was a mistake. It enormously increased Dr Mannix's importance and prestige, and it is doubtful if it brought more than a very slight additional percentage of votes to our side. Those who were likely to be affected by the anti-Mannix cry—chiefly members of avowedly patriotic or Protestant bodies—were already well out on the firing line, doing their best to secure the referendum's success.[7]

That, at least, was how Holman saw it. I make no judgement on the accuracy of Holman's evaluations of Hughes's political strategy except to say that Evatt accepted Holman's statement that the Archbishop was 'set up' by Hughes so as to obtain a sectarian issue around which to organize. However, Evatt came to a conclusion different from Holman's as to the political effectiveness of what Evatt himself blandly christened 'the tactics of sectarianism'. In Evatt's judgement sectarianism probably won more votes than it lost. Evatt was, in fact, so convinced of the success of these tactics in 1916-17 that he made them the foundation of his own campaign against the 'Movement' and the Industrial Groups forty years later. They were to prove equally successful.

Thus provoked, Dr Mannix chose to fight, not on the issue of the morality of conscription—he did not oppose conscription when Australia was threatened during the Japanese War—but on the issue of the limits of Australian participation in a war which was predominantly European. This issue coalesced the ancient emotion of Irish nationalism and the burgeoning realization of Australia's national identity.

The question is whether the action of Dr Mannix was consistent with his primary responsibilities as a bishop. After all, when he became aware of Hughes's tactical gambit, he could have endured one or two rebuffs and simply withdrawn from the lists.

In my own purely personal view, in the circumstances and atmosphere of the time, not to have fought would have contributed to the demoralization of the community for which he was responsible. It was under renewed and sustained attack as a result of the continuing tragedy occasioned by British policy in Ireland. Whether the apparent issue was education, or Ireland, or conscription, it always came back to the same thing. The only basis on which it was possible to reach accommodation with the Ascendancy, as he himself said, was that his community should accept the position of second-class citizens. They would be treated courteously; but they must claim no share in the general direction of the life of the Australian community. That position has not been accepted by the American Blacks in the second part of the twentieth century. Daniel Mannix was determined that it should not be accepted by Australian Catholics in the first: this, not for political reasons, but ultimately for the spiritual reason of their self-respect as free and self-determining Catholic citizens.

One must therefore draw a very clear distinction between the subjective and the objective elements of the dispute: one's judgement on the personal motives of the participants, one's judgement on the issues being decided. As to the former, I cannot condemn the motives of the social group with which Dr Mannix was in conflict. Their loyalties and emotions were just as deeply involved as his own: only theirs were in the fate of England and the Empire. They could see nothing but disloyalty in his position, warranting his deportation. Neither group of participants could reasonably have been expected to act otherwise than it did.

What the socialist elements in Australian society thought about the Archbishop was quite different from the viewpoint of the Establishment. R. S. Ross in the *Socialist* of 30 July 1920, expressed the viewpoint of a philosophical rationalist:

'Twere idle to deny his grip on the popular imagination in the world of things working-class where politics and unionism reign supreme. To their world he speaks as one admired for his courage and his cleverness. Everything he says appears to be in logical sequence and of unerring strength. He rarely blunders. One cannot help feeling for his speeches and his career and wondering Whither? What a figure he has made himself! Unless you take the view that his enemies have made him. Does he march to power and on to prison—or both?

The issue which was, in fact, being determined apart from the emotions of the participants was whether Australia was a separate nation with interests separate from those of Britain. The answer which history has given in our own generation is, in fact, the answer which Dr Mannix gave in 1917: that there is a British interest and an Australian interest and that they are not necessarily the same. John Curtin was to say this directly—and there were no dissentient voices—in the immediate aftermath of the Japanese attack in December 1941, when he publicly subordinated the British to the American connection. In our own time when one sees prominent Federal Ministers, themselves belonging to the Establishment, attacking British shop stewards, are the political profits of Australian nationalism not also present in their minds?

Dr Mannix, however, paid the penalty which is paid by all those who are right before it has become fashionable to be right. 'The general rule', wrote Walter Lippmann in his work *The Public Philosophy*, 'is that a [leader] had better not be right too soon. Very often, the penalty is political death. It is much safer to keep in step with the parade of opinion than to try to keep up with the swifter movement of events'.[8]

For these largely accidental reasons the Catholic minority in Australia was, to a large extent, the matrix of Australian nationalism.

Dr Evatt was largely right in claiming that Hughes 'made' Dr Mannix. Even Hughes, however, could not have achieved this distinction if the qualities of leadership, which include coolness in a crisis, had not been present in the Archbishop. That quality, which he manifested throughout his long life, was best epitomized, perhaps, during the *Wyvern* incident in 1920. Dr Mannix was arrested on the high seas when on his way to Ireland and refused to budge until the captain of the British destroyer *Wyvern* placed his hand on the Archbishop's shoulder formally to apprehend him. He thereupon said coolly: 'This is the greatest British naval victory since the Battle of Jutland, won without the loss of a single British sailor'.

This was the man whom I met for the first time in 1935, when he was already 71 years of age, and I was barely 20.

It might have been thought that one so accustomed to exercising direct personal leadership would be insistent on retaining it to the end, and that if he apparently cultivated the young Catholics of the Campion Society, it would be to fill the rôle of messenger-boys or, at most, lieutenants. It will emerge that this was far from his interpretation of their rôle, and that when he spoke of the necessity of lay leadership, as he frequently did, he meant leadership.

Throughout my first discussion with him, it was apparent that his interest in the initiative shown by a few of Melbourne's Catholic graduates in forming the Campion Society was far more than purely formal. What he already saw in it was the possible fulfilment of that part of the programme he had set for his episcopate when, immediately on his arrival in Australia, he had founded Newman College:

In his Inaugural Address on his arrival in Melbourne in 1913, he had said: 'In the natural course, the men who will make their mark for good or ill will come from the universities . . . leaders of thought and action. . . the leaders of public life who will make or mar the well-being of the Commonwealth'.[9]

What he saw in the Campion Society clearly was the fulfilment of an aspiration, rather than a programme, since the Society was not founded as a result of his own initiative.

# 4 The Spanish War

The issues of the *Catholic Worker* in the early months of 1936 reflect, I suppose, my own priorities. If the first editorial nominated capitalism as a greater enemy than Communism, it was not because of its intrinsic nature. A system which, despite its manifold defects, was based on liberal principles which recognized political, social and religious freedom obviously was not in terms of principle to be compared with totalitarianism. Nevertheless, with Communism still confined to the Soviet Union, the capitalist system could not escape responsibility for the fundamental errors which had precipitated the Great Depression, bringing universal misery in its train.

So we attacked 'sweat-shops' as they were called; the exploitation associated with the old system of 'industrial' insurance where—quite unfairly—we chose the Australian Catholic Assurance Co. as the main villain; the hostility of the Lyons Government to the seamen. Accompanying these direct attacks, there was a demand for a Family Wage, a wage system which would adapt family income to family responsibilities.

There was an attempt in a series of articles entitled 'The Social Primer' to educate the paper's Catholic working-class readership in the history and the main principles of Catholic social thinking as exemplified in the Encyclicals.

The paper owed its immediate success more to the vigour of its expression than the intellectualism of its arguments. In one aspect it was markedly inferior to the American *Catholic Worker* which had inspired it. The founders of the latter, Dorothy Day and Peter Maurin, bore witness to the integrity of their principles by establishing 'Houses of Hospitality' for the down-and-outs of New York, themselves living among them. It was a beautifully Franciscan model which we did not follow, perhaps through the accident of our history, perhaps because we simply were not good enough.

It was the outbreak and course of the Spanish Civil War which reshaped my own priorities and those of most of my colleagues in the

34 | Campion Society. What concerned us primarily was not even the strategic necessity of preventing the establishment of a Soviet client State at the entry to the Mediterranean. It was primarily the matter of freedom of religion from persecution by the State.

On 12 January 1937 W. H. Auden left for Spain to serve as an ambulance driver for the Republican forces. He did not do so. He visited Barcelona and Valencia, returned to England and, twenty years later, wrote:

I found as I walked through the city [of Barcelona] that all the churches were closed and there was not a priest to be seen. To my astonishment, this discovery left me profoundly shocked and disturbed. The feeling was far too intense to be the result of a mere liberal dislike of intolerance, the notion that it is wrong to stop people from doing what they like, even if it is something silly like going to church. I could not escape acknowledging that, however I had consciously ignored and rejected the Church for sixteen years, the existence of churches and what went on in them had all the time been very important to me.[1]

My natural reaction to the fact of religious persecution was complemented by a judgement as to the likely strategic consequence of a Franco defeat. I did not believe in the possibility of a liberal parliamentary State should the Republicans win the war, but rather that the real victor would be the Comintern, through the agency of the Spanish Communist Party; and that 'La Passionaria' and her associates, being loyal adherents of the Soviet Union, would establish a Soviet State in Spain. However one might argue the moral, philosophic or other historical antecedents of both conflicts, I could see no advantage in such a result, nor can I today; any more than I could or can understand how the non-Communist supporters of the American withdrawal from Vietnam can find any satisfaction in the consequence of the policy they pursued more than thirty years later.

Those Australian Catholics who believed that Spain was worth a political fight thus did not share the view—originally held by the European Left—that 'in the morality play of thirties politics, Good was striking back at Evil'.[2] In other words, we did not equate the cause of the Spanish Right with absolute Good and that of the Spanish Left with absolute Evil. We were not ignorant of the brutal injustices of Spanish society, nor of the apparent affiliation of the higher clergy with the cause of the landed aristocracy, very much in the manner of the *ancien régime* in pre-revolutionary France. Nor were we ignorant of the barbarities committed by the Nationalists against their opponents in many parts of Spain, paralleled, of course, by those committed by the other side, although that provided no justification. The brutal killings by the Franco forces of so many of the Basque Nationalists, who, influenced by Basque separatism, sided with the Republican Government, was a particular blot on the conduct of the forces which we were willy-nilly supporting. The more honest of the Left, like Orwell, must also have found it an untidy war which refused to order itself by neat Left-Right formulae, the assassination of leaders of the Trotskyite POUM and of the Catalonian anarchists by the Communist police and militia providing apparent illogicalities similar to the killings of the Basque Nationalists by the Franco forces. It was not a matter of excusing the inexcusable. It was a general *prise de position* determined by our judgement that a defeat for Franco would mean not a Republican Spain, but a Soviet colony, with all its strategic, political and religious consequences. Nor can it be claimed that our judgement was unbalanced. Writing from a Left viewpoint, Auden said: 'The Spanish Government (including the semi-autonomous Catalonian Government) is more afraid of the Revolution than it is of the fascists'.[3]

Dialectical conflict is bloodless. It cost us little except passion and words. The really brave were those on both sides dying on the battlefields of Spain, the victims of the mutual atrocities. However, it did take a modicum of courage to oppose the 'Republican' side in Australia. The propaganda was monolithic, overwhelming, and far more coercive than that which prevailed during the Vietnam conflict three decades later.

The impact of the Spanish Civil War in Britain on a spectacular generation which included figures like Auden, Isherwood, Spender, Orwell and others has been treated so exhaustively in a series of recent works that it appears pretentious to compare the resultant ferment in Australia with that which swept the British and European universities. Yet A. J. P. Taylor was right, as much for Australia as for Britain and Europe, when he wrote:

The Spanish question far transcended politics in the ordinary sense. The controversy provided for the generation of the thirties the emotional experience of their lifetime. It has been rightly said that no foreign question since the French Revolution has so divided intelligent British opinion or, one may add, so excited it. The rebellion was generally supposed to be part of a coordinated Fascist conspiracy against democracy, with Franco as Mussolini's or Hitler's puppet. The belief was in fact unfounded. Franco was nobody's puppet. He had acted without prompting from Rome or Berlin, and displayed later a remarkable independence in asserting Spanish independence. Nor could the causes disputed in Spain really be interpreted in simple terms of fascism and democracy, still less of socialism and capitalism. However, what men believed at the time was more important than what was actually happening.[4]

The atmosphere in Australia was equally electric, although on the European stage the Australian protagonists would have been quite unknown. In an Australia in which literature was the esoteric pastime of a minority, even the names of figures like Vance and Nettie Palmer would have been virtually unknown. Yet it was the conflict of ideas generated by the Spanish Civil War which in Australia transformed the Catholic attitude to Communism from generalized opposition to passionate resistance.

The dialectical struggle over the Spanish Civil War in Australia was an introduction into a world in which to press our ideas meant to be confronted with an almost unbroken wall of hostile opinion, which had deep cultural roots in the English Reformation, the Spanish Armada, the Whig interpretation of history, and the left-liberal ethos dominant in Anglo-Saxon communities from the early years of the twentieth century. If there was a Catholic 'ghetto mentality', it was not Catholics who built the ghettoes. The consequence for those who persisted was the development of a moral and intellectual hardiness which was not overborne by persistent opposition. Without the passionate commitment derived from the issues fought over during the Spanish Civil War, the long fight against Communist influences within Australian Labour, the formation of the Movement and, later, of the Industrial Groups, are alike incomprehensible.

On the side of the Left, the gamut of political positions ran from that of the generous Christian, rightly appalled by the social injustices of pre-Republican Spain; to the agnostic liberal who had placed his hopes of reform in a democratic Republic now attacked, as he saw it, by a reactionary military junta; to the revolutionary romantic in the tradition of Wordsworth and Byron; and from him to the hardline Stalinist, who merged into the category of traitors, like Philby, Burgess and Maclean.

Seemingly the whole of contemporary European literature was politicized in the interest of the Left. Those who upheld Franco's revolt against the Republic had far fewer literary lights of which to boast. As Orwell pointed out, the English dailies, whose literary pages made and broke reputations, were in the hands of editors and journalists totally committed to the Republican cause. As the members of the Campion Society in Melbourne looked around for established figures with whom to confront the literary lions of the Left, they could find only Roy Campbell on the side of the revolt. Among English prose writers the position was held by a small and almost exclusively Catholic group, among whom Douglas Jerrold deserves remembrance. He was not merely a writer but a man of action. It was Jerrold who hired the light plane which transported Franco from the Canary Isles to Morocco, whence he gave the signal for the launching of the revolt.

The 'great Spanish Debate' at Melbourne University was the first major Australian engagement arising out of this conflict. Something between 750 and 1,000 people gathered together in the Public Lecture Theatre, on the night of 22 March 1937. The two sides represented on the one hand the characteristic Left position in relation to the War, on the other what was predominantly the Catholic position in Australia at the time. The Opposition team comprised Nettie Palmer, wife of the Australian novelist Vance Palmer; Dr G. P. O'Day, a former Catholic doctor, well known as a Communist Party candidate; and Jack Legge. The Catholics were Kevin Kelly,

Stan Ingwersen and myself. Of the crowd, many were from outside the University itself, although both academic staff and under-graduates were very well represented. The partisans cheered and hooted their champions and opponents respectively. However, much more than a debate was involved: atti-tudes, philosophies, policies were being fixed and positions hardened. It was not a debate, because there were no assumptions in com-mon. In a sense, what the opposition represented was the confused complex of liberal-Marxist ideas which have been dominant in the West since the days of the French Enlightenment, with their implicit belief in the perfectability of man and society on this earth, if only the Left were given a free hand with the social and political engineer-ing. What we represented was a less Utopian view of man, with a profound belief in the Fall and in Original Sin; imposing the neces-sity of the search for justice, but knowing that the quest for human perfectability on earth was ultimately unrealizable and would be used to justify the most appalling tyrannies. The perfection of man, if it could be achieved, was not for this life, and, as far as concerned the next, it depended on the maintenance of the intimate link with God, which was what the religious freedom denied in Republican Spain was about.

It is a view of man and society which I have never abandoned, although I recognize that it has been used, in Spain as in many other countries, as cover and justification for outrageous injustices perpe-trated by those who control the machinery of the State in their own social and political interests, to whom God is merely a chance ally.

Interesting, perhaps, to note that it was the religious or philo-sophical significance of the encounter, rather than the mere debate, which impressed Professor Manning Clark, later to establish a repu-tation as the leading philosopher of Australian history. On the occasion of the award of an honorary doctorate at Melbourne University on 21 December 1974, he was to recall the occasion as one of the three most significant formative influences in his life.

There was that night in March 1937 when three men—Bob Santamaria, Stan Ingwersen and Kevin Kelly—representing what I will poetically call Catholic Truth—debated with three people, Nettie Palmer, Jack Legge and G. O'Day, who entertained the great hope that mankind has the capacity for better things here on earth, that heaven and hell are priests' inventions, and that we should trust the brotherhood of men. The point at issue was the Spanish Civil War. That was the night when . . . yes, was it Bob Santamaria—a sound Carlton man, but alas wobbly on what my great teacher, Richard Penrose Franklin called mysteriously 'other things', or Kevin Kelly or Stan Ingwersen . . . curious how one forgets the detail in the great scenes . . . raised the cry 'Long Live Christ the King' in 'the temple of Australian secularism'. Well I remember the pandemonium after that . . .
Now, as you know, all writers are deeply divided men. From that time Catholic Truth and the Enlightenment were to engage in never ending war on the battlefield of my heart. That night too, I had the first intimation of what had to be done. I had to

38 | shed the shallow hopes of childhood. to shed secular humanism, protestantism, and liberalism . . . to see them as ideas which would melt like the snow-drift, because they did not stand on entrenched ground. We have been told that the historian, like the hedgehog, knows one big thing about life. It was in the old Arts Building here that I learnt my one big thing about life.[5]

The March 1937 meeting at Melbourne University was followed by a number of similar meetings in different parts of Australia, including Broken Hill, Adelaide and Ballarat. The main organizer and speaker at these meetings was Stan Ingwersen, while I went back to the editing of the *Catholic Worker*.

After the Spanish debate, however, everything was changed. Beforehand, the Campion experience was predominantly an adventure of the mind. It was Spain which imported passion into the enterprise. From it originated the belief that so long as the Soviet Union existed, not only religion, but the liberal culture of the West, reflected in its free political institutions, was in daily jeopardy; and that if the battle was not won within the institutions of individual nations, the world would one day face a major conflagration.

# 5 Apprenticeship

Given so intense a stimulus by the Spanish conflict, Campion organization (or its equivalent) spread to most States. The Assisian Guild of Catholic Teachers was formed side-by-side with the Evidence Guild and the *Catholic Worker*. The Clitherow Society was formed as the parallel of the Campions for women. The Central Catholic Library flourished as never before. (For me, it was not entirely an intellectual pursuit. It was among the young Catholics now flocking around the Library that I met my future wife.)

The Campion idea was new, its expansion rapid. It could not have spread so quickly had the Catholic community not been as prepared to respond to clear leadership in the thirties as it had been during the period of the Conscription controversy. The few hours' voluntary work, which was all that could be offered four or five nights a week by a handful of the more experienced Campions, most of them now at the stage at which normally they should marry and establish themselves in their professions, was obviously inadequate. So the senior members—of whom I was not one—proposed to Archbishop Mannix that the Bishops should set up a National Secretariat, to fulfil the threefold functions of expansion, direction and co-ordination. This plan, at his request, was put into a detailed memorandum which he presented to the Fourth Plenary Council of the Catholic Hierarchy. It was accepted; and so the National Secretariat of Catholic Action for Australia and New Zealand* was duly inaugurated on 13 September 1937. The body, which was to comprise two full-time laymen and a chaplain, would be directed by an episcopal committee headed by Dr Mannix. What was voluntary had become professional, and inevitably was to lose some of the bloom of spontaneity.

---

*'Catholic Action' was a phrase with a different connotation in Italian, but unfortunate in the Australian environment.

40    I had played no part in these developments since, although winning some repute as a result of the successful establishment of the *Catholic Worker* and of participation in the Spanish debate, I was well down the Campion line. It was natural that Frank Maher should be appointed director. No other Campion had his breadth of view and his universal popularity. When Kevin Kelly was unable to accept the second position, no one else was offering. So ultimately it came down to me. I took the job at £5 a week. Having graduated in Arts and Law, and completed my Articles, I was able to present myself on the day the new office opened on 24 January 1938. It was meant to be for two years only. I am writing these words on the forty-second anniversary of that date.

I was not, and am not, quite clear on what we were expected to achieve other than to expand group organization on the Campion model throughout Australia and New Zealand. The disappointments came well before the achievements. One of the main factors which had led me to accept the position was that the entire Hierarchy of Australia and New Zealand had united in forming the Secretariat. Yet only a few months later the Archdiocese of Sydney withdrew from the organization, on the formal basis that a national body would limit the authority which a bishop must, accordingly to canon law, enjoy in his own diocese. The argument was, of course, nonsense, since in practice the new organization could do nothing in any diocese which the bishop did not permit. The real reason was that Archbishop Kelly was unwilling to be part of a national organization with headquarters in Melbourne. In my inexperience of Church politics it came as a shock that any bishop, least of all the Archbishop of Sydney, would break his contract so cavalierly, when two men had put their respective futures in jeopardy with no other security than their confidence in the pledged word of bishops. It was a foretaste of what was to happen, but on a far more serious occasion, seventeen years later. That, of course, was in an unpredictable future.

As we began the preparatory work for the organization of whatever new Catholic lay movements were likely to develop, the storm-clouds which were gathering over Europe presented an emerging threat to the possibilities which lay before us. In mid-March 1938 Hitler entered Vienna and annexed Austria to Germany. The crushing of all non-Nazi organizations, including the Catholic organizations, followed, Cardinal Innitzer of Vienna not being the first prelate to misunderstand the intrinsic nature of totalitarianism. The creation of the Rome–Berlin Axis was the unnecessary and disastrous consequence of Anthony Eden's highly touted diplomacy over Abyssinia and Spain, which led to a breaking of the Stresa Front. September 1938 was the month of the Munich Conference, and of Chamberlain's acceptance of Hitler's guarantee that the Sudetenland was his last territorial claim in Europe, and of the Munich Settlement, which the vast majority of Australians, myself included, regarded as a merciful alternative to the disaster of another world war. Short of the total capitulation of Britain and France, following upon Hitler's occupation of Prague in March 1939, the storms of war were visible on the horizon.

Early in 1939, Pope Pius XII called on Catholics throughout the world to join him during the month of May in a crusade of prayer for world peace. To conclude the month of prayer requested by the Pope, the National Secretariat was asked by Archbishop Mannix to organize a mass demonstration for peace. It duly took place on 28 May.

The result was the most extraordinary single event with which I have ever been personally connected. Sixty thousand people gathered in Melbourne's Exhibition Building in what must have been one of the largest meetings in Australian history. Present, among others, were the Prime Minister (R. G. Menzies), the Victorian Premier (Albert Dunstan), the Deputy-Leader of the State Opposition (H. M. Cremean), the Lord Mayor (Cr A. W. Coles) and all the Victorian Bishops.

The *Argus* reported the Prime Minister's speech which, in days now dismissed as benightedly unecumenical, struck a note to which the entire gathering vociferously responded.

The things which bind us are greater than the things which divide. That is why I, a Presbyterian, can stand here, a non-Catholic, on a Catholic platform, because we all believe that our common Christian faith is greater than any differences of doctrine. All of us, non-Catholic and Catholic, believe that the essence of our Christian faith is in the fatherhood of God, and there can be no belief in the fatherhood of God without a real belief in the brotherhood of man.

The task of statesmanship today is to get people to believe more in the things uniting them than in the things keeping them apart . . .

Let us begin now, and, instead of talking of the inevitability of war, talk of the inevitability of peace . . . [1]

In moving a vote of thanks, Archbishop Mannix said:

. . . We are not pacifists, or rather we are the only real pacificists. Our people will never be guilty of aggression, but they are prepared, if attacked, to defend themselves. If this country were attacked they would fail in an essential duty if they were not prepared to defend the integrity, independence, liberty, and life of the nation.[2]

In its editorial the *Argus* stated:

Nobody who attended the amazing peace meeting at the Exhibition Building last night or who listened by radio to the inspiring speeches could fail to be impressed by the sincerity and emotional depth of the proceedings. The demonstration was arranged by the Central Catholic Peace Committee: but it is safe to say that the huge crowd, estimated at more than 60,000, included thousands who were not of that faith. That fact in itself was a tribute to the essential universality of the cause espoused. The yearning for peace which is to be found in the great majority of Australians far transcends any consideration of sect or creed, and those responsible for the demonstration are to be congratulated upon the broadminded way in which they invited all faiths to share in furthering their ideal.[3]

Platitudes, perhaps, and, in the event, unavailing as a meeting of even 60,000 people held in an obscure State capital in an unimportant country must inevitably be. Yet, even forty years later, it is difficult to recall the event without some emotion, or to forget the lessons. In an age in which highly propagandized ecumenism is so often an expression of indifference, it is worth recording that in 1939, in one Australian State alone, 60,000 people of all religious persuasions and their equally diverse leaders could stand together to demonstrate a common allegiance to the noblest cause to which humanity can dedicate itself.

Within three months the Nazis and the Soviets had signed their Pact; Poland, guaranteed by the West, was invaded across two frontiers; and the 'mighty continent' was once again at war.

Perhaps the most useful services I was able to render in the early years of the National Secretariat, before having to concentrate most of my efforts on the Communist problem within the unions, was the establishment of the National Catholic Rural Movement, and the drafting and publication of most of the annual Social Justice Statements generally produced in the name of the Australian Episcopate from 1940 onwards.

It was H. M. Cremean, MLA*, who originally proposed the idea that the Catholic Bishops should themselves produce, or officially endorse, an annual statement which would seek to apply the social principles of Christianity to a particular national social problem. By the end of the thirties he had become insistent that a systematic opposition should be organized to the depredations of the Communist Party within the trade unions. Under the pseudonym Michael Lamb, he had written a well-documented pamphlet dealing with the sabotage of the war effort by Communist union activists before Hitler's invasion of the Soviet Union. Entitled rather starkly *Red Glows the Dawn*, it sold 35,000 copies.

He was equally pressing, however, that the Australian Catholic Bishops, who unlike their brothers in France and the Latin nations had maintained a close connection with a largely working-class Catholic community, should apply the principles enunciated in the two great Encyclicals, *Rerum Novarum* of Leo XIII, and *Quadragesimo Anno* of Pius XI, to the actual conditions of Australian life.

The Bishops, to their credit, took little persuading and embarked on this policy with the publication of the first Social Justice State-

---

*Deputy Leader, Victorian Parliamentary Labor Party (see Chapter 8).

ment in 1940. This was drafted largely by Archbishop Simonds, coadjutor to Archbishop Mannix.

During the whole of the period in which I remained with the Secretariat the following Statements were published:

1941 *Justice Now*
1942 *For Freedom*
1943 *Pattern for Peace*
1944 *The Family*
1945 *The Land is Your Business*
1946 *Social Security*
1947 *Peace in Industry*
1948 *Socialization*
1949 *Christian Education in a Democratic Community*
1950 *Morality in Public Life*
1951 *The Future of Australia*
1952 *Food or Famine*
1953 *Land Without People*
1954 *The Australian Standard of Living*
1955 *The Big Cities*
1956 *Hunger*

The 1949 Statement on Education was drafted by Frank Maher. *Pattern for Peace* (1943) was prepared in response to a routine request made of the various religious denominations by the Federal Government that they should recommend approaches to the problems of post-war reconstruction. *Pattern for Peace* was the work of a committee which included the future Chief Judge of the Commonwealth Arbitration Commission (Sir Raymond Kelly). I undertook the drafting of almost all of the others.

The normal method of production of the Social Justice Statements was that I would suggest a series of topical subjects to the Episcopal Committee some fifteen months before the date of publication. The Committee would choose one of them. I would discuss the method of treatment with my superior, Frank Maher, research the topic, and prepare the first draft. This would then be submitted to the Episcopal Committee, and the various emendations of its members would be consolidated in a second draft. This would then be issued to every member of the Hierarchy. Once again amendments would be reconciled in a third draft which would then be finalized by the Episcopal Committee in time for publication. The booklets were then sold at church doors throughout Australia on Social Justice Sunday, normally observed in September. Even those which sold worst always reached a circulation of over 100,000. My role was similar to that of a research and drafting officer acting under a departmental committee. It is difficult to see how else the series of Social Justice Statements could have been maintained or have been the success it became.

44  The most successful statement was *Socialization*, published in 1948, which sold over 200,000 copies. Its success was due largely to the topicality of the issue of government intervention and planning in the post-war economy. The Chifley Government, in its 1946 referendum proposals, had obviously proposed a major extension of government control throughout the whole of the economy, confident that the experiences of a war-time economy could be translated to the task of post-war reconstruction. What limits it envisaged were unclear, since Mr Calwell, as an influential member of the Cabinet, in a series of personal discussions had insisted that no guarantee against manpower direction or industrial conscription would be incorporated in the proposed constitutional amendment.

Hence, even before Chifley's Bank Nationalization proposals of 1949, a strong resistance developed among a few influential Catholics located mainly in Sydney, aiming at a declaration by the Bishops that the ALP's Socialization Objective should be condemned. In their minds, it reflected a completely socialist philosophy of the type which had been condemned by a series of Popes. The logic of such a condemnation would be that membership of the ALP should be strongly discouraged among Catholics.

My own view was that the proposition was philosophically mistaken, historically uninformed, and that it completely ignored the fact that the policies likely to be pursued by a Labor Government of that era, whatever Mr Calwell's obduracy, would have little to do with philosophical Marxism. If this were so it would *a fortiori* be extremely damaging to the Church's mission of influencing public life, if Catholics were encouraged to leave a Labor Party with which they had an historic association at a time when Mr Menzies' newly established Liberal Party was still, obviously, a citadel of the traditional Establishment.

The members of the Episcopal Committee accepted this view. The Statement *Socialization* was officially 'published with the authority of the Archbishops and Bishops of the Catholic Church in Australia'. Its Conclusions defined 'the attitude of the Catholic Church to the various systems which demand the intervention of the Government in social and economic life'. Since the Bishops accepted these Conclusions as presented in the original draft, and since I have had no occasion to revise their basic principles in the thirty-two years which have since elapsed, they may retain some interest.

## Conclusions

(a) The philosophy and programme of Communism cannot under any circumstances be reconciled with Christian teaching.

(b) The philosophy and programme of strict Socialism—the taking over and operation by the State of the entire machinery of production, distribution and exchange—are Marxist in origin, and cannot be reconciled with Christian teaching.

(c) Where the meaning which is given to the programme of Socialisation is the same as that given above to Socialism strictly so-called, Socialisation, in that sense, cannot be reconciled with Christian teaching.

(d) Where the meaning which is given to the programme of Socialisation is simply that the State has the right to place under public control those industries which are too vital to the common good to be left safely in private hands, then in that sense Socialisation is NOT opposed to Christian teaching.

(e) The nationalisation of any particular industry within this particular and restricted group is NOT opposed to Christian teaching, so long as it is not intended as one step on the road to total Socialism.

(f) Citizens should always seek to determine whether the nationalisation of an individual industry is legitimate or whether it is really only one part of a more far-reaching plan. There are three methods by which this can be done. They should constantly question their parliamentary representatives as to the real aim of their policies. They should constantly study the published programmes of political parties. Above all they should endeavour to discover whether the overall result of a Government's policy has been to extend the ownership of productive property or to restrict it. In the former case, the nationalisation of a particular industry is far less suspect than in the latter.

(g) On the other hand, the nationalisation of an industry in which numerous small firms operate, or which is capable of being run by small units, is NOT legitimate.

(h) At all times the purpose of Government policy should be, as far as possible, to break up big productive units, particularly monopolies and near-monopolies, so that industries may be operated by small and medium-sized firms. In all industries in which this is possible, it is the only programme fully in accord with Christian teaching.[4]

The 1948 Statement was not without importance to the Labor Party. It was ironic that the benefits of the 1948 Statement, which checked any erosion of traditional Catholic support for the ALP, were substantially thrown away by the events which followed the attack on the Industrial Groups in 1954-55.

By the beginning of the fifties, the Social Justice Statements were being issued annually with an orderly and efficient machinery of composition, publication and general management. It was at this moment that problems began to manifest themselves. In 1953 the Bishops approved a Statement on Commonwealth–State relationships for publication in the following year. The Episcopal Committee supported my recommendation that it should oppose the continuing concentration of power in the hands of the Commonwealth Government and the Canberra bureaucracy. It was already apparent that this process would develop with the speed of an avalanche after the High Court judgements in the Uniform Tax cases. A strong 'States Rights' stand based on decentralist positions was the only one which accorded with the Principle of Subsidiary Function, which Pius XI had defined in the Encyclical *Quadragesimo Anno* in 1931.

. . . On account of the evil of individualism, things have come to such a pass that the highly developed social life which once flourished in a variety of prosperous

46 | institutions organically linked with each other, has been damaged and all but ruined, leaving thus virtually only individuals and the State. Social life lost entirely its organic form; the State, which now was encumbered with all the burdens once borne by associations rendered extinct by it, was, in consequence, submerged and overwhelmed by an infinity of affairs and duties.

It is indeed true, as history clearly proves, that owing to the change in social conditions, much that was formerly done by small bodies can nowadays be accomplished only by large corporations. *None the less, just as it is wrong to withdraw from the individual and commit to the community at large what private enterprise and industry can accomplish, so, too, it is an injustice, a grave evil, and a disturbance of right order for a larger and higher organization to arrogate to itself functions which can be performed efficiently by smaller and lower bodies.* [My italics.] This is a fundamental principle of social philosophy, unshaken and unchangeable, and it retains its full truth today.[5]

The Statement was drafted in accordance with those assumptions and was fully approved when, quite unexpectedly, its publication was opposed by Cardinal Gilroy. Since its influence would be greatly reduced if the Cardinal were not a signatory, and since he made it clear that he would not attach his signature to what had already been approved, the subject had to be jettisoned almost at the moment of publication. Despite great difficulties due to shortness of time, and the need to repeat the entire procedure to obtain approval of a new subject, an alternative Statement entitled *The Australian Standard of Living*, dealing with Australia's methods of wage-fixation, was prepared instead and published in time.

The identical problem manifested itself in the following year. The approved subject was a criticism of Australia's excessive urbanization. The Statement was to be entitled *The Big Cities*. Both subject and contents were thoroughly in accord with the Catholic decentralist philosophy. They were approved by all the other Bishops. Then, once again, almost at the last moment, the Cardinal objected. This time, however, the Statement was published. It carried the individual signature of the other Australian bishops—but not that of the Cardinal.

In retrospect—after the appearance of the divisions among the Australian Bishops in relation to the policies of the Movement during 1954-55—it became clear that winds of change were blowing in the Sydney Archdiocese. These had little to do with the Social Justice Statements themselves, the latter being merely the victims of more wide-ranging difficulties.

Dr Mannix was greatly perturbed by the failure of the original 1954 Statement on Commonwealth–State relations to appear at all. Administering the parish structure of his own archdiocese on a genuinely decentralized basis, with wide autonomy, including financial autonomy, delegated to his priests, he had little confidence in the growth of a centralized bureaucracy in Canberra, which he regarded as inevitable if the income tax power ultimately rested exclusively with the Commonwealth. So in 1954 he published the

pamphlet *The Australian Commonwealth and the States** over his | 47
own name, probably the only moderately lengthy dissertation which
he published after his translation from Maynooth to Melbourne.

The establishment of the National Catholic Rural Movement
during the course of 1939 was a consequence of the same decentralist
impulse. In its first origins, however, it arose from more mundane
considerations. The National Secretariat had developed out of a few
discussion groups organized largely in the metropolitan centres
among university students, with a few professional men thrown in.
The majority of bishops who contributed financially to the maintenance of the Secretariat, however, were country bishops. Naturally
they expected some results in their own areas.

By the end of 1939, a number of farmers' discussion groups had
been organized in the following centres, which would hardly appear
on a map of Australia, let alone the world:

*Victoria*: Bunyip, Leongatha, Pakenham, Morwell, Hansonville, Trawool,
Rushworth, Devenish, Kyneton, Drysdale, Meredith, Coragulac, Purnim, Koroit,
Kirkstall, Dunkeld, Condah, Cavendish.
*New South Wales*: Urana, Oaklands, Urangeline, Lockhart, Milbrulong, Junee, Hall,
Braidwood.
*South Australia*: Naracoorte, Booleroo Centre.
*Queensland*: Ayr.

I had visited most of these centres once or twice, and subsequently
tried to maintain contact by correspondence, since travel was by
train and the distances great. During 1939, one of the more prominent members of the Assisian Guild of Catholic Teachers, Ted
Hennessy, strongly represented his view, based on his experience as
a country teacher, that the programmes developed for these groups
were along the wrong lines. To model them on Campion Society
groups, studying history, philosophy, sociology, would be irrelevant
to their real needs, and kill both the interest of their members and the
contribution which they might make to the practical application of a
Christian rural philosophy. They were farmers. The farm was the
natural habitat of the family. The reproduction figures of rural,
compared with urban, populations proved that they were the real—
indeed the only—domestic reservoir of national population growth.
(It was still seven years to Mr Calwell's post-war immigration programme.) A strongly established and expanding rural community—
of farmers and of inhabitants of provincial towns—was the basis of
political and social stability, and an essential counterpoise to the
problems of mass culture generated by the big cities. Furthermore,
the Church itself had a direct vested interest in the consolidation of
the basic institutions of rural life. There was overwhelming statisti-

---

*Originally published as an article in *Twentieth Century*, Autumn 1954.

cal evidence to prove that religious belief and practice were far more solidly established in rural than in urban areas.

Ted Hennessy's arguments were convincing. He was given a little financial help and administrative support to establish a monthly news-sheet called *Rural Life*. Gradually a kind of vocational cohesion developed around the rural groups, and finally Frank Maher suggested that I might try to weld them together into one of the 'specialized' movements of lay apostolate which, on the French model—in this case specifically of the French *Jeunesse Agricole Chrétienne*—the Secretariat was attempting to develop.

For some reason, it took off. By 1955, at the time when the Labor split threw so many established ideas and organizations into a seemingly unmanageable flux, the NCRM had expanded to twenty dioceses, to every Australian State, with about 200 branches (or rural groups) and approaching 4,000 active—and highly enthusiastic— members. It gained an enormous accession of strength in the interest of its episcopal chairman, Bishop Henschke of Wagga Wagga. A farmer, from a South Australian farming family of German extraction, he commanded total confidence from everyone who worked with him. If I revered Archbishop Mannix, I loved Bishop Henschke. As secretary of this organization, I wrote its Manifesto, its policy statement *The Fight for the Land* (1942), and a larger work *The Earth Our Mother* (1945).

To find myself acting as secretary of an organization of farmers at the age of 25 was a turn of events so bizarre that if anyone had predicted it some ten years earlier, when I began my studies at Melbourne University, I would have laughed. It was one of those things that one was told to do. From those inauspicious beginnings, however, it became the most personally rewarding work in which I have ever engaged before or since.

In the essay dealing with myself in his *Builders and Crusaders* T. R. Luscombe has written:

As an organization the NCRM was, in many ways, the finest fruit of Catholic social effort. It was a movement that literally went to the grass roots of rural problems, social and economic, and the country people who, over the years, passed through its membership, were equal to any in Australia for a combination of practical commonsense, idealism, personal responsibility, and generosity.

The annual National Conventions, held for many years at Albury under the wise and benign guidance of the National President, Bishop Henschke, brought together the cream of the nation's rural Catholics to discuss and enunciate policy matters. Later critics have had much to say concerning an alleged semi-mystical desire to create a peasant proprietorship based on a mythical three acres and a cow. This type of criticism was often a wilful distortion of the facts. Rank and file NCRM members were too experienced and practical to allow themselves to be caught up in a farce of this nature.

However, he also adds:

Looking at it in retrospect, one cannot escape the conclusion that, despite its undoubted achievements in some directions it was an artificial organization created from the city and run by city intellectuals and theorists. At one stage its principal organizers were city-bred university law students. Ideas or initiative rarely came from the ranks. Policies, while debated at considerable length and with commendable vigour, came from Collins Street, or Swanston Street or, later on, Belloc House in Kew.[6]

That judgement is basically correct, the only defence which I can offer being that I did the job because I was instructed to do it. If I had said that it was hardly an appropriate task, it is difficult to see that it could or would have been undertaken by anyone else.

The organizational principle of the NCRM was identical with the one I have endeavoured to apply in every field of activity in which I have been engaged. In each of those fields there are admittedly large areas of change which can be brought about only by the action of governments, through legislation, regulation, financial support. The characteristic form of socio-economic organization in Australia has been that of the pressure group, which uses electoral sanctions, strikes, or the withholding of financial support to compel governments to produce the desired result when a political party has been elected to office. I have never doubted the legitimacy or desirability of this form of action whenever it is relevant. But it appeared to me even then that equally significant changes could be brought about only by the social group involved, through its own activity. The first necessity was to make the social group conscious of the real nature, source and origin of the problems it faced; to show it how many changes could only be wrought by education, local action and, in many cases, by co-operative organization—whether in the fields of credit, buying or selling. This method was not a substitute for political action. It was the indispensable ancillary of political action and, in the long run, perhaps more important. Above all, the basic organizational unit had to be small and local, whatever machinery of regional, State and national organization might be erected on that foundation.

So, using this method, we set about imparting to the farmer and the inhabitant of the country town a vision of what their way of life might be if only they were themselves prepared to shake off the urban image of the rural population as being composed of 'country cousins' and plain ordinary 'hicks', with straw in their mouths and sticking out of their ears. We tried to impart a vision of the land as the natural habitat of man; of the family as the primary and indispensable social unit; of agriculture as the first and most indispensable industry; of a farm economy which, wherever climatically possible, would be based on diversification of crops rather than on the then fashionable one-crop specialization, pressing the point of diversification down to the production of most of the family's own food; of the Australian township as potentially the kind of social, recreational and educational centre which the English and European

50 | villages still remained after centuries of evolution; of an education system which would no longer be directed merely to the production of workers for secondary and tertiary industries, with a consequent depreciation of the status of the agriculturist, but which would also attempt to provide for the children of the farmer the technical skills required by the life of the land; of agricultural co-operatives as a form of economic organization which, if fully developed, would make farmers masters of their own destiny, instead of remaining tied to the apron-strings of city bankers acting through their directorships of the great pastoral companies.

My own approach to the policies of the NCRM was primarily philosophical and only secondly economic. Psychologically, I suppose that it owed something to my own European peasant background. The writings of Gustave Thibon, the French neo-scholastic philosopher, of Herbert Agar and the Southern Agrarians in the USA, thus fell on ground already partly prepared. William Ernest Hocking, Professor of Philosophy at Harvard, had summed up this philosophic viewpoint in his illuminating article in the 1942 Year Book of the US Department of Agriculture, which after many years still retains its intellectual fascination:

There is a great deal of nonsense talked about farming and the satisfactions of farming. It is especially foolish to speak of farming as though it were one sort of thing instead of a dozen very different sorts of things especially in North America. It is peculiarly silly to talk about the joys of being 'next to nature', without distinguishing between the times when Nature is a very agreeable companion and the times when her storms, her winter rigors, her excesses of dryness and wetness, her untamed irregularities turn the best plans into dust and ashes and empty pockets. But it remains true that farming survives, and will always continue to attract men to itself, because the farmer is, among all ups and downs, a successful creator in the sense that the ideas of his brain do get themselves built into visible living products and that this, his personal success, is at the same time an absolutely necessary social good.[7]

He added:

We say that the frontier is gone, the first transformation of the wilderness into the cultivable land. But there is the frontier of the craftsman, that is to say the line where his skill meets the obstacle it cannot yet surmount. There is the frontier of the scientist, the line between knowledge and ignorance. And there is the frontier between barrenness and fertility, the frontier of the farmer, a line that is always being pushed back but which is never banished and forever threatens to return. This line is a line between life and death, both for the farmer and for the community; for unless the farmer can continue to make the soil yield enough living matter for living people, all human life stops. This is the commonplace miracle of the farming process. The city takes it for granted; the farmer knows its incessant risks and perils.[8]

This somewhat philosophic vision of their vocation we succeeded in communicating to a considerable group of hard-bitten Australian farmers in every State in Australia. The task was rendered easier by the constant emphasis on the religious values of rural living reiterated by Bishop Henschke and dozens of devoted country priests. To these factors there was added the contribution of economic theory made by Colin Clark.

I met Colin Clark in the mid-forties, when he was financial adviser and director of the Bureau of Industry of the Queensland Government. Some years later, having left the Queensland Public Service, he became director of the Institute of Agricultural Economics at Oxford. In 1969, having reached the age of retirement at Oxford, Clark returned to Australia, serving for a period of some years as director of the Institute of Economic Progress, which was attached to Mannix College at Monash University in Victoria.

Whether in or out of Australia, we remained close friends, a friendship which continues to the present day. The economic analyses of Colin Clark had a powerful influence on the thinking and policies of the NCRM and, later, of the Catholic Social Studies Movement. Of particular persuasiveness were his ideas relating to closer settlement. He was strongly in favour of breaking up the vast pastoral leases in Queensland's coastal areas and substituting smaller properties devoted to intensive beef production and the production of grain. He was a strong proponent of regional decentralization, believing that it was economically feasible and socially desirable that new cities should be limited to a population of 100,000 people.

With some important qualifications, Robert Murray is generally right in observing that

the distinction should be made that Clark, unlike Santamaria and the NCRM, always used economic analysis in his argument. On economic grounds, he opposed further development of the Queensland sugar industry years ahead of public opinion in the State. Unlike the NCRM, he was opposed to further irrigation—again years ahead of public opinion.[9]

The qualification I would make is that the NCRM policies were not as devoid of economic analysis as Murray's statement might imply. The differences between Clark's views and those of the NCRM were generally differences of emphasis and presentation. Clark spoke as an economist to economists and politicians. The NCRM, being a Movement with a predominantly spiritual mission, spoke the language appropriate to such an organization, although never ignoring the economic arguments and the economic consequences of its policies.

If one realizes that the NCRM's visionary outlook was so much against the current of the time and the canons of a purely commercial agriculture, it was surprising that for more than a quarter-century its ideas generated so much support among a representative sampling of tough Australian farmers. Equally unexpected was the list of distinguished figures who were prepared to appear on NCRM platforms: Barbara Ward; the renowned demographer Sir Alexander Carr-Saunders; Sir Ian Clunies Ross, the Director-General of the CSIRO; Professor Sir C. Stanton Hicks, of the Department of

52 | Physiology at Adelaide University, dealing with 'The Moral Basis of the World Food Shortage' at the 1952 Convention. These are a few random names which come at once to mind. One memorable event was the appearance of Bishop Taguchi of Osaka at the nineteenth Annual Convention. The invitation to a Japanese bishop, who had been Military Ordinary attached to the defeated Japanese Imperial Forces, to speak as the guest of the NCRM in the Albury Town Hall at the 1959 Convention, only fourteen years after the termination of hostilities with Japan, was obviously a gamble, but the cordial reception given to a defeated enemy proved that Australians possessed often unsuspected moral resources.

When the Labor split came in the mid-fifties much play was made of the primitive peasant ideas which I had tried to inflict on honest Australians. Having learnt something of the success of experiments in agricultural colonization by migrants in Latin America, during 1953, I attempted to secure second-grade Crown land for experimental migrant land settlements in Tasmania and Victoria. The Italian and Dutch Government migration authorities had committed themselves to make loan capital available. Both the Tasmanian and Victorian Premiers undertook to make low-quality land available on this experimental basis. The fate of this particular initiative contains instructive lessons in the nature of party politics apart from the admitted difficulties of increasing rural settlement in a predominantly urban community.*

More successful was an NCRM 'sideshow'—the part-time farming settlement for industrial workers which we established on a co-operative basis in 1950 at Maryknoll, some forty miles from Melbourne. Briefly, the idea was to mix urban and rural living. The workers would earn their money wage by either full-time or part-time industrial employment either on the settlement itself (where a joinery and a silk-screen colour printing plant were quickly established) or in a nearby industrial centre. The balance of working time would be given to the development of a small holding around the family home. The homes were built in a concentric pattern around school, hall, and church, creating a natural centre for community activities.

The settlement at Maryknoll still exists today and contains approximately seventy families. St Mary's Co-operative employs about seventeen workers: five women work in the office-store complex, and the men either travel to Nar Nar Goon or further afield on building projects (mainly schools). Sixty-six other people travel from the settlement to work each day. Young people have generally been successful in finding employment. The settlement is more flourishing today than at any previous time.

---

*See pp. 128-9.

It is impossible to say whether the experiment would have been capable of expansion, with different patterns of employment and community living in the myriad environments provided by Australian country towns; just as it is impossible to say whether the proposed rural settlements for migrants could have sustained themselves against the frenetic urbanization of post-war Australia. There was no opportunity to prove or disprove the thesis. Within five years of the beginnings at Maryknoll, with seven families living in temporary homes, the Labor split absorbed so much of our effort that it was impossible to give to the idea the impetus it deserved. The premature death of the founder of the settlement (the Rev. W. A. Pooley) removed the man with the practical knowledge and experience needed to expand the programme.

Those inclined to dismiss Maryknoll as a romantic illusion ignore the fact that, as late as 1980, between 35 and 55 per cent of farmers in France, Britain, West Germany, Italy, Holland, Belgium, Luxembourg, Denmark and Ireland, work according to the same pattern, combining small farming with another job in a nearby provincial town.

With the basic structures of industrial employment likely to change in a number of industries as a result of the present technological revolution, with part-time employment becoming far more frequent than it is even at the present moment, perhaps a reconsideration rather than a dismissal of such new ideas is called for. Must one believe that Australians—unlike Western Europeans—are so much in the grip of blind forces and unthinking habits that the decentralist pattern of rural-urban employment organized around country towns is beyond their ingenuity?

In this chapter, I have not attempted to write a history of the National Secretariat, which would require far more detailed treatment, especially of the work of Frank Maher in providing the overall planning and in establishing the youth organizations associated with it. I have simply attempted to outline my own relatively small areas of specialization. The National Secretariat lasted from 1937 to 1955. While my own connection with the Secretariat continued until the end, from 1942 onwards the time given to the works described was increasingly circumscribed by the necessities of the fight against Communist influences in the Australian trade union movement.

# PART II

# Cold War: an Australian Chapter

# 6 The Climate of the Times

In the immediate post-war decade three Western-style Social Democratic Parties split, while a fourth barely avoided the same fate. Those which split were the Italian, the Japanese and the Australian. It was only with difficulty that Hugh Gaitskell was able to maintain the unity of the British Labour Party against the challenge of the extreme Left in the controversies over Point Four and unilateral disarmament. Nearly thirty years later, the pressures exerted by Anthony Benn and his followers against Callaghan, Healey and the centre of the British Labour Party, raise the question as to whether Gaitskell's success was merely temporary.

Hence the split in the Australian Labor Party, which was consummated between 1955 and 1957, was by no means unique. Although several writers have taken the view that it was the consequence of purely personal rivalries, normally of primary importance in politics, the essential elements were those which occasioned the general post-war crisis of social democracy. The interplay of clashing interests and clashing personalities was both spectacular and important. Without the personality issues which affected Dr Evatt, Senator Kennelly and one or two others, the catalysts which precipitated the Australian split would have been lacking. Equally, however, had there been no conflict of ideologies, a split would have been impossible.

In the four cases both the historical context and the political issues were the same. The context was the Cold War. The issues ranged from divergent attitudes to the American alliance, deriving from the never-ending 'hate America' campaign of the Left, to a deep concern with the penetration of Labour Parties everywhere by Communists and fellow-travellers in the interests of Soviet policy.

British Labour leaders like Bevin and Morrison, American union leaders like Murray, were animated not merely by the desire to hold their own positions, but by their understanding, arising from their

58 own experience, that the aim of the Stalinists was to range the
unions, the party and the nation behind the Soviet Union in its life-
and-death struggle against the admittedly defective, but still 'open',
societies of the West. The form taken by this essentially philosophic
and ideological struggle was the Cold War.

Some knowledge of the events of the period 1945-50 is indispensable to an understanding of the pressures to which Social Democratic Parties were subjected by the international situation. These
events and these pressures do much to explain the urgency with
which a large group of Australian Labour leaders regarded the
struggle against Communist influence within the Australian unions
and the Australian Labor Party.

The emergence of the Cold War within a few years of the defeat of
the Axis by the grand alliance of democratic and Communist States,
could be regarded as remarkable only if the Nazi–Soviet Pact were
treated as an historical accident, and if it were believed that there was
a basic political affinity between Soviet Russia and the Western
democracies. Yet it was not until Hitler invaded the Soviet Union
that the Communist Parties of the West were prepared to abandon
the strategy of 'revolutionary defeatism'. This belated transformation was not brought about by any sense of loyalty to their own
communities, but by their decision to use Western resources to
defend the Stalinist State.

Stalin's speech of 9 February 1946 and Churchill's Fulton speech
may be said to have initiated the period of the Cold War, in the same
sense as President Carter's response to the Soviet invasion of
Afghanistan may one day be regarded as having signalled the end of
the illusions of détente.

The Soviet takeover of Poland had occurred in 1945. It was none
the less shocking because Churchill and Roosevelt had already
conceded Poland to the Soviet sphere of influence, despite Chamberlain's ill-judged guarantee. On 7 August 1946 the Soviet Union
made its first attempt to obtain control of the Dardanelles, by
demanding of Turkey that it be permitted to participate in their
defence, a demand which in the judgement of the US Secretary of
State, Dean Acheson, 'meant the occupation of Turkey'.[1] The US
replied by sending the newly commissioned carrier *Franklin D.
Roosevelt* to join the USS *Missouri*, which was already in Istanbul
and prepared, if necessary, to go to war.

During 1945 and 1946 the major Powers had already come into
conflict in both Iran and Greece. By late 1946 the US administration
had accepted that the attempted Potsdam settlement was a failure,
and had moved towards the reconstruction of the economies of
Germany and Japan, which was the central objective of the Marshall
Plan, announced in 1947. The Soviet Union used its armed forces to
back the Communist coup in Prague, which succeeded in killing

THE CLIMATE OF THE TIMES

Masaryk and toppling Benes in the process of taking over Czecho- slovakia in February 1948. The Brussels Defence Pact was signed by
the Western allies on 17 March 1948. In June, the Soviet Union
announced a full blockade of Berlin. The West replied with the
Berlin Airlift, as an alternative to moving an armed convoy to Berlin
through Soviet-occupied territory. The Berlin Airlift was meant to
demonstrate that the West had the determination to meet and defeat
the Soviet challenge without, at the same time, setting in train a
course of events which could explode into war.

The Western attempt to create a European Defence Force to
counter the conventional military power of the Soviet Union failed.
On 4 April 1949, the North Atlantic Treaty was signed in Washington, bringing NATO into being, basically to guarantee the future of
Germany and to provide a roadblock against a Soviet attempt to
move into Western Europe. Truman signed the ratification document on 25 July 1949.

By the end of the year, however, what had been gained in Europe
was apparently lost in Asia, with the victory of Mao Tse-tung in
China.

These historic events opened up not merely political or ideological, but essentially spiritual, cleavages within Western societies.

On 2 February 1950 Klaus Fuchs was arrested in England and
charged with passing on to the Soviet Union vital information
concerning the atomic bomb. The ramifications of Soviet espionage
were as extraordinary as the exalted positions occupied by British
and American citizens who were proved to be in its service. Alger
Hiss, who was judicially found to have served as part of a Soviet
espionage group, had held office as a high official of the US State
Department and was at different times closely associated with Dean
Acheson; Kim Philby worked in the highest positions with the
British Secret Intelligence Service; Donald Maclean and Guy
Burgess were senior officers in the British Foreign Service. On
Philby's own statement, it was Fuchs himself who identified Harry
Gold as his American contact, while it was Gold who 'fingered' the
Rosenbergs.[2]

Many years were to pass before Anthony Boyle's *The Climate of
Treason* presented the detailed story of the penetration of a significant section of the British Establishment. This operation was originally designed by the future Soviet Foreign Minister, Maxim Litvinov
(who had lived in Britain and was married to an Englishwoman), and
was implemented largely by the Soviet spymaster, Samuel Kaplan.[3]

The significance of the transition effected by this numerically
small section of Britain's *jeunesse dorée* from the position of anti-
Fascists into Communist sympathizers, from Communist sympa-
thizers into Party members, and from Party members into traitors to

60

their own countries, was noted at the time only by those who took the Communist problem seriously. While it remained the fashion to minimize the significance of their treacherous acts, Fuchs' and Nunn May's exploits must have been of considerable significance in the rapid development of the Soviet nuclear weapons programme. As MacArthur himself bitterly remarked, it was clear to him that the enemy in Korea was well aware of the most confidential instructions he was receiving on the battlefield from Washington.[4] Considering Philby's and Maclean's access to important US Cabinet papers, which they cheerfully transmitted to their Soviet masters, this was not remarkable.

The subordination of loyalty to one's own people to loyalty to the Revolution was justified by Philby with the argument that the Western States were not the guardians of the national interests of their own peoples, but an organized conspiracy to defend the interests of monopoly capitalism. Therefore to betray them was not treason, but the mark of a higher patriotism.

Roger Baldwin, one of the two founders of the American Civil Liberties Union, declared that 'a superior loyalty to a foreign government disqualifies a citizen from service to his own'.[5] It was not a view which found much sympathy on the Left.

This total inversion of the values required of its own citizens by any State which hopes to defend its own existence was facilitated by the characteristic illusions of the Western intelligentsia. The intelligentsia, the articulators of ideas and issues, were, as David Caute was later to document, not merely overwhelmingly on the Left but, in disproportionate numbers, defenders of the 'great Soviet experiment'.[6]

On 25 June 1950 North Korea invaded the South and precipitated the Korean War. The conflict finally involved Communist China's military forces, leading to the interposition of the US Seventh Fleet in the Formosa Strait, and the establishment of the 'special relationship' between the US and Taiwan, to which the most influential figures in the Truman Administration, including Secretary of State Acheson, were strongly opposed.

Before the Korean War was over in July 1953, the intervention of the Chinese Communist armies had brought a real threat of a general war in the Far East. An intelligence paper presented to the US Administration in December 1950 reached this conclusion, as Dean Acheson reports in his memoirs:

The intelligence paper made these points: Chinese deployment and action in Manchuria and Korea were aimed to make the US–UN position in Korea untenable. The attitude of the régime and the magnitude of military preparations in China itself indicated an appreciation of the risk of general war with the United States that this effort entailed. It was unlikely that the Chinese would run this risk without some assurances of support from the Soviet Union. Support would probably include, in ascending order: continued provision of material, technicians, and perhaps, if necessary, 'volunteers'; air units and anti-aircraft batteries for defense of targets in Manchuria should US–UN air attack them; appropriate military support under the Sino-Soviet treaty in the event of US–UN operations against other Chinese territory. Furthermore, the Soviet Union must have appreciated and decided to risk the increased danger of both general US–Chinese war and global war, which Chinese intervention on the then existing scale might cause.

Finally, the Kremlin probably saw advantages to it in the US–Chinese war flowing from the diversion, attrition, and containment of US forces in an indecisive theater; the creation of conflict between the United States and her European allies and the obstruction of NATO plans; the disruption of UN unity against the original aggression in Korea, thus also aiding Communist objectives in Southeast Asia. If, however, the United States should decline the gamble of war with China and withdraw from Korea, the USSR might be counting on collecting the stakes in Korea and Indochina. In any event, the United States Government should expect aggressive Soviet pursuit of its attack on the world position of the United States. Other aggressions in Asia and Europe were not to be counted out . . .

Doubtless present-day 'revisionist' writers would conclude that this paper and the agreement of the three of us [Truman, Marshall, Acheson] with its conclusions as a guide to action, represented 'over-reaction' to Communist action.

Even with such help as hindsight gives—which I do not regard as much—I do not agree and am glad that we did not consider the conclusions overdrawn.[7]

In this international climate the Western nations were trying to re-build their shattered economies. They were constantly sabotaged by unions whose policies were dictated from Moscow. Thus the problem of Communist subversion emerged as a major threat in most Western countries, Australia included.

The drive of the Australian Communist leadership to consolidate and expand its influence in the Australian Labour Movement throughout the forties was part of a world-wide conflict which had exploded into war in Greece and Korea; which threatened world war over the Berlin blockade; which evoked the extraordinary achievements of the Marshall Plan; which witnessed the failure of the West to prevent the absorption of Czechoslovakia by the Soviet Union in the same year. The divisions which the conflicts evoked were not only between nations, but within them, especially within their political, trade union and academic institutions. It would have been remarkable if Australia had been completely spared. And it was not.

J. N. Rawling, who joined the Communist Party of Australia (CPA) in Newcastle in 1925, and remained a member until his resignation on 15 December 1939, was under no doubt that the purposes of the CPA had little to do with its professed social objectives, but everything to do with the foreign policy objectives of the Soviet Union.

Rawling, whom I came to know, became a member of the Central Committee of the CPA, was placed in charge of the Party's united front activities, and was thus privy to the Party's most confidential plans. On at least one occasion he carried a substantial amount of money from Moscow to the Australian Party.

When Rawling left the Communist Party, almost twenty years before the general exodus of 1957-60, he wrote:

62 | The Communist Parties of the world are no longer concerned with the interests of the workers of their respective countries. They are merely the agents of the Russian Foreign Office and the Kremlin, ready to frame or change policies and manufacture 'justification' for them on receipt of cabled instructions from Moscow. Stalin decides that they are to go this way or that. Then Dimitrov, Stalin's tame Comintern Secretary (useful because of the reputation he gained by his stand in the Leipzig Court six years ago) opens his office for a few minutes, sends his instructions, closes it again until next time, and returns to listen once more in rapture to the ineffable words of wisdom that ceaselessly fall from the lips of the great Stalin.[8]

The attempt to educate public opinion as to the significance of Soviet policy throughout the Cold War period came up against a major obstacle. The cultural penetration of the Australian intelligentsia during the thirties, which paralleled that of the British intelligentsia, had had three consequences. Public opinion began by being exceedingly favourable to the Soviet Union, naturally enough, because of the appalling casualties suffered by the Soviet forces in the Second World War. The prestige of the Soviet Union rubbed off onto the shoulders of its Australian apologists. Many of those who had been recruited either to the Party or to one or other of the 'fronts' during the thirties had, by the mid-forties, achieved positions of considerable influence, in the press and elsewhere. They used the opportunities their positions gave them to propagandize the public with a view of Soviet Communism which Khrushchev—and Solzhenitsyn—were later to dispel as utterly mythical. Their positions also permitted them to exclude opposing views from debate.

Charles Baumgartner, with whom I formed a friendship, and who in the early forties was assistant editor of the Melbourne *Herald*, confessed himself impotent to preserve any kind of objectivity or balance in a daily newspaper which, in left-wing mythology, was supposed to be the citadel of Australian capitalism.

The position in the Australian press was not dissimilar to that remarked on by George Orwell in Britain:

On one controversial issue after another the Russian viewpoint has been accepted without examination and then publicized with complete disregard to historical truth or intellectual decency. To name only one instance, the B.B.C. celebrated the 25th anniversary of the Red Army without mentioning Trotsky. This was about as accurate as commemorating the battle of Trafalgar without mentioning Nelson, but it evoked no protest from the English intelligentsia.[9]

The pro-Soviet climate, which made it so difficult to mount an anti-Communist struggle in the unions, and to publicize the issue in the Australian press, was in fact an all-pervasive mood which influenced every part of Australian society.

The Australian journalist Rupert Lockwood, who joined the Communist Party in 1939, and who was later to achieve notoriety as the author of Document 'J' before the Petrov Commission, testified to the immediate change in the position of Australian Communists following upon Hitler's attack.

The change was remarkable . . . Among the greatest and most enthusiastic supporters of alliance with the Soviet Union were people like Bishop Burgmann of Goulburn, who was extremely active, Canon Garnsey of the Sydney University, and the Reverend Churchward. There were very, very large numbers of clergymen involved, sitting alongside Rationalists and Communists and very free with biblical texts to show just why we should be in alliance with the Soviet Union. From being on the list that Dr. Evatt had in his possession of people to be interned, I became the National President of the Friends of the Soviet Union. I produced a paper called 'Russia and Us' and turned out pamphlets almost by the dozen to consolidate the alliance with the Soviet Union. At any meeting held then in aid of the Soviet Union, the donations were colossal. The Russian Medical Aid was founded. Lady Jessie Street was the Chairwoman, Mr. Justice Sir Percival Halse Rogers was the President, and I was one of the Vice Presidents. That indicated a sudden upsurge of respectability for Communists in that period.[10]

The effects of this conquest of public opinion as it manifested itself during the forties has been documented by witnesses whose first-hand authority cannot be questioned. Lockwood was later to explain what was going on in the Melbourne *Herald* chain during this period. In 1973, speaking to Tim Bowden, an ABC interviewer, Lockwood cheerfully testified to the double political life he, and so many other leading Australian journalists, then lived.

### Interviewer

Were you making any efforts at all to conceal your left-wing views?

### Lockwood

I should have said that before I left Melbourne and on the day war broke out I joined the Communist Party but I wasn't an open member of the party. In fact I had two faces. I was a member of the Labor Party. Jack Cain, the leader of the Labor Party in Victoria, had actually asked me to stand for a Labor seat in Victoria, but I'd been vetoed by the Right Wing of the Labor Party. They already had me on the list in Victoria in those days. I came to Sydney as a member of the Communist Party. This membership was a semi-secret one . . . [11]

Asked by his interviewer, 'If one can generalise, what sort of people were Communists?', Lockwood replied:

The Communist journalists were mostly of some position, and certainly journalists of some capacity. I remember one Communist who used to be very critical of me for not being fiery enough—he finished up as Editor of Australia's leading daily newspaper. There was such a good basis built among journalists in the newspaper industry that in Sydney, about 1942 or 1943, there were 48 journalists in the Communist Party who worked on daily newspapers, not counting those who worked on the smaller papers. This showed that the party had very, very considerable influence. The membership among the journalists was only a reflection of the strong membership that went in all occupations and industries of any importance.

### Lockwood added:

It's rather a pity that one couldn't do a thesis on what happens to ex-members of the Communist Party in Australia, but one can't break confidences on these things. When I look at how some of the ex-members of the Communist Party that I know have finished up you could almost assume that it would be impossible to run the country without the 100,000 ex-members of the Communist Party in Australia.[12]

64    The Communists did not think it necessary to be modest about their achievements. In his memoirs, *Comrades Come Rally*, John Sendy, former National President of the Communist Party, wrote:

> Yesterday's Communists today occupy some public and private positions of great professional respectability and profit. They are to be found in schools, universities, parliaments, municipal councils, trade unions, law courts and journals throughout the country . . . If an occupant is middle-aged or above and holds radical political views, then it's a fair bet that a story of association with the C.P.A. could be told.[13]

Thus the forties, which were to witness the beginnings of the struggle against the Communists in the Australian trade union movement, were dominated by two contradictory phenomena. In Europe and elsewhere the military and political conflicts of the Cold War were to mount in intensity to the point that World War III could have broken out either during the Berlin Air-lift or during the Korean War. Within Australia, however, the relatively large numbers of influential persons who had been recruited either to the Communist Party itself, or to one of its 'fronts', at the end of the thirties, were now rising to important positions of influence, especially in the media, in the universities, and in the world of literature and the arts.

# 7 Communist Penetration of the Labour Movement

The rise of the Communist Party of Australia in little more than twenty years, from foundations so frail as to invite derision, to a position which could promise considerable returns to the Soviet Union, was the result of the Party's strict adherence to Stalinist discipline both in its internal organization and in its external policies. Rigid totalitarian controls of the internal structure of the Party, allied to a clearly formulated objective—the penetration of the unions and of the Labor Party—pursued through the astute strategy of the united front: that combination constituted a precise formula whereby substantial gains could be registered by a revolutionary party operating within a democratic society.

Early in 1933 Archbishop Mannix sent a handwritten letter to the then Victorian Premier, E. J. Hogan, containing questions arising from enquiries made of him by some unidentified person as to the strength of the Communist Party in Victoria.[1] The Victorian Premier supplied his answers late in February.

The only answers of any significance were those given to Questions A and F.

## Question A

Is there any evidence that Communism has gained a foothold in the State of Victoria? Are there in Victoria any Political Communist Organizations?

## Answer

Yes. The Communist Party is established in Victoria and has no difficulty to carry on, as the organizing and other work is performed voluntarily by people who are practically fanatics. But whatever money is required always seems to be forthcoming. Apart from the Communist Party itself there are the following Communist organizations: Friends of the Soviet Union Industrial Class War Prisoners Aid (Mr. Blackburn, M.L.A., was President of this organization in 1930), Militant Minority Movement, Workers' International Relief, Unemployed Workers Movement. These organizations are political, do not believe in democratic rule, but hold that a militant minority by its energy and force, should establish a dictatorship of the Proletariat. The number of votes recorded for Communist candidates at Parliamentary elections in Victoria has increased, as is evident by the large vote recorded for the Communist candidate, Dr. O'Day, at the by-election for Carlton last year. Branches of the Communist party exist in practically all the principal towns in Victoria. Where no branch is in existence individual members spread Communist propaganda.

## Question F

Do Communists attempt by secret penetration or otherwise, to use Labor, or any other Organization to propagate their views?

## Answer

There is no doubt that the Communists have secretly penetrated the political Labor Party and Labor Unions. At the Labor Conferences in Melbourne on January 28, 1933, 61 delegates voted in favor of admitting the Members of the F.O.S.U. [Friends of the Soviet Union] into the Labor Party and 109 voted against admitting them, and at the Labor Conference in Sydney on February 21, 1933, a motion admitting Communists to the Labor Party was rejected on the casting vote of the Chairman, the voting being 39 for and 39 against . . .[2]

The Depression gave the CPA its real beginnings in Australia. J. N. Rawling classifies the first recruits to the Party as falling into two categories: the adventurers, among whom he includes 'Jock' Garden, who was to become Secretary of the New South Wales Labour Council, and R. J. Heffron, who was later to become Labor Premier of New South Wales; and the idealists, mainly academics, whose imagination was seized by the event which John Reed described as the *Ten Days that Shook the World*. The revolutionary romanticism associated with the name of Trotsky and the victorious achievements of his Red Army exercised a particular fascination on this group. However, as Rawling wrote:

Not all young intellectuals were swept off their feet. Though many were called, few were chosen. There were those who were content to stand on the outskirts to cheer, or, like Peter, to follow afar off and again, like Peter, to deny before the cock crew. The majority of those who were moved, letting perspicacity triumph over emotion, sheered off, though with many a backward glance, e.g. H. V. Evatt.[3]

The somewhat chaotic origins of Australian Communism, due partly to the gyrations of the Comintern and partly to local and personal factors, are sufficiently familiar. Stalin's tactics of head-on collision with the Social Democratic movements did not pay any more in Australia than they did in the various European countries. The Nazi victory in Germany in 1933 convinced Stalin that he must switch Communist policy from outright opposition to the 'social Fascists' of the Labour Parties, to that of the 'open hand' or the 'united front'. The Communist Parties were thus back to Lenin's policy of 1921. The changed policy became effective in Australia through such organizations as the Council Against War and Fascism and the Friends of the Soviet Union. The new policy, with the fertile field for contacts which it offered, paid better dividends than the old.

In France a similar policy was to triumph with the election of Léon Blum's Popular Front Government in 1936.

The effective penetration of the Australian unions, which was begun in the middle of the 1930s, began to bear fruit before the decade was ended. Thornton, refused admission as an Ironworkers Union delegate to the Melbourne Trades Hall Council in February 1935, on the ground that he was not a worker in the industry, had become National Secretary of the Federated Ironworkers' Association; Healy was General Secretary of the Waterside Workers' Federation; Orr was Federal Secretary of the Miners' Federation; Wright was Federal President of the Sheet Metal Workers' Union; Elliott was Federal Secretary of the Seamen's Union. They were all members of the Communist Party. The unions in which they now held the most important administrative positions covered the strategic industries of inland and maritime transport, fuel and power, the manufacture of steel and processing of steel products. Their importance was already considerable by the time of the outbreak of the Second World War in 1939. But the rapid industrialization which accompanied the war effort increased that importance beyond recognition.

The capture of the federal secretaryship of a union did not mean that the union had simultaneously become Communist; but it did enable the process of penetration to proceed faster at all critical levels. In each case, the immediate task of the Secretary became one of strengthening Communist positions on Federal and State Councils and Executives; of expanding shop committees at the point of production; and of creating a Communist majority in the ACTU and in the State Trades and Labour Councils, the representative bodies of the union movement.

While economic sabotage was a significant objective in the Communist union strategy, the fundamental objective was to use the unions not only for their own avowedly industrial purposes but through the weight of their delegations to take over the machinery of the Labor Party—its Conferences, Executives and Branches, at both Federal and State levels. With the control of the national Party machinery in their hands, the Communists would then control endorsements of Labor candidates for both Federal and State Parliaments.

That Communist activities would generate opposition and that they might even cause splits in the target organization were risks to be taken in the necessary task of removing all anti-Communist elements from the leadership of the Labor Party and the unions. 'The revolt now to be seen in the unions should not be allowed to split the Labor movement', said the (Victorian) *Workers' Voice* on 15 April 1939; 'on the contrary, Labor Party members should organize to remove Calwell, Lovegrove, Riley and their group, who are assisting the development of Fascism, and so helping to destroy the Labor Government'.

There was no secret as to the way in which control of the unions could be used to take control of the Party. The trade unions, then as now, were affiliated with the ALP. As a general rule, union delegations comprised more than 75 per cent of the delegates to all State Conferences of the ALP. These bodies elected the State Executives. Each State Conference elected the six State representatives on the Federal Conference and the two State representatives on the Federal Executive of the ALP. Conferences and Executives, Federal and State, in turn laid down the State and Federal policies of the ALP and, directly or indirectly, controlled the endorsements of Labor members of Parliament.

Communist control of a sufficient portion of the trade unions must inevitably mean a powerful influence within the ALP. Decisive Communist influence on the trade unions—even if it fell short of a numerical majority—meant decisive Communist influence on the ALP.

Whether the Communist Party could ultimately create a 'revolutionary situation' and come to power in Australia without direct military pressure from an external ally might well be debated. What was beyond doubt was the danger to the defence and foreign policy positions, as well as to the economy of Australia, which the Communist Party would represent if it were able to consolidate its grip on the ALP. For non-Communist officials and parliamentarians, the embarrassment was both more direct and more personal. They would be deprived of their positions.

At this point significant sections of the leadership of the Victorian ALP and of the unions realized that something must be done if Communist penetration of the ALP in both New South Wales and Victoria was not to result in the destruction of the entire non-Communist position within the Party.

Granted the history of weakness and factionalism within the Communist Party, and their own previously complete control of the Labour machine in Victoria, it is surprising that Victoria's Labour leaders should have lacked the capability to do the job themselves.

In a repetition of the tactic employed with temporary success in New South Wales in 1923, the Victorian Branch of the Communist Party wrote to the ALP Central Executive (31 January 1935) 'that the Communist Party and the A.L.P. on the basis of an agreed upon program and lines of action should carry out joint activity in organizing the workers in the struggle for their urgent demands and interests'. The proposal was rejected on 10 April.[4] The Victorian ALP Executive, despite the pressure now beginning to be developed by the Communists and their fellow-travellers, never quite fell into the situation of the New South Wales Branch in 1923. However, in

New South Wales the Labor Party crisis of the twenties was to recur when the Hughes–Evans group took control of the New South Wales Branch in 1939.

The formal proposal to the Victorian ALP was an example of the 'united front from above'. Having failed with this approach, the CPA, with its relatively new-found professionalism, switched to the 'united front from below', that is, direct pressure by undercover members in ALP branches for joint action 'against war and Fascism' projected through the fraternals, particularly the Victorian Council Against War and Fascism. The Victorian ALP's Central Executive knew exactly what these moves meant, and expelled ALP members who refused to break with the latter body. Nevertheless, it was clear that while the Central Executive was acting vigorously to preserve the integrity of the ALP, the action was purely defensive, and its own positions were coming under constant and more pressing attack from the branches and affiliated unions.

The 1936 Victorian ALP State Conference Agenda paper contained twelve resolutions proposing the removal of the ban on the Council Against War and Fascism[5], while in the following year the Agenda paper contained eleven resolutions, using the success of the French Popular Front as the major argument for a united front between the two parties. The resolutions were forwarded by ALP branches as well as by affiliated unions.

As the Left's most accomplished controversialist, Brian Fitzpatrick, pointed out in his *Short History of the Australian Labor Movement*,

most A.L.P. branches [in Victoria] had small membership and a substantial proportion of this individual membership consisted of persons so diligent and devoted as to be active both in the Communist Party, secretly or quasi-secretly, and in the Labor Party, openly.

The Communist or 'fellow-traveller' membership of the Labor Party, the Communist-directed trade unions, including essential industry unions like the miners', metal workers', waterside workers', seamen's, building trades', which had many Communist officials, and the Communist Party as such through its organs of propaganda, provided much of the organised working class support for Federal Labor policies as important as, for example, the post-war powers proposals.[6]

All of these elements were welded together in the 'Progressive Movement', which made its appearance in a number of Communist-led unions in 1937 and 1938. Members of the new body, it was hoped, would be elected as delegates to the State Labor Conference, and would constitute an ideologically coherent opposition to the Labor Party's 'reactionary' office-holders.

The latter included Dan McNamara, the ageing State Secretary; P. J. Kennelly, who was then Organizing Secretary and McNamara's heir apparent (unless the Communists won); H. M. Cremean, Arthur Calwell, Fred Riley and 'Dinny' Lovegrove. These were the 'power-holders' whose grip on the Party was to be broken. The Communists, who controlled not only the 'Progressive Movement', but the ALP Metropolitan Council, were able to act all the more effectively since they enjoyed the support of non-Communists motivated by their own particular discontents against the Party officials. Amongst these were men like Bill Evans, Secretary of the Federated Engine Drivers and Firemen's Union, later to become Vice-President of the ACTU, and Ted Smith, Secretary of the Clothing Trades Union, who was animated largely by anti-Catholic bigotry.

Most important of all was Don McSween, whom Smith, to his own ultimate detriment, admitted to an official position in his Clothing Trades Union. A strong influence over this group was exercised by the barrister, J. V. Barry, who was later to be elevated to the Victorian Supreme Court, and who was the leading figure in the Victorian Council for Civil Liberties.

The Communists had a perfect understanding of the explosive potential of anti-Catholic sectarianism. E. F. ('Ted') Hill, who had studied at Melbourne University at the same time as myself, by the end of the thirties had become a leading figure in the Victorian branch of the Communist Party. Hill produced a pamphlet exposing a 'conspiracy' by Calwell, Cremean and Kennelly to take over the Labor Party in the interests of the Catholic Church. It was neither the first nor the last of such discoveries to be announced periodically by the Communists and their allies. The real dividend of the strategy of sectarianism was to be collected at the time of the Labor split.

The 1939 ALP Conference launched a further defensive attack on the extreme Left by banning the ALP Metropolitan Council on the ground that the 'Socialization Committees', set up under the aegis of that body through the energy of McSween, were 'merely an institution of the Popular Front'.[7] Since it was Kennelly who had led the attack in 1939, it was natural that McSween should challenge him for his position as Organizing Secretary of the Victorian ALP at the 1940 Conference. What was significant was not Kennelly's retention of his position but the narrowness of the margin. Kennelly, who had been accustomed to defeating all challenges by at least a 2–1 majority, scrambled home by a mere 119 to 104 votes.

This vote was decisive as far as the existing officials were concerned. They now understood that all of their efforts to withstand the Communist forces over the greater part of a decade had merely won temporary victories. They had only the manipulative resources of a party bureaucracy to fight a movement endowed with a coherent ideology, firm discipline and (since Moscow's entry into the Australian scene) a new and competent leadership.

Nor was their prospect greatly altered by the Nazi–Soviet Pact of 23 August 1939, with the subsequent transformation of the CPA into a party of treason, in the sense that it published open attacks on Australian troops in the field. It might have been thought that this policy would have been fatal to the Communists and their supporters. It had little, if any, effect. The non-Communist leadership of the ALP was in fact, half-defeated already. On 15 April 1939, the Communist *Workers' Voice* had clearly stated that the Party's aim was to take complete control of the Victorian Branch of the ALP. The 1940 ALP Conference proved that to achieve their objective, they merely needed to change a handful of votes.

The progress of the CPA within the New South Wales Branch of the ALP was even more marked. In 1937 the Federal Executive of the ALP rejected still another proposal for affiliation by the CPA and declared that 'the Communist Party is in direct conflict with the policy, platform and constitution of the ALP'. When this was reaffirmed by the Federal Executive in 1938, and re-adopted by the Federal Conference in 1939, it was as if nothing had happened. J. R. Hughes and W. P. Evans, leading a left-wing faction which already had the support of the New South Wales Labour Council, took control of the New South Wales Branch of the ALP. At the next annual ALP State Conference, in March 1940—only six months after the Soviet occupation of Eastern Poland, undertaken in collusion with Nazi Germany—the Conference passed its celebrated 'Hands Off Russia' resolution. Although, until the signing of the Nazi–Soviet Pact, the Communists themselves had supported the strongest action against Nazi Germany, the Menzies Government was condemned by the Conference for plunging Australia into a war 'in which the people had no interest'.

The 'Hands Off Russia' resolution was a direct challenge to the Federal authorities of the ALP. Later in 1940, the Federal Conference removed the New South Wales Executive, an action which led the Hughes–Evans group to set up their own State Labor Party.

In New South Wales, as in Victoria, the reaction of the Labor leadership was largely defensive. Since the basis of Communist power in the unions remained largely undisturbed, and since the unions were the dominant force in the structures of the ALP, it appeared only a matter of time before the pressures generated by the CPA must be crowned with success.

# 8 The Movement: Its Origins

H. M. Cremean was a man of remarkable political gifts and moral qualities of the highest order. He had been trained as an accountant, earned his living as a timber worker, and later as a law clerk. He became Mayor of Richmond (Victoria) in 1929, when the Depression hit this highly industrialized suburb with shattering effect. He rapidly mounted the ladder of Labor politics, winning the State seat of Dandenong, also in 1929, but then losing it in the 1931 'Premier's Plan' election which left the Labor Party in ruins. Cremean was Secretary of the Fire Brigade Employees' Union from 1935 onwards. In 1935 he returned to the Victorian Legislative Assembly, representing the safe Labor constituency of Clifton Hill, and only four years later was elected Deputy-Leader of the Parliamentary Labor Party. When State Labor returned to office in 1943 he became Deputy Premier and Chief Secretary. The highest offices in Australia were not beyond him. It was a major tragedy when he died unexpectedly in 1945.

In a few brief years we became close friends. Perhaps it is that which makes me say that in courage, judgement, diplomacy, humour and personal charm, he was the finest man I met in Labor politics. There is every reason to concur with the judgement of former Senator Frank McManus that 'if he had lived, the split of 1955 might never have happened'.[1] He would have exercised a major influence on men like the Victorian Premier, Jack Cain, former ACTU President Percy Clarey, and its Secretary Reg Broadby, men who should never have finished on the other side. Although no one can be certain of what might have been, it is probable that he would have modified policies on both sides sufficiently to keep these essentially non-Communist Labor leaders working in double harness with the Industrial Groups, as most of them had done for so long. Without them, Dr H. V. Evatt and his fortuitous allies could not have pulled off the coup of 1954-55.

It was H. M. Cremean, in fact, who persuaded me that the Communist problem was much more than a generalized philosophic or ideological challenge, and that the events with which we should be concerned were much closer to home than Spain. When Kennelly, whose pragmatic appreciation of the numbers game was to become notorious, held on to his position as Organizing Secretary of the Victorian ALP against McSween's challenge by a mere fifteen votes, even the pragmatists had begun to take the Communist problem seriously, if not out of sheer altruism. Cremean, who was no mere pragmatist, decided that action of some kind had become imperative.

He suggested that I should approach Archbishop Mannix to discuss the Communist situation in the Australian Labour Movement, and to see whether the Archbishop could be persuaded that the Communist challenge to a Party which held the allegiance of almost all Catholics should be resisted through a broader effort than its leaders could organize. Cremean told me that similar approaches were being made by some of his Labor associates to leaders of the other denominations.

There was, in fact, no reason why the Archbishop should listen to me. I had met him only half a dozen times at most, had never been a member of a union or any political party, and could well have been dismissed as long on theory, but extremely short on practice. Hence Cremean's presence at the meeting, and his obvious experience and authority, were critical to the success of any proposal.

We gave the Archbishop the details of the consolidation of the Communist Party's organization since 1930; the rapid gains it had made both in trade unions and in Party branches, first in New South Wales and then in Victoria; the seeming inevitability of defeat of the non-Communist forces despite the rearguard action fought by the Labor Party leadership throughout the second half of the thirties.

Cremean, who, as Deputy-Leader of the Parliamentary Party, might have been expected to adopt the view that the Party bureaucracy, still in control, could handle the situation satisfactorily if given a modicum of temporary help, adopted a quite different position. He had already come to the conclusion that in a struggle between a group of professional political bureaucrats and the votaries of a pseudo-religion, the powers of patronage and manipulation enjoyed by the former ultimately would not equal the vision of a new society proposed by the latter to the more idealistic members of the Left, or the promise of jobs and power it might offer to the opportunists. The professionals were doomed to defeat. What Cremean was asking was thus something quite different from a purely temporary assemblage of delegates at ALP State Conferences.

The Knights of the Southern Cross, much longer in existence, with an Australia-wide organization, would have provided far stronger and more immediate resources than anything which the Archbishop could provide through the newly formed National Secretariat. But what Cremean was asking for was a kind of Catholic 'crusade' against Communism; not one which would be based on mass meetings and ringing pronouncements, but one which would base itself on practical organization within the trade union movement. While its primary aim would be to rescue the position of the non-Communists in the Labor Party and in the unions, its ambit would extend far beyond both.

I was puzzled as to the practical use which Cremean saw in my few colleagues and myself. His answer was that since he had been present at the Spanish Debate in 1937, he had come to believe that we understood the nature of the Communist problem; that as a consequence we realized that what to his professional colleagues was merely a challenge to their careers and positions was in fact a philosophic conflict; and for that reason alone, we were more likely to persist and might ultimately prevail. It was an unusual view for a professional politician. I thought it was a pretty long shot!

Archbishop Mannix dealt at once with the situation as Cremean described it. He said that if we advanced a practical plan of action he would be disposed to back us. Somewhat timidly, I mentioned the question of financial support. What did we need? Unprepared, I could do no better than to say that a piece of propaganda we proposed to produce for the railways would cost £25. He did not even refuse. He simply changed the subject. That, I thought, was his way of refusing. In fact, it was not so. Some months later, when with Cremean I went to the Archbishop with the practical plan of action the latter had requested, I told him that for a start we should need £3,000. He did not demur. When I referred to the by-passing of our original request for £25, he smiled: 'Now, I know that you are serious'.

Since the Federal Labor leadership was at all stages unwilling, and the State Labor machine apparently incapable, it became necessary to devise an organizational structure which would both raise the recruits and keep them in the field. What was needed was something quite different from those nonsensical anti-Communist organizations which publish a manifesto, fly a flag, run a few demonstrations, and engage in ritual denunciations which do little other than expose the ignorance of the organizers.

The first signs of an organized resistance on the part of Catholic trade unionists had indeed already begun to appear, even before Cremean's suggestion for a more permanent organization. A young, energetic and capable Communist, J. J. Brown (who had been born a Catholic), had recently been elected State Secretary of the Australian Railways Union, largely as a result of the lethargy of his opponents. I had been approached by a group of Catholic railwaymen, headed by Jack Desmond, to help them in producing and publishing a small paper designed to circulate among the members of the various railways' unions throughout the State. They approached me because they were strong supporters of the *Catholic Worker*, and were known to me as such. The result was the publication of a miniscule printed monthly, which we called the *Rail Worker*. I generally wrote a good deal of it, on the basis of information supplied by the railwaymen themselves. The purpose of the paper was to build resistance to Brown's control of the ARU.

The task ahead was, however, much more complicated than writing articles either for the *Catholic Worker* or for the *Rail Worker*. The problem was to find the relevant organizational method. For this there were no better teachers than the Communists themselves.

Apart from the 'fraternals' or 'fronts'—whose object was general propaganda, and recruitment of potential fellow-travellers or Party members—the CPA's operational organization was directed to the establishment of undercover groups, cells, or 'fractions' of the Party in unions, particularly the key unions, and ALP branches. Unity of policy and organization was guaranteed by the application of the principle of 'democratic centralism', which ultimately guaranteed control by the party bureaucrats, and through them, by agencies of the Soviet Government.

One critical difference was that there were no 'friendly' governments, either Australian or foreign, who ever offered to play the same 'friendly' rôle as the Soviet Government played with the CPA. The CIA, which is supposed to have played an active rôle in Australian industrial and political affairs and has possibly done so, never contributed a penny to the operation, despite not a few statements to the contrary.

The Communist organizational method had stood the test of effectiveness, and my proposal was that we should copy it. In so far as we had the capacity to give effect to our own proposals, my thought was that the battle to defeat Communist power in the Labour Movement—whether in the Labor Party or the trade unions—should be essentially one of cadre against cadre, cell against cell, fraction against fraction. If the central problem of creating an essentially Catholic organization was the almost inevitable sectarian reaction, Catholics were, on the other hand, in a unique position to build such an organization if only they had the necessary collective courage and corporate determination. In social complexion they were largely working class. They were therefore, overwhelmingly, members of unions, while their political sympathies and membership—in the case of those who were political activists—were almost exclusively Labor.

As Robert Murray points out:

In a party where above half the rank and file were Catholics, their home bases usually lay with people of similar disposition. Particularly at this time . . . they were bound together by a detestation of communism. At the same time, most had a concern for social reform that enabled them to work without misgivings in the same party as the two left groups.[2]

What was involved, therefore, was not the interposition of an extraneous or alien force in the Labour Movement, but the mobilization of a force which was already present, but dormant.

To begin our work, we sought out a few men with knowledge of trade union affairs. The initial meeting of the organization, later known as 'the Movement', which was held on 14 August 1941, had only four people present, two others in addition to Cremean and myself. The next meeting brought together about twenty unionists from twelve Melbourne suburbs. With their help we gradually founded a large number of groups of trade unionists on a district (or parish) basis. The first general gathering of these groups took place on 4 January 1943. Through these efforts, groups of anti-Communist trade unionists were formed in a number of trade unions and in the larger factories. At this stage the work was confined to Melbourne. In that city it developed cohesion and organization under the direction of a small organizing committee of four, two of them being Cremean and myself.

There may be some interest in the practical methods by which this modest effort was maintained. A regular link with the top rungs of the non-Communist trade union leadership was established as a result of a meeting between P. J. Clarey (President of the ACTU), J. V. Stout (Secretary of the Melbourne Trades Hall Council), Norm Lauritz (my first 'recruit') and myself, in a room provided for the occasion by Mr Clarey in Parliament House, Melbourne. At the end of a long discussion, it was decided that we should all, in our various ways, combine our efforts against the Communists. The most regular link was maintained with J. V. Stout, through weekly meetings between himself and Norm Lauritz, since they already knew one another. Their weekly meetings were supplemented by almost daily phone calls. Stout used to tell Lauritz of meetings of any importance in the various unions, so that we would induce members of those unions whom we could influence to attend those meetings. This we were generally able to do. At his end of the operation, Stout kept in touch with a number of non-Communist union secretaries.

The results were quite apparent, even if not of overwhelming importance. The files of the Melbourne press from 1943 to 45 disclose a considerable number of anti-Communist victories in small- and medium-sized trade unions.

Our own members in the various unions, who had previously shared the general apathy in relation to union affairs, now attended their union meetings in numbers and provided the numerical strength which challenged the growing Communist power. Each union which was thus either retained in non-Communist hands or won back from Communist or extreme Left control, provided non-Communist delegates to the Trades Hall Council. These in turn added to the small majority on which Stout's position as secretary had until then precariously depended.[3]

To transform these incipient successes into something more substantial and more permanent necessitated some effort to change public opinion concerning Communism through the agency of the media. In the prevailing climate, it was unreal to expect that the press would provide favourable reports of anti-Communist activities within the union movement. There was no alternative but to try to establish our own weekly paper. It was much more easily said than done. We had no money, few potential writers, and no machinery of distribution. There was, in addition, the almost insuperable obstacle that the Federal Government had established control of all newsprint supplies, making it impossible to establish a new weekly or any other paper without a specially created newsprint licence.

To overcome the difficulties I asked Archbishop Mannix whether he would be prepared to give the Movement one of the two Catholic diocesan papers controlled by the Archdiocese of Melbourne—the *Tribune* (not to be confused with the name adopted much later by the Communist *Workers' Weekly*!). Since the paper had been running quite successfully, under competent editors, for many years, the request was outrageous and was made only because there was no apparent alternative. The Archbishop refused my request, but said that he would discuss the possibilities of obtaining a newsprint licence and allocation with Mr Calwell. It was characteristic of Dr Mannix's policy. He would try to facilitate what he thought was worth doing, but, having provided the opportunity, he left you to succeed or fail on your own account.

His discussions with Mr Calwell were ultimately successful, but only after what appeared a long and agonizing delay. Mr Calwell secured the newspaper licence and the newsprint allocation, and *Freedom* (later *News-Weekly*) was founded. It was the most practical sign he could give that he thought the struggle for control of the Labor Party and the unions extremely important, apparently overcoming a personal antipathy to myself, of which I was not then aware.

This was the beginning of my personal relationship with this strange and contradictory figure, a relationship which in later years was to be increasingly important.

For many years I thought that this personal hostility, which was to become so obvious during the DLP period, had only developed at the time of the Post-War Reconstruction Referendum of 19 August

78 | 1944. The avowed purpose of that referendum was to transfer certain stated powers to the Commonwealth to enable it to meet the problems of rebuilding a shattered economy without the handicap of the centrifugal powers of the States. The editorial board of *Freedom* adopted a policy of a conditional 'Yes', the condition being that the Federal Government should include in its proposals a guarantee against the continued direction of labour (or civilian conscription of manpower) which had prevailed throughout the war. Mr Calwell was enraged at *Freedom*'s refusal to urge an unconditional 'Yes'. More than once he summoned me to his Department of Information office to demand that *Freedom*'s policy be changed to one of unconditional support. Even had I personally supported his position—and I did not—I could not have changed the opinion of the editorial board.

This led to a total breach between us, certainly not of my choosing. Mr Calwell had great abilities and many virtues which nobody should gainsay. His virtues were pre-eminently a genuine sympathy for people suffering hardship. His immigration policy—in which his performance was blotted only by occasional incidents like the O'Keeffe and Gamboa cases, and that of the Manila girls—demonstrated qualities of first-class statesmanship. He was also a good hater, and I seemed to have precisely the personality which aroused that capacity.

Twice I tried to bring about a reconciliation. In 1944 Mr Calwell was sued for libel by Brian Penton, editor of the Sydney *Daily Telegraph*. I sent him a wire wishing him good luck. His secretary, Jack Cremean (a brother of H. M. Cremean), a close personal friend of mine, to his great embarrassment was told to phone me and say that if Mr Calwell had to choose between Penton and myself, he would choose Penton!

Later, in June 1948, Mr Calwell's only son died of leukemia. I shared the widespread sympathy for a father's deep sorrow. By chance, soon afterwards, I ran into Mr Calwell in Robertson and Mullen's bookshop. I hesitated as to whether I should risk a rebuff by speaking to him. I thought of my own feelings after such a loss, went up to him, and offered my sympathy. The agony of loss was obvious on his face. However, nothing had changed. 'I want no sympathy from you' was all that he would say. Whatever I felt it was impossible to blame him for an antipathy which he obviously could not control. If we had been able to come to terms with one another, he would not have vetoed the proposals for settling the conflict between the ALP and DLP in 1965.* Personal hostility, conceivably, deprived him of the prime ministership, which he wanted more than anything else.

* See p. 259.

Apparently the antipathy went back to a period before the 1944 referendum. In his autobiography *The Tumult and the Shouting* Frank McManus says that even before I met him in 1941, 'Arthur Calwell had spoken to [McManus] about [Santamaria] on a few occasions; he had complained of one or two articles in the *Catholic Worker* that criticised the ALP, and accused Santamaria of Fascist tendencies'.[4]

Without Mr Calwell's intervention, however, obviously due to the extremity in which his forces in the ALP found themselves, there would have been neither licence nor newsprint for *Freedom*, whose first issue appeared on 25 September 1943. Among the people directly involved, it was commonly thought that the Archbishop had supplied the initial capital. In fact, I borrowed £700 from my father, who never expected to see it again. It was a satisfaction to me, and a surprise to him, when I repaid it about five years later.

*Freedom* was a pretty poor substitute for regular reporting of anti-Communist union activities by the daily press. As a weekly it lacked the intellectual distinction of Britain's weekly organs of opinion like the *New Statesman* and the *Spectator*. It was, and was meant essentially to be, utilitarian. It informed the Movement activist, the relatively large number of inactive supporters, and other favourable forces in the Labour Movement of events within the unions, the political orientations and convictions of candidates, the campaigns, the results. A deliberate effort was made to provide a balance between the reporting of union activities and articles on positive social policies. The question of post-war reconstruction was always, at least theoretically, in the air.

Political analysis was a permanent feature of the paper. That analysis mainly concerned the Labor Party, simply because that was where the struggle was and where the bulk of the *Freedom* readers had their political home. In any case, Federal Labor was in office from 1942 until the end of 1949. The Liberals were almost completely irrelevant to the problems with which *Freedom* was concerned.

*Freedom*'s journalistic tone has been variously described. 'Strident', 'acerbic' are some of the kinder adjectives. There was some truth in these descriptions, although on the whole the tone was consistently more moderate, for instance, than that of the Leftist English *New Statesman*. The truth was that what was needed was not a literary journal in whose columns academics might discuss the finer points of political science, but a crusading tabloid which would inform the troops of battles to be fought, of the strategems of the enemy, and the ever-changing terms of the struggle.

Ultimately, however, information and propaganda were merely a function of organization. The only type of Movement likely to count was not one which would merely editorialize, but one which would supply trained and dedicated activists to attend the meetings of unions to which they belonged; and, equally, of those branches of the Labor Party which, in Brian Fitzpatrick's delightfully frank phrase already quoted, 'had small membership, and a substantial proportion of this individual membership consisted of persons so diligent and devoted as to be active both in the Communist Party, secretly or quasi-secretly, and in the Labor Party, openly'.[5]

The difference between the two groups was that the Communists entered the Labor Party which, in principle, they opposed and despised as, at best, 'reformist' and, at worst, 'social fascist', for totalitarian and undemocratic purposes; while members of the Movement were traditional Labor Party members or voters, but passive and dormant, activated to protect democratic institutions as the best available safeguard of political, social and religious freedom.

The situation within the Victorian Labor Party and within the Melbourne Trades Hall Council improved fairly quickly as a result of the smooth co-ordination which prevailed from the beginning.

As far as the Labor Party was concerned, H. M. Cremean was the link with P. J. Kennelly, the Organizing Secretary of the ALP, who was a political practitioner of high order. To him was attributed the immortal phrase, 'You can have the logic, so long as I have the numbers', a sensible description of how final decisions were and are made, not merely in the Labor Party. Frank McManus writes that Kennelly 'had an immense capacity for work and intrigue, and a sincere devotion to Labour's cause. He had a keen sense of humour which helped him in many tense situations'.[6] His humour was undoubted, although whether you were in a position to enjoy it depended on whether he was with you or against you, and whether he or you had the magic 'numbers'.

By 1945, the Left was so thoroughly defeated within the Victorian Branch of the Labor Party that Kennelly's position was declared a life-time job, to save him from facing the annual challenge which had almost led to his political extinction in 1940. It was a mistake, as life-time appointments almost always are. It meant that in future he need concern himself much less with the views of those who put him there, while it enabled him to make deals at various times with the extreme Left, justifiable only in terms of pragmatism or of seeking a quiet life.

As a member of the Legislative Council, Kennelly became Minister for Public Works in the 1945-47 Cain Labor Government.

As the anti-Communist vote improved on the floor of the Trades Hall Council, so did the quality of the leadership. A group of union officials who met regularly in the Boot Trades Union office—including 'Dinny' Lovegrove, 'Mick' Jordan, who was Stout's Assistant Secretary, and 'Gil' Hayes, Secretary of the Boot Trades Union—constituted themselves the leadership, and deprived the

Communists of the debating edge as thoroughly as the different floor strength deprived them of 'the numbers'. For the longer term, the most important development was the growth of a new group of union and Labor leaders, many—but not all—connected with the Movement, whose ability and dedication provided some guarantee that the gains would not proved ephemeral. Frank Scully (ARU), John Maynes (FCU), Labor politicians like S. M. Keon, J. M. Mullens, T. Andrews (the last three to become members of the House of Representatives), were beginning to make their mark.

The post-war problem was the direct consequence of the foothold the Communists had gained in the most strategic industries during the War. The effect of the popularity gained by the military valour of the Russian soldiers for the Soviet's Australian associates, particularly those within the Australian trade union movement, was quite dramatic.

The results had become apparent in the desperate moments after the Japanese attack. The Curtin Government felt that it had no alternative other than to deal with Healy, Thornton and the other Communist union leaders, who as acknowledged leaders in possession of the most important sections of the trade union movement, were essential to the efficiency of the war effort. Communism gained respectability and prestige. Other unions elected Communists as leaders. By the end of the war in 1945, the balance of power in the unions had altered decisively in favour of the Communist Party. By 1945, as Professor Crisp witnesses, the Party had 'unprecedented strength'.[7]

The Federated Ironworkers' Association, with 60,000 members, was not only led by a Communist, W. E. Thornton, but the union as a whole was under the effective control of the Communist Party. The FIA had absorbed the Munition Workers' Union, and its 30,000 members, who until the amalgamation were led by a Communist, Sharpley. The Communist grip on the Munition Workers' Union was so strong that amalgamation with the Communist-controlled FIA was pushed through with relative ease, despite strong opposition. The Amalgamated Engineering Union, the third big union in the metal industry, was in fact controlled by the Communist, E. ('Teddy') Rowe. The Miners' Federation, the Waterside Workers' Federation, the Seamen's Union, the Australian Railways Union, were other examples of important Federal unions under Communist control. At the state level, many unions were in the same position.

In all, unions with half a million members were directed or powerfully influenced by the Communist Party—a very large proportion of the work force of a country which in 1945 had only 2,114,000 salary and wage earners.[8] It will be noted that Communist power, concentrated in the important sectors of inland and maritime

82 | transport and the fuel, power, heavy metals and engineering industries, was centred on the focal points of the national economy.

It was not only the individual trade unions which came under Communist control. The State Trades and Labour Councils are, in a sense, the state parliaments of trade unionism. By 1945 the Brisbane, Sydney, Adelaide and Hobart Labour Councils were all under effective Communist control, and only in Melbourne did non-Communists hold a narrow majority.

It was inevitable that the result would be reflected at the apex of the trade union pyramid. In July 1945, at the biennial Congress of the Australian Council of Trade Unions, the Communist Party disposed of a majority of ninety delegates in a Congress with a total of approximately 400 delegates. This majority was not made up exclusively of card-carrying Communists. It included the fellow-travellers and a number of intimidated non-Communist union officials to whom the Communists guaranteed a quiet life if they 'went along', and the opposite if they did not. Whatever their motives, they voted solidly with the Communists.

Thornton, who was the CPA floor leader at the Congress, was reported to have told a cheering crowd of delegates at a Marx House social on the first night of the Congress: 'Today we have passed a vital milestone on the road to proletarian revolution in Australia'.

Sharpley, who had been Communist Secretary of the Munition Workers', was not indulging in idle boast when, much later, he wrote: 'So strong did we become that it was touch-and-go at the 1945 Australian Trade Union Congress whether or not the whole trade union apparatus would fall into our hands'.[9]

If the Communists had been able to consolidate their floor majority at the 1945 ACTU Congress by the passage, through a majority of State Trades Hall Councils, of the two amendments to the ACTU's Constitution, which they passed at the Congress itself, it is difficult to see what further effective action could have been taken.

Fortunately, only one of the two constitutional amendments was carried by the necessary majority, when referred back to the States as they had to be. This amendment made all future decisions of the ACTU Congress binding on the entire trade union movement, which until that time had not been the case unless Congress decisions were validated by a majority of State Trades Hall Councils.

The other amendment, which provided that all members of the Interstate Executive of the ACTU (the permanent executive body between Congresses) should be elected by the Congress itself, instead of being elected in part by the Trades Hall Councils, would simply have meant that whoever had the majority on the floor of a Congress would have total control of the union movement. This amendment was rejected by the majority of State Trades Halls, as the result of a somewhat miraculous chance-majority produced by last-minute organization in Adelaide.

Throughout this period my own work in developing the organization of the Movement went hand-in-hand with my responsibilities to the National Secretariat; to the Catholic Rural Movement; and to the development of work in the general field of social justice, of which the drafting of the annual Social Justice Statements was the most demanding.*

One criticism, proffered much later, was that many of the problems which developed at the time of the Split would not have developed had I left my position in the Secretariat, joined the Labor Party, and pursued the work of organization from within its ranks rather than from outside. I can only say that nothing was more alien to me than membership of a political party. I disliked the necessary compromises of politics, and was only too well aware, from many examples before me, of the consequences of political ambition, once aroused. I did not believe that I was likely to be any better than anyone else in politics. I did not trust myself to resist the temptations involved in the struggle to get to the top.

Nor did the suggestion make much practical sense. The work of organization demanded both an adequate administrative base and some reputation for altruism. Without the administrative back-up, first of the Secretariat, and after 1945, of the Movement, there would have been nothing on which to build. And if a person of such outstanding organizational ability as H. M. Cremean had not been able to organize an adequate resistance from a purely Labor base, how was I to achieve a better result?

Hence, my only personal encounter with party politics was in 1941. On 3 October, Maurice Blackburn, MHR for the utterly safe Victorian Labor seat of Bourke, was expelled by the Victorian Central Executive for refusing to sever his association with the Australia-Soviet Friendship League which the Labor Party—years before there was any Movement influence on its decisions—had proscribed as a Communist 'front'. When the pre-selection to choose his successor for Labor endorsement was announced, the secretaries of two ALP branches in the electorate approached my father in his Brunswick shop to see whether I would be prepared to nominate for Labor endorsement, claiming that their branches could control the selection. My father pointed out that I was not even a member of the Labor Party, or, for that matter, of any other. To my surprise they answered that this was no disqualification! A ticket could be issued and pre-dated. Whether it could have been issued or not; whether they represented anybody other than themselves; whether or not

---

* See Chapter 5.

84 | they could have won—these were all unanswered questions, since, because of the work on which I was already engaged, the proposal could not be considered. That was the closest I got to membership of any political party before the Labor split, and it was not very close.

# 9 Building a National Organization

The general result of the 1945 ACTU Congress could have been predicted long before it happened. The situation of the nascent anti-Communist opposition was absurd. The effort already made in Victoria might show promise. It was nevertheless fiddling with a problem whose dimensions were already nation-wide. It was time to see whether the contacts already made in Sydney could be induced to participate in the work of a national organization and—the key to the issue—to participate in one centrally co-ordinated disciplined national effort.

I took the familiar route to St Patrick's Cathedral to discuss the matter with the Archbishop, since what had to be done needed to be done quickly if we were not to be completely out of time. If quick results were to be gained, it could only be through the extension into all States of the type of organization developed in Victoria. In Sydney Dr P. J. Ryan had proved himself a brilliant controversialist in a series of public debates with the Communist leaders, arousing great enthusiasm which might perhaps be turned into organizational capital. To bring this about, however, would demand both the moral and material support of the Bishops. Dr Mannix said that this could only be gained at a Bishops' Conference if the support of the Archbishop of Sydney (Archbishop, later Cardinal, Gilroy) had been obtained beforehand. In that case, the proposal would be presented to the Bishops with the joint backing of the two Archbishops, thus averting another example of the historic Sydney–Melbourne division.

About this, he took the view that he himself could do nothing, and that I would have to persuade Archbishop Gilroy myself, although he would write beforehand to introduce me to the latter. I did not think I would be able to do much. Archbishop Gilroy had, however, already been persuaded by Dr Ryan as to the nature and urgency of the Communist problem. It was this which led him to give his

86 | support to the project which I outlined to him. He and Dr Mannix thereupon jointly summoned what was called an Extraordinary Meeting of the Australian Bishops, which met in Sydney on 19-20 September 1945—three months after the significant Communist victory at the ACTU Congress.

This was the first time I had met the Archbishop of Sydney. Ten years later, in the mid-fifties, his changing attitudes were to have fateful consequences, not merely for the Movement but for Australia. He was kindly, courteous and charming. I was surprised by his quick response, since it had proved impossible to secure the participation of the Sydney Archdiocese in the work of the National Secretariat eight years earlier, and since, in the Sydney tradition, there was rarely support for lay initiative and autonomy. It was apparent that he was extremely alarmed by the union situation, and that his alarm overcame his native inhibitions. On the other hand, lacking Archbishop Mannix's practical, if hard-earned, political experience, he was unfamiliar with the details of the situation outlined to him, whereas Archbishop Mannix fully understood its complexities.

A small touch of irony was associated with the Bishops' meeting. To give the Bishops the necessary factual material for discussion, I had prepared a detailed report which outlined both the Communist situation in the unions, and the proposed national organization to meet their challenge. Thirty copies only were printed, marked 'Completely Confidential', and delivered by hand to the Bishops of each diocese. Within a few months, this 'completely confidential' document, greatly embellished by the Communists themselves in order to arouse a sectarian reaction, appeared as a Communist Party pamphlet entitled *Catholic Action at Work*. One of the Bishops, travelling by train to the Conference, had carefully placed the statement under the pillow in his sleeper, and when he left the train had completely forgotten the precious but dangerous document. In retrospect the incident was not without humour, although it did not augur well.

Archbishop Mannix was not present at the Extraordinary Meeting of the Hierarchy. That body nevertheless decided unanimously to back the Movement. I had naturally felt that the prospects of winning support would be greatly diminished if he were not present and if the responsibility for presenting the case were left largely to myself. This was in no sense to demean the support which could be expected from such close friends as Archbishop Beovich of Adelaide and Bishop Henschke of Wagga. While both had expressed their unequivocal support for the proposal, they could not have the same knowledge of detail as Archbishop Mannix.

I pressed Dr Mannix as to his reasons for staying away from the meeting. He would say no more than that, at the age of 81, train travel was difficult. This was a reason I had not heard him use before. Many years later, he told me that the real reason was simply to ensure that no bishop would feel under pressure to vote for the project out of personal loyalty to himself, instead of out of conviction as to its intrinsic merits. If it were the former, he explained, that Bishop's support could not be expected to last beyond his own lifetime. And he was 81!

The standard of my address to the Bishops' Meeting, I felt, was abysmal. But there were some strong friends present. The support of the Archbishop of Adelaide (Dr Beovich) and of the Bishop of Wagga Wagga (Dr Henschke) was invaluable. The result of their efforts was that the Meeting gave its 'approval and support to the general principles of the Movement as set out in the Memorandum'.[1] With this declaration of support went two other decisions. The Bishops voted £10,000 per annum to enable the Movement to engage a skeleton staff in each State. Any extra money for expansion had to be raised by ourselves.

At the same time, the Bishops naturally expected to be informed of the conduct and progress of a work to which their material and, above all, moral assistance was basic, since there was no other source to which one could go. They appointed a subcommittee of three to maintain liaison with the organization. These were Archbishops Gilroy and Mannix, and Bishop O'Collins of Ballarat. Partly as a result of strong representations by myself, the latter was asked by the other members of the subcommittee to attend executive meetings of the Movement, now that it was to become national in scope. There were three reasons for the choice of Bishop O'Collins. As a Victorian, he was close to the national headquarters in Melbourne. He had been an active unionist, a member of the Plumbers' Union, before his entry into the priesthood. Furthermore, he was a close personal friend of Archbishop Gilroy. This led to a curious instruction, not without its humour. Archbishop Gilroy told him that if there were any meetings of the subcommittee (which was not anticipated), he did not propose to attend, but wished to cast a vote. On matters on which Archbishop Mannix and Bishop O'Collins were in agreement, his vote would be registered with theirs, thus ensuring unanimity. Should there be disagreement between the two Victorian Bishops, his vote was to be registered with that of Bishop O'Collins. The old Sydney suspicion of Melbourne was not absent even in a venture which, because of singular emergency, had witnessed a rare degree of unanimity.

The terminology of the resolution guaranteeing episcopal support was later to occasion limitless trouble, and was to be a significant factor in the ultimately insoluble difficulties of the fifties. Referring to the functions of the subcommittee, a separate resolution stated that 'The Movement be controlled, both in policy and finance, by a

88 | special Committee of Bishops'. The resolution was drawn up hastily, as the meeting dragged on into the evening, and as several of the older Bishops wanted to adjourn. Its terms were doubtless intended to reassure doubters that any controversial policies or activities on the part of a Movement which the Bishops were assisting would be kept under supervision.

The terms of the resolution must be read in the light of the constant practice of Bishop O'Collins, who attended practically every quarterly meeting of the national executive for the better part of the next decade; and, as far as I can recall, only twice intervened on an issue of substance, and, on both occasions, in relation to the same matter. This was when some delegates were arguing that a number of union ballots were so thoroughly 'cooked' by the Communists that, regardless of effort or deserts, it was impossible to win an election in fair fight. Their claim was that there were thus two sets of union rules, the registered rules, and rules which actually prevailed, which were indistinguishable from Rafferty's. Since the latter were the real rules under which these unions—like Thornton's FIA and Rowe's AEU—operated, it was claimed that those who fought were entitled to act according to the real rules rather than the registered rules in any branches in which they might take control. Bishop O'Collins dealt with that proposal without hesitation, ruling that such a decision would morally involve the Movement in corruption and was, therefore, *ultra vires*. Except for that issue, the principle of lay autonomy in every aspect of Movement life was completely observed.

It was this issue—ultimate control—which precipitated the split in the ranks of the Bishops, which occurred at the same time as the Labor split of the fifties. The judgement of the Rev. P. J. Duffy, SJ*, who investigated the whole matter in close detail for his M.A. thesis, therefore deserves study:

On the face of the wording of the bishops' resolutions it seems that they intended close detailed control of the CSSM's policies and activities, and that the responsibility for them would be theirs.

Yet Bishop O'Collins' declaration of the practical application of the resolutions conflicts with such an interpretation. He also makes it clear that the bishops accepted his interpretation. Subsequent episcopal resolutions in 1946, 1947 and 1953 show that the bishops did not conceive their relationship with the CSSM to be anything like their control over Catholic Action bodies. These latter were explicitly under the bishops' direct and immediate control, and the whole administration of such institutions conformed to that principle.

Some bishops at the 1945 meeting had feared that an episcopal connection with the CSSM would involve the Church in party politics, and had given their support only on two specific conditions. One was that there should be a complete separation of the CSSM and Catholic Action. The other was that the laymen should be responsible for the CSSM.

* Now Provincial of the Society of Jesus in Australia.

One bishop present at the meeting has said that the resolution on 'control of policy' was passed solely to satisfy these few bishops who wanted enough control to stop the CSSM involving the Church in politics if the danger ever arose. He maintains that the rest of the bishops agreed to this, fearing that the misgivings of the few would prevent the immediate creation of the national movement at a time when it was considered urgently necessary to get it started . . .

Whatever their intention in 1945, and whatever the extent of their authority over Catholic laymen to direct them to be active in politics—and their authority was considerable—one thing is clear. From 1945 until 1954 the bishops never acted as though they considered their control of the CSSM to be anything more than a negative watch over faith and morals.[2]

Since I was not present when the matter was debated and decided, I was unware of the resolution, being told of its existence and its terms only some months later.

My own view was then and remains today, that the Movement had been founded and conducted in Melbourne from 1941 to 1945 by a group of laymen; that it was therefore their Movement; that Archbishop Mannix had assisted it, but never claimed to control it; that the same Movement was now being extended nationally without any alteration to its intrinsic nature; that the Hierarchy as a whole had the same relationship to the national Movement as Archbishop Mannix had to it while it was confined to Melbourne and Victoria.

To my mind, there was no other way of running such an organization. The financial and moral support of the Bishops was certainly needed, otherwise it would be impossible to grow quickly. If the Bishops did not accept responsibility for all the policies of the Movement—and they were adamant that they would not—they could not claim to 'control' it. Since they were advancing a not inconsiderable sum they were entitled to reports, while their advice would have considerable influence. Control, however, for their safety as well as ours must remain where it had always been. In the last analysis, if the Movement were to take an unacceptable direction, the withdrawal of their moral and material support would limit the damage which insistence on this principle could occasion.

None of the future problems could be fully foreseen.

November came before Archbishop Mannix received the minutes of the meeting. Having received them he remembered the similar episcopal decision, taken equally unanimously in 1937, to establish the National Secretariat of Catholic Action. He recalled that three dioceses (Sydney, Canberra–Goulburn and Hobart) had later separated themselves from the Secretariat, despite their earlier vote and with little apparent regard for the personal and family responsibilities of the lay members of the Secretariat. Accordingly, on 19 November 1945, he sent the following letter to each Bishop.

I have the Minutes of the Bishops' Meeting in Sydney recently. I find that the Bishops have agreed to make themselves responsible for an annual expenditure of £10,000 approximately, on (1) the work of the National Secretariat of Catholic Action and (2) on what they call the 'Industrial Movement'. I am wholly in agreement with the decision. I am glad that the Bishops show their continued approval of the Australian Catholic Action Movement and that they are increasingly interested in the urgent need for the new Industrial Movement.

I also learn that the Bishops decided to set up a Committee to supervise the policy and the expenditure of the Industrial Movement; and that they wish me, with the Archbishop of Sydney and the Bishop of Ballarat, to be the members of that Committee. The two Bishops associated with me in the proposed Committee were present at the Sydney meeting and had an opportunity of expressing their views. But, before I join the Committee, I think it necessary to provide against any possible misunderstandings later. I shall gladly work on the Committee, on the understanding that the annual financial provision made by the Bishops will remain available as long as the need for the suggested Industrial Movement remains. It would be a waste of energy and of money for the Committee to begin the proposed industrial campaign with the possibility that at a critical time the whole campaign should be abruptly abandoned because the expected financial aid was not forthcoming. The Bishops, I am sure, did not overlook this aspect of the case. But, in any event, I want to make my own position clear at the outset.

Moreover, if the Committee is to give effect to the policy of the Bishops, highly qualified and experienced men must be found to work under the guidance of the Committee. Such men are not easily found. They will be men who have already proved their worth: men who have a good salary and a more or less secure position; they may also have family responsibilities. Such men would not think of giving up their present employment, unless the Committee could offer them a wage and a measure of security comparable to what they already enjoy. From enquiries I have made I am hopeful that highly competent and reliable men can be found to serve the Committee under the conditions that I have broadly outlined.

Having explained my own position, and having tried to provide against possible misunderstandings, I feel that I can now communicate with the Archbishop of Sydney and the Bishop of Ballarat and join with them, if they share my views, in giving effect to the policy endorsed by Bishops at the Sydney meeting.

I am,
Sincerely yours,
D. MANNIX[3]

The most important immediate practical consequence of the assistance thus promised by the Bishops was that it enabled me to make appointments to the national office of the Movement and to create State offices in each State. Except for Melbourne and Sydney, each office consisted of only one official and a typist.

Robert Murray is right in estimating that Movement membership at its peak was closer to 5,000 than to 10,000.[4] But almost without exception they were extremely active and self-sacrificing persons, always prepared to attend their union and Labor Party meetings and above all to stay until the meetings closed. Murray is also correct in writing: 'Movement officials were mostly poorly paid, usually at about the ruling rate for a skilled tradesman. They worked for long hours and the organizers travelled around the cities by public transport'.[5] In speculating that some of the money from confidential American Government sources which was 'certainly . . . available for anti-Communist work in the Australian Labor Movement at this time', 'may have gone to the Movement'[6], Murray, in so far as he commits himself on this question, is completely wrong. There never was any money from that source or from any government source whatsoever. I can testify to that as one who would have had no compunction in accepting financial support from any legitimate source, so long as it was given without strings.

The constitution of the Movement clearly expressed its general objectives:

(a) to inculcate in members positive ideals of Christian social teaching, and to permeate the whole of society with these ideals through the activities of its members;

(b) to adopt all methods necessary for preserving and developing democratic institutions in Australia;

(c) to oppose with all means at their disposal all Movements having as their objective totalitarianism whether of the Left or the Right.[7]

To avoid the impotence which would result from fragmentation of authority in a work in which rapid and clear decisions were the condition of success, proposals that the Movement should be a federation of 'independent diocesan groupings' were rejected in favour of a unitary organization.[8] The constitution provided for strict adherence to decisions of the central authority. That authority was a National Committee with representatives from each region in which the Movement existed and, subject to the ultimate control of the National Committee, of a National Executive. Within this framework it was inevitable that the full-time officials, as the only permanent personnel, would exercise considerable *de facto* authority. It would also be foolish to pretend that as the only remaining member of the small group who had founded the organization, my own moral authority was not somewhat more that that of the others.

It was all done in a hurry without time for debate, for conceptualization, for the working out of the undoubted theoretical problems which must arise in the case of a religiously motivated organization acting in the field of politics, or for the hundred more urgent problems of practice. *On s'engage, puis on voit.* Since by any rational judgement the extension of the Movement from Victoria to Australia as a whole had apparently come about far too late to succeed in what we set out to do, it was hardly practical to add to the wasted time by long theoretical discussions.

# 10 The Sectarian Dilemma

The ultimate health of democratic societies depends not merely on the authority of political parties but on the strength of what Professor Peter Berger has called the 'mediating' institutions. Apart from political parties, the trade unions, the universities, the financial institutions, the Church, the media are the most important. Like the organs of a healthy body, when their members are attacked by a virus, they should produce their own antibodies, and with them fight the disease with which they are attacked. The Communist Party might be regarded as an expression of the totalitarian virus. When it attacks, institutions as strong as both the unions and the Labour Party should be capable of producing their own antibodies, their own resolute defenders, animated by the political philosophy of social democracy, as a response to the totalitarian infection. Between the thirties and the late fifties, this is precisely what happened in Britain between the days of Attlee, Bevin and Morrison, and those of Gaitskell.

It was no mean achievement on the part of the British Labour leadership of the thirties and forties. As George Watson points out, 'between 1930 and 1939 many, and perhaps most, British intellectuals under the age of fifty, and a good many in other Western lands, knowingly supported what may have been the greatest act of mass murder in human history'.[1] This was the crime which led Orwell, again in Watson's words, to hate 'intellectuals not as individuals but as a caste'.[2] It says a great deal for the British Labour leadership that it met this enormous philosophic pressure which seemed to have quite overcome the generation to which they must have looked for their own successors.*

---

* How completely different is the situation in the ranks of British Labour at the beginning of the eighties, following the death of men like Anthony Crosland, the retirement of Roy Jenkins, the withdrawal of Reginald Prentice and David Marquand, leading to the triumph of the Left, headed by Anthony Wedgwood Benn, backed by strong Communist and Trotskyite elements in the TUC.

The developments inside the American labour movement in the mid-forties were almost identical. Philip Murray rallied the anti-Communist elements in the American trade union movement and established the mould which, under the leadership of George Meany and his successor (Lane Kirkland), has endured to the present day: this despite the present dominance of the McGovernite Left within the Democratic Party. It is what ought to have occurred in Australia. Yet by 1940 it was clear that there was no possibility that it would happen.

Professor L. F. Crisp, who idolized Chifley and whose opposition to both the Movement and the Industrial Groups is well known, nevertheless understood the significance of the refusal or the inability of the Australian Labor leadership to follow the example of their British equivalents and to ensure the integrity of their own Party.

Only if Chifley and the whole leadership of the A.L.P., accepting these hard facts, that the Communists had brought party into the unions, and had subordinated union interests to their own local and international party purposes, and measuring the forces they were opposing, had unreservedly thrown the *whole* organisational strength of the Party on the broadest basis, and its fund of goodwill, into a concentrated drive for union power, would they have made both fast and effective inroads into Communist industrial strength. At the same time they would have sustained a broad A.L.P. (rather than made way for a narrowing, increasingly sectarian) character to the anti-Communist drive which was in fact organised in the unions after 1945 by the 'industrial groups' in the name of the A.L.P.[3]

Crisp's prescription was correct. Prescriptions, however, butter no bread. If the Labor leadership failed in its responsibilities, as it did, the critical question was what ought to be done to compensate for its failure. Or was the community to accept the position that nobody else was entitled to try, regardless of the effects of Communist victory in the unions on the community as a whole, as well as on the Labour Movement itself?

This essential point was made by John Kerr, then a member of the New South Wales Bar, later to become Mr Whitlam's nominee—and nemesis—as Governor-General. He wrote:

In Labor Party circles however, there were people like Ward who criticised me for helping the Industrial Groups. I said to Ward: 'If you fellows would give leadership things would be different. If you really believed in the Labor Party, you would give leadership in this. You would not leave it more or less exclusively to active Catholics. You would say, if the Labor Party is fit to run the country, it is also fit to run the unions which are affiliated with it and you would give leadership to people who are setting out to defeat communism in trade unions. But you don't do it; you leave the field exclusively to Catholics, or almost exclusively so, and then you complain because it is Catholics who are carrying on the fight. It's a fight that you don't carry on yourselves and if it were not carried on by them, it would be carried on by nobody. Communist strength would grow in the unions and in the Labor Party through the unions' influence on the Labor Party.'[4]

That problems of incalculable dimensions would certainly arise if a specifically Catholic effort were organized to combat Communism in the Labour Movement was quite apparent from the beginning. A specifically Catholic effort, however sincere its leaders might be in acting for national rather than for purely sectional purposes, could always be side-tracked, isolated and destroyed by the use of the sectarian weapon.

The first quarter of the twentieth century had witnessed two episodes during which the destructive sectarian passion had been consciously aroused for political purposes. The first—immediately before the First World War—had resulted in the expulsion of large numbers of Catholics from the Labor Party in Victoria, because of their association with the Catholic Federation in its fight for educational justice, for some form of governmental assistance to independent schools. The second was during the Conscription controversy, in which W. M. Hughes had, in the judgement of Dr H. V. Evatt, consciously chosen 'the tactics of sectarianism' as the most likely strategy to give him victory in both referenda.[5]

Both episodes were part of the folk-memory of Australian Catholics of my parents' generation. Consequently it was clear that if in the course of a struggle against the Communists in which Catholics were prominently engaged, things went awry, a similar situation might well arise. As Frank McManus was later to write in his autobiography, it was soon after our first meeting in 1941 that he warned me that while Cremean was a most honourable man, some of those who might benefit from the proposal to initiate organized struggle against the Communists were opportunists who would have no hesitation in using the sectarian weapon to disown both myself and those whom I might succeed in enlisting, once they considered their own personal interests secure.[6]

Foreseeing that a problem of this kind might arise even if it did not assume the dimensions of 1912 and 1917, I made an initial attempt to meet the possibility by suggesting to representatives of a number of Protestant Churches that their own interests were equally at stake, and that they might join in a common struggle which would transcend religious differences. This was a personal initiative of my own quite separate from the approaches to leaders of Protestant denominations made earlier by various Labor leaders.

Perhaps to parallel the initiative of the British and American Governments in devising the Atlantic Charter in 1941, the Curtin Government had sent a request to all religious denominations to assemble and forward to the Government a statement of their respective ideas on post-war reconstruction. The Catholic Bishops placed the request in the hands of the National Secretariat. One result was the preparation and publication of a specifically Catholic document, *Pattern for Peace*, the product of a committee, chaired by myself, which included such personalities as Mr Justice (later Sir Raymond) Kelly of the Commonwealth Arbitration Court, Michael

Chamberlin, later to become Deputy Chancellor of Monash University, and Charles Baumgartner, Assistant Editor of the Melbourne *Herald*.

The second consequence was a successful approach to other Christian denominations to see whether we could perhaps produce a joint document, which would thereby have a stonger effect than a purely denominational statement. My colleagues on the Joint Committee originally included persons like L. Biggs, former Editor of the Melbourne *Age*, who was a member of the Anglican Synod, and the well-known peace advocate, the Rev. Palmer Phillips.

The limited enterprise was successful in that, over a series of meetings, we hammered out Twenty Points which represented our joint ideas on the socio-economic structures which should follow the termination of hostilities—at that moment, a somewhat remote future. They were:

1. The public control of monopolies.
2. The public control of credit.
3. The institution of Industrial Councils. These councils were to be self-governing bodies representing the employer, the employee and the public. Their function would be to control all the operations of each particular industry, and they would fix wages, prices, dividends and profits.
4. Assistance to small owners.
5. Part ownership of industry for the workers.
6. The extension of the co-operative movement in all its aspects.
7. The recognition of the principle of adequate income for all, including those on the land.
8. Special assistance to family life, including a marriage bonus, adequate family allowances, child endowment, etc.
9. Adequate wages to be paid before dividends and profits.
10. Equal pay for equal work.
11. Family homes to be available to all who need them.
12. Decentralization.
13. A national campaign for family land settlement.
14. Personal ownership of land and freedom from debt.
15. Revision of farming policy whereby the first principle of farming should be to provide for the sustenance of the farmer and his family.
16. Development of the co-operative spirit in rural communities.
17. Fair return for farm products.
18. The establishment of a self-governing body to direct agricultural development and policy.
19. A national system of education.
20. Religion to be the basis of education.

All of those objectives were idealistic in motive, some more or less scientifically expressed, others so general in expression as to be as meaningless as most political or social slogans.

I suggested to the other members of this committee that it was as important for the churches to guard against the totalitarian penetration of the Labour Movement as it was to propound programmes of social justice and social reform; and that perhaps we might act jointly on this matter as well. The suggestion came to nothing. Mr Biggs, the Anglican representative, viewed the projected Catholic effort with favour, but pointed out that quite apart from other obstacles, most church-going Anglicans were middle-class and non-unionist. The others were simply non-committal. The Methodist representative, the Rev. Palmer Phillips, whom I had learnt both to like and to respect, had his heart on the Left, his association with the Spanish Relief Fund and the Council against War and Fascism being a matter of public record. This approach thus came to nothing.

Frank McManus experienced a similar disappointment. He writes:

> Support was also sought from leaders of other Churches. I was asked to meet a leading Nonconformist clergyman who was said to be interested. I explained the need for Christian men to attend their union meetings and stand for office, and assured him that they would be supported even in preference to Catholic candidates. He said that he could give no assistance, because his people were mostly professional or small business men and did not join unions.
>
> When the split came, the same man issued a blast against the secret Catholic campaign to take over Labor and the unions.[7]

The truth was that, regardless of foreseeable complications, unless the Communists were to be given a free run, there was no alternative but to proceed, if possible minimizing the risks of a sectarian reaction, knowing, however, that they could not be completely avoided.

By 1945 the essential principle of counter-organization which had been pioneered in Victoria—to oppose cadre with cadre, 'fraction' with 'fraction', cell with cell, and to give effect to the entire enterprise with tight central direction—was now being put into operation throughout Australia, without excessive concern as to whether it was not too late.

If the plan worked, the machinery being developed by the Movement to counter the Communist offensive would be successful in rallying considerable numbers of rank-and-file unionists. The fundamental political condition of success was, however, still lacking. Since the organization, in its membership, would be very largely Catholic, it required no great prescience to predict the nature of the counter-strategy which the Communists would use to repel, to weaken, and ultimately to destroy the nascent opposition. The sectarian weapon was always ready to hand.

Nobody was more adamant on the necessity for countering this tactic than J. V. Stout, if for no other reason than that (so those who knew Stout best claimed) he himself had strong anti-Catholic feelings, and his association with the Movement was a marriage of convenience. I was more impressed when similar advice came from Percy Clarey, President of the ACTU. I trusted him, whereas I did not always trust Stout.*

But although Clarey on one, and Stout on several, occasions warned against the danger of sectarian tactics, they apparently had no particular idea as to how the danger could be averted other than to give general advice to be discreet.

The Communist Party understood the tactical position very well. Its campaigns against 'clerical reactionaries masking under the ALP cloak' were continuous, as were its attacks on the 'alliance of the AWU bureaucracy and Catholic Actionists' and on 'the Catholic Action Movement [which] forms an essential part of the campaign to destroy the working class movement'. As G. F. Walsh points out: 'No fewer than 16 articles on this theme appeared in the Sydney Communist *Tribune* during the first two months of 1946: and several larger articles, with the same message, were published in the Communist Party's theoretical review, *Communist Review*, during the same year'.[8] The problem was never far from my mind.

My own conviction grew rapidly that unless we could radically change the terms of the struggle, at the worst we would face total defeat, at the best make merely indecisive marginal gains.

The problem—if not the solution—could be simply stated. If the Communists were able to project the fight in the unions as 'Moscow v. Rome', those who carried the banner of Moscow would defeat those who carried the handicap of Rome. What needed to be achieved, was somehow to transform the struggle from 'Moscow v. Rome' into 'Labor v. Communism', which, in any case, was what it really was.

A solution—which led ultimately to the adoption of the concept of ALP Industrial Groups by the ALP—suggested itself in the course

---

* I believe that Clarey reciprocated that trust, since when he was elected to the Federal Parliament in 1949, he came to my office and asked if I could find a confidential secretary for him. I thought the request strange, since he barely knew me; but I persuaded Cecily Laird, who was employed in my own office, to take the position, which she held until he died on 17 May 1960. But before I recommended her, I pointed out to Clarey that while she would be utterly trustworthy and, once appointed, loyal to him not to me, our mutual enemies would not hesitate to assert the contrary in an endeavour to breed distrust. He replied that he took the point, but would accept her if I recommended her. The event is worth recalling because Percy Clarey was persuaded to oppose the Industrial Groups—and by consequence the Movement—at the time of the Labor split, some five years before he died. It then became fashionable for Labor parliamentarians and officials to deny all previous contact between themselves and myself, but I am not aware that Clarey did so.

98 of discussions with Jim Kenny, Assistant Secretary of the New South Wales Labour Council, early in 1944. Kenny was in general touch with our activities through Dr P. J. Ryan. When the Movement became a national organization, Kenny joined it. The New South Wales union situation was fraught with even greater possibilities of danger than the Victorian: it was in fact in New South Wales that the Industrial Groups were first initiated in 1945.

The underlying principle on which the Industrial Groups were founded was that the Labor Party would form 'groups'—not 'branches'—inside Communist-controlled unions; and that these groups would select and give the equivalent of official Labor endorsement to candidates to oppose the Communist leadership in ways similar to the endorsement of Labor candidates in Federal and State elections. The advantage would not only be that the system would force a differentiation between Labor and Communism in vital union elections, but that fellow-travelling Labor men who stood on the same ticket as Communists would ultimately face Party discipline.

The idea of the Industrial Groups, which like so many others developed out of general discussions, was not immediately accepted because it bore within itself a number of obvious difficulties. The polarization of union elections between Labor and Communist candidates was calculated to lead to the isolation of the latter. But it could not be excluded that in ambitious and unscrupulous hands, the Industrial Group principle might be used in elections in which there were no Communist candidates, those temporarily in control of a State Labor Party machine using the potent weapon of Labor endorsement to get rid of their purely factional enemies and to instal their own friends in union office. It was unlikely, but not impossible. Hence the idea lay fallow for many months.

It was during 1945 that elements in the New South Wales leadership began an active campaign to familiarize the Party membership with the basic principles of the proposed method of organization.

In 1946 the Labor Premier of New South Wales, Mr W. J. McKell (later to become Governor-General) described the foundation of the Industrial Groups.

The Groups had been formed over a year ago for the purpose of strengthening the cause of the Australian Labor Party in factories and workshops . . . Their special function is to keep up a close liaison with the trade unionists and the workers in industry on behalf of the Labor political movement.[9]

J. A. Ferguson, MLC, Federal Vice-President of the ALP (later to become one of the Industrial Groups' most inveterate opponents), declared in the *Industrial Groups Handbook:*

Labor's continued ability to govern depends . . . on the preservation of discipline . . . Over-presumptuous 'leftists' cannot be allowed to use the trade unions as a means of imposing minority anti-Labor political control over our Governments.[10]

My associate, Norm Lauritz, first sounded out Stout as to the prospects of extending the New South Wales precedent to Victoria late in 1945.

To meet the opposition which must inevitably be anticipated at the 1946 Victorian State Conference of the ALP, the first at which the idea could be considered in that State, it was necessary to demonstrate to Labor Party members the arguments for what was without precedent—except in New South Wales. *Freedom* began to campaign on this issue in November 1945.

The members of the Movement at once saw that if the idea were accepted, it would do much to destroy the sectarian tag, as well as otherwise to improve the anti-Communist prospect in union elections. Other Labor leaders with whom they were working within the Labor Party did not take long to conquer their reluctance, as it became clearer day by day that unless the tide were turned they would lose their positions in the Labour Movement, for by this time, the industrial situation throughout the country had become extremely critical. It was this constantly mounting Communist pressure which ultimately persuaded the leadership of the Victorian ALP.

In 1946 the Communist Party adopted a three-point plan:

1 to use their industrial power, especially in heavy industry, to hamper the whole process of post-war reconstruction;

2 to use their control of the transport and mining industries in particular to bring about a coal famine, and so strike not merely at industrial power supplies but at domestic heating in many homes;

3 to sabotage the housing industry and foster general discontent by prolonging the wartime housing shortage.[11]

Action taken by the Chifley Labor Government in sacking Communists from their wartime positions on the Stevedoring and Maritime Industries Commissions, for calling strikes in those very industries, had little effect on the situation. The political pressure on Labor governments was becoming extremely strong. Jack Cain, the Victorian Labor Premier, reacted to the 1946 strike in the engineering industry with strong language which merely disguised essential impotence.[12]

It was all essentially negative. *Freedom*, in a front-page story on the same situation, wrote:

Unless the present crisis is consciously used by Labour to lead an offensive against the Communist aggression, which will result in the removal by unionists of every Communist from office, there will be a recurring series of crises for Labour between now and the next election.

It added:

It is not enough for the Federal Conference of the Labour Party to pass resolutions which dissociate that body from Communism. *The battleground is the factory* . . . A resolution from Labour telling the workers that they must go to their union meetings, that they must eliminate every Communist from any position of trust, would evoke a tremendous response from the rank and file . . . Labour would confirm itself in the estimation of the Australian people.[13]

After a strong campaign which would nevertheless have been unavailing unless the most senior members of the Victorian Labor Party had been previously won to the principle of Industrial Group organization, the 1946 Victorian Conference carried a resolution authorizing the formation of Industrial Groups by a majority of two hundred and seventy to twenty-five. The overwhelming victory of the anti-Communist forces which supported this resolution has only to be contrasted with the near-defeat of Kennelly for the position of Organizing Secretary in 1940 to measure the amount of work which had been done already in the Victorian Branch of the ALP. An ancillary factor was the recent disaffiliation from the ALP of the Victorian Branch of the Australian Railways Union, which was under the control of a Communist, J. J. Brown. This step was rightly understood as a warning that major unions traditionally affiliated with the Labor Party would use the weapon of disaffiliation from the ALP as a kind of financial threat or sanction to compel the Party to obey Communist policy. It was clear, however, that once the step of disaffiliation was taken, even if it were later reversed, the rank-and-file would gradually come to see that there was an alternative to the traditional affiliation with the ALP—namely, association with the CPA.

There were important differences in the constitutional structure of the Industrial Groups in New South Wales and Victoria. In New South Wales, even non-members of the ALP could join, while the control of the ALP State Executive was looser than in Victoria. In the latter State, the control by the Party was close and detailed, membership of the ALP being a prerequisite of membership of the relevant Industrial Group. Needless to say, the penetration of the Groups by left-wing and fellow-travelling ALP members had to be guarded against.

From 1948 onwards, Lovegrove, who had become Assistant Secretary of the ALP, maintained close personal control of the Victorian Groups. The maximum number of groups ever in existence in that State was sixteen. They were restricted quite rigidly to unions which were Communist-controlled or powerfully influenced by the Communist Party, since Lovegrove was determined that relationships with the non-Communist 'centre' of the union movement should be preserved.

The Groups were established in Queensland by the Labour-in-Politics Convention in 1947. They operated under the control of a three-man committee headed by AWU State Secretary, J. Bukowski.*

---

* His switch from outright support for the Groups to outright opposition in January 1955, in the period of the Labor split, took exactly twenty-four hours.

While the Industrial Groups were technically established in South Australia, they enjoyed a merely formal existence until their charter was ultimately withdrawn in October 1951. It was no secret that the withdrawal of the charter was due entirely to the opposition of Clyde Cameron, then State Secretary of the AWU, and later Federal member for Hindmarsh and Minister for Labour in the Whitlam Government (a position from which he was unceremoniously ejected by the Governor-General on the demand of his own Prime Minister). It should be said for Mr Cameron that unlike other prominent members of his Party who were strong protagonists of the Industrial Groups when the wind of political favour was blowing in their direction, and who were to develop severe conscientious scruples about them only when the wind changed, his opposition to the Groups was both permanent and consistent.

If the machinery of the Industrial Groups was firmly in the hands of the constituted authorities in the Labor Party, there can be little doubt that the Groups owed a great deal to the dedicated enthusiasm of Movement members. As to the peculiarities of their structure, there is no need to revise what I wrote in 1971 in reviewing Robert Murray's *The Split*:

> The Industrial Group leaders comprised a number of prominent individuals, some of whom, like Short, Maynes, Hurrell, Ross, Woodhouse, Neill, were outstanding by any standards . . . Alone they could have achieved very little. It was the Movement 'cadres' in their unions on whom they could rely absolutely, who gave them freedom to act. They knew that—whereas a following gained purely on the basis of political advantage and careerist instinct was likely to abandon them in moments of depression, adversity, defeat—the Movement man, to whom communism was to be fought absolutely, would not run away. This quality, mistakenly called ideological, was more important even than the fact that the Industrial Groups, never having any real interstate organization with which to fight Federal union elections (the ALP having prevented this development), the Movement possessed this indispensable logistic support and made it available.[14]

Nobody understood better than the Communist Party what was involved in the formation of the Industrial Groups. The whole front had been turned. They were now fighting not merely the Movement; they were fighting the Labor Party. With the outbreak of the Cold War, the CPA was moving from a policy of the united front to another of its periodic attacks on reformists and 'social fascists'. Now they were being pushed away from the policy of the united front by something other than themselves, and they did not like it.

The first reaction was a recrudescence of the sectarian tactic. The Victorian CPA Secretary, Hill, attacked the decision of the 1946 Victorian ALP Conference:

> No doubt, however, the Catholic Action Movement regards as a good victory the decision of the Conference to set up ALP groups in the factories. It will be remembered that it was precisely this policy that was advocated in the secret report of the Movement (partially quoted in the CP pamphlet, *Catholic Action at Work*).[15]

102     It was a tribute to Hill's powers of observation and analysis that he had seen where the idea of the Industrial Groups first originated. He was not, however, primarily interested in observation and analysis. His primary interest was to use the sectarian weapon against the Groups, so as to force Labor delegates to reverse the decision to form the Groups at forthcoming State and Federal ALP Conferences.

It would be tedious to quote other examples of this campaign. That it was merely a tactic was later revealed by the former Communist Secretary of the Munition Workers' Union, Cecil Sharpley.

In many trade unions and factories, ALP Industrial Groups are effectively combating Communism. When an ALP 'Grouper' is succeeding, the Reds spread the story, by mouth and leaflet, that he is a Catholic Action man, concerned more with popery than the union. The dangerous sectarian activity to which I referred was not, as many readers imagined, Roman Catholic union activity, but the activity of those who fall for the Red bait and denounce ALP Groupers for being, as they so often are, Catholics. Even men within the ALP Groups fall for the Red bait and become involved in sectarian squabbles.[16]

Although the Communist campaign drew the expected reactions in resolutions forwarded to Labor Party Conferences by Communist-led unions and left-wing Labor Party branches, all seeking the disbandment of the Groups, there was never any major crisis until close to the decisive year, 1954.

Two statements made by the National Secretary of the CPA at about that time furnish an interesting reflection on the objectives and the methods of the Communist campaign.

In 1951 Mr R. Dixon, President of the CPA said: '. . . The Industrial groups are the organizations of the Labor Party in the factories and unions. When we deal with the Industrial Groups we deal with the Labor Party . . .'. He added:

It is often sufficient for a worker to oppose us for him to be branded a 'grouper', and a 'Catholic Actionist', or to be given some other tag which means that he is a no-hoper. My experience has been that a great number of workers branded as 'Catholic Actionists' by sectarian Communists have turned out to be Protestants.[17]

# 11 Labor's Reply to Communism

Supporters and opponents of the Groups agree that they were remarkably successful. Ironically, in the light of later events, the Federal Labor leader Dr H. V. Evatt, in his address to the Industrial Groups Rally at Sydney Town Hall on 30 March 1952, correctly placed the Industrial Groups within the context of the social democratic tradition when he said:

A vindication of what has been done by the Labor movement in the industrial field is now apparent to all. It is part and parcel of the democratic Labor policy opposed to the totalitarianism of the Left as much as to that of the Right. The efforts of the ALP Groups to combat Communism and its extremists who have attempted to dominate the trade unions have been completely justified by events.

In the first few years, they concentrated their attention on the consolidation of the anti-Communist elements in many small unions which might themselves be unimportant but whose delegates were vital in Trades Hall Council and ACTU elections. By the end of the decade, Communists had lost control of four of the five State Trades and Labour Councils.

The 1945 ACTU Congress had been followed by a major campaign of industrial sabotage which ended in the national paralysis which engulfed Australia between 1947 and 1949.

The nation which had just emerged from the war against Japan stood in need of everything. In particular, it required coal, iron and steel, and the efficient functioning of the internal and maritime transport which was needed to carry basic materials from the point of mining and manufacture to the point of merchandizing and consumption. Unfortunately, it was precisely in these industries that the Communists had control of the key unions.

With the substantial victory which they had garnered at the 1945 ACTU Congress behind them, the Communists acted boldly to use their industrial strength in a quasimilitary attack on the economic life of the country, facing the Chifley Labor Government with problems almost identical in nature and dimension as those which simultaneously faced the Attlee Government in Britain.

By Christmas 1945, the Communist-led Miners', Ironworkers' and Seamen's Unions, acted jointly to paralyse the eastern seabord of Australia. Already in Victoria, serious transport strikes had broken out ostensibly in pursuit of industrial claims by the Communist-led Railways and Tramways Unions. On the sworn evidence of Cecil Sharpley, who at that time was an important member of the Communist industrial apparatus in Victoria, most of these strikes were 'neither decided on nor directed by the unions. They [were] called and run by the Communist Party'.[1]

The pattern of Communist strike action spread over all of the eastern States. On 13 December 1945, the Sydney correspondent of the Melbourne *Argus* reported the consequences of the industrial situation on the life of the city, on the eve of what came to be known as 'Black Christmas':

Events of the last week have moved rapidly towards a national disaster. At least half a million workers have been thrown idle . . . The wheels of industry are stopping all over New South Wales and in parts of Victoria and South Australia . . .

Lights are going out all over the most densely populated parts of Australia which depend on NSW for electricity and gas. Housewives in Sydney are striving to cook over open fires in crowded backyards. With summer conditions and hot winds, big city and suburban fires might break out at any moment.

Violence and robbery stalk the streets and lanes and parklands . . . This is not scaremongering. The evidence is there for anyone with the eyes to see it. And this is not the worst. The condition of mind among the masses of Sydney, Newcastle and all the County of Cumberland might even contain the elements that can produce riot, civil commotion and the shedding of innocent blood.[2]

The Christmas strike of 1945 was followed by a series of well-ordered stoppages in heavy industry, transport, power and fuel.

1946 saw the Queensland meat industry strike and the metal trades dispute in Victoria. The year ended with a gas strike as well as a general transport strike in Melbourne. This was also the year when the Waterside Workers and the Seamen's Unions, both Communist-controlled, were able to dictate a major aspect of Australian foreign policy with their ban on the loading of Dutch ships for Indonesia.

The Victorian metal trades dispute dragged on for several months in 1947. In defiance of the ACTU, three Communist-led unions, the Ironworkers, the Railways and the Amalgamated Engineering Unions formed a joint strike committee, and J. J. Brown brought the long dispute to its climax by drawing out a handful of key men at Newport railway workshops.

When the strike ended, the Engineers' Communist leader, E. J. Rowe, claimed: 'We have learned a lot in this campaign. We now know the vital points. We will not pull out a lot of men next time. We can cause paralysis with a few'.[3]

1948 opened with the Queensland rail strike, which also involved the AEU, in what was described by ALP leaders as a calculated political attack on the Hanlon Labor government. In Sydney, the FEDFA, the Gas Employees and Ship Painters and Dockers held stoppages. There was the Kemeira coal dispute which cost the country an estimated 200,000 tons of coal. This was organized by the Communist-led Miners' Federation.

The year ended badly for Melbourne, facing a bread strike, a gas strike and a coal strike at the same time. When the Victorian government threatened to invoke the Essential Services Act, the Communist union leaders were able to threaten in return a tram, railway and building strike. This was the occasion when Bird, Communist Secretary of the Victorian Branch of the Seamen's Union, dispatched a letter to the Premier in which he threatened 'a complete blockade on all Victorian ports'. Sharpley stated that 'the Government of Victoria yielded finally under our threat that the next move would be a stoppage of key men (engine-drivers and firemen) at Yallourn. That would have cut off Melbourne's light and power. We won'.[4]

When P. J. Kennelly, as Minister for Public Works in the Cain Government, was trenchantly criticized by senior members of the Victorian Labor Party, like Lovegrove and Broadby, for negotiating with the Communist leader Hill, behind the backs of the officials both of the Trades Hall Council and of the ALP, his defence was simple. The power to end disputes which threatened the economic life of the State and the political existence of the Government, rested not with them, but with Hill.

The culmination of this campaign of industrial sabotage was reached with the great Coal Strike of winter 1949. Once again the joint action of the Communist-led miners, watersiders and seamen had paralysed the most populated areas of eastern Australia. Despite strong left-wing pressure, the Chifley Government sought and obtained emergency powers. Mr Chifley expounded his viewpoint in a broadcast to the Australian people. He said:

The whole economic and social life of the nation is approaching complete disruption.
The miners cannot hope to enforce their claims by the law of the jungle. . .
The people of this country have had imposed on them an intolerable hardship that is completely unjustifiable. Living conditions are for many people becoming completely intolerable, and unemployment will be, and indeed now is, widespread.
It has been suggested that the stoppage has been planned by a Communist section of the Miners' officials for some months. I hesitate to believe that any citizens could be so callous as to plan deliberately for the holding up of the life of the community and the imposition of the intolerable hardships and deprivation of amenities that this stoppage creates. But that is what has happened.[5]

Under its emergency powers the Chifley Government 'froze' the funds of the striking unions, prosecuted and gaoled a number of Communist union leaders, and authorized a security raid on Marx House, the headquarters of the Communist Party in Sydney.

The 1948-49 Report of the Joint Coal Board described the havoc wrought by the Communist offensive. On 18 June, the Board was compelled to restrict coal consumption 'drastically'.

> . . . The steel industries at Newcastle and Port Kembla were directed to shut down forthwith and to limit coal consumption to the minimum consistent with the preservation of plant . . . Non-essential food processing industries. . . were prohibited from any coal . . .
> *New South Wales*: Throughout almost the whole of the strike period there was no electric power for industry or commercial use, except in the case of essential food stuffs. For purposes other than lighting, domestic electricity was restricted to three hours daily. Domestic gas consumption was limited to three hours daily and for one period of several days the use of gas from the company supplying most of Sydney was entirely prohibited. Railway services were cut over 80 per cent and tram services by over 40 per cent. At one stage 86 ships were tied up in Sydney without bunkers.[6]

What was under way was an industrial offensive, carried out in the spirit of a military operation, by an organized group as clear on their objectives as on their methods. Over the greater part of the period from 1945 to 1949 the resistance was too newly organized to be very effective. By the time of the 1949 ACTU Congress, the situation was beginning to change. The Communists, who had held a majority of ninety at the 1945 Congress, found it transformed into an anti-Communist majority of 100. The Communists recognized the significance of these events, J. McPhillips, who had become their leading union organizer, pointing out the lesson. He wrote that the 1945 Congress was the last congress at which the 'progressive' forces in the trade unions 'had majority support'. In 1947, 'the influence and numerical strength' of these forces was 'declining', but at that particular congress the anti-Communist opposition of the Industrial Groups was only in its early stages.

> . . . Their disruptive influence was just commencing to be felt. Consequently that Congress (1947) was not as adverse for the progressive forces as were later Congresses in 1949, 1950, 1951, 1952 and 1953 when the Groups were at their height and their worst.[7]

Although some Labor leaders, journalists and reviewers were later to deny the achievements of the Industrial Groups, the Communists were in no doubt as to the source of their defeats. They were in the best position to know.

Once the Communist defeat was accomplished in the Trades Hall Councils and the ACTU, the Industrial Groups carried their offensive into the key unions. In these unions the 'clean ballot' legislation, introduced first by Mr Chifley, later amended and improved by the Menzies Government, was the essential complement of the Industrial Group method. Without the simultaneous operation of both factors, victory in these unions would have been impossible. The reason was made clear by the Commonwealth Arbitration Court in its finding in relation to the 1949 elections in the Federated Ironworkers' Association, that there had been 'forgery, fraud and irregularity on a grand scale',[8] as the National

Secretary of the union—the Communist, Ernest Thornton—fought off a strong Industrial Group challenge. What was happening in the Ironworkers' Federation was known to be happening elsewhere. Sharpley was later to describe how he personally had participated in ballot-rigging in a number of unions as part and parcel of his functions as a Communist 'specialist' in these matters.[9]

Of course, these allegations of ballot-rigging were copiously denied, and were regarded as symptomatic of the exaggerations in which my associates were said habitually to indulge. If we had permitted the protests of the Communists and Left-liberals—who alleged that our story of Communist ballot-rigging was the result of anti-Communist phobia—to prevail, the results in the major union ballots in the early fifties would have been radically different. But we were not inhibited, since we knew what was happening.

Sharpley, the former Communist secretary of the Munitions Workers Union, on his defection from the Party in 1949, supplied the necessary evidence.

In a series of articles in the Melbourne *Herald*, which he later expanded into his autobiographical study *The Great Delusion*, Sharpley stated:

When I became one of the leaders of the Australian Communist Party, I found that the following instructions were issued to trusted leaders of union groups:
1  See that a Communist or at least a sympathiser is elected as a union returning officer.
2  See that the union's ballot papers are printed at Party printing works, or at printing works in which we have contacts or where Party members are working.
3  Party members concerned with the union ballots must see that many more ballot papers are printed than voting members.
4  If necessary, and where required, organize Party members and sympathisers to vote in the names of union members who will not be bothered to exercise their votes.

He added:

I could name at least a dozen union officials in Melbourne and Sydney today (1952) who hold their positions because of rigged ballots. Between 1946 and 1948 I witnessed the rigging of union ballots, in the Amalgamated Engineering Union, the Federated Ironworkers' Union, the Federated Engine Drivers' and Firemen's Association, the Blacksmiths' Society and the Federated Clerks' Union.[10]

The orthodox justification for the shameless ballot-rigging of the forties appeared much later—in May 1978—when Daphne Gollan wrote of what, with delicious sensitivity, she called 'adjustment of ballots'.

Another problem which was never mentioned in the union or party branches was that of ballot rigging. But we did discuss it in private. Those who argued for adjustment of union ballots, recognizing it as an evil necessity, of course, said that, beleaguered as we were in the unions with the reactionaries constantly attacking, we could not allow the enemy into policy-making bodies. Everyone knew that if their returning officers presided over the ballot boxes, the vote would never give victory to the left.

Above all, the long-term objectives of the socialist movement could not be jeopardised by the errors or failures of our short-term policies, or halted because the rank and file were temporarily misled by the overwhelming barrage of lies from the reactionaries.[11]

The first 'clean ballots' legislation was passed in 1949 by the Chifley Government, which took a long time in overcoming its scruples against any 'interference' with unionism. A deputation from the Industrial Groups led by E. Peters (later MHR) and J. Maynes of the Clerks' Union, together with F. Scully of the ARU, approached the Government after this principle had won the support of the 1948 Federal Conference of the ALP. The weakness of the new Chifley legislation was that before the Arbitration Court was empowered to intervene to set aside a union election, on grounds of malpractice, the onus of proof of malpractice rested on the shoulders of the aggrieved party. While there was no reasonable doubt that there were many instances of malpractice, it was another matter to obtain evidence amounting to judicial proof.

The amended legislation, introduced by the Menzies Government in 1951, made it possible for a substantial proportion of the membership of a union, on petition. to secure the supervision of a union election by the Industrial Registrar before the election took place. As a result, it was possible for the Industrial Groups to meet the Communists in fair fight.

Ballot-rigging was not the sole remaining obstacle to victory in the unions once the Labor Party had decided to give official endorsement to the Industrial Groups. Victimization of anti-Communists on the job and acts of physical intimidation were frequent. Particular attention was given by Victorian Communists to three trade unionists who had the temerity to provide leadership on the job—Scully, Lloyd and Miller. Although these examples excited great indignation among the relative minority which was prepared to take an interest in union affairs, the individuals concerned regarded victimization as par for the course and got on with the job.

Although the strategic situation, as it were, changed very much for the better with the ALP's endorsement of the Industrial Groups and with the 'clean ballots' legislation, it would not have been practical to expect any rapid change in the overall control of the union movement. Nothing could stop the impetus which the Communists had gained from years of organization, and from the many hundreds of union positions already in their possession. However, the development of co-ordinated opposition to Communist union power within the Labour Movement itself gradually raised the level of the performance of the Chifley Government in other ways as well. As Professor Crisp has pointed out, had the Chifley Government itself undertaken the leadership of a nation-wide struggle by the Labor Party itself, the results would have come far more quickly. Mr

Chifley, however, refused to undertake this responsibility. The best that could be done was to win concessions from a grudging government—so that rank-and-file unionists could win a battle in which the main beneficiary would be the Labor Party itself!

Yet the Chifley Government had been put to the test as far back as 1947. A challenge to its defence power was launched by Communist-controlled building unions when they banned the construction of the Woomera Rocket Range. The object of the strike was clearly political, a contribution made by Australia's Communist union leadership to the strategic necessities of the Soviet Union. The black ban followed a campaign (since reproduced in the anti-uranium agitation of the late seventies), which had as its ostensible and emotive theme the welfare of the Aborigines, whose sacred sites would be disrupted by rocket testing.

Face to face with its international responsibilities, the Chifley Government was not slow to pass legislation which dealt not merely with the black ban, but, despite the inevitable 'free speech' issue, also with the propaganda used to support it.

Dr Evatt, who was given the responsibility for drafting the necessary legislation, did not use the Crimes Act, which had ready-made provisions for dealing with such contingencies. The campaign of vilification of the Crimes Act which the Communists had undertaken for years had been successful, and provided an object lesson in the way in which legislation passed by Parliament can be rendered unenforceable. Dr Evatt therefore fashioned the Approved Defence Projects Protection Act, 1947.

Its salient clauses are worth recording:

4-(1)  Any person who—
　(a)  without reasonable cause or excuse—
　　(i)  by boycott or threat of boycott of any person, property, work or undertaking prevents, hinders or obstructs, or endeavours to prevent, hinder or obstruct, the carrying out of an approved defence project;
　　(ii)  publishes any declaration of a boycott or threat of a boycott by means of which the carrying out of an approved defence project is prevented, hindered or obstructed or is sought to be prevented, hindered or obstructed; or
　　(iii)  by speech or writing, advocates or encourages the prevention, hindrance or obstruction of the carrying out of an approved defence project; or
　(b)  by violence or threat of violence to person or property or by other unlawful means, prevents, hinders or obstructs, or endeavours to prevent, hinder or obstruct, the carrying out of an approved defence project,
shall be guilty of an offence.[12]

The Act was immediately effective. Perhaps the most significant event associated with the passage of this legislation was Dr Evatt's speech, which was published as a pamphlet entitled *Hands Off the Nation's Defences*. There can be few more accurate descriptions of the problem represented by the growth of Communist influence within a democratic community than that given by Dr Evatt in the course of this address:

Some of those opposing the construction of the range took an utterly unjustified and sinister step when they proceeded to attempt to give effect to their own international policy by bringing about a trade union boycott to declare black a work finally adjudged by the Government, and impliedly by Parliament, to be an essential defence project.

Just as the endeavour to change decisions by open expression of opinion is of the essence of democracy, so attempted boycott to prevent the Government carrying through a defence project, approved by Parliament, or by the Government responsible to Parliament, would be the antithesis of democracy, and no Government could tolerate it.

Fortunately, the matter has not reached the critical stage. But if it does, then those people who attempt to block the defence project by obstruction and sabotage will have placed themselves within the reach of Commonwealth criminal law. To them, the law says: 'Hands off the defences of the Nation'.

One outstanding lesson of the whole affair to date is a warning to many who have too readily lent their aid to communist-inspired political slogans. Their socialist sympathies are played upon with the argument that anything and everything done in the supposed interests of Soviet Russia is justifiable, even though the defences of Australia may be imperilled. This is dangerous doctrine, and every trade unionist and citizen, whatever his political views may be, will repudiate it.

Those who permit this false doctrine to capture their minds may proceed from step to step until, to their own dismay, they find themselves engaged in courses operating against the safety of their native land and therefore seditious in character and intent. I assert that any political group or party becomes a menace to the safety of Australia whenever it allows its desire to forward the interests of Russia or any other foreign country to induce it to take steps interfering with the conduct of undertakings which are vital to Australian defence security.[13]

The climax of the situation was reached with the Coal Strike called by the Communist leadership of the Miners' Federation during winter 1949. It did not take the Chifley Government long to realize that the strike, while nominally industrial, was essentially political. It was meant to destroy the arbitration system by proving that industrial power used by a key union could override the decision of any tribunal, even if that tribunal was backed by the Government. There was strong resistance to the strike within the Miners' Federation itself, the resistance being publicly led by George Neilly, but actually being planned by the Northern Districts Organizer of the New South Wales Industrial Groups (Frank Rooney), who was also an outstanding Movement member.

This time the Government went in 'boots and all'. It was Dr H. V. Evatt who as Attorney-General froze union funds. The New South Wales Branch of the Railways Union (whose secretary, J. A. Ferguson, was also State President of the ALP), relying on the refusal of the New South Wales Labour Council and of the ACTU to give any support to the strike, carried 'black' coal. Mr Chifley himself ordered the troops on to the northern fields. These inexperienced tyros were to register production records against which the previous Federation performance looked poor indeed. But while the 'boots and all' policy gave a dispirited public the necessary public leadership, the truth was the Government's victory would have disappeared if the Communist leadership had continued to hold sway in the Miner's Federation. The real victory was won by the Industrial Group Movement, whose ticket, headed by George Neilly, was swept into office in the first Federation election which followed the strike.

The 'boots and all' policy did not represent a sudden transformation on the part of the Labor leadership, although Chifley, who had been a striker himself in 1917, was always reluctant to pursue any policy which seemed to restrict the union movement. The practice run which it had had over the Woomera Rocket Range enabled the Chifley Government to handle the Coal Strike with greater effectiveness than it might otherwise have shown. Its action was decisive. It changed the whole public atmosphere in which the anti-Communist campaign was conducted from 1949 onwards.

For myself, there was only one discordant note in the entire campaign which was waged around this critical issue. My departure from the editorial board of the *Catholic Worker* in 1941 had inevitably meant a physical separation from those who had been among my closest friends in the Campion Society. In addition, the long hours which had to be devoted to handling the sheer volume of work which developed with the organization of the Movement (while my responsibilities with the Rural Movement remained) meant that I completely lost the familiar contact which might have softened the differences which had developed between us. We became strangers.

A new generation of young Catholics, who seemed to me to lack the same solid roots in Irish Catholicism which had been the mark of the first generation of Campions, had made its appearance on the Board of the paper. They quickly established a substantial influence on the policy of the *Catholic Worker* and, as far as it related to myself, an extremely unfriendly influence. This was understandable since, with them, the old Campion links did not exist.

It was clear that over a period the *Catholic Worker* group had become more and more critical of the policies with which I was associated in the Movement. The first serious public manifestation of these differences was during the Coal Strike. On the very eve of the aggregate meetings on the northern fields which were to determine whether the miners would vote to go back to work, the *Catholic Worker* published an editorial which strongly attacked the Chifley Government's legislation 'freezing' the funds of the Miners' Federation:

To prevent men by law from using the funds of their own vocational organization for their own maintenance is a grave infringement of personal rights.

. . . This tyrannical law, the evil social consequences of which will be felt by Australian workers for generations to come.

. . . There is no logical distinction between seizing the miners' savings held collectively and seizing them when held individually by the workers. Will the next move by the Government in this or any subsequent dispute be to seize the private bank accounts of individual miners?

... The 'C.W.' must now record its conviction that the principle underlying the Coal Strike Act, together with its application as a first instead of a last resort, represents another step towards forced labour and the Servile State.[14]

The editorial might have influenced the result at the aggregate meetings. The Communist leaders could be expected to use it to split the vote of the Catholic section of the miners, who were generally supporters of the Industrial Groups, by showing that there was Catholic backing for the strike.

My first instinct was to let the matter pass. But the margin at the aggregate meetings could have been close. *News Weekly* therefore strongly criticized the *Catholic Worker* statement:

The technique of the 'fellow-traveller' has never been better exemplified than in this article of the *Catholic Worker*. Pious protestations against Communism are followed by a deadly attack on any concrete Government measures to fight a Communist revolutionary strike.

This is not to say that the *Catholic Worker* is written by 'fellow-travellers'. Far from it. It is simply written by a group of academic individuals who persist in applying to a war in defence of the nation (in which the unions are simply the battleground) a set of principles valid only when unions and employers are engaged in a bona-fide industrial battle.[15]

It was the beginning of a new and, at least as far as I was concerned, a most unpalatable conflict.

The deep reluctance which I felt in attacking the position of former close friends was overcome by my conviction, which was identical with that of Mr Chifley, that the objectives of the Coal Strike were political and revolutionary, while the *Catholic Worker* held that they were genuinely industrial. It took many years before the truth was admitted by the Communist leadership itself. At the time of the strike, Edgar Ross was editor of *Common Cause*, the organ of the Miners' Federation. Twenty-eight years later, writing in *The Socialist*, the organ of the pro-Soviet Communists, he naturally continued to claim that the strike was the result of the spontaneous mood among the miners themselves. He nevertheless added:

True, leading members of the Communist Party, including myself, occupied a key position in the working out of tactics, and the party itself saw the clash, when it came, as providing an opportunity for it to display its concepts and leadership, while testing the rival ideology of the Labor Party, that of reformism. That's the grain of truth in the charge of 'communist inspiration'.[16]

That the strike was not only political in purpose—in challenging the 'reformism' of the Chifley Labor Government—but also a function of an internal power struggle within the Communist Party itself, may be gathered from Ross's further observation:

As a sequel to the strike, if it took some years to be 'worked out', J. C. Henry and J. D. Blake lost their positions on the CPA secretariat, being charged with succumbing to anarcho-syndicalism against the background of a sectarian attitude towards the Labor Party, with undertones of a bid for personal power by supplanting Sharkey and Dixon ...[17]

The Chifley Labor Government was defeated in the Federal elections of 10 December 1949. There is little doubt that the long history of industrial dislocation caused by the Communist union leadership had counted heavily against the Ministry. It had finally been converted to a policy of strength in 1947 over the Woomera issue, and in 1949 over the Coal Strike. These episodes did not have time to register their effect in the public mind. Chifley's attempt to nationalize the banks provoked a major reaction among hundreds of thousands of Labor and swinging voters who felt that their savings were imperilled. The decision to continue petrol rationing was the final factor which defeated the Labor Government.

It was self-evident that the accession to power of a Liberal Government would greatly complicate a struggle which had barely begun. With Labor in opposition, the superficial interest of Labor politicians was to embarrass the Liberal Government by exacerbating industrial disputes. There was a clear potential for conflict between short-sighted Labor parliamentarians still smarting from electoral defeat, and the Industrial Group leaders to whom the defeat of the Communists was vastly more important than the embarrassing of the Liberals.

It is traditional that Labour Parties in opposition go to the Left, whereas Labour Parties in government, if the state of their internal machinery permits it, are driven by administrative responsibilities to the Right. If a Menzies Government took no stronger steps against the Communist union leadership than those which the Chifley Government had taken when in office, there would inevitably be the strongest Labor protests of 'oppressive and anti-working class legislation'.

The inevitable conflict would arise from the fact that the machinery of the Industrial Groups could not simply go into abeyance until a Labor Government was re-elected to office. The impetus would be lost. Those who, with such great difficulty, had been persuaded to lend their support to the anti-Communist struggle on the basis that it was a national issue which transcended politics, would have had their will destroyed by what could only be regarded as a shameful display of partisan politics on the part of their own leaders. For those reasons and despite the difficulties which were not long in manifesting themselves, the impetus of the Industrial Group and Movement attack on Communist control of the unions was kept up.

The Communists were defeated in the Federated Ironworkers' Association (50,000 members). In this union, Laurie Short fought an outstanding campaign in which legal action, judiciously undertaken, was not only legally successful but contributed brilliantly to the propaganda war, largely through strategies worked out by Short's barristers, Eric Miller, Q.C., and John Kerr, and solicitors, C. O'Dea

114 and, later, J. McClelland. Despite the brilliance of their campaign, it would have counted for little if the machinery had not existed to 'get out the vote', since voting in union elections could attract as little as 5 per cent of the membership.

Associated with the victory in the FIA were victories in the Clerks' Union (60,000 members); the Amalgamated Engineering Union (70,000 members); and in one or more branches of the following bodies: Australian Railways Union, Boilermakers' Union, Waterside Workers' Federation, Builders Labourers' Union, Electrical Trades Union, Painters' Union, and Amalgamated Postal Workers' Union.

John Douglas Pringle, who was then editor of the *Sydney Morning Herald*, summed up the achievements of the Groups:

Slowly, slowly, the tide turned. Taking advantage of the Menzies Government's Act providing for a secret ballot in union elections if a sufficient minority demanded one, well advised by industrial lawyers, mobilising the Catholic vote, the Industrial Groups expelled the Communists from one union after another. A decisive victory was won in 1949 when Mr Short, after a long and heroic struggle (he was once beaten up by Communist thugs), defeated the Communists in the Ironworkers' Federation. By 1950 the Communists were in full retreat, and the Industrial Groupers were everywhere advancing to the relief of the nation.[18]

The general method which had to be adopted, at least in the case of the great national unions, is illustrated by what had to be done to win back the AEU which, at that time, although it had 70,000 members, was still technically a branch of the British union of the same name.

The rules of the union were handmade to ensure that those in office were never beaten. It had one 'democratic' rule, for instance, that candidates were prohibited from issuing printed propaganda of their own, being restricted to a very limited statement on their personal qualifications in the columns of the union journal. In practice this meant that the Communist office-holders had the advantage of the journal for the entire three-year period, with ample personal publicity, and with persistent propaganda in favour of their policy positions, embellished by continual abuse of any potential opponent. To all of this, the latter could reply only with a short *curriculum vitae*.

Once the clean ballot legislation had been utilized to ensure that the election was by postal vote—the ballot papers being addressed to the home of every member, the returns being counted by the electoral officer—it was somehow necessary to back the anti-Communist candidates in the AEU with a substitute for the nationwide exposure which Short and his colleagues in the Ironworkers' election had enjoyed through their spectacular legal actions. Since printed propaganda in the AEU was not permitted, the Movement organized the writing and posting of 70,000 handwritten letters, one to every member of the AEU, to reach them by the same mail as would bring each of them his postal vote. In addition, more than one thousand members of the Movement were deployed in different cities throughout the country to canvass almost every AEU member. The period was, in a sense, the first time that union elections had been organized according to the methods of democratic politics and not according to a system which was designed simply to keep oligarchies in office. The oligarchies could not of course be expected to enjoy the situation, and cries of 'Fascism' and 'anti-union methods' swept the land.

Whatever the inevitable attacks, the fact was that by the beginning of 1953, Communist power was to all intents and purposes broken in the Australian trade union movement. The fact that the Melbourne Branch of the Waterside Workers' Federation, one of the two great Communist citadels, protected by the power and prestige of Jim Healy, the Communist Federal Secretary, had been won by anti-Communist forces headed by 'Gus' Alford, indicated that nothing was impossible. Communist power could be beaten in a clean-up operation. After that what was needed was a machinery which would, on the one hand, guarantee the continued exclusion of the Communists, and, a far more difficult task, that the victors would not develop into an oligarchy in their turn.

So, at the beginning of 1953, when my wife, who had borne the burden of raising a family then numbering six children with very little money and not much companionship to ease her task, asked for the first time whether this abnormal life-pattern was to last forever, I felt confident in saying that within two years the position would be so strong that I could resign my task and devote myself to my family. I could hardly have been more mistaken. The difficulties had not really begun.

# 12 The Menzies Challenge

The Liberal victory on 10 December 1949 created a completely new situation, destined to have a harmful effect on the fortunes of the anti-Communist effort in the trade union movement. While a Labor government was in office, the campaign of the Industrial Groups to defeat Communist power in key unions had inevitably to be treated even by the non-Communist Left as a signal contribution to the strength of a Labor government. The Labor Left was not favourably placed either to defend its normal associates or to attack those who were inflicting defeat upon them in the unions. To pursue the same programme successfully with Mr Menzies and the Liberals in office, and thus to ease the industrial challenges facing a Liberal government, was a totally different proposition. The fellow-travelling Left now enjoyed a freedom to attack those who by virtue of their union activities were assisting what was now a Liberal, rather than a Labor, government. The consequence was to exacerbate the normal Left–Right divisions within the Labor Party. The tactical difference was partly foreseen by the Movement leadership. It was one thing, however, to analyse the problems which were likely to arise, but quite another to devise a satisfactory solution.

All of the incipient difficulties created by the Liberal victory were multiplied by the transformation of the international situation in the Far East, as a result of the conquest of the Chinese mainland by Mao Tse-tung during 1949. The Communist seige of Peking concluded in January 1949 with the entry of the Communist armies into the ancient Chinese capital. The collapse of Chiang Kai-shek's armies followed. The People's Republic was proclaimed on 1 October 1949.

Although the overwhelming majority of Australians had no interest whatsoever in international affairs, within the narrower confines of the Labour Movement the tensions created by the

Communist victory in China were greatly to heighten the ideological conflict.

The British Government moved at once to recognize the new régime. Yet although formal recognition was accorded by Britain in January 1950, the British did not actually succeed in having their Ambassador accepted in Peking for another twenty years, the British diplomatic office in Peking being accorded the status only of a 'negotiating mission'. The entire Australian Left, inside and outside the Labor Party, launched a major campaign to compel the Australian Government to follow the British policy. Although the Australian Diplomatic Mission was withdrawn from Nanking in October 1949, no step was taken by the Liberal Government, after its accession to power in December, to follow the British step. The Left at once represented this failure to follow the British example as a sign of Liberal submission to the policies of the USA. Washington had refused to accord recognition to the new Peking Government, a position which it was to maintain until 15 December 1978. The evidence given to sustain the charge of subservience has been shown to be without substance.[1] A bare twelve months later, the Chinese Communist forces were involved in hostilities against Australian military forces, which were part of the UN forces in Korea.

The confusion following the flight of Chiang Kai-shek thus merged quickly into the Korean War, creating a situation in which both the USA and Japan refused to give diplomatic recognition to the new rulers in Peking.

The Movement's position was based on the view that Australia could expect little from Britain in the future, that it needed to align itself as closely as possible with the USA and Japan, and, if necessary, to do so against Britain. The Soviet and Chinese leaderships were united. The Sino-Soviet split lay well in the future. The British position was not taken on the high ground that the British were wiser in their understanding of international affairs. It was taken to keep open Britain's trade with the Chinese mainland. What was a matter of trade and economics for Britain was a matter of national security for Australia, whose only potential allies were the Americans, while the latter were simultaneously building up Japan.

The Movement attitude was based, however, on a more general factor: its calculation of the international factors likely to prevail in Southeast Asia as a result of the Communist victory in China, and thereby on the security of Australia.

The Communist insurrection in Malaya had formally begun in June 1948, after a prolonged period of violence. The aim was to declare a Communist Republic of Malaya on 3 August 1948.[2]

The establishment of the Cominform in September 1947 clearly signified the end of the wartime alliance between the Soviet Union and the Western Powers. The Asian strategy of the Cominform had been the subject-matter of two conferences held in Calcutta in February 1948. The first was the Southeast Asian Youth Conference, which was held under the auspices of the so-called World Federation of Democratic Youth. The next was the Second Congress of the Communist Party of India.

The Movement had particular reason for noting two events which might otherwise have passed unnoticed. L. L. Sharkey, the General Secretary of the Communist Party of Australia, who was present at the Calcutta meetings, was actually chosen by the Cominform to carry the decision to begin the armed insurrection in Malaya to the leaders of the Malayan Communist Party. Cecil Sharpley, at that time a leading CPA member, noted in his autobiography published after his defection: 'It is therefore no coincidence that only a few months later [i.e., after Sharkey's fortnight stopover in Singapore] the Communists began open revolt in Malaya'.[3]

Simultaneously, the decisions of the Calcutta Conference, which were communicated to the Indonesian Communists by the two Indonesian delegates, Francisca Fangiday and Supeno, led to the beginning of a policy of armed struggle by the PKI (Partai Kommunist Indonesia), which was to issue in the ill-fated Madiun rebellion of 18 September 1948.

The strategic significance of these developments, particularly those within Indonesia, was obvious to those who were formulating the Movement's attitudes. Since they had none of the military qualifications of those who advised the Australian Government, they relied on elementary common sense, and were duly dismissed as alarmist. However, the Australian Cabinet papers for the years 1945-46, which were not published until thirty years later, included the assessment then made by the Chiefs of the General Staff, the Naval Staff and the Air Staff, on the long-term security of Australia of enemy control of Indonesian territory:

The NEI [Netherlands East Indies] is of extreme importance to Australia both strategically and economically.

A hostile or non-co-operative government or governments established in the area would prejudice Australian defence with the possible denial of resources both desirable in peace and vital in war--oil, rubber, quinine, etc.

Furthermore, the imperial intercommunication and air routes network must of necessity pass over the area.

Denial of facilities and resources in this area may have grave results in war.[4]

The bitter revolutionary struggles thus launched in Malaysia and Indonesia were much closer to Australian territory than the mainland of China.

In the light of these events, the developments on the Chinese mainland were of great strategic significance. The mobilization of the most populous nation in the world by an efficient, ruthless and totalitarian government must provide a further stimulus to the policy of armed rebellion in countries immediately to the north of Australia. If these succeeded in their objective, potentially hostile great powers would acquire bases close to Australian territory.

The strategic situation in 1949 bore no resemblance to that of 1980, when the Sino-Soviet conflict has given the Western Powers the opportunity to play the 'China card', although—despite the often uncritical nature of the discussion of the current policy—the permanence of the new diplomatic phase is no more certain than that of any other. In 1949, despite previous tensions between Mao and Stalin, and the ambiguities of Soviet policy towards the Chinese revolution, the alliance between the Chinese and the Soviet Communists had not been called into question.

Liu Shao-chi's 1948 article, 'On Nationalism and Internationalism', condemned Tito, root and branch, for breaking with the Soviet Union, and assured the Soviet that the Chinese Communists would never take the same road.[5] At the Czech Party Congress in 1949 (soon after the Communist takeover in Czechoslovakia), the Chinese Party again reassured the Russians: 'The C.C.P. recognizes proletarian internationalism as one of her main principles. There is no trace of bourgeois nationalism in Mao Tse-tung's teaching'.[6]

At the beginning of the fifties, the Sino-Soviet split, while always a possibility in the sense that everything is a possibility until the opposite occurs, was not seriously foreseeable, let alone inevitable. At the beginning of the eighties, even if no great Sino-Soviet intimacy can be predicted, it does not follow that the present active hostility will necessarily last. Major internal conflicts are still under way inside the Chinese Communist Party. No one can predict either the ultimate victors or the foreign policy which they will pursue.

The sounder judgement at the beginning of the fifties was to regard Chinese Communism as a revolutionary force, likely to act in conjunction with the Soviet Union at least for a considerable period, likely to pursue a revolutionary policy in Southeast Asia, and likely to exercise a considerable influence both upon the Chinese population and the Communist Parties of Southeast Asian countries.

This was, in fact, the role of Chinese Communists during the massive Singapore riots of 1955; during the Malayan insurgency which lasted from 1948 to 1960; and during the period of the supremacy of Aidit and the PKI with Sukarno before the attempted Communist *coup d'état* of 30 September 1965 which, with the massacre of six Indonesian generals at Halim Air Force Base, came close to success.

Whatever the Movement's influence was worth in the development of a sectional Australian public opinion concerning diplomatic recognition of the new Peking régime, there was thus every justification for the policy it adopted.

120

The issue was to open up schisms in the Labour Movement, which were partly hidden while the Industrial Groups were in the full flood of their trade union victories.

The attitude of the Movement naturally had a considerable influence on that of the leaders of the Industrial Groups, and of a new Labor parliamentary group which entered the Federal Parliament as a result of the 1949 election. Among these Messrs S. M. Keon (Yarra), J. M. Mullens (Gellibrand), and T. Andrews (Darebin) were the most prominent.

Thus within the Labour Movement there was a separate flashpoint for ideological conflict. The Left, on the defensive as a result of the disruptive union activities of the CPA which had contributed to the defeat of the Labor Government, found itself on more favourable ground on a foreign policy issue which was rationally arguable on a variety of grounds. It was undeniable that the Communists controlled the Chinese mainland. The Left cleverly set about confusing public opinion with the specious claim that diplomatic recognition must follow the physical control of national territory. A dispute about diplomatic recognition appears improbable as a factor in a split within a political party in a nation as decidedly anti-intellectual as Australia. That dispute did, however, help to divide the Left and its opponents within the Labor Party from 1950 to 1954.

The division which was to isolate the latter group and to secure the expulsion from the ALP of the greater part of the Industrial Group leadership began, however, with the attempt of the Menzies Government in 1950 and 1951 to ban the Communist Party. The Communist Party Dissolution Bill, which Mr Menzies introduced into the Parliament on 27 April 1950, which was passed by that body but struck down by the High Court in March 1951, was publicly justified by the Government as necessary to reduce Communist power within the union movement.

The Bill precipitated the internal conflict within the Labor Party which the Movement had feared as a likely consequence of the defeat of the Labor Government.

A new situation had in fact arisen with the election of the Liberal Government, with which it was necessary to deal if for no other reason than that its leaders must see their own party-political interests in widening the Left–Right divisions in the ALP, regardless of the consequences on the anti-Communist forces.

Towards the end of December 1949, an opportunity unexpectedly arose. I had a phone call from Mr R. G. Casey (as he then was). Having served as Australian Minister in Washington from 1940 to 1942, and later as a member of the British War Cabinet, and Governor of the Indian State of Bengal from 1943 to 1945, he had returned to Australian political life at the end of the war and been given the portfolio of National Development after the Menzies victory in 1949. I had never met him, and was surprised at his wanting to talk to me. It was the beginning of an acquaintance which lasted until Lord Casey's death in 1976.

The first conversation was about the industrial situation which confronted the Menzies Government on its assumption of office. The Communist Party, through the agency of Jim Healy, Federal Secretary of the Waterside Workers' Federation, and of the Communist majority on the Federal Council of that union, was in process of organizing a national waterfront tie-up. Earlier in the year the WWF and the Seamen's Union (controlled by its Communist Federal Secretary, Eliot V. Elliott) had affiliated with the Maritime Unions International of the WFTU. The Federal Council of the WWF, at its November 1949 meeting, had decided on a programme of rolling strikes, that is, a regular sequence of strikes at different ports on consecutive days. In January, Healy's Assistant Federal Secretary, Roach, who was also a Party member, explained the significance of the new tactic: 'International experience and the lesson from last year's Coal Strike has taught us that the workers must fight in an entirely new way'.[7]

Before the end of December, the new government understood that it would be challenged on the waterfront in exactly the same way as the Chifley Government had been challenged on the coalfields.

Casey said that the Federal Cabinet had just finished a meeting which dealt exclusively with the forthcoming industrial crisis. It had, he said, come to the conclusion that, despite all of the habitual talk about 'strong government', there was singularly little which a government could do when faced with a continuous programme of serious industrial sabotage fostered by a revolutionary party deeply embedded within the structures of the union movement. It could declare a state of emergency: but even if the resultant measures helped in meeting the immediate situation, they could not be repeated again and again. It was his conviction, he said, that there was no long-term solution other than the method of changing the control of the trade union movement from within. He had sought the conversation, he added, so that I would know directly the importance which at least some members of the Cabinet attached to the work in which my associates were engaged.

The views Casey expressed were quite different from usual Liberal Party rhetoric about 'getting tough with the unions'. I did my best to strengthen his conviction. The political problem was already evident. Diehard supporters of the Liberals would demand 'strong action', without specifying concretely what that action would be. The Liberals might hold and even win votes by proposing 'tough' legislation reflecting the demand for 'strong action'. I stressed as strongly as I could that these measures would be counter-productive, if the net result was to isolate the moderate leadership of the ALP in its struggle with the extreme Left.

Although Casey understood the position, he was faced with the fact that some members of the Federal Cabinet were strongly committed to proposals for legislation which would impose a legal ban on the Communist Party. He asked me to meet the Minister for Labour and National Service (Mr Harold Holt), whom he phoned while I was still in his office. As a result of this second discussion, Holt suggested that I should put my views in a memorandum which he and Casey would discuss with other members of the Cabinet. The memorandum, dated 7 January 1950, carried a letter of endorsement from Archbishop Mannix, with whom I had discussed the two interviews.

Dr Mannix's letter said:

Needless to say, I am glad that your Government proposes to give no quarter to Communists. For with me the Communist menace is no mere political matter: it threatens the Christian way of life.

Those who have drawn up the Memorandum are the same people who a few years ago, almost single-handed, tackled the Communists in their chosen battleground, the industrial unions. I have been in close touch with this fight, and I venture to say that there has been a large measure of success. Indeed, anything that the late Government was able to achieve against Communism was made possible because, by quiet but effective work, the mass of the unionists were gradually won over to sanity. A definite cleavage was made between them and the Communists.

Of course the battle is not over. The Communists will now try to undo what has been done, and set up a common front against your Government. Any unwise move would play into their hands. Like the author of the Memorandum, I have more faith in securing clean union elections than in banning the Communists, or making strikes illegal. Above all, I fear that any attempt to hamper unionists in the election of their officers might just be the one thing that would line up the mass of unionists in a common front with the Communists. At the moment certain repressive measures may be quite logical, but yet unwise.

You will pardon me for writing at such length. The Memorandum speaks for itself, and I shall be grateful if you can bring it before the Prime Minister and the Cabinet.

Faithfully yours,
D. MANNIX[8]

The memorandum itself warned against precipitate action which would lead to the isolation of the anti-Communists within the Labour Movement.

It was necessary to convince the non-Communist unions that this claim to union solidarity was false, and that the Communist Party was mis-using it with one end in view—to capture the union movement and the political labour movement as well.

After a long and sustained effort this task was largely accomplished. *It cannot be overlooked, however, that the major factor in this work of political education was the fact that the Communist strikes occurred at a period when a Labour Government was in power in the federal sphere.* It was possible to present all of these strikes as a Communist attack on the Labour Party with which the unions were generally affiliated.

In this way the Communists in the trade unions were gradually but definitely isolated. *This isolation was, and is, the indispensable prerequisite of their destruction.*

It was to be anticipated that the Communist Party would use the fact that the Liberal and Country Parties had won the election in a supreme endeavour to end this isolation. If they could succeed in reversing this trend of the past five years, they would again be on the way to the achievement of their major objective—the unification of the Australian trade union movement under Communist leadership.

The line, of course, is perfectly clear. Every intervention by the new Government designed to limit Communist power in the trade unions will be labelled as an attack, not on Communism, but on trade unionism. It is absolutely vital that the persons concerned should realize how easily this 'line' can spread among non-Communists . . .[9]

The memorandum then proceeded to make positive recommendations on several government proposals.

In the light of these factors, the following observations on the projected legislation are advanced for consideration.

A. *The Ban on the Communist Party*:
Frankly, we do not believe that it will be effective in dealing with the Communist problem, a problem which depends on the degree to which Communism can control the trade unions . . .

B. *The Reform in the Method of Conducting Union Ballots*:
This is the key to the situation. While there will be much union opposition to any intervention in this field, we feel that reforms should be carried through . . .

C. *Banning Communists from Holding Positions in the Public Service and in the Trade Unions*:
*This is the critical proposal.* In relation to the public service, the issue is not contentious. In relation to the unions however, the worst consequences are feared. Granted the psychology of Australians, there is no doubt that unionists, even non-Communists, would elect and continue to elect a person banned by the Government from holding office. An effort to enforce this ban by positive sanctions would involve all other unions. Communist isolation would be broken, and the fatal consequences we anticipate would be realized.

We therefore respectfully recommend that the Government should assist the forces which are successfully and relatively speedily purging the unions from within by natural process. This can be done by the institution of a proper system of union ballots. We respectfully request that the direct banning of Communists from union positions should not be attempted, for the reasons stated.[10]

Although the Government did proceed with the first stage of 'clean ballot' legislation, nevertheless when it introduced the Communist Party Dissolution Bill, on 27 April 1950, it was evident that the tactical recommendations submitted to both Ministers had been rejected. The Bill, as its name indicated, proposed to ban the Communist Party. As this, however, was a largely useless ritual, it went further. It provided that a person 'declared' to be a Communist by a committee of five senior officials, whose 'declaration' was proclaimed by the Governor-in-Council, could not hold office in any industrial organization considered by the Governor-General to be vital to the security of Australia, or hold employment with the Commonwealth, unless he discharged the onus of proof that he was not a Communist or engaged in subversive activities. The legislation was certainly capable of being abused; yet, as Murray indicates, 'it is

124 | difficult to see how the ban could have been made effective without the "onus of proof" clause'.[11]

The reasons which prompted Mr Menzies to introduce the Bill have always been, and remain, a puzzle. There was the difficulty of establishing Federal legislation of this kind on the constitutional basis of the defence power. Apart from this, it was hard to see how so intelligent a Prime Minister, with a deep understanding of internal Labour politics, could present a Bill which at the best promised only a temporary and partial solution to the problem, at the long-term cost of weakening the anti-Communist position within the Labour Movement. Some believed that it was a normal exercise in partisan politics, promising a dual dividend to the Liberal Party in providing them with an issue to divide the Labor Party internally, while simultaneously maximizing Liberal votes in a subsequent Federal election. When I put this to Sir Robert Menzies many years later, during his retirement, he said that he was motivated by neither reason, but simply by the need to deal with Communist union leaders by direct legal action so that in the event of war they could not repeat their treacherous conduct during the early months of the Second World War.

There is evidence that this argument did weigh considerably with Mr Menzies. In the early months of 1950, some weeks before he introduced the Communist Party Dissolution Bill, he had summoned a Special Premiers' Conference to deal with defence, stating in his opening speech: 'We have not a day more than three years in which to get ready, and that time may well be shorter'.[12] His prediction seemed borne out by events. The Bill was introduced on 27 April 1950, and the Korean War broke out on 26 June.

Perhaps the most impelling motive was that the Liberal electorate expected something to be done about the Communist problem. If the High Court invalidated the Bill, at least the Government could claim that it had attempted to do what lay in its power.

Mr Chifley, on the other hand, saw the purpose of the legislation as a cynical political manoeuvre to prepare the electorate for the next Federal election—in which Menzies must seek the Senate majority he did not yet have. In fact when this election did take place at the end of April 1951, although Menzies lost five of the Representatives' seats he had won in 1949, he won control of both Houses, gaining a Senate majority of thirty-two to twenty-eight.

The result of the ill-fated Menzies legislation was precisely what had been anticipated. The Communist Party Dissolution Act was taken to the High Court on 14 November 1950. Dr Evatt led the attack on the legislation, which was finally invalidated by a majority of six to one. Only the Chief Justice, Sir John Latham, ruled in favour of the Act, the other judges, including Mr Justice Dixon, ruling that the defence power could not sustain legislation of this type in a period in which Australia was at peace. The Federal Government's subsequent attempt to acquire constitutional power by way of referendum failed on 22 September 1951, even though the 'No' majority won only 50.48 per cent of the vote.

The decision of the Menzies Government to ignore the advice given to it in the memorandum of 7 January 1950 had placed the Movement in a difficult position. Its first reaction was to stick to its guns, holding firmly to the position that a ban on the Communist Party would not only achieve nothing in the union arena, but would be counter-productive in giving the useful status of martyrdom to the Communist leaders. We moved from that position as a result of two arguments. The Korean War appeared as a warning sign that more general hostilities might be imminent. (The Federal Government had transmitted British Government advice to the Department of Supply that this was likely.)[13] Furthermore, it appeared too difficult a distinction to establish with our own members that while they engaged in their struggle with the Communists in the union movement, we would apparently be helping to guarantee legislative protection to their right to continue the industrial depredations of 1947-49. There was a clear logical justification for maintaining the distinction. What was difficult was to make the logic comprehensible in practice. Dr Mannix believed that we should not move from our original position, that we should continually re-state it and oppose the Menzies legislation. As always, having made his point, he did not press it. We went against his opinion. In retrospect, he was right and we were wrong.

Murray's account of the internal struggle which the Menzies Bill precipitated in the ranks of the ALP is substantially correct. It provides a valuable documentation of the intricacies of a struggle in which, as he rightly observes, the Menzies legislation 'had the support of a wide right-wing opinion, in which the Movement was not unduly important'.[14] However, the Movement was greatly affected by the polarization of forces within the ALP at both the Parliamentary and 'machine' levels. Its organ *News Weekly* made strong criticisms of parliamentarians like Evatt, Ward, McKenna and Pollard, who led the ALP opposition to the Bill and to the subsequent referendum proposals. For this, it was banned by the Federal Executive of the ALP on 19 November 1951.

# 13 High Noon

The invalidation of the Communist Party Dissolution Act and the defeat of the subsequent referendum proposals brought Dr Evatt to the peak of his career. It was at this moment that this extraordinary man decided to make another of his strategic switches in political tactics. This time his switch was to the Industrial Groups, for whose blood his supporters were howling as the 'guilty men' who had originally supported the Menzies Bill and then allegedly failed to support the Party's policy in opposing the Menzies referendum proposals.

Speaking at a meeting in the Assembly Hall, Sydney, organized by the Industrial Groups for the Ironworkers' national elections, and referring to the 1949 coal strike, he said: 'No Labor Government can tolerate a situation like that again, and we are not going to do it . . . The Labor Party is just as much entitled to fight in trade union elections as the Communist Party'.[1]

Dr Evatt's gestures took more tangible form as well. He was helpful in getting the ALP Federal Executive to lift the ban on *News Weekly*. He was prepared to attack the Menzies Government for permitting his own former secretary, Dr John Burton, to lead a delegation of five to a 'peace conference' in Peking at the height of the Korean War! (Evatt was, of course, aware of the fact that, in November 1949, a few weeks before the defeat of the Chifley Government, at the WFTU Asian Labor Conference held in Peking, a WFTU Liaison Bureau for Asia and Australasia had been set up in the Chinese capital. This was followed in October 1952 by the setting up of the Secretariat of a 'Peace Liaison Committee' in Peking.)

It was not difficult to see what Dr Evatt was at, although, as always with this complex man, his motives were obscure. Although he had incidentally served the interests of the Communists and their allies in the whole long campaign over the Menzies Act, and the subsequent referendum, it was Dr Evatt who, as a member of the Chifley Cabinet, had introduced the Approved Defence Projects Protection Act in 1947 to defend the Woomera Rocket Range against Communist black bans. Likewise, during the 1949 Coal Strike, the legislation which 'froze' union funds and gaoled the Communist leaders had been in his hands.

The truth was that after the referendum the extreme Left had no alternative other than to support Dr Evatt. With this force safely corralled, it suited the Labor leader to make a play for their opponents, with whom he could have had no ideological sympathy whatsoever. He knew that he had to face a Senate election in the autumn of 1953, and a general election approximately a year later. His popularity among his own Federal Parliamentary colleagues was extremely limited, since few trusted him. If, then, he permitted the ALP to continue to rend itself apart by a continuation of the controversies initiated by the Menzies legislation and the subsequent referendum, it was doubtful whether after the inevitable electoral defeats he would be able to maintain his leadership.

His surprising change of tactics was extremely useful in the union struggle against the Communists, and the victories of the ALP Industrial Groups redounded greatly to the electoral credit of the ALP. The Left could not be expected to admit the connection, but it has been—and remains—clear that if the ALP permits itself to appear too closely aligned with, let alone dominated by, the extreme Left, its electoral prospects are negligible. If it appears a moderate Party, dedicated to progressive social reforms but prepared to stand up to the Communists in the trade union movement, its electoral prospects are greatly improved and those of the Liberals diminished. This was a major factor in the election of the first Labor Government ever to govern Victoria in its own right in the State election of 9 December 1952, three years almost to the day after Mr Chifley's disastrous defeat on 10 December 1949. Victorian Labor added 7 per cent to its vote and won thirty-seven out of sixty-five Legislative Assembly seats.

The new Premier, John Cain, was a moderate. He was indistinguishable from the veteran parliamentarians whom he led.

Within the ALP Executive, however, serious divisions were already developing between Lovegrove, the State Secretary, and Stout, Secretary of the Trades Hall Council. Among the Labour parliamentarians, the conflict was between those who remained faithful to the old John Wren 'machine'—most Labor parliamentarians, regardless of professed ideology, had been beneficiaries of the Wren generosity—and those who wished to break away from it. Neither of these divisions appeared sufficiently significant to disrupt the Government.

S. M. Keon, member for Richmond, a close personal friend but not a member of the Movement, who had pursued a strongly anti-

Wren line in the previous Parliament, had moved to the Federal seat of Yarra in the 1949 Federal election. He was succeeded in the Richmond seat by a strong Movement member, Frank Scully, who had been an able and courageous secretary of the ALP Industrial Group in the Railways Union, and of the Young Labour Association. Scully had great promise. It took much persuasion, however, to have Cain and his senior colleagues accept him in a minor position as Honorary Minister in the new Labor Cabinet. When he was finally selected, Cain had a comfortable majority within the Cabinet. There were about seven Cabinet Ministers, however, who were influenced by Movement ideas, although Scully was the only member.

The Cain Cabinet had a good record of social reform, in the characteristic Labour tradition, with electoral reform, improvements in the Workers Compensation Act and in long-service leave standing to its credit. Through Scully, the Movement succeeded in interesting the Cabinet in passing a Co-operation Act based on similar New South Wales legislation, to provide a legislative and administrative structure for the organization of co-operatives of every type, but particularly of credit unions. There are today no less than 199 credit unions and co-operatives registered under the Act in Victoria.

The post-Korean recession of 1952 left many migrants, particularly Italian, unemployed, not merely in Victoria. Through the National Catholic Rural Movement, I approached the Dutch and Italian Governments, and ICEM, the international migration organization, to seek loan capital for land settlement co-operatives which would be secured by government guarantee according to the provisions of the Co-operation Act. After many difficulties, these approaches proved successful. Simultaneously, again through the NCRM, I approached the State Governments of Victoria, New South Wales, Queensland and Tasmania, for grants of second-grade land which would not be required for soldier settlement, as the site of one experimental Australian-migrant civilian land settlement in each State. The New South Wales Labor Government was not interested. Mr Gair in Queensland turned down the idea, despite the interest of Colin Clark. Mr Cosgrove in Tasmania promised to make land available in the northwest of his State. The Victorian Premier was obviously under pressure from anti-Catholic elements in the community. There was dark talk about 'peasantry' and 'foreign [meaning Italian] enclaves'. Cain, however, agreed to supply some low-quality land in the vicinity of Caradale in Victoria. With Frank Scully, I had a friendly interview with the Minister for Lands (R. W. Holt), who was under direction from the Cabinet to include in his forthcoming Land Settlement Act a clause permitting the establishment of a migrant settlement.

It was a satisfactory result. Two State Labor Governments, two foreign governments, and an international migration organization had agreed to attempt a new type of migration plan (although there were precedents in Venezuela and one or two other South American States). Everything had been done through correct official channels. On 12 August 1952, in the course of his Budget speech, even Dr Evatt proposed that land settlement and migration should be linked together. The explosive eruption of anti-Italian and anti-Catholic feeling which accompanied Mr Holt's introduction of the Land Settlement Act on 24 November 1953, with his flat refusal to include the vital amendment which had been decided on by the Cabinet of which he was a member, was completely unexpected. The incident led to the resignation of the Minister, while the outbreak of sectarian and racial feeling which it generated made it a major event in the chapter of unpleasant incidents which led to the Labor split less than a year later.

During 1952-53, however, that disastrous development lay well ahead. The prospect was extremely favourable. By 1953 Communist power had been broken within the trade union movement. Dr Evatt's changed attitude both helped the Industrial Group cause and contained the Left. The Victorian, New South Wales, and Queensland State Executives of the ALP were strongly influenced by the Groups and, even apart from the few Movement members on them, were disposed to favour a number of Movement ideas.

1953 accordingly seemed an appropriate time to capitalize on the situation. The first avenue was an attempt to widen the horizons of some of the more thoughtful contacts formed among Labor men, both among the parliamentarians and the members of executives and conferences. The method chosen was to run what today would be called 'seminars', although to have given them that name in 1952-53 would have been to guarantee non-attendance.

The Premiers of Queensland (Mr Gair) and of Tasmania (Mr Cosgrove), each attended at least two of these seminars, giving the seal of their prestige to the new initiative. There was talk that Mr Cahill, Premier of New South Wales, was interested in coming to the third, but this did not eventuate.

The objects in mind could be simply stated. Most of those who attended were men who had chosen Labor politics or trade unionism as a career. They were neither more nor less disinterested than any similar persons. Presumably they wanted to 'get on'—into Parliament, Cabinet, or some equivalent position. Hence there was a limit to the risks which they could afford to take. Nevertheless, they were men with a broadly similar outlook on public affairs, as they had shown during the several years of the Industrial Group effort. Very few of them, however elevated their political position, had had the opportunity of devoting time to detailed study of international affairs, economic and financial policy, even of major policy developments in the trade union field, however intimately they might be associated at the organizational level with the latter. As a result, if they acquired high responsibilities in government, they would inevitably be deeply influenced by departmental heads, who would in many cases be acting on an entirely different set of philosophic assumptions from their own. It was likely that Labor governments in which they might exercise influence of some kind would be indistinguishable from any other at the level of policy, subject *de facto* to the instructions of the Treasury, and with little if any impact on the serious social, economic and international problems which were obviously accumulating for Australia.

I thought that in bringing them into contact with people like Colin Clark, Barbara Ward, Paul McGuire, as well as with some of the senior Movement officials whose experience was not to be despised, it would be possible to accomplish, although on the basis of a different philosophy, what the Fabian Society had accomplished within the British Labour Party. The Left within Australian Labor had its own avenues of intellectual formation. It was time to equip those whose philosophy was quite distinct from that of the Left with the factual knowledge and the philosophic assumptions which lay at the foundation of their activity in and around the Industrial Groups.

The three or four seminars which were held before the Labor split were highly successful in every way. If they could have been continued I believe they would have rendered a signal service to the Labour Movement and to Australian government and administration. They would have helped to infuse a different school of thought into the formulation of Labor policy, instead of permitting the Marxist Left and its fellow-travellers to enjoy their habitual monopoly.

Had the Labor split not eliminated the possibility of continuing with this enterprise throughout the sixties and seventies, Australian Labor might have appeared as a party broadly similar to the German Social Democrats. 'The anti-communism of the right-wing in the Labor Party in the early 1950s has few advocates in the Labor Party today', wrote Judah Waten in his review of Don Watson's life of Brian Fitzpatrick.[2] He is right. Instead, it is lost in the quicksands of Socialist Left control of the 'machine' and the constantly increasing domination of its parliamentary representation by wealthy left-wing trendies. Even a serious apologist for Soviet policy like Judah Waten can surely find little to praise in this.

It was therefore with good reason that Murray regarded 1953 as the 'High Noon' of the Movement/Industrial Group effort.

# 14 Asian Interlude

The second major step which was taken during 1953 was an attempt to harness the intellectual and organizational energies of the Catholic Church in different parts of Asia to the cause of the political and economic development of their newly independent countries. It was for this purpose that the Pan-Pacific Social Action Conference assembled in Melbourne at the end of June 1955. By then, the Movement had felt all of the traumatic consequences of the Labor split. As we struggled desperately to survive, an international conference of this type was almost the last event we wished to have on our hands. Yet the need remained, the preparations had been completed, and the Australian commitment given, although by the date at which the Conference was held it was fairly clear that my own future relationship with the Australian Bishops was, at least, conjectural.

Preparations had in fact been in hand since April 1953 when, at the National Eucharistic Congress at which, on the invitation of Cardinal Gilroy, I spoke in Sydney, I had met Cardinal Gracias, the Archbishop of Karachi. He had taken the opportunity to inform himself thoroughly about the work of the Movement in Australia, and was impressed by the fact that it was not a talking shop, but was engaged in practical political and social work, of which India, whose independence was then less than five years old, stood greatly in need. When it was pointed out to him that the Communist Party of Australia, through its leader, Sharkey, had been the transmission belt for the instructions given at the Calcutta Conference of the Cominform in February 1948 (nominally the South East Asia Youth Conference) to launch the Malayan insurrection in June 1948; that there was an international organization of Communist Parties in Southeast Asia in being, in which both the Indian and the Australian Parties were involved, he at once saw the point that international organization should be met by international organization, however unprepared, uninfluential and possibly ineffective the Catholic effort might be. On the basis of these discussions it was decided that an international Social Action Conference should take place in Melbourne, of which the Holy See would be informed, and which would seek representatives nominated by the Catholic Hierarchies of India/Pakistan, Ceylon, Malaya, Indonesia, Burma, the Philippines, Japan, USA, New Zealand and Australia.

The June 1955 Conference was successful in terms of realistic discussions on the political and social situations of the highly disparate countries represented. There were no illusions as to the likely effectiveness of the relatively small Catholic communities in all these countries, unless in a common resistance to Marxist elements they could secure the co-operation of representative Islamic, Buddhist and similar groupings. Nor was it likely that an orientation based exclusively on resistance to Marxism would commend itself to social forces much more concerned with overcoming the results of economic under-development, which was regarded as the inheritance of European colonialism rather than of the Soviet Union or Communist China. The emphasis would need to be on the latter rather than the former.

To ensure the future of the international organization, it was decided to hold a second conference in Manila, probably in May 1956, and to place its organization in the hands of a Temporary International Committee, of which the Indian, M. Ruthnaswamy, was elected chairman, with myself as secretary, and with the temporary international office in Melbourne. The most significant member of the Committee other than M. Ruthnaswamy was Jeremias Montemayor, President of the Federation of Free Farmers of the Philippines, which was already developing into a significant mass organization.

In order to place the new international movement on a sound philosophical basis from the very beginning, a draft statement was prepared by Ruthnaswamy and myself, which was to be submitted to the Bishops' Conferences of the various Asian Catholic countries, in the hope that they might issue a united declaration. This would thereupon serve to give future direction to Catholic thought in those countries in so far as it could be effective in contributing to the development of the new nations. As there was nothing specifically Catholic about its contents, it might be expected to gain the support of the various non-Christian intellectual and spiritual currents which had shaped the life of Asia.

The subsequent vicissitudes, which for a decade were to prevent the development of the international organization envisaged at the Melbourne meeting in 1955, militated against the fulfilment of the plan that the Statement should be issued on an Asia-wide basis. However, it was issued by the Indian Catholic Hierarchy in January 1956. Since it represents a considered approach to the joint problems of economic development and social justice in developing countries, prepared a quarter of a century ago, it is perhaps worth reproducing.

## Statement of the Catholic Bishops' Conference of India

1  The movement for political and social change which in one way or another has swept every Asian country over the last half century has been in its essence an expression of the legitimate aspirations of the Asian peoples for national independence, political democracy and social reform; as such, it merits the support of Christian forces throughout the world.

2  This movement, which in its authentic expression was a legitimate protest against out-dated colonial imperialism and economic exploitation, and which has, to a great extent, liberated the Asian continent from these parasitic evils, now finds itself menaced by a new and mortal enemy—the imperialism of international Communism. Just as the peoples of Asia protested against the ancient evil of colonialism, so now they repudiate the efforts of Marxist Communism to pervert Asia's movement towards liberation for its own sinister ends.

3  The normal bases of Asian society—the family as the basic social unit, the village as the primary centre of communal life, and a sound agriculture as the foundation of a developing economy—have stood the test of time and must at all costs be preserved. Hence, all of those techniques which may and should be imported into Asian countries to increase the efficiency of economic life should be used to strengthen and not weaken these basic institutions. Excessive and unbalanced industrialization, anti-social capitalism in all its forms and the domination of Communism are equally destructive of Asia's traditions and must be resisted. Family farms of economic size, peasant proprietorship, co-operatives, craft and cottage industries, small decentralized factories, are to be encouraged.
Government enterprises in the clearing of land, the drainage of swamps, the construction of irrigation works and power projects, and the provision of credit, should serve the latter rather than the former objective.

4  Absentee landlordism which denies security of tenure and ownership of land to the tillers of the soil is diametrically opposed to the type of society which Christianity wishes to inspire.

5  The newly-developed Asian societies are threatened not only by Communist imperialism and the remnants of colonialism, but by incipient national antagonisms among the various Asian peoples themselves. It would be a betrayal of the aspirations of Asia's millions if the final result of the struggle for national freedom should be an exaggerated nationalism.

6  To stimulate all that is good in the movement for Asia's liberation and to repel the evils which threaten it both internally and externally there is need for a dedicated group of men and women who, offering themselves completely to the service of God whatever may be their vocation, loving their neighbour, and placing the common good before any party loyalty, will devote themselves to the cause of Asia and her millions. In this regard a special role awaits, and a special responsibility rests upon such a group in every Asian country. This responsibility is acknowledged in a particular way by those who have brought forward this proclamation.[1]

The possibilities which were inherent in this venture became manifest during 1958-59. I met the leader of the Indian Praja Socialist Party (Asoka Mehta) during his visit to Australia at that time. Before we met, he had been aquainted—by friend and enemy—with their respective versions of Australian events before

134 and during the Split. Unlike almost everybody else, however, he had taken the trouble of reading our publications and otherwise informing himself about the Movement. The result was a series of discussions, in the course of which I showed him the statement which had been prepared for and issued by the Indian Bishops, and in which I explained to him the purposes of the projected international organization. Of the Statement, he took the view—which I had expressed to the Melbourne Conference—that there was nothing specifically Catholic about it and that it might well appeal to Hindus, Moslems or Asian Socialists. Mehta gave me a copy of his own book *Studies in Asian Socialism*, remarking in the covering letter at 'the considerable agreement in our approach to contemporary problems'. In the correspondence which passed between us in 1959, I outlined the difference between my own view and what, from the late sixties onwards, came to be regarded as the characteristic economic doctrine of the 'new conservatism'.

> ... Those who favour a decentralist political and economic structure, as we do, must face up to what I regard as the basic cause of economic concentration—the grant of the privilege of incorporation to private individuals who associate for private profit. Without the concept of the joint stock company, which has had a relatively recent history in the English-speaking world, economic concentration would have been impossible ... It was only the legal concept of the joint stock company which made possible the concentration of capital, materials and manpower necessary for the economics of large-scale production in the last century. The question which I ask myself is whether some other legal form cannot be devised which makes the pyramiding of ownership impossible. Unless we deal with economic concentration, it will be impossible, in my judgement, to deal with the concentration of power in the fields of administration and government.[2]

Understanding the practical purposes of the new international organization, he suggested that through it I might be able to help in the immediate problem of the elections in the Indian State of Kerala. In a letter of 25 March 1959, he suggested that a visit might be useful. 'There is', he wrote, 'a large Catholic population in Kerala, and your visit there would have considerable significance in organizing public opinion in favour of democracy against the Communist Government in power. In case you decide to come you can count on our welcome and co-operation'.

The importance of Mehta's letter was that it indicated that there was a basis for effective co-operation between Christian and non-Christian bodies in defence of democratic institutions, and that the situation, properly handled, need occasion no fear as to the isolation of Catholics in overwhelmingly non-Christian communities. By this time, however, because of Australian developments, the possibility had passed. In a subsequent letter of 18 May, I felt it necessary to point out to him how different my own position had become in Australia. I told him that 'elements in the Catholic Church in Australia who are opposed to what I am doing, did prevail upon

Cardinal Gracias to be very cautious in his attitude to us'; and that, as a result, I knew 'that certain sections of the Church in India are so concerned that the divisions which have developed in Australia should not be imported into their region that they might be quite unenthusiastic about a visit by myself'.

As far as the Kerala election was concerned the visit would have been quite unnecessary since there was a strong local reaction which replaced the Communist government of that State. The incident is reported, however, to illustrate the difficulties which led to the postponement for almost ten years of a plan from which much good might have come.

The difficulties associated with the Labor split in Australia in 1955-56, accompanied by divisions in the ranks of the Australian Bishops, had two consequences. It became impossible to give the necessary attention to the new organization which its establishment demanded. In addition, my own credit both with the Vatican and the Asian Bishops who had been interested in the project was greatly diminished.

The venture was revived in quite different form on a non-denominational basis in 1964, in the immediate aftermath of the assassination of President Ngo Dinh Diem of South Vietnam. On this basis, as a centre of information rather than joint action, it has maintained a useful, if quite different existence, ever since.

# 15 To the Labor Split

The first visit of Cardinals Gracias and Agagianian to Australia, which led to the calling of the Pan-Pacific Social Action Conference in 1955, took place in April 1953, on the occasion of the National Eucharistic Congress in Sydney. On 26 April, they were both given a reception in the Exhibition Building in Melbourne with Archbishop Mannix presiding, although he was suffering from a severe attack of pneumonia on the night. No less than 25,000 people were in attendance. The occasion is recorded simply because it was on that night that I met Dr Evatt for the first time. It was my task to deliver the address of welcome to the Cardinals. It was supported by Mr R. G. Casey, then Minister for External Affairs, and by Dr Evatt, the Leader of the Opposition. In the foyer after the reception, Dr Evatt approached me and, with what I thought was routine courtesy, said that he hoped we could meet again and discuss some of the issues raised in my address of welcome which had some incidental relationship to Australia's international position. I did not expect anything to come of Evatt's remark, although the attitude of the Leader of the Opposition in his newly expressed friendship with the Industrial Groups was obviously of critical importance. The Twentieth Federal Conference of the ALP had already taken place in Adelaide in January 1953. While in form or to outward appearances it witnessed quite substantial achievements on the part of the Industrial Groups, and was therefore satisfactory to the Movement, the events which were associated with it made it clear that serious trouble was brewing within the ALP.

The Group position had never been stronger than it was among the Conference delegates. The six Victorian delegates were all anti-Communist, although it was clear that there was trouble in Victoria between Lovegrove and Stout, for reasons largely personal relating to their respective status and power within the two sections of the Labour Movement. The New South Wales delegation was now as strong as the Victorian. Gair had become Premier of Queensland about a year before, following on the death of the former Premier Hanlon. The Australian Workers' Union leadership, Dougherty and Bukowski—and consequently the delegates whom they could influence—were working closely with the Groups.

The central objective was to give the Industrial Groups an acknowledged Federal organization, recognized by the ALP, and within the framework of the Party. It was known that Kennelly would labour might and main to prevent this. It was because Kennelly had made no secret of his determination to destroy the Groups, if he could, that two attempts had been made to reduce his influence. His position in Victoria depended on the salary which he drew as a member of the Legislative Council. The pre-selection for his safe seat of Melbourne West was due early in 1952. For some time, Kennelly had been waging a bitter war against all Group supporters in the ALP branches within his particular electorate. They decided to try to defeat him in his next campaign to win ALP endorsement for his seat. Deprived of this salary, he would find it difficult to carry on as Federal Secretary, which was an unsalaried position. It was likely that he would then seek endorsement—successfully—for a Federal seat. However, without the federal secretaryship, his opportunities for damaging the entire Industrial Group effort would be severely limited. The plans made to defeat him in Melbourne West were complete when, only two and a half months before the plebiscite, his son was tragically killed in an accident on 18 December 1951. There are limits which political conflict should not exceed. Had it been possible to call off the challenge at that late stage, it would have been called off. There were too many interests involved, however, and it was not possible. It was an accident of fate, similar to that which had occurred on 13 June in the same year. Mr Chifley died suddenly of a heart attack on that day. One of the strongest editorials which *News Weekly* had published against his policies appeared on that precise date. As with a weekly paper, it had been printed one day, and written three days, before his death. It could only contribute to a reputation for insensitivity on the part of the Movement, which I do not believe to be deserved.

Kennelly's defeat in the plebiscite by Bailey—1,335 votes to 1,058—was generally unexpected. The loser's grief and anger can be imagined. He was tireless in his organizing efforts against the Industrial Groups throughout 1952, in the period of the run-up to the 1953 Federal Conference. The result was apparent. Although Industrial Group delegates were in the majority; although Industrial Group policies were prominent in the debate on foreign affairs; although the ALP, for the first time in its history, came out in support of a policy of State Aid for independent schools; their

138 | attempt to lay the foundation of an interstate Groups' organization failed. Kennelly diverted the proposal with a successful motion which he induced his friend, E. J. Walsh, who was Gair's State Treasurer, to move:

> That as communism is accepted as an enemy of the working class movement, Conference congratulates all sections working within the Labor Movement in the persistent fight against communism. Conference commends to all state branches the necessity for full . . . support to any section working within the ALP and/or the trade union movement, consistent with the principles, rules and platform of the ALP for the complete elimination of communist influence.[1]

Although they had a majority the Groups had failed in their essential objective. If their leaders had understood the ferocity of politics as well as Kennelly did, they would have done to him what he was later to do to them at the time of the Labor split, when he drove them out of the ALP. There were, in fact, one or two who thought that this would be the only solution to the perennial problem to the anti-Communist cause which Kennelly represented. In fact, the 'numbers' would have been there to bring about this result at the 1953 Federal Conference. One person who would have shed no tears over the event would have been the Labor leader, Dr Evatt, as he made it clear to me only a few months later. Nevertheless, Kennelly's bereavement was in the minds of those whose assent to this solution would have been necessary. They forebore. Later, when Kennelly himself, in a different situation, asked me whether the Industrial Group delegates did not know that they had the numbers to expel him, I assured him that they did. When he then asked why they did not act, I told him that it was his bereavement which motivated them. His answer was, 'Well, you're a bloody fool'. Which, if politics are everything, is probably right.

Once the Conference was over it was clear that the partisans of both sides were heading towards a major conflict, although its form and dimensions were unpredictable. The Communist Party, which had sustained terrible losses in the trade union movement, brilliantly adapted its strategy to the new situation. A series of statements by representative leaders clearly indicated what that strategy was.

R. Dixon, President of the CPA wrote:

> Many Communists say that the Industrial Groups are small and that the workers will not have them on. Facts, however, completely refute this latter point. The Groups may be small in number, but in all recent Union elections, the Industrial Group candidates have commanded a big support among the workers. Why this support? *Because the Industrial Groups are the organisations of the Labor Party in the factories and Unions. When we deal with the Industrial Groups we deal with the Labor Party.* [My emphasis.] Most workers, as yet, are members or supporters of the Labor Party.
>
> It is often sufficient for a worker to oppose us for him to be branded a 'Grouper', and a 'Catholic Actionist', or to be given some other tag which means that he is a no-hoper. My experience has been that a great number of workers branded as 'Catholic Actionists' by sectarian Communists have turned out to be Protestants.[2]

L. L. Sharkey said:

Our comrades in the Trade Unions should assist the reformist Trade Union leaders who are not connected directly with the Industrial Groups. In Trade Union elections *we should be very careful whom we oppose in this period.* [My emphasis.]

He added that the comrades should

in particular work closely with the ALP workers who are antagonistic to the ALP Industrial Groups and must be helped in every way. That is to say, we must further all the time, a united front with the Labor Party from top to bottom, with the Labor Council delegates, Sub-committee members, Shop Stewards who are Labor Party, but not Industrial Group.

He concluded: 'The conditions for success in this struggle are becoming increasingly favourable'.[3]

Since the government in office was Liberal, the advantage of exposing the Left's campaign as a danger to the continued existence of a Labor Government was not available. Hence the correct counter-strategy for the Groups was to consolidate the positions they held and to attempt to smother the conflict within the ALP. This proved impossible. The faction opposing the Groups was now strongly organized. It had the solid, even if subdued, support of the Communist machine throughout the country. But above all, it had Kennelly, who was both indefatigable and courageous. He had won a Federal Senate seat in the 1953 Senate election and it was quite clear that unless he could be removed from the federal secretaryship of the ALP there would be no end to the conflict; while, if it continued, the future of the Industrial Groups, the key to the many victories against the Communists, would be jeopardized.

Nor was there any doubt that a majority existed on the Federal Executive to bring this about. In addition there were Federal parliamentarians, who were not concerned with the fate of the Industrial Groups, who strongly objected to a member of the Federal Parliamentary Party holding the position of Federal Secretary as well. On 26 June, the Victorian Central Executive gave notice of its policy when Lovegrove moved 'that delegates advise the Federal Executive that the office of Federal Secretary should be vacated'. When the Federal Executive met in Melbourne on 13 July, the resolution which was carried was that a Federal parliamentarian should not fill the position of Federal Secretary. However, the resolution was not to take effect until the following meeting of the Federal Executive in November.

Industrial Group supporters now occupied the positions of Federal President (with Lovegrove of Victoria) and the two Vice-Presidencies (Boland of Queensland and Colbourne of New South Wales, the latter having been chosen to take Kennelly's position when it was vacated). As far as I was concerned, however, the most important incident was one which was not reported: the absence

140 from the Federal Executive meeting of Cosgrove, the Tasmanian Premier. He had been elected one of the two Tasmanian delegates, but he phoned me on the morning of the meeting to state that as a result of some emergency relating to his responsibilities as Premier he would be unable to attend. Nevertheless, his substitute, Eric Reece, could be relied on. Nothing that Reece said or did at the Federal Executive meeting justified this confidence. I wondered whether the Tasmanian Premier was as committed as we had believed. It transpired much later that he had been warned to break his association with the Movement, and had decided to do so.

Kennelly's energies redoubled. Working in particular with Clyde Cameron (MHR for Hindmarsh, SA), a strong personality who detested the Groups and the Movement, and with the New South Wales opposition, Kennelly welded a formidable machine. As a result of his strenuous organizing he reversed the July decision at the November Federal Executive meeting. It was now decided that the July resolution, stating that a Federal Parliamentarian could not also be Federal Secretary, was unconstitutional. To achieve this result, Kennelly had to undertake to stand down from the federal secretary-ship voluntarily after the next Federal election, which was scheduled for the latter months of 1954. He had won valuable time, and could be expected to use it. The decisive factor in this serious reversal for the Groups, was that Reece once again represented Tasmania, thus confirming that Cosgrove, as Premier, had effectively pulled out of the fight; while Chamberlain, who later, as Federal President, was to preside over the judicial execution of the Victorian and New South Wales Executives, made his appearance from Western Australia.

When Dr Evatt publicly attacked the Groups on 5 October 1954, and thus initiated the chain of events which led to the split in the Labor Party, his indispensable ally was Kennelly: indispensable precisely because the latter understood the science of 'numbers' in a way that Evatt never did. Yet at the November 1953 Federal Executive meeting, Kennelly had allegedly stated that 'if he was reinstated he would set out to break Dr Evatt's leadership of the Party'.[4] No statement better illustrated the fundamental divisions between those who were eventually to unite to destroy the Groups.

In April 1954, with all of the issues unresolved, a new and urgent factor entered into the situation. Federal Parliament had re-convened on 6 April. Menzies announced that the rolls for the coming election would close on 23 April, and that nominations would close on 6 May.[5] At the end of February, I had received a phone call from one of Dr Evatt's secretaries, Albert Grundeman, previously unknown to me, stating that the Parliamentary Leader of the ALP wished to meet me in Melbourne. I recalled the vague wish he had expressed at the meeting in the Exhibition Building, Melbourne, some ten months before: but I had not heard from him since. It was much later that I discovered that, during this period, he had sounded out the prospects of such a meeting with Lovegrove and Keon, neither of whom gave him any encouragement. When Grundeman's phone call came, I had no wish to accept the invitation. I understood that Evatt's 'right-wing' *démarche* of the last two years was a tactical manoeuvre. My own feeling was that he was not to be trusted, and that to enter into any discussions with him, especially discussions at which there were no witnesses, was giving hostages to fortune. I raised the matter with Dr Mannix, whose view was that I could not refuse an invitation from the Leader of the Opposition without insulting him: and his support for the Groups, however motivated, was important.

The three discussions which I had with Dr Evatt, each one of them at his request, comprise a most extraordinary episode within a twelve months period. Since the basis on which the discussions were held was that they were confidential, I treated them as such until long after his open attack on myself on 5 October 1954, when he stated that he had only recently discovered a 'plot' with which I was connected to 'take over' the Labor Party.

As we walked down the magnificent stairway of the Hotel Windsor from Dr Evatt's private suite, after a discussion which had lasted more than an hour, he came directly to the point of the factional struggle within the Labor Party machine. He said that he was well aware that my friends were trying to remove Kennelly from the federal secretaryship. He expressed complete support for this enterprise. The only criticism he could make, he said, was of the decision to fill the federal secretaryship with Colbourne of New South Wales. Colbourne, he said, was weak, and he would ultimately let down anyone who trusted him. Lovegrove or McManus were greatly to be preferred. I replied that 'my' friends were actually members of 'his' party of long standing. As for Colbourne, I felt that Evatt was being unjust to him. 'Nevertheless', he replied, 'you'll find out that I'm right'. In the light of this single incident, it might be understood why I thought the honest indignation expressed by Dr Evatt in his statement of 5 October 1954, at the discovery of a 'plot' to take over the Labor Party, somewhat synthetic. If as Parliamentary Leader he represented his party, never was there a maiden more willing to be ravished than the ALP.

The discussion in his suite began with the most outrageous flattery directed to the speech he had heard me give at the reception to the two Cardinals a year before. The speech, he said, indicated that I had a knowledge of foreign affairs of which he would like to avail himself, as he expected to form a government. I suggested that one who had occupied his positions could learn little from me. He persisted. I said vaguely that I was deeply concerned at the dangers represented by the Communist movements in Southeast Asian countries, and that, in broadest outline, Australia's attitude should favour Asian nationalism while rejecting Asian Communism. 'I would be more cautious', replied Evatt. 'I think that we have to be careful about Asian nationalism as well.' He was persistent in his demands that I discuss with him the type of measures I would like to see a Labor government introduce if it came to power, which, he maintained, would not be long delayed. I did not really believe that he needed to be told, but it would have been embarrassing to be reticent. Hence I told him of my anxiety that Labor should strengthen the 'clean ballots' provision in union elections. His answer was that he intended to solve the entire question of Communist power in the union movement in a most dramatic way. All union elections would be conducted on the same day, with voting compulsory for union members, the ballot to be conducted and the votes counted by the Commonwealth Electoral Office. When every unionist voted in a clean ballot, he said, the Communists would have as little chance in union elections as in political elections. There was never a more complete rapport. He was strongly in favour of an expanded migration programme. He would make £2m available as a capital contribution for land settlement projects to complement the loan capital promised by the Dutch and Italian Governments. He would solve the financial problems of the independent schools. He would make Keon a member of his Cabinet. It was all rather disgusting. When I went home that evening, I told my wife that I had encountered the impossible—a man without a soul. Archbishop Mannix thought that my reaction was quite mistaken. What mattered, he said, was that political necessity had compelled Dr Evatt to rely on the support of the Industrial Groups within the ALP, if and when he became Prime Minister.

A second interview at my own office in Gertrude Street, Fitzroy, went over similar ground. When Menzies announced the date of the 1954 election, Evatt threw himself energetically into the campaign. His first task was to draw up his policy speech. He rang me at home, asking me to fly to Canberra the very next day to help him (and presumably the group around him) to draw up his policy speech. I had no wish to be drawn into Evatt's entourage and made the excuse that it was undesirable that someone who was not a member of his party should be involved so directly in his campaign. He was extremely annoyed with my reaction. However, some time later, he had recovered his good humour and phoned me once again while he was on his way to an election meeting in the Latrobe Valley. I was actually called out of a meeting of the Movement National Executive to take his call. He said: 'Santa, things are going very well. If your people "stick", we are past the post'. I walked back to the Executive meeting and told the members of the Executive of that sentence, adding: 'I believe that Evatt made that call to establish his alibi. If he is defeated, he will say it was because "we" didn't "stick" to him'.

I have entered into such detail concerning this unexpected and—on my part, unwanted—association with Dr Evatt, simply to establish how dishonest were the terms of the attack he made on the Industrial Groups, the Movement, and myself personally on 5 October—only five months later—and over the following years. I do not know any political associate of Dr Evatt who has ever believed that there was anything inherently improbable in my version of the discussions with him.[6]

The truthfulness of my account of the conversations which Evatt sought with me has naturally been called into question since only Dr Evatt and I were present at them. It may therefore be useful to repeat Murray's judgement.

Evatt followed up his public campaigning with three private conversations with Santamaria in the autumn of 1954. As only the two of them were involved, Santamaria was the only living witness to the nature of these talks when this work was being written. Nevertheless, the general outline is widely accepted. Dalziel tells in his *Evatt The Enigma* how Albert Grundeman, a member of Evatt's secretariat, used to say that he accompanied Evatt to a private meeting with Santamaria . . .

Santamaria's version of the incident accords with the impressions of others who heard about it later, and who could be expected to be reasonably critical in their approach to vital statements by Santamaria.[7]

In his review of Sir Paul Hasluck's *Diplomatic Witness*, Professor W. Macmahon Ball, who worked directly under Evatt as consultant to the Australian delegation at the 1945 San Francisco Conference, as political representative of the Australian Government in the Netherlands East Indies in the same year, and as Australian Minister to Japan in 1946-47, declared: 'Evatt was completely untrustworthy'. Then, quoting Hasluck, 'He did not scruple to destroy or withhold papers which might contradict his own story . . . He was quite unblushing, or seemed to forget, that officers had been at his elbow . . .'[8]

In the light of after-events it seems likely that in all this period the seeds of the mental disturbance which later overwhelmed him were already present, and that in his conduct there was perhaps diminished moral responsibility.

Evatt should not have lost the 1954 election. The strong and successful attack which the Labor Party, through its Industrial Groups, had made on Communist power in the unions, compared with the purely theoretical—and unsuccessful—approach made by the Menzies Government in 1951, had lent considerable prestige to the Labor Party. One result was that by the time of the 1954 Federal election, Labor was in power in all States except South Australia, where Sir Thomas Playford's unique electoral system kept the Liberals in office.

144

In fact, Labor made a net gain of four seats, entering the new Parliament with fifty-seven seats compared with sixty-four for the Liberal–Country Party coalition. It improved its share of the popular vote from the 47.63 per cent it had gained in 1951 to 50.03 per cent. Evatt's own explanation for his defeat, and one which for the next twenty-five years remained as the powerful left-wing orthodoxy, was that Menzies entered into a conspiracy with ASIO (Australian Security Intelligence Organization) to exploit the defection from the Soviet Embassy of its Third Secretary (Vladimir Petrov) and his wife. Whether the Petrov affair cost Dr Evatt the half-dozen seats which he would have needed to gain a working majority, I cannot judge. If Dr Evatt had won the election, he would never have launched his attack on the Industrial Groups or the Movement, since he would have needed their support as Prime Minister.

What is more important is that since the publication of *Truth will out: ASIO and the Petrovs* by Michael Thwaites, then Director of Counter Espionage with ASIO, perhaps the central figure in the Petrov defection, no commonsense person can believe what for a quarter of a century has been the Australian Left's great historical legend: that there was a Petrov conspiracy, that it was Australia's own McCarthyist experience; and that the Movement was involved in this non-existent 'plot'.

The scenario, sedulously furthered by Dr Evatt and the entire left-wing 'apparat' throughout Australia for the next twenty-five years, was that Menzies himself carefully timed Petrov's defection, of which he was aware beforehand, so as to create an anti-Communist issue for the May 1954 Federal election, which he had also timed to profit from the situation; and that in this plot he was joined by distinguished members of the judiciary and by the right-wing of the ALP. If consistent repetition could establish history, the left-wing legend of the Petrov conspiracy would be history.

As J. B. Paul, Senior Lecturer in Political Science in the University of New South Wales, pointed out after the publication of Thwaites's book, the twentieth Commonwealth Parliament would in any case have expired on 12 June 1954. The election was called by Menzies for 29 May, almost the last possible date. On 6 April Menzies confirmed a previous broadcast announcement that 23 April was the date for issuing the writs and 6 May the closing date for nominations. Menzies thus 'announced the date for issuing the writs for the closing of nominations for that election fully a week *before* that "dramatic revelation" . . .'[9] Thwaites effectively disposes of Alan Renouf's allegation that the establishment of the Petrov Royal Commission was 'largely (but not totally) a function of domestic politics'[10], by showing that it was, in fact, Colonel (later Sir Charles) Spry, then Director-General of Security, who on 3-4 April advised Menzies to establish a Royal Commission to pursue enquiries into Petrov's revelations, on the model of the Canadian Royal Commission, which was appointed to examine Gouzenko and the documents which the latter had removed from the Soviet Embassy in Ottawa.[11]

As Paul remarks, however:

> It does not detract in the least from Thwaites's account to say that the absurdity of the legend he demolishes has been obvious from previously published sources, nor that some will still cling to its supposed orthodoxy, smelly as it is, as tenaciously as a Pharisee would cleave to his phylacteries.[12]

In the immediate aftermath of the election, Dr Evatt gave no indication that he intended to change his pro-Industrial Group orientation. He was very well received by more than four hundred delegates to the Victorian ALP Conference in June. The Melbourne *Sun* reported him as being 'visibly moved'.

Dr Evatt's own position as Parliamentary Leader must in any case have been in some doubt after the loss of two elections as leader, but there was no immediate threat to his position. The Industrial Group forces then dominant in the Party had no reason whatsoever to prefer Calwell, Dr Evatt's Deputy. Careful calculations on both sides would have dictated a continuation of this marriage of convenience. With five Labor governments in the States, four seats gained in the recent election, and Labor still pursuing an anti-Communist course, Dr Evatt, even with the Kennelly–Calwell forces against him, might have considered that by playing for time he could still have achieved the prime ministership.

During the month of July, however, I was filled with deep forebodings that this would not be the course which events would take. In the internal Party conflict, hostility was reaching a hitherto unimaginable level of hysteria. Dr John Burton, who had once been Dr Evatt's private secretary before becoming Secretary of his Department of External Affairs, had published a strongly ideological attack on Movement influence in the ALP in his *The Alternative*. Great play was being made of an address entitled 'The Movement of Ideas' which I had given to the National Conference early in 1954.

Murray, having analysed the text of the address, summarized its import:

> In this typically Santamaria speech Santamaria analysed with brilliant ideological clarity the situation that was developing as the anti-communist battle in the unions neared its end. He said the battle in the unions had had absolute priority, and the next task was to beat, in ideological argument, those inclined to a 'soft', anti-American attitude on foreign policy and reduced defence spending. Santamaria made frequent use of the words 'we' and 'us' and the speech had the clearest possible implication that he expected Movement members to influence the ALP on these questions. It could have been construed as hinting that Santamaria wanted the Movement to 'take over'

146 | the ALP, but only by assiduous 'reading between the lines'—a practice that was prevalent on this question at the time, however, and was to become more so.

In one resounding political gaffe, Santamaria referred to the foreign policy softliners using what he called the 'Chifley legend' to reinforce their viewpoint. 'People might not follow Dr Evatt or Mr Calwell, but the Chifley legend is held to be strong enough to make orthodox any policy that they put forward and to condemn any policy that we put forward', Santamaria said. He said Movement members should work to destroy the 'Chifley legend' and replace it with the pro-American 'Curtin legend'. Within a few months, Santamaria was to be dubbed throughout the country as the man who had not only tried to subvert the Labor Party, but perhaps worse crime, the 'Chifley legend' as well.[13]

What was meant by the 'Chifley legend' was not the inheritance which Chifley had actually left to the Labor Party, but the travesty of his ideas as a charter of anti-American neutralism, which the Left was sedulously propagating.

At the non-ideological level, the argument was that the Groups had exceeded their charter, embarked on objectives never envisaged, and become the band-waggon on which ambitious careerists might thrust their way to power. A few weeks later, Alan Reid, the best-informed of Australia's political correspondents, put the increasingly familiar thesis in these words:

Santamaria, like the medieval Fulk of Neuilly, who preached the 13th century crusade that was to founder abortively in opulent Constantinople, fostered a crusade for the eradication of communism from the trade union movement.

Men of all creeds and men of none, and men of all political hues (except communists) came to him for help and support, and got it.

The ex-Trotskyist Laurie Short, an ex-communist like Koestler, Silone, and a host of others who are today bitterly anti-communist, and effectively so, was aided and supported by Santamaria in his long-drawn-out struggle with communist topliner Ernie Thornton for the national secretaryship of the Ironworkers' Union.

When Short triumphed and replaced Thornton, it was the worst disaster and the first major set-back for communism in the trade union movement since it first obtained its industrial bridgehead in the 30's. Success followed success . . . In its way, it was a fantastic success story.

But along the road towards its goal, the crusade, like its historical predecessor, got diverted. It started to intrude into unions that were not communist controlled . . .

It began to become known that if anyone climbed on the groupers' bandwaggon he would go places. The bandwaggon started to get crowded with careerists, some of them trading upon qualifications that had nothing to do with politics, even of the cynical machine variety . . .

So the opportunists started to look around for Constantinoples to conquer. Whereas, previously, a man had to be a communist, or at least a proven communist sympathiser before moves were made against him, the pattern changed. It was enough now that he was not sufficiently violently anti-communist in his attitude . . .

It is to these formidable stresses that Labor is being currently subjected, and which could cost it its stability, possibly its native character.

For, like their historical predecessors, the crusaders who set out with such noble intentions, may unwittingly, as was the case centuries ago, be destroying a bastion against the inroads of modern infidels.[14]

The legend of the twentieth century crusade which lost its way and permitted itself to become diverted to the fleshpots of a latter-day

Constantinople was brilliantly conceived. In far more plebeian versions it became the vogue. There was some truth in what Reid wrote, but on balance not very much. The inevitable difficulties of success were magnified into an argument against the whole principle of action on which an indispensable enterprise was based.

On 1 August 1955, at the Victorian State Convention of the Movement, in the presence of Archbishop Mannix and Archbishop Carboni, I expressed my anxiety. 'There are many forces previously for us which are now against us. If they unite, and find a common leader, we will find ourselves in trouble, deeper than we have ever experienced before.'

Everything changed with Dr Evatt's appearance before the Royal Commission into the Petrov defection. Fergan O'Sullivan, a member of Evatt's staff, admitted that he had been the author of 'Document H', a detailed survey of the lives and times of a number of Australian journalists which, he said, he had prepared at the request of the *Tass* representatives in Canberra. (Most *Tass* representatives, as is well known, are members of the KGB.) Further evidence was given that some of the facts contained in the far more serious 'Document J' had come from O'Sullivan and other members of Dr Evatt's staff. On 15 July Mr Justice Owen, one of the Commissioners, stated: 'It is very disturbing that the writer claims to have got information from the secretariat of a man who holds a very high position in public life'.[15]

Thus, Dr Evatt himself became directly involved, through allegations against members of his personal staff, by mid-July. The post-election ballot for the position of Parliamentary Leader of the ALP took place on 3 August, in the heat of the controversy generated by the statements in the Petrov Commission. Although Evatt comfortably defeated his opponent, Tom Burke of Western Australia, it was apparent that his deposition was only a matter of time. He had lost two elections; his staff had been named by the Commission; and finally Evatt himself entered the lists as counsel for two members of his staff, Dalziel and Grundeman, on 16 August. On the morning of the sixteenth, when Evatt's likely appearance was still only a matter of conjecture, the Melbourne *Age* had reported that 'senior Party members, when they heard rumours that Dr Evatt might appear before the Petrov Commission, said that if he did he would lose the leadership within 48 hours'.[16]

In the subsequent battles Evatt did not lose the leadership. His mind gradually fell prey to another delusion, that the Industrial Groups, the Movement, his right-wing Parliamentary colleagues who had been in collusion with Menzies and ASIO during the Petrov affair had now combined in another plot, this time to deprive him of the leadership of the ALP. If the new delusion was the symptom of a growing mental disorientation, the political strategy he and his

148 associates devised was brilliantly conceived. What he did was to change the whole of his political strategy. Since his centre and right-wing colleagues in the parliamentary Caucus made it clear that they were determined to remove him, he set out to guarantee his political survival by switching his policy from support of the Industrial Groups to leading an outright attack on them. He thus based the whole of his future career on the support of the Communist and extreme Left machine, with Kennelly, in an equally epic reversal, becoming the campaign director of the leader he had sworn to destroy! It was a *tour de force*.

The subsequent Evatt campaign set out to ban the Industrial Groups (thus guaranteeing the support of the Communists and the Left); to destroy the existing control of the three State Executives which were under Industrial Group influence—Victoria, New South Wales, Queensland—and thus to change the representation from these States at the Twenty-first Federal Conference, which was to take place in Hobart at the end of January 1955.

At the end of the affair, the Industrial Groups (and the Movement) would be destroyed; the Communists and their allies would regain the unions; Dr Evatt, thus guaranteed their support, would have retained his leadership of the Parliamentary Party; Senator Kennelly and his allies would once again control the Labour machine. The only point on which the new-found allies were not at one was on the issue of Dr Evatt's own future. For while he, perhaps already in the midst of the intellectual decline which ended only with his own death, believed that he would retain the parliamentary leadership, Senator Kennelly and Mr Calwell had a different objective. They would use Dr Evatt to destroy the Groups, and then they would remove him.

The formal details of this imaginative—and destructive—operation have been recounted elsewhere.[17] There is no need to recapitulate them. The critical sections of Dr Evatt's initial attack are worth quoting once again:

At the recent Federal elections on May 29 we put forward a policy of development and we polled a majority of the people in Australia. We made gains in every State except Victoria.

All this was achieved by the self-sacrifice of tens of thousands of voluntary workers for Labor.

It was achieved, too, despite the thinly-veiled use against Labor of the opening speech before the Petrov Commission—the statement of which seemed to be distant many poles apart from the truth of the matter so far as it has been more recently revealed by the sworn evidence of many witnesses.

But in the election, one factor told heavily against us—the attitude of a small minority group of members, located particularly in the State of Victoria, which has, since 1949, become increasingly disloyal to the Labor Movement and the Labor leadership.

Adopting methods which strikingly resemble both Communist and Fascist infiltration of larger groups, some of these groups have created an almost intolerable situation—calculated to deflect the Labor Movement from the pursuit of established Labor objectives and ideals.

Whenever it suits their real aims, one or more of them never hesitate to attack or subvert Labor policy or Labor leadership . . .

Since the elections, nothing has been done officially to deal with those responsible for the disloyal and subversive actions to which I refer.

In addition, it is my clear belief that in crucial constituencies members of the same small group, whether members of the Federal Parliamentary Labor Party, or not, deliberately attempted to undermine a number of Labor's selected and endorsed candidates, with the inevitable and intended result of assisting the Menzies Government . . .

It seems certain that the activities of this small group are largely directed from outside the Labor Movement. The Melbourne *News Weekly* appears to act as their organ. A serious position exists.

Since the referendum of 1951 Labor leadership has become very patient with some of these outbursts, solely in the interests of solidarity. But our patience is abused and our tolerance is interpreted as a sign of weakness.

The Labor Party cannot yield to the dictates of any minority which functions in a way contrary to the overwhelming majority of the rank and file of the Labor Movement . . .

Having in view the absolute necessity for real, and not sham, solidarity and unity within the movement, I am bringing this matter before the next meeting of the Federal Executive, with a view to appropriate action being taken by the Federal Labor Conference in January.

Ninety-five per cent of the rank and file of the Parliamentary Labor Party are absolutely loyal to the movement. There is not the slightest reason why their efforts should be undermined by a tiny minority.[18]

# PART III

# Struggle within the Church

# 16 The Two Camps

Between 5 October 1954, the date of Dr Evatt's first attack on his opponents within the Labor Party, and his retirement as Parliamentary Leader of the ALP in 1960, the most important single issue in Australian politics was the struggle between the Evatt forces and the Industrial Groups (later to take parliamentary form as the Democratic Labor Party). It is the result of that conflict which even now is still decisive as to the character of the Labor Party.

The intense feeling aroused by this conflict involved far more Australians than those normally interested in political affairs. The emotions—at once racialist and religious—fomented by Dr Evatt arose naturally enough from a national psyche that was still largely Anglo-Saxon. The racialist elements in Evatt's campaign have been remarked on by Robert Murray, whose book *The Split* is the best comprehensive analysis of the factors leading to the Labor split of the fifties.

Innuendo built up a public 'image' of Santamaria associated with all that Anglo-Saxondom instinctively disliked about Southern Europe. Santamaria had often mentioned that the Lipari Islands, where his parents came from, had had a considerable influx of Spanish blood at one time, and this enabled not only the build-up of a 'stiletto' legend, but coupled with his name an inference of association with the Spanish ultra-clerical tradition stretching from the Inquisition to Franco. The *Australian Worker*, often referred to 'Santa-stiletto' or 'cloak and stiletto', usually associated with the attack on the 'Chifley legend'.[1]

It was in this vein that a Victorian Catholic parliamentarian, Malcolm Gladman, who sided with the Evatt forces, speaking at Warrnambool on 12 May 1955 with the Premier, Cain, on the platform, said: 'The Santamaria group would make Hitler's Blackshirts and Mussolini's Fascists pale into insignificance'.[2]

The profoundly sectarian passions invoked in his attack, which combined so effectively with its racial overtones, were evidenced by

154 | Evatt himself when speaking on the Victorian Labor Hour program on 15 May 1955.

Sixteen members of the Barry Party in the Victorian Parliament are Roman Catholics and only one is a Protestant, and but for the efforts of the legitimate ALP the sectarians would have gained control of the party. It is the duty of all non-Catholics to smash the Catholic influence in the Labor Party. Defeat it.[3]

It has been suggested that the struggle was merely a squalid contest for parliamentary leadership and seats, and for control over the Labor 'machine' which ultimately controlled Labor endorsements for parliamentary candidature. From one aspect it was. But it is worth recalling once again that in the same epoch as the Split in Australia, the Socialist Parties split in both Italy and Japan on the identical issue of Communist influence; while a split was averted in Britain only because the moderate social democrats under Gaitskell defeated the Left extremists within the British Labour Party. However, Gaitskell won only because the largest British trade unions, which controlled the Party, were then in strongly anti-Communist hands.

The Australian episode therefore was only one chapter in a world-wide story of the issues raised by the Cold War. What makes the Australian chapter so interesting is the fact that in the end it was decided less by political than by ecclesiastical factors, especially by the outcome of a struggle within the Catholic Church. For I have no doubt at all that if the Catholic Bishops had maintained in the time of its adversity the same unity in support of the Movement which they had demonstrated so admirably during the many years of its success, the struggle within the ranks of the Labor Party would have ended quite differently. Even more, the future of the Labor Party itself and of Australia would have been altered radically and, in my view at least, for the better.

Once the Evatt attack was launched, the Movement attempted to confront Dr Evatt and his supporters with a united front, transcending religious allegiance, in tactics, strategy and programmes. The leaders of the Movement gradually became aware, however, that the national organization which they had so carefully built up was being divided from within. The most critical months, during which their abilities should have been entirely devoted to meeting the tactics of the Evatt forces, were wasted in the prolonged effort to maintain the internal unity of the Movement itself. Effective unity of direction was destroyed.

Many non-Catholic political leaders (for instance, D. Lovegrove, the Victorian State Secretary of the ALP, whose position depended considerably on Industrial Group support) were demoralized by growing evidence of Catholic disunity. On the other hand, Dr Evatt, who might otherwise have hesitated to challenge the Industrial

Groups and the Movement, could only feel greatly encouraged when a Catholic like J. P. Ormonde, closely connected with Catholic officialdom in the Sydney Archdiocese, was able to assure him on the eve of his attack, that the Cardinal's influence would be thrown against the Movement if only Evatt would grasp the nettle.[4]

There is no doubt that those Catholic Bishops headed by Cardinal Gilroy, who threw the whole of their weight against the Movement, believed that they were acting in the interests of the Church.

As de Gaulle had written of an incomparably more significant occasion:

... Men, divided into two camps, had claimed to lead the nation and the state toward different goals, by contradictory paths. From that moment, the responsibility of both groups was measured . . . not by their intentions, but by their acts, for the country's salvation was directly at stake.[5]

# 17 Beginnings of Conflict

Throughout 1952 and 1953 a well-organized Catholic opposition to the Movement established itself, particularly in Melbourne and Sydney. It provided the atmosphere without which the eventual split in the ranks of the Hierarchy would have been impossible to achieve.

The Newman Societies in both universities, although, as always, representing only a small minority of Catholic graduates and undergraduates, then enjoyed an exceptionally gifted group of leaders—which included a person of such distinction as the poet Vincent Buckley—and they were almost uniformly opposed to the Movement. The Melbourne leaders of the Newman Society were rapidly becoming, if they were not already, the dominant influence on the *Catholic Worker*, so that the university opposition had a regular monthly organ. The links between this group and the Young Christian Workers' Movement, whose episcopal chairman was Archbishop Simonds, were informal but close. Dr Mannix's obstinate refusal to die had inevitably delayed Dr Simonds's accession to the Archbishopric of Melbourne, creating natural frustrations inseparable from such a situation.

The Melbourne group had also enjoyed a strong fellow-feeling with Mr Calwell, who was Federal Deputy-Leader of the Parliamentary ALP; while the Sydney group found its political link-man in the future Senator, J. P. Ormonde, who in turn was associated with the group of Labor-oriented priests surrounding Dr James Carroll, who was to be consecrated Auxiliary Bishop to Cardinal Gilroy early in 1954.

It was a formidable combination. Although I was far more familiar with the Melbourne than with the Sydney group, I had no doubt that this informal alliance represented a considerable danger, and that it was necessary to devote a good deal of attention to the problem it was likely to create. As Murray points out:

In Sydney, the more vocal dissidents had talks with Ormonde and with the anti-Movement, anti-Grouper front building up around him. The obsessive Ormonde worked frantically at his cause, creating hostility by word of mouth and warning a number of Protestant leaders. Some of the statements by Protestant leaders, warning against 'Catholic Action' in 1953 and 1954, can be traced to Ormonde's zeal.[1]

To determine what motivated the hostility was, and remains, a complex question. In part, of course, it was a product of differences between generations. There was also a legitimate grievance in the case which the opposition represented to the Bishops. In 1953 the Melbourne *Catholic Worker* group sent a letter to all of the Bishops, while the Sydney group (perhaps acting in combination) presented their complaints to Cardinal Gilroy. The gravamen of their joint complaint was that the Movement 'line' on what they regarded as a purely political issue was being presented to Catholics in such a way as to represent a religious, and specifically Catholic, orthodoxy. Hence a Catholic who opposed the Movement 'line' on purely political grounds was in danger of being regarded as less a Catholic for doing so.

It was already apparent that the Movement and its critics were really intent on two quite distinct objectives. The critics, in so far as they were motivated by the principles they expressed, were primarily concerned with the freedom of the Catholic to hold differing viewpoints on political issues, without their Catholicism being impugned. Movement members were primarily concerned with the fight against the Communists in the trade union movement, which they believed affected national security, with which their opponents appeared not to be concerned at all. They felt, therefore, that Catholic unity was necessary to the achievement of objectives which were ultimately concerned with the nation's security, which involved politics but ought to transcend them. On that view some sacrifices of individual liberty were worthwhile in an emergency which had lasted more than a decade. If the emergency had begun to recede with the turning of the tide in the unions in 1952-53, that was not by chance, but as a result of a concerted Movement campaign. Communist influence would certainly reassert itself if division were allowed to set in.

The judgement of the Rev P. J. Duffy, SJ, who unlike most of the critics knew the Movement from the inside, was in my view closely related to the political realities of the era:

Given Communist exploitation of sectarianism . . . if tactics against the Communists in the unions were to be successful, there was a case for submerging differences for the sake of that organizational unity that gave strength to the anti-communist cause. It can be argued that this was a period of emergency when, like governments in wartime, those actively opposing the Communists in the unions had some right to expect a unified support from their Catholic colleagues.[2]

Personalities were of course deeply involved as well as questions of principle. Just as there would have been no Labor split if the

Petrov Commission had not threatened to terminate Dr Evatt's political career, so there would have been no split in the Church in the fifties if certain powerful personal emotions had not been involved. Archbishop Simonds, whose theological views were conservative, and who was, in a sense, a 'clerical', found himself heading a professedly liberal reaction, largely through the frustrations which resulted from Dr Mannix's longevity. His disappointment was increased by the fact that there was no real intimacy between himself and Daniel Mannix.

In Sydney, the influence of the opposition probably would have remained minimal, had it not been for the antipathy of Ormonde and his close connections with a circle of priests who were close to the Cardinal and thus were able to play upon the latter's not always latent suspicion of 'Melbourne'.

I attached much more significance to this newly concerted opposition than did Dr Mannix. Approaching his ninetieth year, he had lived through many great events, including the Conscription crisis of 1916-17. Dr Mannix had seen oppositions come and go and was disposed to be philosophical.

On the other hand, I made some attempts to deflect the opposition, but owing to a variety of circumstances, my attempts failed. I attempted a direct personal approach to Father Lombard, the National Chaplain of the YCW, relying on the friendship we had had when he was a young priest in the thirties, and pointing to the damage which must be done to the Church if his hostility were to proceed to its logical conclusion, whatever that might be. It was unavailing.

Belatedly, I approached Archbishop Simonds. That approach was equally fruitless. The reason seemed to me to lie in the close friendship which existed between Archbishop Mannix and myself, whereas between Dr Mannix and his coadjutor the relationship was correct but formal. That judgement may be mistaken, but I believe that it is correct.

I had already attempted to tackle the more general problem of the 'secrecy' of the Movement, which became a major campaigning issue during the Labor split. 'Secrecy' associated with the name 'Santamaria' could always be relied upon to produce a *frisson*.

The Movement was about as secret as the Sydney Harbour Bridge. Its existence and activities were known to friend and foe alike: not least to Dr Evatt, who had attempted to use it for his own purposes; and to Mr Calwell, who had secured the wartime newsprint licence for its organ *News Weekly*.

The pledge demanded of members that the proceedings of the Movement should be regarded as completely confidential, which was the foundation of all of the allegations of 'secrecy', had originally arisen as a result of two factors.

The Victorian Trades Hall Council Secretary, J. V. Stout, had understood the force of the secretarian weapon and insisted that nothing should be said or written about the Movement in any way. In addition, in the climate of the time it was as much as anyone's position in the trade union movement was worth to be labelled a Movement member. The arguments for total confidentiality were overwhelming. By the end of the forties, however, it was apparent that the alleged secrecy of the Movement would become a serious issue. Hence I proposed that the Movement establish an open and public position, using the name Civic Committees, on the model of a similar organization which had been effective in the Italian elections of 1948.

I first proposed the change to the Episcopal Committee at its meeting on 3 April 1951. As the Movement had been greatly dependent on the financial and organizational support of the Church since its foundation, it was practically impossible to make so radical a change without the general concurrence of the Bishops. The Committee rejected the proposal, probably for reasons similar to those of the Victorian trade union leaders. In this situation it was not practical to pursue the matter further. Nor indeed would a change have made much difference. When in 1957 the National Civic Council was formed to continue the work of the disbanded Movement, the charge of secrecy exercised a powerful fascination, which still remains to the present day. How an organization whose president has appeared weekly for twenty years, on a television circuit which ultimately embraced some twenty channels, can still be classified, at least by its opponents, as secret must be left to students of language to determine.

It was to be expected that some of the absolutism associated with the views of the more 'straight-up-and-down-the-line' Movement members would provoke a reaction. Nevertheless, my first attempt to modify it had an unexpected and quite counter-productive conclusion. At the beginning of 1952 I read a paper to the National Conference of the Movement to which I gave the title 'Religious Apostolate and Political Action'. The paper had a single purpose: to put some limit to exaggerated claims that since the Bishops had unitedly expressed their support for the Movement and had supported its particular commitments, Catholics were bound by that decision and had no right to oppose the Movement.

I understood and sympathized with those who expressed this exaggerated view. It was not easy to arouse the normally apathetic to persistent and organized activity within the union movement. Such activity interested them as little as it interested the rest of the community. It involved repeated absences from home and family, and not infrequently the threat of discrimination and occasionally of personal physical danger. As far as one can see, from that day to this, no other similar force has been able to achieve this 'grass-roots' anti-Communist resurgence in the union movement in any Anglo-Saxon country.

Nevertheless, the idea expressed was an exaggeration, and a potentially harmful one. The best way to attack the thesis, without hurting its proponents, was indirectly. It was for this purpose that I prepared the paper 'Religious Apostolate and Political Action' and delivered it to the National Conference.

In the first draft of the paper, as it was presented to the National Conference, I argued that in certain clear and specific situations it was proper for the Church, as represented by the Bishops, to be involved in political matters. If a country were threatened by a totalitarian movement, the triumph of which would mean persecution for the Church, the Bishops would be failing in their duty if they did *not* resist that movement, even if the only method of resistance was political. If governments legislated on matters related to marriage and the family, with laws which clearly had unfavourable moral connotations and consequences, how could the Church, through the Bishops, not be involved? If a society permitted grievous violations of social justice to take place, could the Church be neutral in that situation?

It is worth noting that few Catholics today would deny the second and third propositions at least, and assert that the Bishops should keep silent on laws which facilitated abortion, or should remain neutral on the question of aid to underdeveloped countries.

The central question, of course, related to method. In what way should the Church intervene? How far should it come down from the level of general principle to that of policy and method? Could it, with propriety, be linked, in whatever way, with a lay organization which acted as a political force in the political order to bring about practical results?

My answer—to sum it up quite briefly—was:

1  That the Church could not opt out of such situations simply because the issues were on the mixed ground of religion, morality and politics.

2  That the Bishops, representing the Church, could be 'linked to' a lay organization seeking, by legitimate and democratic methods, to bring about political results. These methods might include the permeation of the policies of political parties.

3  That the policy decisions of that organization bound only its own members; and bound them, not by virtue of any authority delegated to it by the Bishops, but simply by virtue of their own membership of the organization. This membership, and the resultant obligations, they freely entered into and could freely terminate—as many did in the case of the Movement itself. In this there was no essential difference between the contractual obligations assumed by a person when

he joined the Movement and when he joined a football club. It certainly did not involve the conscience or the loyalty of any other person, through any presumed ecclesiastical authority.

The protagonists of liberation theology—among whom would be numbered some of the intellectual descendants of the liberal and progressivist opposition to the Movement during the fifties—are today most insistent on the necessity of the involvement of the Church, through its Bishops and priests as well as its laity, in the political struggle. The difference appears to be that they regard the intervention of the Church to support left-wing causes in the name of justice as both legitimate and necessary, whereas its intervention to preserve the civil order against revolution is regarded as both reactionary and illicit. In this way they are the mirror-image of the European Right of the nineteenth century. The European Right also believed that the Bishops should intervene to assist the 'forces of order' against the 'forces of revolution', but had little sympathy with their intervention to ameliorate the worst excesses of the industrial system, which ultimately delivered the French, Spanish and Italian working class to revolutionary parties.

The central purpose of the paper was, however, not merely to assert the right of Bishops to act politically for moral purposes, or to defend their association with a lay political force engaged in those activities. As its concluding sections showed, its purpose was also to put an end to the claim that ordinary Catholics were bound to support Movement policies because of some presumed authority devolved upon the Movement by the Bishops. The only persons bound to support Movement policies were those who freely undertook to do so, and—even these—only for so long as they did so.

The paper had some considerable effect within the Movement itself. It did eliminate the more extreme claims which it was intended to curb. Nevertheless, in the light of what ultimately happened to the paper, it would have been far better to have left well alone, to act on the view that it is better to live with mistakes and to explain nothing.

The paper was prepared for private reading and study within the Movement to deal with a particular problem. It was not intended for publication.

Nevertheless, it was published in edited form by Cardinal Gracias of Bombay, who obtained it from me during his visit to Australia in 1953, and who thought so well of it as to reprint it in his *Bombay Examiner* (18 and 25 June 1955).

My rather clumsy attempt to meet one of the reasonable objections of the Catholic opposition became decidedly unprofitable when Cardinal Gracias gave a roneoed copy of my paper to an Australian visitor to India who expressed interest in seeing the full original text after he had read the edited version in the *Bombay Examiner*. On his return to Australia he passed the paper to Dr Evatt

162 | through Mr Ormonde and Mr Calwell. Large numbers of roneoed copies were made, distributed by his supporters, and spread throughout the country.

The paper spoke of 'permeating' political parties and other social organizations. Dr Evatt saw how explosive such terms could be and exploited them skilfully. He later gave his own sidelined copy to Malcolm Muggeridge, who pressed the damaging words on me in a Channel 7 (Sydney) television interview. Muggeridge showed me the copy after the interview. While several paragraphs in Dr Evatt's copy are simply sidelined with a single stroke, the sentence which included the word 'permeation' had been marked with three strokes, showing the importance Evatt attached to it in building up his media campaign on the iniquity of the Movement's activities.

The constant attribution of a sinister meaning to the word 'permeation' was ironic. I had borrowed the word from the British Fabian Society, which used it to describe not merely its educative functions, but the organizational work of its members. Alas! I was to discover that a word permitted to an English Fabian was forbidden to an Australian Catholic!

The university Catholic opposition also, of course, seized its opportunity. The contents of the paper were represented as an arrogant expression of ultramontane claims, more fitted to the age of Innocent III and the medieval doctrine of the 'two swords' than to the age of Pius XII.[3]

Thus the attempt to dispel the gathering storm-clouds which cast a deep shadow over the undoubted achievements of the years from 1951 to 1953 had largely failed.

# 18 The Movement Divides

How much depended upon maintaining the unity of the Catholic Bishops in their support for the Movement was illustrated by a conversation I had with the Secretary of the Victorian Branch of the ALP (D. Lovegrove) during the first week of August 1954. I had not spoken to—nor even met—Lovegrove since that brief meeting in the Melbourne Trades Hall in the far-off thirties, when having recently left the Communist Party, he had given the 'inside-story' of Communist penetration of the Labour Movement to a young and politically innocent group of whom I was one.

In August 1954 we met for lunch at the Latin Restaurant, at the invitation of a mutual friend, Frank Hurst, Secretary of the Fibrous Plaster Manufacturers' Association. (Lovegrove had been Secretary of the Fibrous Plasterers' Union in the same industry.) Lovegrove came at once to the point. Dr Mannix, he said, had already passed his ninetieth birthday. He could not be expected to live much longer. He had no doubt that while Dr Mannix was alive, the position of the Movement—and my own position—were relatively strong. But what would happen afterwards? It was common talk, he said, that when Archbishop Simonds took over the entire policy of the Archdiocese would change. What then? He asked me to weigh my answer carefully since a good deal depended on it.

He and the Victorian ALP Executive were already in a position of open conflict with the Trades Hall Council and its Secretary, Stout. Hence I thought that he was merely referring to this. In retrospect, it seemed more likely that he knew something of the storm that was to break before the end of the year, and was considering his own position and prospects.

I gave him as truthful an answer as I could. I said that I was sure there would be a good deal of trouble for us when Dr Simonds became archbishop. But I felt that we could weather this trouble, since the great majority of diocesan priests and members of religious

164 orders favoured the Movement; that they were closely in touch with their people; even more, that they would for a long time ahead regard themselves as trustees of the Mannix tradition. In any case, while Victoria was the base, and therefore indeed uniquely important, the Movement was nation-wide, and there was no reason to expect changes in other States.

Lovegrove accepted my answer, and was greatly relieved by it. He seemed to be particularly impressed by the thought that the death of the great Archbishop, whenever it came about, while profoundly important in other ways, was unlikely to affect the convictions of the diocesan and religious clergy; that they were not zombies to march up a hill at the behest of one archbishop, and obediently down the other side when so instructed by his successor.

In the era which followed Vatican II, when the mentality of a large proportion of the younger Catholic clergy has been revolutionized, it is difficult to convey how far the struggle inside the Catholic Church at the time of the Labor split was a struggle for the mind of the ordinary clergy. Although it was being rapidly Australianized both in national origin and in training, it was still profoundly influenced in its attitude by its Irish racial and cultural ancestry.

The assurances I gave Lovegrove concerning the likely consequences of Archbishop Simonds's eventual accession were, I believe, well founded. What I underestimated were the consequences of Bishop (later Archbishop) James Carroll having become auxiliary to Cardinal Gilroy at the beginning of the same year. I did not know him personally, nor did I know his background, nor his political viewpoint, nor even that he had one. That ignorance turned out to be a major handicap. When informed that the Cardinal had given him some responsibility in relation to the Sydney branch of the Movement, I was assured that ultimate responsibility still rested with Bishop Lyons. This was not in fact true, but I had no reason to doubt it.

Bishop Lyons, who had previously represented the Cardinal in these matters, had originally been a Melbourne priest, Administrator of St Patrick's Cathedral, Melbourne, and then Bishop of Christchurch (New Zealand) before being translated to Sydney as auxiliary to Cardinal Gilroy. He idolized Archbishop Mannix—not an unqualified advantage for one who had to spend the latter part of his life as an auxiliary bishop in Sydney. We had been friends for many years. Throughout his life he was faithful to that friendship, as I tried to be in return. Yet even his best friends recognized that in his handling of personalities, particularly some of his priests, he was sometimes less sure than diplomacy demanded.

The tensions—if they can be so dignified—which exist between Sydney and Melbourne extend from football to cricket, from 'our 'arbour' to the Stock Exchanges and the business establishments. It was part of the tradition of inter-city rivalry that it extended to the archdioceses of Sydney and Melbourne. When the Catholic Church formed a national body, like the Society for the Propagation of the Faith, or the National Secretariat of Catholic Action, the location of the headquarters generally became an issue, as the location of the National Companies and Securities Commission has done in more recent times. Hence there was always a good deal of Sydney–Melbourne tension within the Movement.

Difficulties of the normal type with the Sydney office of the Movement had existed at least since the beginning of the fifties. When Bishop Lyons was given the Sydney appointment in May 1951, I informed him of some of the difficulties.[1] One was the appointment of totally unnecessary research officers to the New South Wales office of the Movement, in an obvious endeavour to duplicate the staff of the national office and thus lay the foundation of a claim to parallel authority. This was foolish, since whatever research work was needed was already being done in the national office; since the Cardinal had made it quite clear to me that he would be extremely sensitive to increasing financial demands; and since the efforts required to expand research facilities were at the expense of actual organization in the field.

The appointment of Kevin Davis as State President of the Movement in New South Wales early in 1952 offered an opportunity of remedying certain organizational weaknesses which had developed in Sydney by that time. To help him, the Rev. H. A. Lalor, SJ, was 'seconded' to Sydney, basically because he was an effective speaker, and an outstanding 'motivator'. The results manifested themselves in the fields of recruitment, organization and training.

A massive and extremely successful finance-raising campaign was initiated in a majority of Sydney parishes and in country areas as well. The Sydney office was then reorganized and expanded and several extra organizers, rather than research workers, were engaged. An extensive recruiting campaign was undertaken which greatly expanded the number of district groups and, as a consequence, of union groups. Training schools, seminars, and live-in week-ends were also introduced with beneficial results. *News Weekly*'s circulation was greatly increased. These were substantial gains.

There was, predictably, a price to be paid for this virtual re-creation of a vigorous and increasingly successful Movement in New South Wales, after some years of decline. It was a strong anti-Melbourne, anti-Movement backlash, especially among sections of the clergy in Sydney. But that was not obvious 560 miles away in Melbourne.

In this successful programme of reorganization, Bishop Lyons helped greatly, since—at least in the early stages—he satisfied the Cardinal that progress was being made. He not only kept the

*Above:* Fr B. T. McLaughlin, Archbishop Mannix, Fr W. Hackett, SJ, with the Santamaria family, Mandalay, Portsea, 1954

*Left:* J. T. Kane

Cardinal informed of everything that was happening. He encouraged Davis to see the Cardinal once a month to discuss activities in other States, as well as in New South Wales. The Cardinal demonstrated extreme sensitivity in money matters, a fact which was not fully realized at the national office. However, he was temporarily placated by a situation in which the Movement raised almost all of its own funds. Bishop Lyons was able to secure fairly widespread assistance (or compliance) from the clergy, with the money-raising and group-building programmes in the various parishes.

The Bishop was single-minded and demanding. He ignored the existence of the traditional Sydney–Melbourne feeling. Whenever he sensed the slightest opposition or even reluctance to give undiluted loyalty to himself or to the Movement he felt that there was no alternative but to face the situation with the full weight of episcopal authority. This, naturally, generated a reaction.

The reaction came to a head early in 1953, when he insisted on the removal of Fr P. J. Ryan, MSC, from the position of Sydney chaplain to the Movement and the appointment of the Rev. H. A. Lalor, SJ, in his place. Although there was no doubt that even by early 1953 Dr Ryan had constituted himself unofficial leader of the opposition to the Bishop, so that his continuation in office would have meant paralysis, his removal led to worse consequences than his retention might have occasioned; his great services to the anti-Communist cause were remembered, as a consequence of which he had a deservedly strong following. The removal of Dr Ryan coalesced with the interstate Sydney–Melbourne factor since Fr Lalor was regarded as a 'Melbourne man'.

The Bishop was considered by many of the clergy to be a Melbourne, a 'Mannix–Santamaria man'. His confrontationist tactics were looked on as typical of the crude Melbourne approach. In short, the Bishop did not have many factors working for him.

The same was true—although to a lesser extent—of Fr Lalor. He was opposed, variously, as an Order man; as a Melbourne man (he was actually a West Australian); as being apocalyptic in his preaching; as stripping the parishes of what then seemed to be an extraordinary amount of money; and of having taken Dr P. J. Ryan's position in, of all places, the Sydney Archdiocesan offices.

At the time, the transformation of the Sydney operation produced substantial immediate gains which quite outweighed its disadvantages. In any case, none of us at the National office had any real understanding of the strength of the Sydney–Melbourne factor, which seemed to us a triviality compared with the magnitude of the issues really at stake.

However, as the events of 1954 were to show, these factors, slowly but persistently building up beneath the external successes of 1953, created the climate in which Bishop Carroll in less than six months was able to end the national cohesion, identity and operation of the Movement, and so to determine the ultimate result of the Labor conflict throughout Australia. Just as the Melbourne opposition inevitably found a voice in meetings of the episcopate, whether official or private, in a frustrated Archbishop Simonds, so the Sydney opposition, based far more on the clergy than it was in Melbourne, found its episcopal head in the new Auxiliary, who was appointed in February 1954.

In this regard Bishop Carroll's appointment had a dual significance. He had direct access to the Cardinal. It would have been remarkable if the Cardinal's well-known difficulties with the Movement—its lay control, its capacity to win generous financial support from Catholics by its own efforts, and the location of its national headquarters in Melbourne—were not magnified as a result. As Bishop Carroll had close personal contact with Dr Simonds, and through him with the Melbourne opposition, the Movement was certain to face a serious challenge.

The June 1954 State ALP Conference in New South Wales— which took place some four months before Dr Evatt's attack—was rendered notable by the refusal of both Dougherty and Oliver, Federal and State Secretaries respectively of the AWU, to re-nominate for the State Executive. In retrospect, this was important, although it did not seem remarkable at the time. Whether or not it was true, Dougherty's refusal to nominate was put down to the fact that he, having until then worked closely with the Industrial Groups, felt that his chances of winning endorsement for the Lord Mayoralty of Sydney had been eliminated by an amendment to the rules, and had decided to revenge himself.

J. T. Kane, Assistant Secretary of the New South Wales Branch of the ALP, and the strongest of the Industrial Group leaders, went on holidays to Brisbane during August 1954. While in Brisbane he called on Bukowski, the Queensland State Secretary of the AWU, who was also a member of the Industrial Groups Committee and in frequent contact with the Movement office in Brisbane. Bukowski told Kane of a visit Dougherty had made to Cardinal Gilroy. Bukowski gave Kane what purported to be an account of the discussions. Bukowski claimed that it was as a result of Dougherty's representations to the Cardinal that Dr Lyons had been dismissed from his position as the Cardinal's representative with the Movement. Dougherty had claimed to Bukowski that henceforth 'things would be all right'. Kane did not believe that the Cardinal would discuss such a matter with Dougherty, even if he had given him an interview. So while still in Brisbane, he raised the question with an old and strong Movement and Industrial Group associate, a Labor member of the Queensland Parliament, M. Brosnan, who was a former State Secretary of the Electrical Trades Union and a member of the ALP Industrial Groups Committee. He asked Brosnan, who had been given the same story by Bukowski, whether Brosnan thought that Bukowski believed what he was saying. Brosnan replied that, extraordinary though it seemed to him as a Catholic that the Cardinal would discuss such a matter with Dougherty, he had no doubt that Bukowski did believe it.[2]

None of these developments was known to us in the national office at the time. At a most critical moment, I proceeded to develop ideas as to the way in which to meet the Evatt attack, fortified by a double misunderstanding. If I acted in close liaison with Dr Mannix and Bishop O'Collins of Ballarat, the support of the Cardinal could be assumed for matters on which they jointly agreed. As far as Sydney itself was concerned, Dr Lyons could still be relied on as the final link with the Cardinal, rather than the new Auxiliary Bishop.

What was to happen between 1955 and 1960—in the course of the struggle between the Movement and a section of the Hierarchy, headed formally by Cardinal Gilroy but in reality by his Auxiliary, Bishop Carroll—centred on the issue of the real control of the Movement: whether the lay officials of the organization were in final control of the political and industrial policies of the Movement, with the Bishops maintaining a cautionary supervision in the field of morality of policies and action, or whether final directive control rested with the Bishops.

At every point, the Movement fought for the principle of lay control of what was essentially a voluntary lay organization merely linked with and supported by the Bishops. Bishop Carroll, in the name of the Cardinal and originally supported by only a small group of Bishops in New South Wales, fought to impose the directive control of the Bishops over policy and action, on the basis that the organization was fundamentally ecclesiastical.

Every effort to meet the reasonable objections of the critics, which a successful organization inevitably attracts, had failed by the time Bishop Carroll was allotted his responsibility towards the Movement in Sydney by the Cardinal at the beginning of 1954. Perhaps with more time and more concentration on the problem, the effort might have succeeded. The failure was due, not least, to the fact that throughout 1953 by far the greater part of the attention of Movement officials, particularly in Sydney and Melbourne, had to be devoted to consolidating the gains made in the trade union movement in the two previous years. It was necessary to seek, attract and train suitable persons for the large number of committee positions which had to be filled as the Communists and their associates were displaced from office. Throughout 1953 the developing struggle within the Church was to the Movement officials only a side-issue, their main concerns being with policy and action. To its opponents, however, the struggle was apparently almost a full-time occupation.

170   Throughout 1954 and the early months of 1955, it was extremely difficult for me to achieve a working relationship with the new Auxiliary Bishop, who rapidly assumed administrative control of the entire Sydney organization of the Movement: difficult because there was no basis of past acquaintance on which to work, and because I knew nothing of the policy he intended to pursue.

Sixteen years later the reason was made explicit, as it was not explicit during the years when it really mattered. In 1970 Robert Murray interviewed Bishop Carroll personally, and summed up the Bishop's views, as they were in 1954, in these words:

> He set out to study The Movement—and became convinced that, in its existing form, it had to go from the Diocese. He became an influential proponent of a growing view that it should be placed under firmer episcopal control and emasculated to an innocuous body for the social training of Catholics.[3]

To be fair to Bishop Carroll, he doubtless felt that the traditional alliance between the Catholic Church and the Labor Party was the best arrangement open to the Church; that it was only through the Labor Party that Catholics could enter political life; that the best way of containing Communist influence was simply through the existence of a mass Labor Party, whose leaders could be trusted to defend their Party against Communist influence; that the Movement's organizational efforts were, in the last analysis, unnecessary; and that because of the Movement's activities, the *de facto* alliance between the Church and the Labor Party could easily be broken. While I disagreed fundamentally with this viewpoint, it was at least tenable.

If the Bishop's intention to 'emasculate' the Movement into 'an innocuous body for the social training of Catholics' had been conveyed to the Movement in 1954, the events which followed would have been different. His design would certainly have been opposed, but in the last analysis, if both the Cardinal and the Bishop were determined to exclude the Movement from Sydney, there was little in practice that the rest of the Movement could do about it. The real situation would have been known not merely to Mr. Ormonde, Mr Calwell and ultimately Dr Evatt—the enemies of the Movement. It would also have been known to the other Bishops and to Movement officials who, after all, had sacrificed their careers on the strength of the promise of a united hierarchy.

The rest of the Movement would have been able to formulate a realistic plan based on facts as they were, rather than as they were believed to be, to meet the Evatt attack in October. The otherwise inexplicable defections—of R. F. Cosgrove, Premier of Tasmania, in 1954; of Anderson, New South Wales State Secretary of the ALP in the same year—could have been understood and even anticipated. Sixty parliamentarians would not have been put in the position in which their only alternative was to sacrifice either their principles or their parliamentary seats, and, to their credit, if not to their human advantage, choosing the latter. As far as the formulation of a political strategy to confront Dr Evatt was concerned, there was only one choice—either to counter-attack, or to retreat in good order to fight another day. The former was the correct policy to follow if the Movement was united throughout Australia; the latter, if its Sydney Branch was acting separately and could not be relied on. On this most critical matter of all, our initial 'intelligence' was not only defective but wrong.

In the light of after-events, the policy pursued by the Sydney Branch of the Movement from the time of the mid-year National Executive meeting (July 1954)—three months before the Evatt attack—ought to have spoken for itself. At this meeting, the Sydney representatives briefly announced that the Sydney region no longer intended to regard itself as bound by national decisions on political (as distinct from industrial) matters. If we had been disposed to accept this challenge at its face value, this should have been regarded as an outright defiance of the Movement constitution. The Sydney region should—if it persisted in its new position—have been removed from the organization.

Even if we had had full knowledge of the new Sydney situation the arguments against such a course of action were overwhelming. The new Sydney position—if ultimately persisted in—could not have been taken without the support of the Cardinal. In practice there was no basis for reconstituting an expelled branch, especially if it was that of a major region like Sydney, and that branch had the concurrence, if not more, of the Cardinal. The only practical response was to refrain from consummating the division and to hope that time and persuasion would somehow restore a fractured unity.

The dealings which now began between Bishop Carroll and myself were, as can be seen in retrospect, dealings between two people with diametrically opposite purposes.

In re-examining the correspondence which passed between us from early 1954 to the end of 1956, one can only pay tribute to the Bishop's tactics. He was no mean antagonist.

His general position was that we should all co-operate in a joint endeavour to reconsider the nature of the organization in its entirety. He offered the prospect of 'well-founded hopes of prudent as well as fruitful development of the organisation, provided that bishops and priests are kept informed and that close liaison is maintained between them and representatives of the organization'.[4] He would work closely with Archbishop Simonds to end the latter's general reservations concerning the Movement. The main burden of his approach was that a new relationship should be struck between the Movement and the Bishops. The discussions were, as it turned out, preliminary skirmishes concerned with what appeared to be constitutional abstractions. If significant constitutional alterations were to be made to an organization with a history of ten years under a single constitution, the process would be long, and would require mature deliberation.

Everything changed, however, when Evatt launched his attack on 5 October. From that moment onwards, the constitutional reforms hinted at by the Bishop were no longer matters of the future. Exactly how the Movement's authority was to be exercised; what role bishops would claim; these became matters of the most urgent practical importance, with potentially disastrous effects on the lives and careers of dozens of parliamentarians and other men in public life.

# 19 The Movement Unwinds

On the morning after Evatt's attack, I phoned each of the Movement's State Presidents and tried to explain Evatt's strategy, as I assessed it. From the form of words chosen by Evatt, against the background of the developments of the last six months within the Federal Labor administration, I suggested that he had three tactical objectives in view, in what was clearly to be a terminal struggle. He would seek:

1 To isolate the Victorian Branch of the ALP within the Party, before turning his attention to other States, particularly New South Wales. In the meantime, he would make it appear that if the New South Wales and Queensland Executives refrained from helping the Victorians, they could save themselves;

2 To isolate Catholics within the general Australian community by using the weapon of sectarianism; and

3 To isolate the Movement within the Church by spreading the rumour (as *I* thought it to be, though *he* knew the truth of the matter) that there were Bishops who did not support the Movement.

I had no doubt that we were in for an assault comparable with that which accompanied the conscription campaign in 1916-17.

My submission concluded with two broad alternatives. The policy which the Industrial Group leadership would ultimately follow was not the Movement's to direct. The Movement could, however, influence the decision by knowing its own mind. That is to say, if Movement members at every critical level in the unions and the Labor Movement in general were united in following a rational policy, that policy would be the foundation of a consensus which could be created with the other Industrial Group leaders. That consensus would certainly win the support of other non-Communist leaders who belonged to neither section, since the latter had been accustomed to following the policies of the Industrial Group leaders.

174 | That force would constitute a majority up to the level of the Federal Conference of the ALP.

In this sense, the position taken by the Movement would be critical.

The Movement might, on the one hand, capitulate to Evatt's demands, which were certain to include the elimination of the Industrial Groups, the dismissal of the Victorian Executive of the ALP, and ultimately the dismissal of its opposite number in New South Wales (since Ormonde, Dougherty and others were concerned primarily with what went on in that State). On the other hand, the Movement could decide to resist. Resistance would take the form of persuading the three major State Executives—New South Wales, Victoria and Queensland—to defy Evatt, leaving him, at the most, with the South Australian Executive, which was under the influence of Clyde Cameron, and with split party branches in West Australia and Tasmania. If this situation could be reached, Evatt could not win, and he himself would be removed from the leadership of the ALP by his fellow-parliamentarians.

I asked all State Presidents to consult their respective State Executives in emergency meetings during the day.

What we were attempting to decide was simply our own policy as a Movement. The decisions of the several ALP State Executives would naturally be made by their own members. The Movement's own prior decision would, however, be influential not only with its own relatively few members, but also with the larger number of sympathizers and associates on those bodies.

By the afternoon of 7 October I had answers from all States, all agreeing with a policy of resistance, whatever tactical form such a policy might take from day to day. This unanimous vote included New South Wales.

I had already sent a written analysis to Dr Mannix, and saw him myself at Raheen that evening. I had consulted the Bishop of Ballarat during the day. His attitude was that he would endorse any view which might be acceptable to Dr Mannix. In a discussion which lasted three hours, every aspect of the political dispute, including my anxieties concerning the role of the Catholic opposition which now had some kind of episcopal leadership, was considered.

At the end of the time there was only one important question—what was to be done?

The discussion was not only important in itself. It also illuminates the Archbishop's real views as to where—as between Bishops and laity—the control of an essentially political operation should lie.

I put it to the Archbishop that I understood that the Movement leaders had to take their own decision. But if their decision was in favour of resistance, it could be predicted there would be a major sectarian campaign which would bring down great hostility on the whole of the Church, in centres far removed from any political interest. Once the sectarian passion was set alight, even Catholics who had never been involved in the struggle against the Communists would find their professional positions and even their social acceptability brought into jeopardy. Since the whole of the Church—and not merely the Movement—was likely to be involved, I went to the point of insistence that the Archbishop should advise us, and that regardless of our own views, we would adopt his advice as our decision.

I was *not* taking the position of the Sydney ecclesiastical authorities—that the Archbishop, by virtue of his office, should make a political decision for a lay movement. I was expressing my faith in the wider political judgement of a man named Daniel Mannix, regardless of his position as archbishop, and was ready to make his political judgement my own. (On an earlier occasion, I had already put my own position in different words: that I was prepared to follow the then Archbishop of Melbourne because he was Daniel Mannix, although I was not necessarily prepared to follow Daniel Mannix because he was Archbishop of Melbourne. That distinction ceased to be purely theoretical when Daniel Mannix died, and was succeeded by his coadjutor.)

Dr Mannix flatly refused to declare his preference between the two policies to meet the Evatt attack. I argued with him, sometimes heatedly. I stressed the point that I was perfectly prepared to make up my own mind on an issue which had consequences only for the Movement, its members and its associates. But it was not up to me or them to make decisions which would have profound, and extremely serious, consequences for the Church.

'Nevertheless', he said, 'it is your decision, keeping all of those consequences in mind'. At the end of three hours it was clear that he would not budge. 'Well', I said, 'it is the unanimous view of my colleagues and myself that we should resist with all the force at our disposal'. To which he answered: 'Never forget that it is you [by which he meant all of us, rather than myself personally], who have made the decision. But now that it is made, I will tell you that it is precisely the advice I would have given you myself'.

By the night of 7 October—only forty-eight hours after an attack of which we had no prior notice—I felt that we had established a position with commendable speed, thus leaving those who depended on our support in no doubt that that support would be forthcoming for a policy of resistance. Nor was it a decision made without consideration. Every State Executive of the Movement had been consulted. The two members of the Bishops' Committee whom I could consult personally in an emergency had been consulted.

On the morning of 8 October, all State offices were informed that the policy to which they had given unanimous assent would be carried out.

A week later—on 15 October—an urgent phone call came from the Sydney office to say that Bishop Carroll wanted to see the Federal Secretary of the Movement (Norm Lauritz) and myself in Sydney three days later, on 18 October, to meet the leaders of the Sydney Movement and 'consult about the situation'. When we arrived at the meeting, we discovered that the Sydney leaders did not include Anderson (who had walked out of both Movement membership and his position as State Secretary of the ALP), Colbourne, Kane, Rooney or Kenny, the Assistant Secretary of the New South Wales Labour Council. Instead, the meeting was chaired by a Mr A. Roddy (the Bishop's nominee) who had never played any major part in Movement affairs. Davis, the New South Wales State President, for some mysterious reason was not in the chair. Later we were told that he was no longer State President, but merely in charge of 'public relations', and that from the moment of the imposition of Bishop Carroll's authority he had been informed that the Bishop would be the only contact with the Cardinal. The remainder of those in attendance were a number of Movement officials and local organizers.

It was apparent that those Movement members who were in the position to influence events, and who were in greatest need of a clear policy decision to which they themselves would have contributed, were simply excluded. They were precisely the people with whom my personal connections were closest and who were most likely to be influenced by the arguments—counselling active resistance—which I would present to them.

Instead, the decision at the meeting was left—nominally—to a handful of Movement officials and voluntary organizers, none of whom had much outside political experience, and few, if any, had any actual responsibilities in the field. In the meantime, it was made clear that if I communicated directly with the really significant personalities, and not through the Sydney office, it would be against the wishes of the Cardinal, on whose attitude the future of the Movement in New South Wales might well depend.

The policy decided on for New South Wales, despite the protests of Lauritz and myself, was to urge general caution, in the anticipation, as Bishop Carroll was later to suggest on 27 October, that the Evatt attack would 'burn itself out if no fuel is added to the flames on our side'.[1]

Along with the cutting of the links between the national officers and their associates on the New South Wales ALP and Trades and Labour Council Executive, who would have to carry on the fight when the New South Wales State Executive came under attack, as inevitably it would, *News Weekly* was systematically cut off from its New South Wales readership. This was achieved by the simple expedient of stating that the Sydney office was too short of staff to handle the distribution of *News Weekly* any longer. The attempt to establish a separate office for the paper, originally agreed to by the Bishop's representatives, was vetoed by the Cardinal himself.

Thereafter the general policy orientations to which its readers in New South Wales had become accustomed over the years were simply removed from their notice. Since the re-staffed Sydney office was now sending out its own policy directions to local branches, directions which were contrary to national policy, the rapid elimination of the sale of *News Weekly* meant that its New South Wales readers did not realize that the policy being fed to them through official channels was the opposite of the national policy. Yet it was portrayed as the national policy! In the general confusion, it became increasingly difficult for New South Wales members to reconcile the policy they were called on to pursue in New South Wales with what the press reported concerning Victorian developments.

For lack of servicing, the circulation of the paper rapidly declined in New South Wales while it increased equally rapidly in other States. (In fact, Dr Evatt had proved the best salesman *News Weekly* ever had, the national circulation rising by nearly 12,000 in the first few months after his attack, despite the rapid decline in New South Wales.) Bishop Carroll attributed the decline in circulation in New South Wales to the acid tone of political comment in the paper's columns[2], a tone which appeared to assist its circulation in other States.

The problem of opening a *News Weekly* office for Sydney dragged on throughout 1955, while the Movement, the Industrial Groups and the Victorian Executive were engaged in a life-and-death struggle for existence, and the first assaults had been made on the New South Wales Executive.

The *News Weekly* affair well illustrated how far relationships with the Sydney Bishops had deteriorated. While intensive negotiations as to the future of the Movement as a national body continued at the episcopal level until the end of April 1956, I realized at last, but far too late, that the Bishop was not really concerned with what he claimed to have in view—some general reform of the Movement. What he was aiming at was its elimination as an effective operational national organization.

In any case, it is difficult to see what could have been achieved even if I had realized it earlier. The views of the Bishop and the Cardinal being what they were, they would inevitably have had their way in Sydney and the greater part of New South Wales.

These developments resulted in the Bishop writing to me on 28 November, stating that while I should 'accept the situation that two diverse solutions are in process of being applied . . . [there was nevertheless] large scope for harmonious co-operation between

178 | those responsible for the diverse policies'. The letter 'begged' me to 'use [my] influence for unity and against division in our ranks'. 'Let nothing be done', concluded the Bishop, 'to set Catholic against Catholic'.[3]

My own reply, dated 7 December 1955, in effect represented a final breach. I believed that there was little to be done except to re-assert my position with whatever firmness and dignity could be preserved, even if it were unavailing. So, *inter alia*, I wrote:

... I did not consider that I needed to be reminded in the peremptory language used by Your Lordship in the first paragraph of the letter that I should carry out directions with 'obedience and respect' regardless of my 'own views or wishes'. I have served the Hierarchy of Australia for almost twenty years in a field of work, which, in the judgment of friends and enemies alike, has been of not inconsiderable importance. Throughout this period there is no Bishop to whom I owed a duty of obedience who can claim that I failed him in that regard. I have a clear concept of my responsibilities in the matter of obedience and when I feel that I am unable to live up to that concept, I will surrender my charge, before it is necessary for a Bishop to remind me of my obligations ...

I regret that Your Lordship should have seen fit to ask me to 'use my influence for unity and against division in our ranks'. I cannot but support Your Lordship's sentiment that 'to present united strength in the name of the Church is the first principle of action and perhaps history will judge us of this generation according to our achievement in this sphere'. They are the very echo of the words which I used myself at the fateful meeting of the National Executive in July 1954, when the national unity which we had built up by consistent and unremitting effort over ten years was suddenly broken by the statement that one diocese would no longer be bound by decisions arrived at by the National Executive, if it disagreed with those decisions.

For eighteen months we have been through disaster after disaster, a long and seemingly unending agony, as a result of that decision. In all of this time I have opposed the attitude taken to the organization by the Sydney Region because I believed that these unilateral actions were in fact destroying national unity, even though they were accompanied by appeals for national unity. How can there be any national unity in the plain meaning of the word when even one Region says: 'We will not carry out policies with which we disagree, even if they are voted by overwhelming majorities'? I have always worked for national unity. But it is not in my power to achieve it. It can only be achieved if and when those who broke it and who continue to break it decide to change their attitude. When they decide to concede unity they will find that I, for one, have not changed.

... Finally, I cannot understand what Your Lordship means when you say: 'Let nothing be done to set Catholic against Catholic.' I feel that those words would be better addressed to those Catholics who have publicly repudiated the policies of the Bishops rather than to those who, with all their many faults and failings, have tried to build up the loyalty of Catholics to the collective judgement of the Bishops. The very words of the Joint Pastoral* with their trenchant criticism of certain Catholic public men, the subsequent statements of a number of Bishops in the same vein, surely can only mean that the Bishops wish Catholics to oppose the policies of those public men, even though those men happen to be Catholic ...

I have never understood that the personal charity which we all owe to our opponents extends to toleration of the evil which, perhaps unknowingly, they do. 'The bond of peace' of which St Paul spoke in Your Lordship's quotation, surely can only be established on the foundation of truth and justice.

---

* See pp. 190-1.

Your Lordship will realise that this has not been an easy letter to write. I have kept clearly in mind the respect I owe to your high office and in addition the personal sadness I feel in opposing, however respectfully, the views of a Bishop for whom I have a high personal esteem. The easy thing would be to say and write nothing. Yet I have a duty and a responsibility to all the Bishops and I would feel that I had shirked my responsibility if I simply looked to my personal comfort and did not deal candidly with these issues, so vital for the Church and for Australia, in the way in which I see them . . .[4]

The Bishop's reply was simply to indicate that my 'narration of facts and events does not present a complete picture' which, in a sense, was true since there were many 'facts and events' which only the Bishop himself knew.

The Bishop's strategy had thus proceeded at several levels. There was one set of dealings with my old associates in the Sydney office, who were likely to favour the continuation of the national connection. There was another set of dealings with myself and the national office. Here the purpose of the discussions was always about re-structuring in the interests of greater unity and therefore efficiency.

There were two sets of dealings with the Bishops. One was with Archbishop Simonds, and most but not all of the New South Wales Bishops, the purport of which remains unknown but may be guessed. With the second group—the Bishops who supported the original concept of a national organization controlled by its own lay leaders, who at that stage were still the vast majority—the line was the same as that with the national office: that re-structuring would bring about unity and efficiency and would certainly be accomplished amicably.

There was a line of communication with one set of politicians, located in New South Wales, who were in touch with both Evatt and Calwell. Ormonde had felt himself able to assure Evatt with the greatest confidence that a number of Bishops would not back the Movement if Evatt went ahead and attacked.

Finally there was another line of communication with politicians who were Movement supporters—like Colbourne, Kane, Rooney— all of whom, with the exception of Colbourne, were mounting continual pressure in favour of resistance to the attacks of the Federal Executive on Victoria which, as practical men, they knew would be followed by attacks on New South Wales. These were continually 'fobbed off' with arguments about the requirements of canon law in relation to lay movements, accompanied by constant injunctions that the supreme interests of the Church demanded 'prudence' at all costs. The supreme criterion of 'prudence' was obedience to the wishes of the Cardinal, as communicated by the Bishop himself!

By the end of 1955 it had become clear to the Bishop (and through him, presumably to the Cardinal) that although he had made con-

180 siderable ground with a group of Bishops in New South Wales and, later, in South Australia, he was as far as ever from a majority. At this point the conflicting arguments about the nature of the Movement and its position in canon law began to assume increasing importance. This is not to say that the legal arguments were the real, as distinct from the formal, factor. As is not unknown even in the behaviour of some members of the judiciary, the decision is made for practical reasons, and the law is found to suit.

# 20 The Principles at Stake

The argument advanced by the opposing sides depended fundamentally on whether the Movement was in fact a lay organization, ultimately controlled by lay people but acting with the support of Bishops, or whether it was a Bishops' organization in which the laity ultimately did what they were told. The repective arguments were not abstract essays in a purely legalistic constitutional conflict. They had the most practical consequences. To meet Evatt's attack on the entire anti-Communist position within the Labour Movement, the former principle alone offered the prospect of a concerted national resistance. The second simply offered division, the *reductio ad absurdum* of the Cardinal's position being simply that there could be as many strategies as there were Bishops.

The documents on both sides lack the legal precision which such as issue deserves.[1] From the viewpoint of the national office there were two good reasons for this. In all of this period it, too, was concerned with a practical result. That was to maintain the widest degree of agreement possible among the Bishops until the Evatt onslaught had run its course. Throughout the whole of this period its main effort had to be devoted to conducting the political struggle to give the requisite backing to the Industrial Group leaders, both until and after the Hobart Conference. This involved maintaining whatever unity of action could be maintained between the Industrial Group leadership in Victoria and their colleagues in other States. The latter, after the expulsion from the Labor Party of the Victorians, could not afford to be publicly too closely associated with their erstwhile colleagues. As a consequence, they depended largely on the Movement to keep open the channels of communication. The supreme necessity was, of course, to hold the support of the Movement's Catholic members and supporters—episcopal, lay and clerical—throughout Australia, during a conflict with leaders of a party to which their sympathies had traditionally gone.

Hence in a number of letters, memoranda and reports, there are offers of concessions by the national authorities of the Movement on the critical issue of episcopal authority which, in terms of strict principle, and in the light of later events, should never have been made. They were made in the endeavour to hold whatever unity of policy could be held on the practical issues raised daily by the threatened political destruction of the Industrial Group leadership in the three major States.

Face-to-face with these necessities the task of the Cardinal and of those who spoke in his name was relatively easy. They had merely to ensure that the national organization was paralysed, so that they could pursue their own policy in New South Wales. To achieve this, they simply needed to cut the links which had previously bound the members of the Sydney branch of the Movement with those to whom they had generally given loyal support in the past; at all costs to stop any communication of ideas as well as policy proposals; and to float the notion that the basic principles of canon law demanded that they follow the lead of the Cardinal rather than that of laymen in another State.

Hence the canonical arguments, while never central to the determination of the real issue, came to absorb more and more time. When they were completely formulated, they guaranteed a fundamental conflict.

The National Movement, which until 1957 was supported by the great majority of Bishops, held that the Movement was a lay organization, supported by the Bishops, with priests acting as chaplains (much as they did in the Army) to ensure the moral formation of those engaged in industrial and political activity. The practical decisions, particularly those in political, industrial, financial, organizational and administrative matters, were the business of the laity.

When the Bishops had given their support in 1945, they had not altered the fundamental character of an organization which had already existed for four years. A committee of Bishops had been appointed to establish an official link between the Bishops and the organization so that the Bishops would have direct knowledge of what was being done with their support. (In fact it was I myself who had brought the greatest pressure to bear to secure the presence of the Bishop of Ballarat at our meetings, so that the Bishops would not be fed by rumour but would have their own direct source of knowledge.) The Bishops had nothing more than a precautionary supervision to ensure that nothing proposed or carried into action contravened the moral principles of the Church. A Bishop could certainly refuse to assist the organization: but once he accepted it, he accepted it as it was, constitutional structure and all.

In this way, it had been possible for the Movement to maintain the decision-taking structure which was fundamental to its effectiveness. Majority votes of a National Conference or a National Executive, representing the organization in every part of Australia, were binding on the organization in every part of Australia. It was because of this basic principle that, say, New South Wales members could afford to take the necessary risks involved in union activities within their own State in confidence that they would not be let down by their colleagues in Victoria and Queensland. It was a principle which ran athwart the federalist principle which was so strong in Australian organizations of many types; but it was indispensable, particularly in the field of unionism, in which the Communists had shown that they were quite prepared to press the authority of Federal bodies to take over State branches in defence of their Party's position, thus rendering useless all the efforts which might have been exerted to defeat the Party's candidates in a State branch.

This principle was never breached until the meeting of the National Executive of July 1954, when the Sydney Region broke new ground by stating that it would be no longer bound by national decisions insofar as they affected political matters. It would in future make its own decisions.

To justify this radical change of position, the Cardinal, and those who spoke for him, claimed that the Movement was in fact an episcopally controlled organization, not merely in the sense that the Bishops would guard the moral and doctrinal orthodoxy of decisions that the organization might take, but in the sense that the Bishops would themselves assume responsibility for the most important practical decisions even in political and industrial matters. If this were the exact position of the organization, he claimed, then under canon law it followed that each bishop would be finally responsible for the decisions taken in the organization within his own diocese, for in all ecclesiastical matters a bishop was finally the supreme authority in his own diocese.

The argument for this position was that the organization had come into being in response to the call of the Bishops; it was therefore an 'ecclesial' rather than a lay organization. In purely historical terms, therefore, the Bishops were entitled to govern what was essentially their property. Furthermore, a Catholic organization dealing with such highly sensitive subject-matter could—indeed would—affect the welfare and reputation of the Church. It was therefore critical that the Bishops should govern it.

The first—historical—argument was not accurate since there was no doubt whatsoever that the organization was established in 1941 by a few of my own colleagues and myself.

The second argument—that the policies of a Catholic organization which operated in the most sensitive areas of community life could seriously affect the standing, reputation and well-being of the

184

*Above:*   A. A. Calwell

*Left:*   Cardinal Gilroy

Church—was put most strongly in the letter sent by Cardinal Gilroy to all members of the Australian Hierarchy on 2 August 1956. In the course of a long letter reviewing every aspect of the situation from the viewpoint of the Sydney authorities, the Cardinal wrote:

As to the right of Catholic laymen to act in the manner indicated, while it is true that any Catholic citizen is entitled to engage in political activity in his role of citizen, without reference to ecclesiastical authority, the men in question cannot be considered independently of the Church, in the light of their activities on behalf of the Church up to date, their well known association with it, and their frequently repeated claim of support from the Hierarchy. Moreover, as they propose to carry the Catholic name, surely their decisions and activities would commit the Church and its Hierarchy, even though in point of fact, they would have no right to speak on behalf of the Church, or of the Catholic people generally. To suggest that in Australia with its strong background of Catholic and Protestant, the activities of a body of Catholics bearing the name Catholic, acting presumably with some encouragement from Bishops, would not involve the Church, is surely unrealistic. But insofar as the interests and reputation of the Church would be involved, how could Bishops shed their responsibilities, leaving matters in the hands of laymen? The proposal seems calculated to make a Bishop's position equivocal. The very nature of the Episcopal Office requires that Bishops exercise their authority with all due providence, even in matters touching the temporal order.

In the same letter, the Cardinal indicated that his position was no mere abstract assertion of episcopal authority without immediate practical political content.

The so-called Episcopal Veto to which they [i.e. the National office] raise objection has never been invoked except in reference to one issue, namely the organization's political action . . . A particular instance was a course of action which it was decided the Movement would pursue in A.L.P. affairs in Queensland, New South Wales and Victoria in March 1955. This decision made by the National Governing Body of the Movement, was rejected by the representatives of Sydney at the meeting of the Governing Body. Further it was condemned as imprudent and damaging to the Church, and at the same time harmful to the cause of combatting Communism, not only by ecclesiastical authorities, but by leading lay officers of the organization in New South Wales, and by the overwhelming weight of mature Catholic opinion within the State of New South Wales. Thus, the question of the Bishops overruling some decisions of the governing body of the Movement has resolved itself in practice into the question of the mode and extent of political activity.[2]

The Cardinal's assertion—that the national policy was rejected 'by the overwhelming weight of mature Catholic opinion within the State of New South Wales'—was no doubt believed by the Cardinal on the basis of information supplied to him. Factually, it was mistaken. At the only decisive moment—in the first months of 1955—the policy of resistance, rather than submission to the Federal Executive, was supported for different reasons by all Movement men on the New South Wales State Executive of the ALP (including, at that stage, even a wavering Colbourne); by J. Kenny (Assistant Secretary of the New South Wales Labour Council), and even by the Premier, Cahill, whom Kane had persuaded to follow a course which accorded with the policy of resistance.

That factual inaccuracy apart, the letter of 2 August is important as expressing the viewpoint of the Cardinal and of the minority of Bishops who then supported him, as to the prerogatives of Bishops in the control of what was essentially an organization with political and industrial objectives.

The Cardinal would not have propounded this position unless he believed it to be the true one.

At the practical level, however, the principle asserted did in fact also guarantee national paralysis, which was a sufficiently practical outcome to satisfy his advisers. For while the argument would be of purely abstract significance if acted upon by the bishop of a minor diocese, when acted upon by the archbishop of one of the two major State capitals—Melbourne or Sydney—it prevented the formulation of any uniform national policy and interposed a veto on what might have been unanimously decided by all the others.

The argument was first advanced, in fact, by Bishop Carroll himself at the meeting of the National Executive which he had attended in July 1954. On that occasion, it had almost no support at all. It was opposed by all but the Sydney delegates in the room. Of the Sydney delegates, the State President (K. Davis) had previously been forbidden to speak on the matter. Among the Bishops themselves, the Cardinal's view had the support of Bishop Carroll of Sydney, Bishop Toohey of Maitland (who had previously been the Cardinal's secretary), Bishop McCabe of Wollongong, Bishop Farrelly of Lismore, and, probably, Archbishop Eris O'Brien of Canberra–Goulburn.

As we have seen, a national policy was formulated within forty-eight hours of Evatt's attack, after consultations with every State including New South Wales. That policy could not succeed unless resistance in other States was backed up by the strongest resistance on the part of the New South Wales Executive. It was quickly indicated to the Sydney office by the episcopal authorities, however, that this policy must not be pursued in New South Wales.[3]

It was December 1955 before the Bishops collectively were able to express their view as to the propriety of the Sydney instruction. When they did so, they very properly expressed no view on the political strategy adopted by the Movement to meet the Evatt thrust. By an overwhelming majority they merely stated that the organization was a lay body, and that as far as they were concerned those decisions which were validly and constitutionally made by its constitutional bodies bound all regions of the organization. (Naturally it did not bind bishops.) The Sydney decision, they maintained, constituted a unilateral alteration of the basic character of the organization from a national to a greatly weakened quasi-Federal body.

While the Bishops collectively were confronted with a conflict which they had never envisaged, and with making the necessary declarations of canonical principle, Bishop Carroll used the period decisively to alter the structure in New South Wales and, as we have seen, to break the links between the Sydney and the national organization.

A series of meetings—and documents—followed. An effort was made to placate Sydney by attempting to compromise at the purely legal level in order to meet its view on the canon law position, in the hope that if this were done in principle, Sydney might not insist on exercising the prerogative which it claimed in practice. These attempts at compromise led to inconsistencies in the national position. They were foolish concessions, although at the time and for the reason given I not only agreed with them but sponsored some of them: foolish concessions since, as it eventuated, Sydney was adamant on practicalities, not on theories.

# 21 The Plan of Campaign

The Industrial Group leaders and supporting Labor politicians, in most cases, had no knowledge whatsoever of the bitter struggle which was being waged within the Catholic Church, although it did, in fact, profoundly affect their prospects. With the issue unresolved, both the Movement and the Industrial Group forces in the ALP went through the December 1954 decisions of the ALP's Federal Executive which dissolved the Victorian ALP Executive. They were dismayed by the defection of Lovegrove, who finally succumbed to Evatt's repeated persuasions to abandon his allies of many years standing. The Federal Executive sought to replace the Victorian State body by summoning a Special ALP Conference in Victoria, to which the Federal Executive admitted even non-members of the ALP. This was the only way in which Dr Evatt could ensure that the new Victorian State Executive would be to his own specifications. The process concluded with the Hobart Federal Conference, which began on 15 March 1955.

The effect of the paralysis created by Sydney's stategy and tactics on the fighting spirit of important personalities is perhaps best illustrated by their impact on Jim Kenny, Assistant Secretary of the New South Wales Labour Council. During January 1955—before the holding of the Victorian Special Conference, and some two months before the Hobart Conference—Kenny called on me in the national office. He was feeling deeply depressed. He complained bitterly that there had been no effective communication between the national office and himself about our plans. Consequently, even by January, he had concluded that there was no plan and that the fight was all over. The Hobart Conference would simply bury both the Groups and the whole enterprise to which he had been loyal since he joined the Movement. His loyalty was most noteworthy because he had won his position by his own efforts and did not owe it in any way to the Movement.

I told him that this was not my reading of the situation and that, depending on which Victorian delegates were admitted to the Federal Conference, Evatt could be defeated at Hobart. I went through the position of the delegates one by one. His attitude changed. Stating that he could not understand why he had been kept in ignorance of the true situation, he added: 'If we have the numbers, we should use them'.

In his Notes, Kane records:

Another discussion took place with Jim Kenny prior to the holding of the Hobart Conference. Kenny had returned from Melbourne and was firmly convinced, or at least seemed to be, that if the New South Wales delegates stood firm with their friends from other States, the Federal Executive could be forced to observe the Party rules at this Conference. Colbourne, however, put up his usual arguments about not being able to beat the Federal Executive.

Kenny spoke to me later and expressed concern at the attitude of Colbourne (at this time a daily visitor to C.U.S.A. House, i.e. the headquarters office of the Sydney Movement). Kenny said that he [Kenny] had not won his trade union position as a result of Movement support. His association with it came long afterwards. After attending a meeting at Abbotsford* [Melbourne] where he was convinced that the church and the nation were faced with a crisis he was prepared to put his career on the line if necessary. Now it seemed that certain people who had done this very thing were considered expendable and were about to be 'dumped'. He said if this practice prevailed the Movement might finish up with a team, but it would be a very small one, and he wouldn't be in it.[1]

Just as the Hobart Conference was decisive for the future of the conflict within the ALP, so it was decisive for the future of the internal conflict within the Church. The issue within the Church assumed critical proportions.

On his way back to Brisbane, the Queensland Premier, Gair, saw me in Melbourne. He was a man of a different mould from his brother-Premier, Cosgrove, who had scented the wind in mid-1954 and cut his connections. Gair himself was in a serious position, since he could have no illusions as to his own future in Queensland now that Dougherty, Bukowski and the AWU had decided to make common cause with Evatt, and therefore with Gair's own strong left-wing opposition in that State. His judgement, both at Hobart, and afterwards back at home, was that he could not safely do more than his Treasurer, Walsh, was prepared to do, and had to act slowly while events 'educated' Walsh as to what was really afoot.

In this situation, Gair met me specifically to explain that if the New South Wales Executive supported the Victorian Executive, he would be able to bring the Queensland Executive and the Labor parliamentarians in behind both of them. But if New South Wales abandoned Victoria, there was nothing, at the moment, that he could do. Some of the Victorian Industrial Group leaders were disposed to criticize Gair for not acting more strongly on his return to Brisbane. I

---

* See pp. 129-30.

was not, since I had no doubt about either his dispositions or his courage, and felt that he was the best judge of his own immediate situation.

However, his position made it clear that the New South Wales Executive was the key to the situation. If the three Eastern States Executives hung together, the Evatt operation was finished. Without united support even in the three minor States, he would have been compelled to rely on the Communist-led unions and the rump of their supporters. My view still remains that it would have been the end of Evatt and of the attack on the Industrial Group position.

During the month of April 1955, the external position of the Movement (which did not yet reflect the divisions within the Catholic Church), its policy, and its backing, thus appeared surprisingly strong. In the immediate aftermath of the Hobart Conference, but before the Victorian State election, the Hierarchy, despite the serious differences which had already manifested themselves in its own ranks, surprisingly issued a Joint Pastoral, which declared strong support for the Industrial Groups and expressed an equally strong condemnation of those who had destroyed them.

The proclamation of the Pastoral was, in all the circumstances, an unexpected event. Archbishop Mannix, then in his ninety-first year, was not present at the Bishops' meeting. It was understood that one of the main advocates of a strong stand was Dr Guilford Young, Archbishop of Hobart. Before 1955, he had expressed serious reservations concerning the Movement. He believed that the Movement leadership itself had not been sufficiently clear in asserting that a lay organization acting in the political order should be clearly separate from the jurisdiction of the Bishops, except insofar as the latter were concerned with strict matters of faith and morals. He was genuinely interested in establishing the correct legal relationships between the Bishops and the organization. He carried his principles to the point of refusing to vote for the otherwise unanimous resolution of support for the Movement, carried at the general meeting of the Hierarchy at the beginning of 1954. His attitude did not change until the Movement made it clear that while it rightly insisted on controlling its own policy, it would not claim to represent the Church, the Bishops or even other Catholics. From that moment his support for what the Movement was doing in practice was clear and strongly expressed.

In its strict terms, the Joint Pastoral of April 1955 gave some reason for hope that there would be united episcopal support for those who found themselves in an apparently unbroken climate of hostility. Until its publication, almost their only public support came from Archbishop Mannix and one or two other Bishops.

Among other things, the Joint Pastoral said:

At the moment there is one outstanding issue for the Nation and the Church. It is the immediate Communist threat to the security of the people and to the freedom of religion in Australia . . .

It is a well-known fact that during the last ten years Catholics in Australia have endeavoured to form a strong public opinion against Communist activities in our community. This was a noble undertaking, patriotically directed to safeguard our Fatherland, the rights and liberties of our fellow-citizens and the free exercise of religion . . .

We recognize that this courageous campaign saved our civil and religious freedoms at a period when they were in grave peril, and we take this opportunity of paying a warm public tribute of gratitude to all who have engaged in the struggle.

This great work of fighting and stemming Communist aggression wherever it shows itself has our full support and approval. It is therefore most deplorable that the only effective way yet found of defeating Communism in industrial life has been destroyed for the moment by political intrigue . . .

It is very regrettable that highly placed public men, including some Catholics, seem to have closed their eyes to the great issues involved in the present upheaval. They do not appear to realize that they are forwarding the interests of Communism . . .

We are alarmed at the attitude of those who, without finding an adequate substitute, have seen fit to disband a well-proven means of fighting effectively the Communist threat to the nation. If they fail to provide such a substitute they will have failed in their duty to Australia. Mere generalized declarations of hostility to Communism are completely futile in these times.[2]

Of course, the Joint Pastoral was welcome; but I was by no means reassured. The words 'a well-proven means of fighting effectively the Communist threat to the nation' could only be interpreted as meaning 'Industrial Groups' and 'The Movement'. Dr Evatt certainly interpreted it in that way, calling it 'an attempt to justify or excuse the Santamaria faction [which] will arouse widespread criticism from those who rightly regard that faction as having demonstrated its anti-Labor character'.[3] However, the Joint Pastoral mentioned neither the Industrial Groups nor the Movement by name. Since nothing had been done to rescind Sydney's declaration of independence at the July 1954 National Executive meeting, it was fairly obvious that generalized declarations of support might not mean as much as they were popularly thought to mean.

Dr Evatt had naturally attacked the Joint Pastoral since it was published not long before the Victorian State election, in which the Victorian ALP (Anti-Communist), later to become the Democratic Labor Party, was opposing the official Labor team, led by the Premier John Cain.

The political position of the Industrial Groups within New South Wales Labor, somewhat surprisingly, appeared almost as strong as in Victoria. With the defection of Anderson as New South Wales State Secretary of the ALP, Kane had been appointed Acting Secretary. His Hobart Conference delegates were behind him. He told me that even Premier Cahill could be relied upon, although he had played no part in Industrial Group affairs. The Premier was in an extremely difficult position within his own Caucus. His members were waiting for a lead, all equally dependent for their endorsement on the New

South Wales State Executive, but facing the major risk that that body would be turned out of office by the Federal Executive. Those who pledged their allegiance to the existing State body, if it was ultimately defeated, would face political extinction.

The tensions were so great that Colbourne, New South Wales State President of the ALP, and therefore the person who should have kept contact with the Premier, simply went incommunicado. His dilemma was understandable. He had been a main figure in the New South Wales Labor split of the thirties, having been General Secretary of the Federal Labor Party from 1930 to 1936. He had been ultimately thrown to the wolves by those whose side he had taken, and for some months was without a job. To be involved in a second split was asking too much of him.

To Cahill's importunate requests, made immediately on Kane's return from Hobart, to be informed of the New South Wales State Executive's likely policy, Kane replied that he proposed to place a resolution before the State Executive, asserting that within the Federal Labor structure the State branches were fundamentally autonomous bodies; that Federal Executive intervention would be resisted; that the date of the State Conference would be advanced; and that it would elect the next New South Wales Executive, whatever the Federal body might decide. Cahill asked Kane whether he felt that he could obtain an Executive majority for that proposition. Kane said that he would have an overwhelming majority. Cahill's reply was instantaneous. He said that he was prepared to base his own position on that resolution. So much so, that he asked Kane to allow him, as Premier, to 'father' the resolution in his own Caucus, to win a Caucus majority, with Kane then putting the Caucus recommendation to the Executive.

Whatever the arguments about canon law with the Cardinal and the Bishop, and the new staff the latter had appointed to the Sydney Movement office, I felt that the practical position among the men who would have to take the real decisions was quite strong. Despite the attempt to break my links with them I had some kind of communication with them through Kane.

However, Bishop Carroll had a representative in Melbourne on other business, who assured me quite specifically that if I had any hopes that the New South Wales Executive, by passing Kane's (or Cahill's) resolution, would make common cause with Victoria and reject the Hobart Conference resolutions, I was deluding myself. The New South Wales Executive would, in fact, reject the Hobart Conference resolutions, whatever manoeuvres might be initiated by Kane or anyone else.

Understanding that the Bishop could cause considerable damage to Kane's position, I pleaded with the Bishop's representative to leave matters where they stood. Had it not been one of Bishop

Carroll's arguments that Movement officials in the national office were a group of amateurs and that political decisions should be left in the hands of the political professionals? Well, here were the political professionals freely at work. 'It won't happen' was all that he would say as to the prospect that the New South Wales Executive would support the Victorians and thus open the way to Gair to bring in Queensland as well.

His prediction was borne out, but only narrowly. Despite his apparent overwhelming majority, Kane did not succeed. This was largely because of the efforts of Kennelly's *alter ego* in New South Wales, R. R. Downing, Minister for Justice in the Cahill Government. His powers of persuasion were exercised on a group of New South Wales Executive members who had normally supported the Industrial Groups, without any deep attachment to them. Downing's initiative was part of a concerted policy of chipping away at the weakest members of a team, which is always likely to be successful if the strongest are paralysed by indecision. Downing, by persistent efforts, gradually turned Colbourne and Shortell* from being proponents of resistance into proponents of compromise, gradually isolating Executive members like Short who had a clearer understanding of what was at stake.

In the event, the New South Wales Executive, at its meeting of 5 April, voted to accept the Hobart Conference resolutions—by the narrow majority of two. The result could hardly have been closer, but we had lost. The acceptance of the Hobart decisions by the New South Wales Executive was followed by withdrawal of official ALP endorsement from the thirteen union and nine factory Industrial Groups in New South Wales. Yet Labor endorsement had been the key to the great series of union victories in 1951-52.

With the failure of the New South Wales Executive to repudiate Hobart, however slight the majority, it was impossible for Gair to bring the Queensland Executive behind the Victorians as well.

The narrow defeat destroyed the original strategic plan which I had regarded as unanswerable—the united resistance of the three Labor Executives in the eastern States, leaving Dr Evatt with only the three smaller States, and only divided loyalties even in these. I believed—and over the years nothing has altered my conviction—that if the few Movement members on the New South Wales State Executive had been left alone to act in accord with their own convictions, the result of the conflict initiated by Dr Evatt would have been entirely different, as would the subsequent history of the Labour Movement, and of Australia.

The failure of the first plan simply meant that the Victorian Industrial Group leadership had to contest the Victorian State

---

* President of the New South Wales Labour Council and of the New South Wales Branch of the ALP (1955).

194 | election as a breakaway party without any official support from any other ALP State Executive.

The general result of that election, fought under such circumstances, was not unforeseen, although the severity of the defeat was not envisaged. The Australian Labor Party (Anti-Communist), later to become the Democratic Labor Party, lost twelve of its thirteen sitting members, the one exception being Scully in Richmond. While it would have been unrealistic to believe that many of the parliamentarians who had taken their stand with the old Executive could have saved their seats, so bitter was the sectarian atmosphere in which the campaign was conducted, nevertheless the fact that only one seat was saved was demoralizing. The magnitude of the loss added to the difficulty of explaining the main objective of the strategy on which the entire DLP experiment was based. Furthermore, the defeat of all but one of the Victorian candidates naturally played into the hands of Bishop Carroll and his supporters in New South Wales, who used it as an argument against the 'imprudence' of the national strategy.

# 22 The Assault on New South Wales

The Sydney Catholic authorities naturally took advantage of the result of the Victorian election to illustrate the wisdom of the Sydney policy compared with the foolhardiness of that followed in Victoria by the national body. The *Catholic Weekly*, organ of the Sydney Archdiocese, devoted a front page to an analysis of the Victorian elections in its issue of 2 June 1955. It duly paid a tribute to the Victorian parliamentarians who had lost their seats for 'displaying a brand of courage rarely encountered in politics', a brand of courage which, needless to say, it did not recommend for emulation. What the election showed, said the editorial writer, who was clearly representing the official view, was that splinter parties had no hope; that what was faintly praised as courage was in fact bad judgement; that it opened the Labor Party to the penetration of the Left; and that there was no alternative but to repair the error.

One could understand the *Catholic Weekly*, as the vehicle of a purely State policy, taking advantage of the Victorian election to prove the wisdom of Sydney's 'prudent' policy compared with the 'reckless' national policy. It was hardly likely that it would point out that the Victorian Industrial Group leaders had been forced to fight a State election as an isolated breakaway party only because the New South Wales Executive was prevented from taking its stand with the Victorians, as even Cahill, the New South Wales Premier, was originally prepared to do, and as Gair, the Queensland Premier, had promised for his own State, if only New South Wales 'stuck'.

Nor was it likely that the *Catholic Weekly* would explain what underlay the national strategy once the Victorians were compelled to face an election as a breakaway party and on their own: namely that the purpose of the operation begun in Victoria was not to build an alternative Labor or Centre Party, but to wage a guerilla war against the ALP, to deprive it both of seats and of government, until in the end it was driven to seek acceptable terms of re-unification.

196   Those who formulated the original strategy of the DLP had no other object in mind, those among them who wished to establish a party of the Centre being always in a small minority. It may sound callous to say so, but it was understood that winning or retaining parliamentary seats was not strictly necessary to the strategy. Nevertheless, the loss of seats, especially when this was extensive, was always a blow to morale, whether in the first Victorian election, the Federal election later in 1955, the Queensland election consequent on the overthrow of the Gair Government in 1957, or the loss of the Senate seats during the sixties. Seats in Parliament served as a banner to remind both supporters and opponents of the existence of the DLP, a factor for which there was no substitute.

Because it did not affect the essential strategy, the Victorian election was far from decisive as far as the external political struggle was concerned. Thus as a result of several defeats, in 1963 Evatt was brought to make an offer to resign the leadership if the DLP would give its first preferences to the ALP; and again, Senators Kennelly and McKenna felt impelled to enter into discussions to heal the Split as late as 1965.

Where the Victorian State election was decisive, however, was in relation to the inner struggle within the Church. Since effective communication between the national leadership of the Movement and the anti-Communist leadership of the New South Wales branch of the ALP (with the exception of Kane and Rooney) had been cut off, the Movement leadership gradually lost authority with many of its former New South Wales associates. It was even more important, however, that the allegiance of some other Bishops began to waver in the light of what could only appear as a major political defeat, justifying doubts as to the wisdom of the national policy, a defeat accompanied by a degree of sectarian bitterness which had not manifested itself in Australia since the conscription years.

A little earlier the Archbishop of Adelaide (Dr M. Beovich) had taken his stand against the national strategy, and ultimately against the national organization itself. This was a major blow in the political sense, since it meant the loss of another State branch of the Movement, even though two out of the three lay officials stayed with the national body. Moreover, in a personal sense, this loss was quite different from those in New South Wales. Dr Beovich had been an old and close friend, who had obviously trusted me for many years, both officially and personally. He had now become an opponent. It was a loss which I felt greatly.

With the Victorian DLP (as it later came to be called) apparently defeated, the long-anticipated action of the Federal ALP authorities against the New South Wales Executive now began in earnest. However, the defeat of a Labor Government in Victoria did bring about a fundamental change of tactics on the part of the Evatt forces.

The Victorian experience had shown that the ruthless overthrow of a State Executive might lead in New South Wales, as in Victoria, to the establishment of an alternative Labour Party. If this led to a State election in New South Wales, as in Victoria, the New South Wales State Labor Government would inevitably lose office. This consideration induced greater circumspection in the handling of New South Wales affairs by the Federal Executive.

The attitude of the extreme Left in pursuing the Communist Party's strategy of expelling the entire anti-Communist force from the ALP was as ruthless as ever, and it was backed by the sectarians. The moderates, however, who included men like Percy Clarey, MHR, previously President of the ACTU, and Reg Broadby, ACTU Secretary, who had previously been associated with the Groups, but who had joined Evatt for a variety of reasons, now believed that things had gone too far.

Two pressures modified both the situation and the timetable in relation to the projected Federal action against the New South Wales Executive. The first pressure—the possible defeat of another State Labor Government—was felt by Evatt and the Federal Executive. The second—and contrary—pressure was felt by the New South Wales Labor Premier, Cahill. If he persisted with his original display of solidarity with the Industrial Group Executive, he would leave the Federal Executive with no alternative but to act in New South Wales as it had in Victoria, regardless of consequences.

Between the two contradictory pressures, there lay a question. If the Federal Executive did dismiss the State Executive, would a breakaway party on the Victorian model, with a sufficient mass following to jeopardize the existence of a State Labor Government, establish itself in New South Wales?

The immediate result of this conflict of pressures was soon revealed. The division in Movement ranks created by the Sydney policy meant that the New South Wales Premier no longer knew whether Kane and his associates had any final backing. Since he was constantly being informed that the Church had changed sides, it was not surprising that the Premier gradually worked his way over to the side of the Federal Executive. The manoeuvres which went on in New South Wales on the part of both sides lasted from April 1955 until September 1956. A significant and, in the end, decisive, role was played by those who spoke in the name of the Cardinal.

The Federal Executive effectively began its intervention in New South Wales in April. The Federal authorities, driven to be cautious in their approach, agreed that the normal State Conference to be held in August should elect the new New South Wales State Executive. The Federal authorities altered their original demand to lay down special rules for the Conference and agreed merely to supervise its proceedings. Although the resultant State Conference

saw the victory of the Evatt nominee, Campbell, for the position of
State President (defeating the Industrial Group candidate, Dr Lloyd
Ross, by 329 to 295), it also witnessed a substantial victory for the
Industrial Group candidates for the majority of Executive positions.
The reason lay in the difference of policy pursued by the Federal
body in prescribing the rules for the composition of this New South
Wales Special Conference, compared with the rules which it had felt
strong enough to impose in the case of the Victorian Special Conference in February 1955. In the case of the Victorian Conference,
non-members of the ALP were admitted as delegates, clearly
indicating that the Federal authorities were determined to pack the
Conference with as many nominees as necessary to give them a
majority. There was therefore little point in the attendance of those
who supported the Industrial Groups who by their attendance would
validate decisions which must go against them, however strong their
positions in the branches and the unions. In New South Wales, as a
result of the defeat of the Cain Government in Victoria, the 'packing'
procedure was not followed. Hence it was possible for the Industrial
Group supporters to win.

It was obvious that the Federal Executive could not accept the
result of this New South Wales Special Conference as a final settlement. The Industrial Groups would consolidate their position at the
next ordinary State Conference. It would be impossible to act against
Gair in Queensland. Ultimately it was not impossible that the
expelled Victorians somehow would be brought back.

A second Federal intervention in New South Wales accordingly
was brought about. A most remarkable set of charges was formulated
against the newly elected State Executive, which duly led to another
'enquiry' which began on 18 April 1956 and lasted for slightly more
than a fortnight. The State Executive , although elected by a conference summoned by the Federal Executive itself, was dismissed by
the Federal body on 15 June 1956. Soon after Kane and Rooney
were removed from their positions. Personalities as different as
Chamberlain and Oliver, aware of the likely consequences of Kane's
removal, declared that he could retain his position as long as he
would accept the Hobart decisions in the spirit as well as the letter.
Kane saw Bishop Carroll on the night of 22 June. The Bishop,
obviously well informed, told Kane that he should remain in his
position. Kane, however, refused to give the required undertakings.
Expulsions from the New South Wales branch of the ALP duly
followed. The DLP was ultimately initiated in New South Wales.
The difference from the Victorian DLP was that the latter was a mass
party which was joined by the great majority of old ALP branches. In
New South Wales, on the other hand, the DLP, while it had some
immediate voting success in the Burwood by-election, was little
more than a rump which, when matters settled down, could attract

only about 5 per cent of the total vote. Even that 5 per cent was not of the same socio-religious complexion which was to guarantee apparently permanent support for the Victorians.

The steps by which the pro-Industrial Group Executive was finally dismissed provided an all too perfect illustration of the problems which had dogged the Movement from the beginning of the crisis.

The consequences of the 1956 Federal Executive enquiry into New South Wales were extremely serious. Yet the enquiry itself was not without its amusing moments. By way of light relief, it included evidence by J. P. Ormonde that 'in 1926 Santamaria had organized a "Rexist" movement in the University of Melbourne'.[1] Answering the rather stunned questions of the Executive members, Ormonde, evidently unaware that the 'Rexist' Movement was a Belgian organization set up during the Second World War by Leon Degrelle, answered that it was an Italian organization which aimed to set up a monarchy in Australia! Mr Ormonde apparently did not go on to explain whether I—in 1926 aged eleven and still at primary school—intended to install the British or the Italian Royal House. This somewhat fanciful accusation was apparently listened to solemnly.

The more serious aspects of the enquiry revolved around what may be regarded as the official cases for the prosecution and the defence respectively. A. C. Platt (State Secretary of the Transport Workers' Union) and R. J. Williams (Federal Secretary of the Builders Labourers' Union) led the attack. Shortell (now State Vice-President of the ALP) and North (an official of the Textile Workers' Union) defended their own Executive. Neither of the latter was connected with the Movement.

The second Federal intervention in New South Wales revealed the intentions of the Federal Executive beyond argument. They had tried and failed to destroy the State Executive leadership in 1955. Now they were back again to make sure of it. The same popular indignation as had manifested itself in the Victorian ALP in October 1954—when it became clear that the Left aimed at the dismissal of the State Executive—now manifested itself, and to the same degree, in New South Wales. As a kind of preliminary barrage, inspired press stories began to appear that the New South Wales Executive would be dismissed, and that Kane, Rooney and others would be removed from the party. Some said that the removal would be by way of expulsion, others that Kane would be offered a Board appointment of one kind or another. (On Mr Calwell's original suggestion, he was actually offered a position as Chairman of the Board of Fire Commissioners—and, to his credit, refused it.)

To prepare for the anticipated attack, Kane, as Assistant Secretary, sought a legal opinion through Jim (later Senator)

McClelland. The latter obtained opinions from several counsel, including one from Sir Garfield Barwick QC. McClelland's advice was that the Federal Executive had no power to dismiss the elected State Executive, replace it with any other body, abrogate its rules, or interfere with the holding of the forthcoming June Conference.

However, when the renewed Federal enquiry into the New South Wales Executive began, the Sydney Catholic authorities again used the *Catholic Weekly* to give advice to the main characters.[2] The burden of the advice was quite simple. Evatt was responsible for beginning the fight in the Labour Movement. The Communists had certainly profited from it. Nevertheless there was one overriding rule which had to be observed. There must be no repetition of the events of Victoria. There must be no split. Where a split had been averted, as in New South Wales and Western Australia, Labor was still in office. 'Infinite tact' was needed to avoid the ultimate disaster of a split in New South Wales.

It was advice which might have been expected from an official organ of the Labor Party or a trade union journal. It was strange to read it in the official organ of a Catholic archdiocese which had once called on the men now facing political execution to do their duty as Christians in political and industrial life. Since the advice to preserve 'infinite tact' was hardly likely to be heeded by the Evatt forces, whose intentions were transparent, it could only be addressed to those likely to be influenced by the *Catholic Weekly*. 'Infinite tact' thus meant that the Industrial Group forces, and particularly the Movement members, should accept the political destruction of the Executive, the dismissal of Kane, Rooney and others, and complete capitulation.

Thus fortified by the assumption that, in view of the withdrawal of support by the Catholic Bishops, there would be no repetition of Victoria events in New South Wales, and that they could therefore act with impunity, the Federal Executive on 12 June 1956 decided to dismiss the New South Wales Executive and replace it with a body selected by itself and composed to its own satisfaction.

The method of action was for the Federal Executive to meet again in Sydney on 15 June, and to choose a subcommittee of five which would submit a panel of names for the new Executive. Of the five, four—Chamberlain, Toohey, Schmella and Campbell—were committed opponents of the Industrial Groups. The fifth—Colbourne—had made his peace with the Federal authorities for a complex series of reasons. Among them, his bitter memories of the Lang split, already referred to, and pressure from Bishop Carroll and his associates that this was the policy desired by the Cardinal, were predominant. Colbourne was permitted by the Evatt forces to continue as State Secretary of the new ALP, and he was to retain this position for a number of years. His retention was a shrewd move since, as a well-known and respected Movement member, he served to divide and immobilize some of his former colleagues in the Movement. The winning of Colbourne was as significant to the future in New South Wales as the winning of Lovegrove by the Evatt forces had been in Victoria.

Equally shrewd was the far more cautious approach to the reconstruction of the State Executive, compared with that which had been employed in Victoria the previous year. The necessity of avoiding the loss of another State Labor Government which, on the Victorian precedent, would become inevitable if a DLP were established with a mass base in New South Wales was always clearly understood by the Evatt forces. In this sense, it was the sacrifice made by the Victorians which ultimately saved whatever was saved in New South Wales.

The new New South Wales State Executive, carefully chosen by the selection panel, had a clear Evatt majority, but it was restricted to approximately twenty to fifteen. The State Premier Cahill, having understood that as a result of the policies of the Sydney ecclesiastical authorities, Kane and his supporters were isolated, had already adjusted himself to the new realities. The advice he gave the Federal authorities was that, while assuring themselves of an overall majority on the State Executive, and a majority on the three key committees—Credentials, Disputes, Organizing—the Executive should retain a sufficient facade of known right-wing personnel to give the appearance of a broadly based party. From the viewpoint of the Evatt forces, the Victorian lesson had been well and truly learnt.

The decision of the Federal Executive to replace the New South Wales body was made on 12 June and executed three days later. On 20 June a letter was sent to all key Movement organizers in Sydney and in other New South Wales dioceses favourable to the Sydney position. The letter was sent on behalf of the Sydney ecclesiastical authorities:

... In April 1956 the Federal Executive came to Sydney to hear charges against certain officials and against the administration of the State Executive. After a most undemocratic process of investigation no decision was made and the matter was referred to the Federal Conference.
The decision to dismiss the State Executive and appoint a Caretaker Executive had already been made and it was merely a question of implementing the decision through the machinery of the Federal Conference and Federal Executive meeting.

Having thus castigated the Federal investigations as 'a most undemocratic process'; called the action of the Federal Executive 'dictatorial, overriding the rules of the Party, and a decision of the rank and file'; praised the State Executive which 'never failed to defend its right to act as an autonomous body within the State . . .', it then came to the crux of the question of what was to be done.

In this situation in which the decision of the Federal Executive to dismiss the State Executive was inevitable, the members of the latter body showed generosity and

202 | wisdom in accepting the decision in order to preserve unity and to increase the effectiveness of the Party's activities in the interests of the Nation and the State of New South Wales . . .

To guide our members at this juncture, it has been thought necessary to give directions for their assistance.

Various consultations have taken place, even with those in the highest authority (i.e. the Cardinal and the Bishop) and these directions are conveyed to you with confidence.

It has been decided that the objectives of the organisation can be achieved by working within the official political organisations. To remain outside or to attempt to maintain discord at any level of the party organisation will only further the aims of the Communists who have already profited from the split in the Labor Movement in Australia. The Christianisation of the organisations within our society can be more effectively promoted by people with an intimate knowledge of these organisations working within them. Men have made sacrifices and will continue to make them. Men have worked in unfavourable situations and they will do so again awaiting the time when we can exert an influence which will benefit our nation and the Church . . .

Yours sincerely,

P.S. Your attention is directed to the article in the Catholic Weekly of Thursday 21st June 1956, which is an excellent analysis of the present position.[3]

The 'excellent analysis of the present position' duly appeared in the *Catholic Weekly* of 21 June. Its full front-page editorial stated that in the course of the second and decisive Federal intervention in New South Wales 'wisdom rather than vengeance prevailed and peace with honour could be acclaimed'. The evocation of Chamberlain's celebrated 'peace with honour' declaration on his return from Munich was no doubt accidental but not without its wry humour. Eight days after the *Catholic Weekly's* 'peace with honour' editorial, on 29 June, Kane was in effect dismissed by the new Executive, with Rooney following on 27 July. The reason for those dismissals were well summed up by Murray.

Kane and Rooney thus disappeared without the charges against them ever being pressed or specified . . . Rooney had long been regarded as an enthusiast for The Movement, but Kane's character was more complex, though he was close to Santamaria then. For most of his career, he had had the knack of being a thorn in the side of established union leaders—for many years, for basically 'left' rather than 'right' reasons. His real sins may have been that he was competent, less inclined than Colbourne to compromise, and said what he thought. He had shown little inclination in the fight to be 'bought off' with a Government job. But by the winter of 1956 there was a compelling political reason to get him out of the A.L.P. office. The 'pro-Evatt' faction simply had to get their own man into the office to avert the danger of it being used as an organising point for a Grouper return to power in 1957. For the same reason, they needed a sympathetic country organiser.[4]

That the attitude of the Sydney ecclesiastical authorities had been decisive in the total overthrow of the Industrial Group position in the New South Wales Branch of the ALP was, of course, perfectly obvious to all the key people in the Sydney branch of the Movement. No one should underestimate the intensity of the spiritual conflict experienced by those who were enjoined simply to stand by as all of the gains of recent years were—quite avoidably—destroyed one by one, while the paralysis against which their spirits rebelled was backed by enormous pressure to 'be loyal to the Cardinal' and the Church.

Their bitterness was all the greater as they began to witness the consequences of the political débacle in the union field. In April the Communists won back the Political Committee of the Amalgamated Engineering Union—a union even more important than the Iron-workers in the metal industry. This was followed by the decision of the Communists and their allies on the Australian Council of the Australian Railways Union to take over the New South Wales branch of that union, thus striking directly at the position of its New South Wales State Secretary, Dr Lloyd Ross, whose intellectual consistency in dealing with the purely ideological aspects of the Split had been flawless.

Since Sydney Movement members were not people without spirit, there was intense indignation in their ranks at the results of the 'wise policy of moderation'. It was likely, therefore, that the same mass defection from the ranks of the ALP which had occurred in Victoria, leading to the formation of a DLP with a mass base, would be repeated in New South Wales. It is impossible to understand why the Victorian development was not repeated in New South Wales without some appreciation of the internal factor.

When the Federal Executive began its second assault on the New South Wales Executive, the first reaction of the New South Wales body was one of overwhelming opposition. On 11 May the State Executive—by twenty-six votes to five—had carried the following resolution:

That the Executive of the N.S.W. Branch of the A.L.P. accepts the authority of the Federal Conference to determine Federal policy, and the authority of the Federal Executive to implement and enforce such policy.

This Executive, however, asserts the right of the rank and file in Conference assembled, in accordance with the Rules of the N.S.W. Branch, to elect its State Officers and Central Executive, and urges the Federal Conference, in the interests of unity, to adhere to the principle of rank and file control in any decisions arrived at concerning the affairs of the N.S.W. Branch.

This Executive therefore resolves:

(a) That in an attempt to maintain the unity of the Party in this State, we, under protest agree to postpone the holding of the Annual Conference of the N.S.W. Branch until after the Federal Conference set down to commence on June 11th.

(b) That the Annual Conference of the N.S.W. Branch due, in accordance with the rules of the Branch, to assemble on June 2nd, 1956, be postponed until June 30th, 1956.[5]

Kane's papers note that 'there was considerable difficulty in getting firm decisions taken at Movement meetings. Colbourne was always able to muster support. Roy Boylan and Father Bird (Bishop Carroll's representative) were doing their best to keep the team together, and despite their anti-Melbourne attitude, did not want to see the Executive surrender'.[6]

At this point, despite Kane's doubts as to the ultimate fortitude of his Executive, it was in fact demonstrating surprising strength.

The political strength of the State Executive as it prepared to face Federal intervention depended on a series of interlocking influences. If Movement members were strong, the strongest non-Movement Industrial Groupers, feeling solid ground under their feet, could also afford to be strong—as they wished to be. If both segments were strong, the weaker Industrial Groupers would be disposed to hold firm. If the three segments were strong, their strength would determine the line of the non-Group right-wingers, and thus ensure an overwhelming majority. If, however, the Movement foundation collapsed, everything above it and around it collapsed with it.

A firm statement of the Executive's position, entitled 'The Future of Labor' was prepared for the Special Federal Conference which was scheduled to meet in Melbourne on 11 June. Again, this was carried by twenty-five votes to five, and accordingly published.

When the Federal Executive had met in Sydney on 15 June and appointed its panel to select a new State Executive, the latter body was faced with the necessity of meeting its crisis in one way or another. Accordingly the New South Wales Executive met on the same night, the fifteenth. It divided between two groups. The first was made up of those who favoured resistance to the Federal Executive, backed by the implicit threat that if the Executive were removed, the Victorian situation would be repeated in New South Wales with quite calculable consequences to the Cahill Government. This would have passed the buck back to the Federal authorities.

There was a group, however, centred on Colbourne, who was in the confidence of Bishop Carroll, which took the view that the Executive's number was up, that even the threat of a split should be avoided, and that they should save what they could.

By the night of 15 June, Colbourne had changed his position. He had been 'adopted' by the Evatt forces to act as new State Secretary of an anti-Industrial Group Executive. There his presence would naturally signify that something had been saved. The majorities of twenty-five to five enjoyed up till then by Kane and the 'resistance' forces had been completely transformed, the Executive now dividing on all critical issues at approximately twenty-all.

Kane's notes indicate what had occurred.

The pressures were now really on. Colbourne, Gavan Sutherland and Dr P. J. Ryan were lobbying executive members with the view to their accepting the Federal Executive decisions.

This line was that if the decisions were accepted a reasonable Executive would be appointed; pre-selections would not be interfered with; there would be no head-hunting; and even Kane would be permitted to hold his job. To reject the decisions would be to make the same mistake as the Victorians; the A.L.P. would be handed on a platter to the left-wingers; the State Government would fall; good Labor men would lose their seats and union officials their jobs; in the end only the Communists would benefit.

Ernie O'Dea (State Secretary of the Shop Assistants' Union) who, as mentioned earlier, was one of our strongest supporters, after he had been contacted by Dr Ryan, now became an opponent. He had directed Keith Murphy, an organiser for the Shop Assistants' Union, that if he voted with me at this special Executive meeting, he would dismiss him.

Lindsay North, Jack Bale, Milton McCarney, Les Druce and Jack Holmes, all union officials, and Jim Blackburn who had supported our stand against the second interference by the Federal Executive, now switched sides.

Jim Shortell on the morning of Friday June 15, told me that he did not feel that he could urge union officials to take a stand that would cost them their jobs, knowing that within a few weeks he would be appointed to a position in the Stevedoring Industry Commission. He did, however, stand up when the Premier, late in the same day, did everything possible to get him to support the Federal Executive decisions.[7]

The intervention of Dr P. J. Ryan was—rightly—regarded by the Catholics who were at the top level of New South Wales Labor politics as reflecting the official policy of the Archdiocese. Colbourne's switch was—rightly—regarded as part of an arrangement, with an implied promise that something would be saved from the wreck. Movement members, supporters and non-Catholic Industrial Group leaders, who naturally could not really understand what was taking place, suddenly found that the ground on which they had stood for so long and so courageously was fragmenting under their feet. What was remarkable was that so many Movement members stood firm on the night of 15 June, leading to the rejection of Colbourne's 'Federal takeover' motion by twenty-one votes to twenty. Those who stood firm included Kane, Allport, Crane, Henry, Holmes, Kenna, McCarney, McGrane, Marsh, Murphy and Lynch. However, five other Movement members followed Colbourne in supporting the Federal takeover.

Although rejection of Federal Executive intervention thus still remained the majority view of the State Executive, the narrowness of the majority on the night of Friday 15 June—only twenty-one to twenty—led to the adjournment of the meeting until Monday 18 June. A meeting of the Sydney Executive of the Movement was held at 7 a.m. on Monday. Here Kane's notes offer important evidence as to what occurred:

About 7 a.m. on Monday June 18, Boylan rang me to say that a special meeting of the Movement Executive had been held the previous night. He said he was not a member of the Executive but, on the Bishop's instructions, had attended. This meeting . . . had decided to advise the 'moderate elements' of the Movement to accept appointment to the caretaker State Executive.

Boylan said he would not tell the men concerned of the decision, but would merely advise them to see me. What Boylan apparently did not realise, of course, was that Colbourne would be appraised of the decision and would be in a position to advise Chamberlain and Co. how to act. In giving me this information Boylan asked me not to involve him.[8]

With the Sydney Movement switch complete, by the night of 18 June, it was all over.

The *de facto* dismissal of Kane nine days later, and of Rooney within the next few weeks, created a furore in Sydney Movement ranks. The furore became even more intense as a series of expulsions from the ALP followed. Alan Manning, fiercely anti-Movement, and a writer for the left-wing magazine *Voice*, had been disgusted by the Federal tactics and said so in the correspondence columns of the *Sydney Morning Herald* in July. That there was a mass base for resistance, equal to that proved to have existed in Victoria, was shown in the large number of invitations received by Manning to address ALP branches throughout the metropolitan area. A meeting summoned by the *ad hoc* 'Rank-and-File Rights Committee' formed to defend the State Executive attracted more than 1,000 persons. As Murray puts it: 'With a *Voice* man defending the old Executive so strongly and attacking the "Evatt-Chamberlain dictatorship" so eloquently, the "Santamaria" story started to sound thin'.[9]

The threat of general reaction against the policies of the Sydney Archdiocese mounted in intensity when it became known that Kane and Manning were proposing to form a new party, which inevitably would be modelled on the Victorian body. To meet this threat, the whole of the Sydney Movement was called together at the Sacred Heart Monastery, Kensington, on Sunday, 30 September 1956.

The meeting was chaired by Ambrose Roddy, the principal speakers being Bishop Carroll, Dr P. J. Ryan and Roy Boylan. Between 700 and 800 people were present at the Kensington meeting. That it was a meeting of extraordinary importance was shown by the presence of almost all the leading members of the organization in full-time union positions.

Three years after these events, the *Sydney Morning Herald* published two articles under the title 'Labour and Roman Catholicism' from a 'special correspondent'.[10] The articles stated *inter alia* that, at the critical moment in the ALP struggle, 'Catholics were adjured to stay in the A.L.P. *as a matter of loyalty to the Cardinal*' (my italics).

The *Catholic Weekly* of 17 June 1959, speaking as it always did for the Sydney ecclesiastical authorities, understood how fatal such a statement was to the claim that the Sydney authorities had always pursued a non-political course as distinct from the highly political course of the Archbishop of Melbourne. Hence, in defending the position against certain 'misguided Catholics', it stated—'categorically'—that the *Sydney Morning Herald* claim was untrue.

On 24 June the *Sydney Morning Herald* published a letter from a correspondent who signed himself 'Misguided Catholic'. He had been a senior organizer of the Movement in Sydney and, to that point, had remained loyal to the Sydney policy and organization. He wrote:

I am a member of what the *Catholic Weekly* calls 'a small number of mis-guided people who have never forgiven the Cardinal for refusing to become the very thing they now allege he is—a political partisan'. These latter 'were not content to feed a daily newspaper with information injurious to the Church; they gave false information.'. . . It is of course impossible for a person of my political outlook to have a protest published in the *Catholic Weekly*. One has only one alternative in this State—the columns of the daily press . . . The *Catholic Weekly* categorically states that the allegation 'That Sydney Catholics were adjured to remain in the A.L.P. "as a matter of loyalty to the Cardinal" is untrue'. I categorically state that it is true, and if necessary, and if it is again denied I am prepared to quote chapter and verse.

I was present at a number of meetings when it was said on behalf of the Cardinal that members of the Movement should 'remain in the A.L.P. ("Stay in and Fight") out of loyalty to their Bishop'.

If this is denied I am perfectly prepared to sign my own name as a mark of the authenticity of my evidence and also to give the names of the ecclesiastics and laymen who spoke at the meetings, and also of the most prominent of the members who were present and heard what was said . . .

Misguided Catholic[11]

The episcopal intervention was quite effective in its main purpose. The appeal to loyalty to the Cardinal was powerful, as it must be with Catholics who are—rightly in the great majority of cases—loyal to the views which their bishops express as to the interests of the Church, since the ordinary Catholic cannot expect to know many aspects of highly complex situations which are known to bishops in the course of their duties.

The repeated assertion that bishops had authority of undefined extent even in matters of political judgement confused ordinary lay people. This confusion was deepened by the obvious conflict of opinion between what was being said publicly by the Pope's representative, in the person of the Apostolic Delegate (Archbishop Carboni), and what was being said by their own local bishops.

True to the tradition that Apostolic Delegates were primarily concerned with maintaining contact between the Holy See and the national episcopate to which they were accredited, Archbishop Carboni had not entered the controversy in its earliest stages in late 1954 and early 1955. A son of central Italy, powerfully built, of independent temperament, he now believed that the Australian laity were being misled as to their rights and responsibilities, and was prepared to say so.

As far as its purely political aspects were concerned he never did enter the controversy. His sole contribution, as he saw it, was to correct the exposition of canon law as to the relationship between the bishop and lay movements organized to pursue policies in the temperal order.

In an address to the men of the Neutral Bay (NSW) parish on 15 August 1955, he pointed out that there was a vital distinction

*Top:* Archbishop Romolo Carboni, Apostolic Delegate to Australia, and B. A. Santamaria at National Catholic Rural Movement Convention, Canberra, 1956

*Bottom:* B. A. Santamaria and Bishop Henschke, 1956

between organizations dealing with specific social and political policies and objectives and official organizations of Catholic Action, which, it was not disputed, were legally dependent on the bishops. Organizations dependent on the bishops, he said, were precluded from elaborating detailed policies in the socio-economic or socio-political fields, or pursuing practical political objectives. They were limited to studying, understanding and teaching the general principles of social justice.

It was perfectly open, he said, to individual Catholics to formulate practical policies and embark on practical programmes, and to seek to give effect to them within their own communities. By the very nature of that activity, it could not be directed by the bishops. In this field Catholics must 'act on their own responsibility and personal initiative, not formally as mandated by the Church'. Organizations of the latter type were juridically regarded not as 'Catholic Action', but as 'action of Catholics'. Driving this distinction home to the very point at issue in the Australian situation, the Apostolic Delegate added:

> The hierarchy could give a mandate to Catholic Action to fight communism in the apostolate of ideas, through the press, by propaganda, by persuasion, and so forth. [But] if it were necessary to extend the resistance to policies, programmes, organizations, institutions, etc., in the industrial, professional, political and other domains, . . . Catholics would then act on their own responsibility, as explained above, not as mandated by the hierarchy.[12]

To Tom Truman, lecturer in Political Science in the University of Queensland, this was a distinction without a difference, offensive to the eyes and ears of non-Machiavellian Anglo-Saxons.[13]

The truth, on the contrary, was that in seeking to establish the distinction in the very heat of controversy, the Delegate was not merely elaborating a doctrinal abstraction. He was risking the whole of his future career.

In form a theoretical discussion of the various types of Catholic organization, it was in practice, and was understood to be, a public repudiation of the Sydney position. It was an act of exceptional courage and integrity: for while Archbishop Carboni was an Apostolic Delegate, he was an archbishop coming into conflict with a cardinal, in the latter's domain. The risks involved in such a conflict were all the greater because the cardinal in question was known to be highly regarded in Rome by Cardinal Fumasoni-Biondi, the Prefect of the Congregation of Propaganda, within whose jurisdiction the Australian Church fell.

The intervention of the Apostolic Delegate was even more courageous since it occurred after, and not before, the Victorian State elections in April 1955, with their damaging results. If his address had been delivered before the elections, it would have been possible to represent his public intervention as a gesture of support for what a

210 united Australian Hierarchy had said in the Joint Pastoral of 27 April 1955. But speaking in August 1955, after the Victorian elections in April, when all the sitting DLP members other than Scully had lost their seats, and the Cardinal's spokesmen were condemning their 'imprudence', he was committing what some might have regarded as the supreme folly of backing a losing horse.

The Apostolic Delegate pursued his campaign in several addresses during 1955 and 1956, as the divisions were widening. As the Evatt onslaught moved into New South Wales, no doubt the aim of the Apostolic Delegate was to outline to lay people the extent of their rights. The conflict of viewpoints led merely to a general paralysis, not only among those of the laity who had not been directly involved in the conflict, but among the less single-minded Movement members. One could not blame them.

That paralysis was effective in the main objective of the Sydney episcopal intervention. It countered the plan of aligning the New South Wales Executive with the Victorian, and leading Queensland in its train. Next it stopped the groundswell of indignation from manifesting itself in a major flow of members into the DLP, thus depriving that party of any mass base in New South Wales. On the other hand, the conflict generated a widespread reaction among many New South Wales Catholics against activity of any kind associated with the Church, creating a climate which could be summed up as 'a plague on both your houses'.

By the end of September 1956, the Sydney authorities had won their essential point: which was to ensure in practice that national decisions did not operate in Sydney and most of New South Wales. They had defeated the original national strategy which sought to persuade the three eastern State Executives to align themselves together against the Evatt attack. When that strategy was successfully aborted, they were equally successful in defeating the subsequent strategy of attrition involved in denying office to Labor by building and supporting the DLP until Labor re-traced its steps. Granted their premises and even allowing for the advantages of a Cardinal over laymen, they had acted with exemplary political skill.

Unfortunately, as the national Movement sought to defend both itself and its policy, the Sydney objective widened. This divergence was to usher in a series of events which led to the disintegration of the Movement, and, ultimately, through various intermediate stages, to the formation of the National Civic Council, a purely civic body which ceased to have any connection with the Catholic Hierarchy and which ceased to be exclusively Catholic in membership.

# 23 Rome has its say

The Extraordinary Meeting of the Hierarchy, which had decided to give the support of the Australian Bishops to the Movement in September 1945, had, as has been indicated already, formed an Episcopal Committee of three Bishops to maintain contact with the organization. Its rather peculiar *modus agendi* has already been outlined. As two of its members—Archbishop Mannix and Bishop O'Collins—were disposed to agree, and as they were both my close personal friends, the relationship between the Movement and the Episcopal Committee raised no problems. However, in 1955-56, as difficulties with Sydney were mounting, the Cardinal persuaded the Hierarchy, in the interests of conciliation, to increase the size of this Committee from the original three (the Cardinal, Archbishop Mannix, Bishop O'Collins) to seven. Of the seven Archbishop Mannix, Bishops Brennan and Stewart supported the national concept. The Cardinal himself, Coadjutor-Archbishop O'Donnell (Brisbane), Bishops Carroll and McCabe supported the Sydney position. From the viewpoint of the Cardinal, the change in personnel was understandable. The original committee gave Archbishop Mannix a two-one majority, and he was in favour of the national policy. The expanded committee gave the Sydney policy a four-three majority. In so far as the decisions of the Episcopal Committee were influential in determining the attitude of the Hierarchy as a whole, the change was significant. There was now overwhelming pressure on the more malleable elements to fall away from the stronger policy, not necessarily because of any defects in the policy, but in the interests of 'unity' and 'peace'.

The last meeting of the enlarged Episcopal Committee took place on 13 April 1956. By June 1956 the collapse of the New South Wales position was complete.

Neither I nor my colleagues were any longer prepared to work in an organization whose national unity had ultimately been destroyed

212 | as a result of a long and persistent campaign. The rock on which the ship had foundered was the wish of the crew that, while insisting on independence of decision, they should maintain their traditional connection with the Bishops. This decision was naturally influenced by traditional loyalties. It was also influenced by practical considerations. The period of crisis in the affairs of the Labor Party and the union movement, initiated by Dr Evatt on 5 October 1954, demanded a strengthening rather than a weakening of the Catholic supports on which the Movement rested, since no other supports were available.

On 18 July 1956, with the exception of two or three of the Sydney officials and of one in Adelaide, all Movement officials resigned. They communicated their decision to the Bishops:

In our view the Sydney region cannot be exonerated from responsibility for this collapse. The policy of the Sydney region is that enunciated in the main article in the *Catholic Weekly* of 21 June 1956. This article makes the truth in relation to the present situation abundantly clear. Although the Joint Pastoral describes the Industrial Groups as 'a well-proven means of fighting effectively the Communist threat to the nation', although the Evatt Labor Party has failed completely to provide any alternative; although it has actively collaborated with Communists on 'unity tickets', the Sydney Region did not even consider the Industrial Groups to be worth a fight.[1]

Resolving to continue the fight against Communist influences in Australian life, those who had just tendered their resignations thereupon formed a new organization, the Catholic Social Movement. Its name was meant to imply continuity in the nature of the work it would undertake. Its constitution, however, was clearly based on lay control of policy and strategy in the political, industrial, and other public avenues, with national decisions taken by majority vote being binding on all.

While, in terms of pure logic, the organization would have been entitled to establish itself in any part of Australia, its proponents did not wish to widen the serious divisions which had opened up. Accordingly, in communicating their decision to all the Bishops, they stated that they would not establish the organization in any diocese in which the Bishop did not wish it to exist. But when the Bishop decided to accept the organization, he would take it with its constitution based on national decisions and lay control.

The organization was thereupon accepted by all the Bishops of Victoria; Brisbane, Toowoomba, Townsville and Rockhampton in Queensland, Cairns being the only abstention in that State; Hobart, the only diocese in Tasmania; Wagga and Armidale in New South Wales; Perth, Geraldton and New Norcia in Western Australia. The Bishops of Bunbury (WA) and Port Pirie (SA) were absent from Australia at the time.

Thus, territorially, the new Movement was considerably weakened compared with its predecessor, since it had lost Sydney and the greater part of New South Wales, and South Australia. Yet it was felt that it was preferable to accept the geographic losses, so long as the basic principles of the organization were maintained in what was left, in the (perhaps vain) hope that when the bankruptcy of the opposite policy had been proved, it might perhaps be possible to regain some of the ground which had been lost.

It was in this hope that a name as close as possible to the original name was chosen—to preserve identity and continuity. In the light of after-events it was a mistake. It would have been far better to have made the complete break, which was made in fact in December 1957 with the formation of the National Civic Council.

The attempt at compromise was futile. By October 1956, the Cardinal and Bishop Carroll had effectively won their way in New South Wales. The old ALP Executive had been replaced without any mass exodus to the DLP. Nevertheless, so long as the Evatt initiative had not run its full course, the Sydney ecclesiastical authorities could not be certain that their victory was final. The Cardinal therefore called a general meeting of the Hierarchy to consider what he chose to regard as a rebellion against the authority of the Bishops in the resignations from the old Movement, and the creation of a new one.

There were, in 1956, twenty-five dioceses in Australia. The Bishops of only twelve of these dioceses responded to the Cardinal's invitation. This meeting thereupon appointed three of its number—the Cardinal, Bishop Carroll, and Coadjutor-Archbishop O'Donnell of Brisbane as a delegation to the Holy See to seek a final adjudication of the dispute. Archbishop Mannix and his supporters repudiated the delegation, and pointed out to Rome that the majority of Bishops had deliberately absented themselves from the Conference which appointed it. Rome obviously took the view that, whatever the legalities, the divisions in the Australian Hierarchy had gone too far and were creating a public scandal. Hence the matter was referred to a Commission of Cardinals.

What the Australian episcopal delegation said in Rome, we never knew. Dr Mannix sent a 'Letter on behalf of Certain Bishops' to the Roman authorities in late 1956, which reiterated the well-traversed ground that the Movement was a lay rather than an episcopal organization, in which the laity had complete freedom and responsibility in formulating its policies; that is, there was to be no episcopal veto. The Bishops, he said, had a duty to support the Movement members and their collaborators in the Industrial Groups, especially those parliamentarians who had lost their seats and who had suffered loss for defying the actions of the Federal Executive in Victoria and New South Wales. This duty flowed from the fact, he said, that these men had acted in accord with the Bishops' own exhortation to them in their Joint Pastoral of April 1955.

The Bishops who had absented themselves from the meeting which selected the delegation took the position that it was a matter for Australian rather than Roman decision. Hence they did not send a counter-delegation, confining themselves to the written representations contained in Dr Mannix's letter. This turned out to be a mistake, since written representations could not undo what was said face-to-face over many weeks in Rome.

It may appear incongruous that while those whose official fate was being decided were a group of laymen, some of whom had at considerable cost foregone their ordinary careers to offer their services for fundamentally spiritual reasons, at no stage was a single one among them invited to Rome to state their collective case. Yet had they sent representatives to Rome without such an invitation, they would have had little standing against a delegation comprising a cardinal, an archbishop and a bishop.

As far as Rome could determine the issue, it was determined in two letters from the Congregation of Propaganda Fide. The first conveyed the decision of the Commission of Cardinals and was dated 27 May 1957. The second, in reply to a request for 'clarifications' by Cardinal Gilroy, was dated 25 July 1957. On 21 August 1957 Dr Mannix appealed directly to Pope Pius XII. On 3 November the Cardinal Secretary of State (Cardinal Tardini) sent the Pope's reply.

It would be most useful to publish the entire correspondence. However, in default of any permission to do this, it must suffice to publish the summary points, as I was authorized to do by Archbishop Mannix in the quarterly *Twentieth Century* in 1960.[2]

In sum, Rome laid down the following points:

1  The Holy See is concerned with the need and urgency for continuing the struggle against Communism, and with eliminating such motives and attitudes as might weaken it.

2  In this struggle the role of the Hierarchy as a body is the spiritual and moral formation of the laity, not direct or indirect intervention in the trade union or political struggle.

3  Lay organizations which juridically depend on the Hierarchy are logically in the same position as the body of the Hierarchy itself—both in their function of spiritual and moral formation and their exclusion from the active struggle in union and political fields.

4  The Catholic Social Movement was to be reconstructed as an organization confining itself to spiritual and moral formation. It would be subject to the bishops. It would exclude from its programmes all direct or indirect action in relation to trade union or political life.

5  A confessional political party, or confessional trade unions, were not desirable in Australia.

6  Laymen are free to act, and indeed are under an obligation to act,

with determination in pursuing their civic duty within trade unions and political bodies.

Through all the apparently Byzantine distinctions, it was obvious that Rome was not primarily concerned with the fight against Communism within the Labour Movement in Australia. Although a series of Popes had called the laity to participate in that struggle, it was apparent that in an Australia which was both small in population and distant in geography, the struggle was not regarded by the Holy See as of the same importance as the question which was really central. What mattered was that the divisions in the ranks of the Bishops should come to an end, regardless of other consequences.

The Pope's reply, which was signed by Cardinal Tardini and was dated 3 November, effectively rejected Archbishop Mannix's appeal. As far as the Holy See was concerned, the matter was now closed.

When the Pope's letter came, it was apparent that even Archbishop Mannix believed that it was the end of the road. There was an informal gathering at Raheen. As far as I recall, in addition to the Archbishop, those who were present were Bishops O'Collins, Stewart and Lyons, all from Victoria. I was invited to attend what seemed uncommonly like a 'wake'.

After a certain amount of desultory discussion, I took the responsibility of saying to the Bishops that it was apparent that the Holy See had been primarily, almost exclusively, concerned with ending the conflict in the ranks of the Australian Bishops. This was natural enough. In my view, however, it had given little if any consideration to what concerned us as Australian citizens. This was that Communist influence, which had been reduced in Australia's political and industrial organizations, should not be permitted to revive. As to how this was to be done, the Roman documents were completely silent. In view of the Communist resurgence in a number of major unions in the course of the last eighteen months, the problem promised to grow to even more serious proportions. If the organization with which I had been connected now for sixteen years went out of existence, what was left with which to face the Communist Party? The Labor Party? Even if it were accepted that Dr Evatt would not have a long future, could it be left to a Labor Party headed by his putative successor, Mr Calwell, who even in the thirties had proved singularly incapable of handling the problem in Victoria? Was the responsibility to be carried by the adult education organization which Sydney was now authorized to establish in place of the Movement? Even that organization, if it were formed, was now forbidden to expand its activities beyond the field of education in social principles. In the meantime, what was to happen to the men who had taken the supreme risk of establishing the DLP, a parallel to

216 which had now been formed in the northern State, after the smashing of the Gair Government?

In brief, I said that I was certain that my colleagues would wish to continue the fight. If it turned out to be beyond us, deprived now of the support of the Church, as we were faced with the general hostility of a community aroused by the sectarian campaign, at least we would go down fighting. I would therefore propose to my colleagues that we break all connections with the past, and establish a new, completely civic organization to face the problems of the future.

The words were stronger than the somewhat faltering spirit behind them. The truth was that although in ordinary decency we had a continuing responsibility to the men who had formed the DLP, basically the issue we had set out to fight still remained.

I pointed out that the Roman documents provided those who so wished with ample justification to continue the fight, so long as they acted completely on their own responsibility.

On any reading the Vatican documents recognized—as indeed they had no alternative but to recognize—that laymen were citizens with citizen rights. They were entitled to organize if they so wished. All that the Vatican could withdraw from them was the organized support of the Hierarchy.

As far as the remaining 'friendly' Bishops were concerned, the only point at issue was whether those still personally attached to our cause would interpret the Roman resolutions as demanding a complete termination of relations, as Archbishop Prendiville of Perth had decided that they did. Dr Mannix, having listened to what must have appeared rather an abstract proposition, with few chances of success, said that he would not change his personal attitude. Whatever his constitutional responsibilities as a bishop, as a man he was still with us. The other bishops who were present took the same view, as did old friends like Bishops Henschke (Wagga), Doody (Armidale), Brennan (Toowoomba), Tynan (Rockhampton), Gummer (Geraldton) and Archbishop Young (Hobart).

In December 1957 all of the former officials of the Movement, with the exception of some of the Sydney and one of the former Adelaide officers, took the step of creating the National Civic Council. It was designed as a purely civic body with no connection whatsoever with the Church, completely independent of the Bishops, making its own decisions on its own responsibility. As a sign of its different status it would seek suitable persons of other persuasions to become part of its membership.

What it meant in practice was that by far the greater part of the Movement membership in Victoria, Queensland, Western Australia and Tasmania formed the nucleus of the new body. A not inconsiderable number joined in Sydney, but strong and effective episcopal action reduced potential membership in New South Wales and practically cut off recruitment in South Australia. In New South Wales strong nuclei remained in the Riverina and on the Northern Tablelands. Quite simply the NCC retained the bulk of the membership in the designated areas, almost all of the old officials, and the same structures of organization. In terms of effectiveness it was however greatly weakened, as far as an effective industrial and political role was concerned, in New South Wales and South Australia.

When the NCC began to seek members in Sydney, as was obviously its right according to the Roman dispensation, it might have been thought that the Sydney authorities, in obedience to the very decision they themselves had sought, and in any case having gained all of their practical objectives, would have permitted their own laity to have that freedom. What actually occurred was the opposite. A special meeting of the clergy was called to inform them that the creation of the new body was just as 'episcopal' as its predecessor, and that it was a cover for the policies of Archbishop Mannix, enabling him to interfere with the authority of the Cardinal in his own archdiocese. The truth—that it was exclusively a lay initiative, independent of Dr Mannix—naturally could not be demonstrated until the death of Dr Mannix. The test would be whether it continued. It is a matter of record that it did, and that it has.

# 24 The 'Conscience' Issue

Two or three incidental episodes deserve to be recorded as significant, only because they provide illustrations of the spirit of various participants in the conflict.

1955 provided Dr Evatt and his supporters with two vital tests. What they did to the Industrial Group forces within their own party was a matter internal to the ALP. How the people as a whole reacted would be witnessed not only in the Victorian State election but, at the end of the year, in the Federal election which was to be held as well.

As a pipe-opener for the coming attack on the New South Wales Executive of the ALP, on 24 March 1955 a pro-Evatt rally of some eight hundred people was held, not in Sydney, but in Wollongong. It was significant that the rally was called by the Port Kembla branch of the Waterside Workers' Federation, which was Communist-controlled, and by the South Coast ALP branches which were effectively under the same influence.

It was the first meeting addressed by Dr Evatt since the Hobart Conference. One of the parliamentarians on the platform was Gough Whitlam. To thunderous cheers—not surprising considering the ideological affinities of the South Coast audience—Dr Evatt announced that 'the Menzies–Fadden–Santamaria–Fascist cell' was engaged in a diabolical conspiracy to push the Labor Party 'even further to the right than the Liberal Party'.[1] Dr Evatt's honest alarm at this 'Fascist threat' to Australia's democratic institutions underwent a rapid metamorphosis with the approach of the 1955 Federal election. Kane, who by definition was part of this hydra-headed conspiracy, records in his notes:

With the opening of the Federal Election campaign Evatt who had not spoken to me for over a year, was now suggesting that we should forget our past differences and be friends. He said that I knew the 'right people' to see, and he was sure a good result could be obtained if I co-operated with him.

Vince Gair told me that Evatt had asked him to see Archbishop Duhig, but Gair declined reminding him that he was opposed to 'outside influences' in the Labor Party. To cap it all he [Evatt] asked [Senator] Nick McKenna to approach Archbishop Mannix.[2]

Evatt's virtuosity was apparently limitless. However it failed to quell the animosity which his outspokenly sectarian attacks had caused. The 1955 Federal election saw the Menzies Government returned to office—on the strength of the DLP's preferences.

It was well understood that Dr Evatt, having survived the 1955 defeat as leader of the ALP simply because it was politically impossible to drop the pilot in the midst of the storm, could not hope to survive another defeat in 1958. Dr Evatt had bravely stated that his electoral strategy was based on the estimate that while he would lose a large number of Catholic votes, he would gain two Protestant votes for every Catholic vote he lost.[3] There was little sign, however, that this mathematical estimate would be realized. By the end of 1958, it was apparent that unless he regained some of the lost Catholic vote in all States, but particularly in the three largest eastern States, he would get nowhere. (It was the same plaintive plea as Mr Holding, elected Parliamentary Leader of the Victorian ALP in May 1967, was to give as the explanation of his failure to become Victorian Premier, when he resigned in 1977.)

The desperation with which the ALP leadership faced the 1958 election, after a decade in the wilderness, was responsible for a piquant series of events. As a result of the outright support given to 'unity tickets' (that is to say, electoral alliances between members of the ALP and of the Communist Party in union elections) in Victoria, the issue was raised as to whether Catholics could in conscience vote for a political party which either authorized or connived at association between its members and the Communist Party. The issue was relevant for Catholics, since in 1949 Pius XII endorsed the following Declaration of the Holy Office:

The Supreme Sacred Congregation of the Holy Office has been asked:
(1) Whether it is lawful to enlist in or show favor to the communist party?
(2) Whether it is lawful to publish, read, or disseminate books, newspapers, periodicals, or leaflets in support of communist doctrine and practice or write any articles in them?
(3) Whether Catholics who knowingly and freely perform actions as specified in Nos. 1 and 2 above may be admitted to the Sacraments?
(4) Whether Catholics, who profess and particularly those who defend and spread, the materialistic and anti-Christian doctrine of the Communists, ipso facto, as apostates from the Catholic faith, incur excommunication reserved especially to the Holy See?
The most eminent and reverend fathers, charged with the defense of matters pertaining to faith and morals, after having previously heard the opinion of the consultors at a plenary session held on Tuesday, the 28th day of June, 1949, decreed that the above-mentioned questions be answered as follows:

To No. 1—In the negative, for communism is materialistic and anti-Christian. Besides, communist leaders, although they sometimes verbally assert that they are not opposed to religion, show themselves nevertheless, both by doctrine and by action, to be in reality enemies of God, of the true religion, and of the Church of Christ.

To No. 2—In the negative, inasmuch as this is prohibited by law itself (of Canon 1399, *Corpus Juris Canonici*).

To No. 3—In the negative, in accordance with the common principles governing refusal of the sacraments to those not having proper dispositions.

To No. 4—In the affirmative.

And on the following Thursday, the 30th of the same month and year, His Holiness Pope Pius XII, when informed of the decision in the usual audience granted to His Excellency, the Most Reverend Assessor, approved and ordered to be published the above answers in the *Acta Apostolicae Sedis*.[4]

In 1959, this was to be re-stated and even strengthened by Pope John XXIII, who issued a new decree from the Holy Office which forbade Catholics to vote for any politician or party who or which supported the Communists either in theory or in practice.

The question which was strongly canvassed was whether, in the light of these documents, it was open to a Catholic, aware of the failure of ALP Executives to police their own policy against unity tickets, in good conscience to vote for the ALP. Bishop Fox, Auxiliary to Archbishop Mannix, stated his own personal opinion that it was not.

It was highly embarrassing to the leadership of the ALP as it limbered up for the 1958 election on which depended so much, for Dr Evatt in particular. Accordingly, in still another convolution of policy in relation to Communist association, he indicated his strong disapproval of the conduct of Labor men who embarrassed the Party by acting in this way. Mr Calwell simply denied that ALP members had supported unity ticket candidates in Victoria, stating that in any case the ALP was perfectly capable of looking after its own affairs on this matter.[5] In 1958—only two years after the suppression of the Hungarian rebellion and fully ten years before Soviet tanks invaded Czechoslovakia—he stated his view that Communism was dying all over the world.[6]

In a veritable *tour de force*, the ALP sought to use the conscience issue to its own advantage. A little more than a week before the 1958 polling day, ALP advertisements appeared in newspapers all over Australia blazoning a statement of Cardinal Gilroy, who had declared that Catholics could in conscience vote for any party except the Communist Party. In a further display of virtuosity, the ALP published full-page advertisements in most if not all of the nation's dailies, claiming that every DLP voter had a duty to examine *his* conscience in the casting of his second preference vote. The *Catholic Weekly* operated once again, this time in offering advice to the DLP that it should think again as to its policy of preventing the ALP from forming a government, since this would deprive Australians, including DLP members, of the new social services which Labor had promised.

It was a neat turning of the 'conscience issue'. The advertisements alone must have cost thousands of pounds. This expenditure was supplemented by the publication of tens of thousands of leaflets offering the self-same advice, many of which found themselves under windscreen-wipers of cars parked outside Melbourne Catholic churches for Sunday Mass.

Strong representations were made to Archbishop Mannix that the use of the Cardinal's statement could be quite harmful to the DLP. For while the continued presence of Dr Evatt as Parliamentary Leader would keep the original issues more alive than would have occurred in the event of a change in the Labor leadership, nevertheless three years had passed and memories might well have been dulled in the process. In any case, it was an altogether more moderate Dr Evatt who presented himself on this occasion. Dr Mannix, however, was unwilling to involve himself at all. The popular image of a political prelate anxious to re-enter the heat of the battle was quite the reverse of the truth.

Cardinal Gilroy officially deplored the use of his name 'for political purposes' but said that he would take no action to prevent the ALP using it in advertisements.[7] When the Cardinal refused to take action, Dr Mannix reluctantly changed his mind. On the following afternoon, using a torn wrapper from one or other of the papers which reached him daily, he wrote out his own statement which was then published:

Amid the turmoil of the election, one thing seems clear. Every Communist and every Communist sympathizer in Australia wants a victory for the Evatt Party. That is alarming. It should be a significant warning for every Catholic, for every decent Australian. Hitherto, I have not deemed it necessary to sound a note of warning. The Communists have long been falsely suggesting that Cardinal Gilroy stands for comparatively neutral benevolence. Of course, the Cardinal ignored their malevolent use of his name. But now that the Evatt party, forgetting all about sectarianism, is trying to shelter under his name in nationwide advertisements and in pamphlets distributed outside Catholic Churches to congregations on Sundays, I deem it timely to recall the official attitude of the Cardinal and of all the Catholic Bishops of Australia.

Writing at a time when the menace of Communism was not as pressing as it is now, and writing, not in the pressure and heat of election time, but in the calm, restrained atmosphere of a national pastoral letter, the Cardinal wrote and all the Bishops signed the following words:

At the moment there is one outstanding issue for the nation and the Church. It is the immediate Communist threat to the security of the people and to the freedom of religion in Australia.

The Cardinal, with the Bishops, went on almost prophetically to say:

It is very regrettable that highly placed public men, including some Catholics, seem to have closed their eyes to the great issues involved in the present upheaval. They do not appear to realize that they are forwarding the interests of Communism.

It seems to me timely to recall these calm and weighty words.

AGAINST THE TIDE

It is needless to add that the Democratic Labor Party, Protestant and Catholic alike,
at heroic cost to themselves, have stood, and stand consistently for the principles
espoused in that Pastoral Letter.

Can the same be said of others?[8]

Dr Evatt was alarmed by the reply his supporters had provoked.
He issued a statement that Labor had always been opposed to
Communism, and proved it by placing Communist candidates last
on ALP how-to-vote- cards.[9] His deputy, Mr Calwell, stated that the
Archbishop was being used by those who wished to damage the
ALP.[10]

In the event, Dr Evatt lost the 1958 election, going down by
twenty-eight seats. Whether the Mannix statement was a decisive
factor cannot, of course, be estimated with any accuracy. The result,
however, was sufficient to lead Dr Evatt to abandon the moderation
he had shown before the election; understandably, since it was
obviously the end of his political career. Ignoring the fact that his
own party officials, certainly with his knowledge, had precipitated
the whole incident by using Cardinal Gilroy's statement, Dr Evatt
launched another characteristic attack. Dr Mannix's statement, he
said, was a 'time bomb' strategically issued too late to permit Labor
to issue an effective answer. The Archbishop's letter, he added, was
conceived on the lines of the Zinoviev letter. Its publication was
determined by the interest Dr Mannix had in the active sponsorship
and patronage of the Santamaria political movement, which was
increasingly associated with the DLP. It was a perfect illustration of
'the Mannix–Menzies' axis.[11]

Evatt's statement was not without irony. Presumably he would
have seen no problem of principle in what could, with equal
inaccuracy and irrelevance, have been called by his opponents an
'Evatt–Gilroy axis'.

A second postscript to the conflict within the Church took place in
1959. Cardinal Agagianian, who had succeeded Cardinal Fumasoni-
Biondi as Prefect of the Congregation of Propaganda Fide, the
Vatican Department with administrative responsibility for the
Church in Australia, visited Australia for the second time.

I had met him first, in earlier and happier days, on the occasion of
the National Eucharistic Congress which was held in Sydney in
April 1953, to which I had been invited by Cardinal Gilroy to speak
on the question of social justice at one of the mass gatherings of the
Congress. At the conclusion of the Sydney Congress, Cardinal
Agagianian and Cardinal Gracias visited Melbourne and, as already
described, were given a magnificent public reception by more than
25,000 people in the Exhibition Building, in the presence of the
Governor of Victoria (Sir Dallas Brookes), with Archbishop Mannix
as host of the occasion.*

* See p. 136.

Cardinal Agagianian asked me to call on him at Raheen on the morning after the Exhibition reception. The interview took place in the small suite which had been allotted to the Cardinal. He had obviously just concluded Mass. With hardly a word of introduction, he asked me to sit down while he went over to the altar. He opened a book at a page in which there was an excerpt from St Jerome which, he said, began with the phrase 'either an apostle or an apostate'. Then, to his congregation of one, he spoke to that subject for fully fifteen minutes. It was the most compelling spiritual talk to which I have ever listened, before or since.

Cardinal Agagianian questioned me in some detail as to the work in which I was engaged which, in the year 1953, before the development of the troubles, seemed to have reached a high level of material success. The Cardinal expressed his satisfaction with what was being done.

When he returned in 1959 the situation was entirely changed. Rumours were widespread thoughout the Church that the real purpose of his visit was to make his own assessment of the constant allegations that, at the age of 95, Dr Mannix had become senile, was being manipulated by a Machiavellian layman, and that it was therefore overdue that he should be replaced by his coadjutor, Archbishop Simonds.

Dr Mannix was certainly well aware of the rumours. The Cardinal was invited by him to attend two Melbourne functions while he was in Australia. The first, on the afternoon of Sunday, 14 September, was the opening of the new Corpus Christi College, the seminary for Victorian priests. The other was to be present on the same night at the opening of the annual Christian Social Week, on which occasion I would be delivering the paper entitled 'The Price of Freedom', later published in the book of the same name.

The strongest pressure was put on the Cardinal not to appear on the stage at Wilson Hall, since this would be regarded as supporting my own position in pressing ahead with the organization of the National Civic Council, despite the opposition of Cardinal Gilroy and many of the Australian Bishops. The issue was strongly contested for some days. Finally Cardinal Agagianian did not appear which, granted the over-riding desire of the Holy See to preserve the peace among the Australian Bishops, was in all the circumstances understandable.

Nevertheless, his absence did not please Archbishop Mannix. So, as it turned out, only a few hours before the Wilson Hall meeting, at the Corpus Christi College opening, with Cardinal Agagianian sitting on his right hand on the platform, the 95-year-old prelate spoke of the importance of the meeting at the Wilson Hall that night. 'Every Catholic man worth his salt', he said, 'will be present on this occasion. If I were 59 instead of 95, I would go to this meeting tonight and take the Cardinal with me'. Linking the struggle in Australia with that which had gone on for centuries in his native Ireland, he added that the fate of the Church in both countries had always, at the most critical moments of their history, depended on the laity. The Holy See had not always understood or been sympathetic to the sacrifices of the Irish people. Bishops, he said, and sometimes priests, had not infrequently failed in their responsibilities, but in both countries the laity had not, and its fortitude had been the strength and salvation of the Church.

It was painfully pointed, and could have lost whatever sympathy a lesser man than Cardinal Agagianian might have had for him. That night, in deference to his house guest, the Archbishop did not attend the meeting at Wilson Hall either. Some 1,600 people did, crowding Wilson Hall to its doors.

I was asked to call on Cardinal Agagianian at Raheen once again on the following morning, which I did in considerable anxiety at his likely reaction. He spoke at once about the Archbishop, stating how remarkable it was that at his age he could have spoken for as long as he did at the Corpus Christi opening. And then, with an unaccustomed smile, he added: 'He is certainly not senile!'.

It might have been enough to close this small episode with a wry reflection on the Psalmist's dictum 'Put not your trust in princes'. However, the two interviews I had had with Cardinal Agagianian, with an interval of more than six years between them, convinced me that his private dispositions, as distinct from the policy he had to enforce, were friendly. He might be able to do little to help in a positive sense, but if it were open to him to prevent harm or injustice which might be occasioned by others, he would do what he could. Which was something!

In fact, so it turned out, as was shown by a curious event associated with the next *ad limina* visit to Rome by Bishop Doody of Armidale (NSW), one of the ten or so Bishops who had never failed in their support. He passed through Melbourne after his return, asked me to see him, and told me what happened.

He had concluded his visit to Rome and was returning to Australia via the United States. He broke his journey at Lisbon in order to meet a former Apostolic Delegate to Australia, Cardinal Panico, who had become Papal Nuncio to Portugal.

When Cardinal Panico was in Australia, he had shown himself to be a quite intransigent enemy of Archbishop Mannix. In bringing about the appointment of Archbishop Simonds as Coadjutor to Daniel Mannix, without even mentioning the possibility of such an appointment to the latter, he had been guillty of a needless act of venom, which had hurt the old Archbishop and had cost his successor (who remained a coadjutor for twenty-one years) two decades of frustration, decades which could have been put to great use in his earlier position as Archbishop of Hobart.

As the incident was recounted to me by Bishop Doody, over dinner in his Lisbon residence, Cardinal Panico expressed his deep concern for the Church in Australia where, he said, an ambitious layman was using his influence over the ailing Archbishop to create what would inevitably be a schism. Cardinal Panico's statement greatly alarmed the Australian Bishop. He knew that the talk of 'schism' was highly-coloured fantasy. What he did not know was whether it reflected the opinion of the Australian situation held in the Vatican, or a view which the Vatican might come to accept.

So, instead of proceeding with the next stage of his journey to the USA, Bishop Doody told me that he returned immediately to Rome to see Cardinal Agagianian. The Cardinal told him not to be concerned, that he knew me personally, and that as long as he was alive he would not permit false impressions to be created in Rome.

A third episode connected with the events of these critical years concerned the award of a Papal honour to Mr Calwell in 1963. It was widely advertised as a 'signal' that the Vatican had decided to give public support to Mr Calwell, and thereby indirectly to approve the policy of the Sydney authorities in their contest with the National Civic Council. This propaganda provoked an interesting exchange of letters between the Australian poet, James McAuley, and the new Apostolic Delegate, Archbishop Enrici.

On 23 March 1964, McAuley wrote to Archbishop Enrici:

I have delayed carrying out my intention of writing to you on the subject of the award of a papal knighthood to Mr Calwell until I had time for reflection. Very probably, the effect on Australian political developments and on the fortunes of Mr Calwell will in the long run be slight. Unfortunately, the greatest immediate effect and one which will not wear away quickly, will be the lowering of the prestige of the Holy See and the value of its honours in the eyes of great numbers of Australians, both Catholic and non-Catholic, to whom this gesture, whatever its intention, must seem painfully inopportune.

Unfortunately also, there is an effect, which I have observed on all sides, of shock and bewilderment and sadness among those who have felt that, while the Church should not necessarily be asked to intervene on behalf of any particular political party and its programme, it could nevertheless be asked to treat with general encouragement those who regard politics as a field for apostolic endeavour. I am sure that I do not have to supply to you the manifold reasons why the singling out of Mr Calwell for conspicuous commendation must have a disheartening effect, which is not to be disregarded because it cannot easily be assessed.

For my own part I should like to say in addition, that the characteristics one has looked for in actions of the Holy See have been paternal solicitude combined with prudent circumspection. Among the rare public gestures of the Holy See aimed at this part of the world, the only two recent ones which stand out in my mind are: firstly, the apparent withdrawal of support from Diem [Ngo Dinh Diem, President of South Vietnam 1954-63] in the hour of his peril when he was subjected to cruel calumny; and secondly, the apparent endorsement of the position of an Australian politician whom great numbers of Australians consider to be guilty of cowardice and naked opportunism in regard to both the fight against Communism and the fight for

226 | educational justice for Catholics. One waits with some disquiet the next manifestation of the paternal solicitude and prudent circumspection of the Holy See in regard to Australian Catholics and their concerns.[12]

## The Apostolic Delegate replied on 2 April:

I wish to acknowledge the receipt of your letter of 23rd March, 1964, concerning the Papal Honour granted to Mr Arthur Calwell.

As you will know, I am sure, the composition of the Extraordinary Mission from Australia to the Coronation of Pope Paul VI was determined by the Australian Government.

It is the custom to grant a Papal Honour to members of these Extraordinary Missions, no matter from what country they come, as a token of appreciation for the courtesy extended to the Holy Father. To have failed to do so in the case of Mr Calwell would have been a grave discourtesy on the part of the Holy See both to the members of the Extraordinary Mission and to Australia. This will, I hope, help you to understand better the situation with regard to this Honour.[13]

## The episode was closed with McAuley's reply:

I am grateful for your letter of 2nd April in reply to my comment on the Papal Honour granted to Mr Arthur Calwell.

You will recall that the Honour was accompanied by a citation concerning Mr Calwell's services to the Church. I understand that this too can be taken as a purely formal gesture. However, I would point out that your explanation amounts to saying: 'There is no cause for comment on this particular incident, because this is the kind of mistake we make continually and intentionally. We expect the people of every country in the world, Catholics and non-Catholics alike, to understand that our citations are meaningless—the sort of routine compliment that a Caribbean banana republic may hand out.' I do not see how the Holy See's reputation can be improved by this.

I would point out also that the gesture in this case was very widely misunderstood, and continued to be the subject of puzzlement and annoyance not merely to laymen but also to many clerics, who might be expected to understand more easily. It seems that an official statement may be desirable, assuring all Catholics that Papal Honours have no significance.[14]

# 25 In Retrospect

How should one evaluate this entire—largely hidden—episode in the Australian history of the mid-fifties? The historian will make his own assessment. Perhaps a participant, looking at events admittedly from his own viewpoint, may have something to contribute by way of judgement.

The simplest judgement would be the pragmatic one. The national Movement and its basic principles of lay control and binding majority decisions were challenged by the Sydney ecclesiastical authorities. The latter were originally alone in their opposition, but gathered support, for a multitude of reasons, as time went on. In the end the Vatican, importuned by the rebels, intervened to restore peace within the ranks of the Hierarchy. The issues which had originally brought the Movement into existence were treated as of only secondary importance. The consequences for the Labour Movement and the political well-being of Australia were political matters beyond the Vatican's concern. So the Sydney authorities won, the national Movement was defeated—and that was that!

The Vatican's short-term pragmatism can be understood in the light of its dealings with Ireland over the centuries. All that mattered, as in Ireland, was to get the Bishops 'out of politics' and to restore peace with any party likely to become the government of Australia, with which the Church would have to deal. But as I objected later to a Nuncio serving in another country who had previously served in Australia, what if that policy should contribute in the long term to the weakening of, and eventual danger to, Australia and its two million Catholics?

The light-hearted answer was that Rome had lost many more than two million Catholics in many countries over the long course of the history of Christianity. I could only remark that one could not expect the potential victims to be equally philosophical.

The Roman 'finding of fact' as to the nature of the Movement was

228 that it was actually an 'arm' of the Bishops. Consequently it should not engage in trade union struggles or internal party political activities which were not proper to Bishops. The 'finding of fact', in my view, was mistaken: for I knew that the Movement had originally been founded by a tiny handful of lay people, who had simply asked the Bishops for their support (which it was certainly open to them to accord, to refuse, or to accord and then to withdraw), but not for their direction. Nevertheless, there was a great deal of written 'paper' which could be interpreted differently. This was due originally to the fact that future problems were not foreseen. In the later stages of the dispute it was due to the unavailing attempt to meet Sydney in terms of abstract principles, while hoping that, as a result of concessions in principle, Sydney would forbear from seeking to direct practical policies in the midst of an emergency. That was a mistake. It arose from my original conviction that the Sydney authorities were serious when they claimed that they wished merely to 'reform' the Movement, but not to destroy it. It was only after a long period of frustration and adversity that I understood what Murray claims to have been told directly by Archbishop Carroll himself in 1970, that destruction, not reform, was intended.

This matter raises, of course, the issue of propriety. If the elimination of the Movement was the aim of the Sydney authorities, it would have been proper, even if admittedly difficult, to say so: so that apart from the consequences of the Industrial Group defeat on the future of the nation, those who had committed themselves to the Movement, who included not merely its officials, but parliamentarians, union officials and others in public life, might have retreated from exposed positions in good time and good order. That almost sixty parliamentarians should be placed unnecessarily in a situation in which they must sacrifice either their principles or their seats, and that having chosen the latter alternative, so many should have suffered grave economic hardship, was, and remains, inexcusable.

I felt, and feel, that after that particular episode, it will be a long time before parliamentarians, or others in public positions, will be prepared to risk their careers for moral and political principles regarded by the Church as fundamental. The performance of a number of Catholic parliamentarians on the question of abortion, during the seventies, is not unconnected with the crisis of the fifties.

The conflict, of course, was not merely, or even primarily, between different concepts of lay apostolate or different interpretations of canon law. It was a conflict over practical policies to be pursued, once it was known that Evatt and his associates intended to launch a major attack on the entire anti-Communist position. The Sydney position was quite simply that, regardless of any casualties, nothing should jeopardize the unity of the ALP, or the position of Catholics within it. There was considerable force in that argument and I do not blame Archbishop Carroll or anyone else for holding it. Very little is voluntarily conceded to minorities in democratic societies, whether they be Jews, Catholics or Aborigines. As far as Catholics were concerned, their experience in the United States and in Australia was the same. Largely because they were overwhelmingly Irish and working-class in background, they were excluded from many public and professional positions, and, in both countries, from political representation in the parties representing the 'Establishment'. (It would be an interesting exercise, even today, to count the number of Catholics in Liberal parliamentary seats or Cabinet positions.) Hence it was their association, in the USA, with the Democratic and, in Australia, with the Labor Parties respectively which opened up positions in public life previously largely inaccessible to them. The Church ought not to be concerned for the social advancement of its followers. Nevertheless, long centuries of Irish history illustrated the point that if religious allegiance blocked the road to all social advancement, inevitably defections would follow.

This was the Catholic interest in its connection with the ALP, and it was more strongly felt in New South Wales than in other States because in that State Catholicism had originated in the most depressed conditions of a convict society. It was open to any Catholic leader, ecclesiastical or lay, to judge that interest as too valuable to be jeopardized.

Recognizing the force of this argument, quite as much as the Sydney authorities—since my own background in the industrial suburb of Brunswick had built this argument into my blood—I nevertheless disagreed with that judgement in this particular case. This, on two grounds. We were entering into the most revolutionary period in Australian history during which, as a result of both external and internal pressures, the security of Australia would be called into question. In such a period, the Labor Party was not only the political party most at risk, because of Communist penetration of the affiliated unions and the party branches; it was also the party which in office could command the greatest sacrifices from the working-class section of the community, which would be resistant to appeals for national unity if voiced by Liberal governments. It was, by the accident of history, a party with a high proportion of Catholic members who, because of this, had an opportunity of serving the national interest, if only they were shown the road.

Furthermore, while even the best-conceived political strategies had to take their chance on the field of battle, my view was that there was no ultimate risk if either of the two strategies, put to Movement members in different States, were pursued unitedly and resolutely. If the first strategy—the banding together of the three eastern State Executives of the ALP—Victoria, New South Wales, Queensland—behind the Industrial Group position had been permitted to operate,

230 as it could easily have done, it was Evatt and his supporters who would have been faced with the responsibility of effecting a split. I did not believe that they would pursue this course. A split based only on the three smaller States, with considerable defections in each of these, could not possibly have succeeded. Indeed, the Communist organization, so important in the Evatt infrastructure, would have been opposed to it.

When this plan was prevented from being put into operation and the back-up plan—the DLP's guerilla war of attrition—had to be invoked instead, it must have succeeded in bringing the ALP leadership to terms, if the voting exodus to the DLP had not been prevented after the fiasco of the 'peace with honour' settlement in New South Wales in 1956. The proof of this is that even with the DLP reduced to practical insignificance in New South Wales, its strength in Victoria and Queensland in particular was such as to instigate Dr Evatt's offer to resign in return for DLP preferences in 1958. This was followed by the approaches made by Senators Kennelly and McKenna in 1965. With equal strength in New South Wales, it is difficult to believe that the Evatt forces or their successors would not have been brought to terms.

The alternative plan, that the Movement should cut its losses from the very beginning and instruct its members to 'stay in and fight'—the title familiarly given to the alternative strategy—necessarily involved the sacrifice of some of the most prominent Movement and Industrial Group leaders, who would certainly have been expelled from the ALP. These would have had to be abandoned. One argument against this course was that it was dishonourable. Another was that men with deep political interests were hardly likely to associate themselves with a Movement which apparently used them in good times and abandoned them in times of adversity. However, a case could be made for the proposition that the best plan was to accept the casualties, stay inside, and live to fight another day. That plan depended however, on one assumption: that it was acted on unitedly throughout the nation. The adoption of this plan, or any other plan, by the Movement as a national body, would equally have raised the central question. Who was entitled to make binding national decisions? It was because of Sydney's insistence on unilateral and episcopally directed action that it was impossible to solve this fundamental question.

One argument used against the 'back-up' strategy—support for the DLP—revealed a complete misunderstanding of the real objective of the strategy. This was the belief that what was being attempted was the formation of an alternative 'workers' party' which would seek to deprive the ALP of its traditional role as the mass party of the workers, or at least of the organized trade union movement. For this belief there was no justification whatsoever, as was clear to any serious student of the situation.[1]

Whether the reasoning on which the national strategy was based was good or bad, whether the strategy would or would not have succeeded, will never be known. That it was not put to the test was determined not by rational argument, but by moral compulsion relying on a misleading exposition of canon law. Moral compulsion was more effective, and we are assured that effectiveness is the test of political success.

In the broadest terms, the problems involved in the relationship between a political organization and a Church, especially a Church as disciplined as was the Catholic Church until the last fifteen years, are probably insoluble. What begins as an amicable relationship— when the Church needs its laity to organize for a political purpose regarded by the Church as seriously necessary, even though ancillary to its mission—is difficult to maintain for very long. In proportion as the organization is successful, its enemies tend to approach the Bishops with an offer of concessions which to the political organiza- tion appear minimal, but to the Church's leadership, sufficient. The Church's leadership is generally prepared to trust the future to the reopened channels of communication. The temptation to 'do a deal' over the head of the leadership of the organization whose work secured the concessions in the first place is so pressing that only the strongest minds can resist it.

It was so in the case of the Mexican Revolution of the late twenties and early thirties. It was so with the German Centre Party, whose lay leaders saw their party split beneath them when Hitler's offer of both a Concordat and education subsidies to the Vatican and to the German Hierarchy, if they would only ensure that the Centre Party voted for Hitler's Emergency Laws, was accepted.

The problem which faced the Movement in Australia once its leaders became convinced that it was necessary to concert resistance to Communist penetration of the Labour Movement, was that with- out Church backing it would have been impossible to obtain the support of Catholic unionists in sufficient numbers across the nation. Yet that backing could both be given and withdrawn.

The problem was fully understood by Archbishop Mannix and the Bishops who supported him. As a result, he kept close to the lay leadership of the Movement, listened to their estimates and their advice, offering a moderating word in season; refused to interfere with their decisions, and backed them in days of adversity as well as of success. This constant personal friendship, without heavy-handed directions based on his status as an archbishop, was the foundation of a working partnership without which the laity could have made no solid contribution. There is no other sensible approach to an otherwise insoluble dilemma. But it demands a magnanimous mind.

232 | 　　With all of this behind us, we set out, with the name of the National Civic Council, to face the unpredictable challenges of the sixties, the seventies and the eighties. They were to include the building and maintenance of the DLP; the revolutionary changes within all Western societies which accompanied and followed the war in Vietnam; the impact on Australia's strategic situation which arose from the shattering of US military supremacy in the world; and the convulsions which faced Catholic Christianity after the Second Vatican Council.

　　In the midst of all of these great historical events, we were nothing more than tiny minnows, swimming in great and turbulent seas. But even the minnow must do what he can.

# PART IV

## The Sixties and Seventies

# 26 Camelot in a Provincial Setting

The decade of the sixties was a historically significant period not merely for Australia but for the whole of the Western world. It witnessed the highwater mark of American military and political power during the Cuba crisis of October 1962, and its rapid eclipse, marked by the fall of Saigon on 30 April 1975. It is that theme which may perhaps lend a somewhat dubious unity to a period of spreading anarchy.

The spurious grandeur of the Camelot era ended only one year after the Cuba triumph. Camelot was important to one section of Australians since it was this tawdry edifice of sophisticated unreality which Mr Whitlam, with the zest for imitation of the true provincial, attempted to recreate in Australia after his victory in 1972.

The essence of Camelot was the substitution of 'style' for substance. The vocabulary of the intellectual sophisticates with whom the Kennedys delighted to surround themselves placed a disproportionate emphasis on the word 'power' and its uses. It led them to involve the US in the Vietnam War—in my opinion, rightly—which they thereupon insisted on fighting according to a no-win strategy, which brutalized the battlefield, and handed a significant proportion of the US forces over to the drug-pedlars of East and West.

When the enterprise turned sour, they rapidly abandoned the commitment which they themselves had initiated, seeking to shift the responsibility for failure on to the head of Kennedy's Texan successor, Lyndon B. Johnson, whose lack of style they seemed to regard as a personal affront.

The substitution of style for substance was a major factor in the total disaster of Vietnam: total in that, within five brief years from the fall of Saigon, the most powerful nation in the world was seen to be vainly threatening an Iranian mullah in an attempt to recover fifty-odd US Embassy staff whom the latter had taken as hostages, risking a world nuclear confrontation in the process.

236    The disillusionment of Vietnam bred the reaction to Watergate. The American people repudiated the president who had negotiated the withdrawal of American troops and a new *de facto* relationship with Communist China. In his place they elected a president with a minimal knowledge of foreign affairs—according to his National Security Adviser Dr Brzezinski, Carter had no acquaintance with foreign affairs until 1975!—who staffed the White House with a posse of former anti-Vietnam demonstrators; announced that fear of Communism had been banished as a formative influence in US foreign policy; and then, less than four years later, threatened the Soviet Union with nuclear war if it took one further step after the occupation of Afghanistan.

The period of twenty years was marked by a thorough-going revolution in the characteristic attitudes, values and institutions of the Western world. Madison Avenue appropriated the word 'revolution' as still another gimmick in the advertising campaigns of powerful clients trying to separate the hedonist young from their money. It was impossible to disguise the fact that it was a revolution more real than many of the bloodier historical events described by that name. Central to the 'revolution' was the breakdown in the concept of authority, the cement both of ideas and of institutions, in both Church and State.

The specifically religious aspect of that disintegration was witnessed within the Catholic Church. It had entered the Second Vatican Council apparently sure both of itself and of its doctrines, set to attract many of the best minds who might well have been drawn to it as an island of stability in a world of progressive disillusionment. Surprisingly, the Catholic Church was then seen to undergo the self-same crisis, and to fall prey to the self-same disease: the general loss of faith in authority, ideas and institutions.

In the whole of this great drama, the last act of which has yet to be written, and the ultimate upshot of which is unpredictable, Australia and Australians played a very small part. But the revolution of the late sixties affected every aspect of Australian life, modifying the political, social and economic calculations which could validly have been made in 1960, in ways which no one could have foreseen. Hence it furnishes the essential context of seemingly disconnected events, as much in Australia as in every other part of the Western world.

It was perhaps the unexpected incursion of the Vietnamese and Cambodian boat people which intruded a sense of reality into the minds of some Australians. The genocide of Cambodia, which reputedly destroyed something between two and four million out of the seven million inhabitants of that deceptively beautiful oasis of tranquility; the imprisonment, death, or forcible migration of one million Vietnamese, victims of Dr Cairns' celebrated 'quiet revolution' in Vietnam, led to a tragic flight of refugees to Australia and other countries.

There was evidence, although not much, that some Australians were beginning to realize that a tragedy of such magnitude, occurring as close to Darwin as Darwin was to Melbourne, raised questions about Australia's external security. There was no evidence whatsoever that the participants in the demonstrations against the Vietnam War, proportionately as large in Australia as anywhere else in the Western world, ever questioned themselves as to their possible responsibility for what had followed the Communist capture of Phnom Penh and Saigon.

In estimating the significance of the main factors in the revolution of the sixties and seventies, this failure of the intellect was ultimately more disquieting than the failure of authority.

# 27 The National Civic Council

With the 1958 election over, and the defeat of Evatt accomplished, it was only a matter of time before a graceful exit would be arranged for him. The Labor Government was still in office in New South Wales and it duly appointed him to the vacant position of Chief Justice of the Supreme Court.

It was an act of mercy. Whether it was wise as well as merciful so to reward a political leader who, to save his own political life, had been ready to divide the nation along sectarian lines, and to hand his party over to the domination of the euphemistically labelled Socialist Left, was a different question.

In any case, it was not of long duration. As Murray expresses it:

Even the final years were not to be dignified or free of tragedy. Evatt's mental condition had deteriorated markedly, if unevenly, throughout the second half of the decade. Many of the New South Wales Labor men who organized the job for him as a dignified exit from politics, had grave misgivings afterwards. There were many stories of his strange behaviour on the Bench. In 1962 he took leave of absence for a trip abroad, but collapsed while the ship to Europe was still on the Australian coast. His mind had broken down completely. He withdrew from public life and was an invalid until his death in the spring of 1965.[1]

That Dr Evatt was deeply affected by this instability throughout the period in which his actions as Parliamentary Leader of the Labor Party had so profound and deleterious an effect on the future of Australia was known to members of his own staff. It was clear enough that throughout the decisive years he had suffered from some form of psychological disorder so that he is less to be blamed than those who took advantage of him.

At this time, however, the mental health of Dr Evatt was not among our particular concerns. These were essentially practical.

The objectives before us could be briefly summarized:
1 To sustain and extend the National Civic Council, which had taken the place of the old Movement, and to ensure that the

political defeat we had sustained was seen simply as the loss of one battle in a long and continuing war. This involved the establishment of a new basis of legitimacy for the NCC to replace that which had disappeared with the withdrawal of episcopal support for the old Movement.

2 To hold the basic organization and voting strength of the DLP.

3 To maintain a base in the unions, despite the highly unfavourable political situation, and somehow to seek the minimum necessary links with the former Industrial Group leaders in New South Wales. The latter, having managed to survive within the ALP, were naturally afraid of any public association with DLP forces in Victoria, since links of any type might be used to secure their expulsion from the ALP.

4 To overcome the sectarian climate which threatened each of these objectives.

In establishing the NCC, with only a part of the support previously given to the Movement, we had taken a new stand in the conviction that not only had the old union problem revived in virulent form, but that the next twenty years would see the external security of Australia threatened by international factors of a type new to Australia's historical experience.

It was a great advantage that the central corps of officials of the NCC itself had not been seriously affected by defections. Thus the maintenance of the national office, and of national lines of communication, was in a sense the easiest task of all. There were no differences in relation to the basic philosophy of the organization. Hence there were few differences in defining both the major policy objectives and the new processes of organization which a new situation demanded.

The loss of 80 per cent of the Movement membership in New South Wales and 90 per cent in South Australia was compounded by the unremitting hostility of the Catholic ecclesiastical authorities of these States. This alone would make any effort at re-building exceedingly difficult. In overcoming this weakness, the most difficult problem was not even primarily the recruitment of new members to replace the old, but, with the breaking of the links with the Bishops, to discover a new basis of 'legitimacy'.

Many of those who had joined the Movement in the fifties did so primarily out of a sense of religious obligation to meet and, if possible, defeat the Marxist forces which had proved themselves to be the inveterate enemies of Christianity. If the hostility of some Bishops and the enforced neutrality of others would militate against the recruitment of Catholics to the new organization, the bitter sectarian atmosphere which still prevailed militated even more powerfully against the involvement of other members of the community who, despite the Movement's religious basis, might be

*Top:* Malcolm Muggeridge interviewing B. A. Santamaria on television, ATN 7, April 1958

*Bottom:* B. A. Santamaria at National Catholic Rural Movement Convention, Canberra, 1956

attracted by its realism in relation to questions of national security.

The magnitude of the task was constantly emphasized by the additional difficulty of maintaining the DLP, a political party which was new to Australia; whose political strategy was not understood by the community at large; and which constantly laboured under the dual handicap of sectarian antagonism on the one hand, and official Catholic opposition in New South Wales and South Australia on the other. Yet if the DLP was to build up a sufficient electoral following for its guerilla operation to be successful, it had not only to consolidate the branch structure in Victoria, but develop into a genuinely national organization.

Somehow it had to overcome the interstate differences which arose inevitably from the feeling of some Victorian DLP leaders that their allies in New South Wales and Queensland had not joined them at the time of the Hobart Conference, but only belatedly when they themselves were expelled from their own State branches of the ALP. Somehow it had to build up a sufficiently strong, but independent, financial base, to maintain not only its offices and officials in each State, but to run election campaigns in the new and expensive age of television. The Left, of course, said that the money came from either or both the oil companies and the CIA.

Above all, there was a most difficult educational task: to instruct what were originally about half-a-million voters that in marking their ballot papers in Federal and State elections the second preference was as important as the first; and to secure sufficient conviction among the great majority, who had been traditional Labor voters, that they should mark their preferences in favour of the Liberal and against the Labor candidate.

The final task was, of course, to maintain the anti-Communist position in the trade union movement in what was now a position of political isolation. The entire *raison d'être* of the establishment of the Industrial Groups by the Labor Party had been to change the terms of reference of the union fight: from Catholic versus Communist (as it had originally been represented, with the consequent sectarian factor working against the anti-Communists) to Labor versus Communism (in which the balance of opinion would move against the Communists). The loss of ALP endorsement for the Industrial Groups meant the end of the vast advantage which that endorsement represented. That was an advantage compulsorily foregone. In contesting union elections, however, the fact that unionists known to be DLP members belonged to a party which was regularly throwing its preferences against the ALP, and thus preventing the formation of Labor Governments, was an even more formidable handicap. The withdrawal of ALP endorsement from the Industrial Groups brought us back to square one. To mix the metaphor, the casting of preferences against the ALP put us twenty yards behind scratch.

All of the above objectives had to be achieved, if the work which had led us originally to band ourselves together was to continue. We were also at the beginning of what were to prove the two decades of most rapid change in modern history with new and unanticipated responsibilities.

The interests of the NCC were soon to move beyond the political and trade union spheres. From the beginning of the sixties, it became increasingly aware of other institutions which were exerting an increasing influence on public opinion and public policy. Television, introduced into Australia in 1956, was obviously about to revolutionize the impact of the media on public affairs, although the full extent of that influence would not become apparent until the end of the decade, with the reporting of the Vietnam War. The enormous expansion of the Australian universities, and of tertiary education in general, as a result of the policies of the Menzies Government, was to create a new and major influence on public affairs. The products of the rapidly expanded universities and of other tertiary institutions were not only numerically significant in elections, especially in the more affluent suburbs. They possessed almost a monopoly of the education of the members of the political class, the bureaucracy, the media, the teaching and educational services, and even of the clergy. With the expansion of the Welfare State, the greatly inflated Federal, State and municipal bureaucracies would become a major political influence primarily because their leaders were both more permanent and more able than the politicians. The white-collar intelligentsia ever more perceptibly emerged as the class in possession of the new society: and it was the product of the universities which thus gained the political influence they had traditionally held in several European countries but not, until the sixties, in Australia.

In short, the business of seeking to influence public policy was no longer merely a matter of political parties and trade unions. The NCC attempted to provide adequate training, research, and other back-up material for those of its members who found themselves within these agencies and institutions. Granted the paucity of the resources of the NCC, it was arguable that it would have been better to confine oneself to one or two tasks, such as helping the DLP and carrying on the work in the unions. Naturally those of its members who were engaged in each of these fields strongly urged that total priority should be given to the work in which they were engaged. But, as the decade of the sixties wore on, it was apparent that the political and union arenas were ceasing to be decisive in the influencing of public policy. If it was to be an 'information society', it was the repositories of 'information' who mattered increasingly.

So while the ground gained within the traditional areas of action had to be retained, and the necessary work there had to be done, it was necessary to draw a line.

The essential obligations of members of the NCC were thus more clearly formulated than they had been in the earlier Movement days. They were to accept both the opportunities and responsibilities which attached to membership of public organizations; to participate in the formulation of their policies; to accept the task of regular attendance at meetings of the union, the political party, or the other public organization of the member's choice, and in this way to seek to influence the policy of that body, but only within the ambit of its own objectives and its own constitutional processes.

It was the extension of a theory of action which had been learnt originally through membership of the trade unions and the ALP. It offered an opportunity for effective action to almost anyone.

The NCC kept regular contact with its members and supporters primarily through *News Weekly*. Its circulation before the Labor split was approximately 18,000. Dr Evatt's attack sent its circulation up by 11,000. The calculated destruction of its circulation in New South Wales cost it 8,000 weekly copies. Ultimately, through many vicissitudes, it settled down at a more or less regular 20,000 readers, among them a small group of not uninfluential persons in various Southeast Asian countries.

Money remained, of course, the perennial problem. The former access to Catholic parishes was all but completely cut off, even in dioceses of the Bishops who continued to give moral support to the NCC. This was, among other reasons, because we had no wish to embarrass the friendly Bishops in their relationships with the Holy See. However, a strong internal financial organization was set up. The gatherings which had previously been conducted on a parish basis to raise money were now conducted on a community basis instead. It was slowly found that other sections of the community were prepared to give financial support to assist work in which they gradually came to believe, especially as they were often disappointed by the irrelevance of local branches of their political party to national issues. The method of the bank-order was used in an attempt to acquire a permanent financial base without the necessity of constantly going over the same ground. The method has proved generally, although not outstandingly, successful.

With the framework of the NCC thus kept in being, although with varying strength in different States, the immediate practical tasks were those which have been outlined already.

# 28 The Democratic Labor Party

The DLP considered as a political party had its own *raison d'être*, its own policy, constitution, organization and objectives distinct from those of the NCC: and so, in time, it must have its own history, distinct from these personal observations which, while predominantly covering the period of the sixties, begin with the establishment of the DLP in Victoria in 1955.

Since its essential *raison d'être* was to carry through the strategy of attrition, the aim of which was to bring about the re-unification of Labor on the basis of acceptable principles, the DLP also sought objectives similar to those of the NCC in so far as the latter was concerned with matters of defence, foreign, social and economic policy.

While both in Victoria and the other States several of the most prominent figures in the DLP were neither members of the Movement nor even associated with it—Joshua, Riley and Little are Victorian names which come at once to mind—by far the larger part of the work of basic organization had to be done by NCC members. The political leaders of the DLP had to concentrate on the specifically political aspects of their fight—raising money, running elections, making a contribution in the Senate.

A medium-term problem of the DLP was already apparent. It was impossible to ignore the effect of Catholic episcopal support and hostility, respectively, on the electoral fortunes of the Party. Just as the support of Daniel Mannix powerfully assisted in the building of the DLP vote in Victoria, so the opposition of the Cardinal and those who spoke in his name operated equally to limit the effectiveness of the DLP in New South Wales. In Queensland, even the prestige of a State Premier in V. C. Gair could not prevent a rapid erosion of the vote between the 1957 State election—the first after the expulsion of Gair from the ALP—and the next in 1960. In the former, the Queensland Labor Party gained 162,533 votes to elect eleven members of the State Parliament. In the latter it gained 88,724 votes to elect four members.

Victoria was the real heart of DLP support. It must be accepted that the support of Daniel Mannix was a major contributing factor. By 1958 he was already 94 years of age; his expectation of life was limited; and his death, whenever it should occur, would exacerbate the problem of the continuing validation of a political strategy which involved voters who were traditionally Labor in the—to them— distasteful task of preventing the election of Labor governments.

The primary objective in assisting the DLP was to keep it in being for a sufficiently long period to allow its strategy of attrition to work, if ultimately it could be made to work. Because of this limited objective, the DLP vote must be regarded as a wasting asset, which would retain strength only so long as the memories of the issues of 1955 remained alive, and as long as the major issues did not change, as they must if too much time was permitted to pass.

Something over two hundred branches of the old ALP had turned over to the DLP in Victoria as soon as the split was confirmed. The organizational base of the DLP was thus secure throughout that State. There was also a small union base with the affiliation of unions like the Federated Clerks, the Federated Ironworkers' Union and the Motor Transport Union.[1] While the majority of the unions remained affiliated with the ALP, not a few signified their dissatisfaction by refusing to affiliate with either party. For the Victorian branch of the DLP, therefore, the problems of electoral organization and finance, while always severe, were never insuperable.

The need to expand into New South Wales was evident from the beginning. If the DLP had been content with manning the Victorian redoubt, it would have become insignificant. Its strategy needed to be effectively nation-wide, if a sufficiently large number of seats were to be decided by its preferences to make the strategy effective.

When the break came in the New South Wales branch of the Labor Party, the new Party which emerged was entirely different in nature from that in Victoria. It was not a mass party, but a chance collection of persons without any particular ideological unity, held together largely by the strong personality of the State Secretary (and later Senator) J. Kane, and the respect which he and his associate Frank Rooney had won through their dogged fight in the unions and the ALP.

The Movement had been quite strong in Tasmania in the days before the Split. After the Split, it faced none of the problems of the organization in New South Wales. Archbishop Young had always maintained a meticulously strict attitude in relation to the independence of the Movement. He had been prepared to court misunderstanding for years by his insistence on the joint principles: the Movement should not use the authority of the Bishops as an argument to win support for its policies; the Bishops should not interfere with the existence or autonomy of the Movement. Once the Movement clearly took this position by separating itself from the Bishops, he made it clear that he favoured its stand and that of the DLP. The whole of the old Movement organization in Tasmania was put at the disposal of the DLP without any conflict of loyalties. The adherence to the DLP of the Tasmanian Senator, Cole, meant that the DLP had parliamentary representation in that State from the beginning.

The strength of the DLP in Tasmania, and indeed beyond it, was increased because of the persecution of two ordinary Tasmanian watersiders, the Hurseys—father and son—by the Communist–ALP leadership of the Waterside Workers' Federation. The two Hurseys were driven out of their union and consequently out of their water-front employment because, as members of the DLP, they refused to pay a political levy which went to the ALP. It was a particularly dis-graceful reflection on the condition of Australian law at the time that it furnished no protection to them, nor ensured that they were restored to their employment. It was ironic that the 'small l' liberals who had agonized over the performance of the Petrov Royal Commission, allegedly because it had damaged the careers and prospects of innocent people—although no single example of such a person has ever been given—never once made any protest concern-ing the Hurseys. The Hursey Case gave the DLP a strong local issue, clearly associated with the more general issue of Communist influence, around which to campaign. The initial position of the DLP in Tasmania was therefore relatively strong.

While smaller branches opened up in South Australia and Western Australia, it was Queensland which was critical to the national structure of the DLP. I had little doubt that while Dr Evatt would have wished to call it quits with the dismissal of the Victorian and New South Wales Labor Party Executives, without carrying the Split further into Queensland—his approaches to Archbishop Duhig providing some evidence of this—the strong Queensland branch of the Communist Party, which had controlled the Queensland Trades and Labour Council for years, was in no mood to be left without its share of the spoils of war.

Gair, as Premier of the State, was well aware of the situation and knew that the day of retribution would come for him as well. His belief was based on his judgement that both parties to the unnatural alliance of previously hostile forces—the Australian Workers' Union and the Communist-led unions—would demand tangible rewards as the price of their participation in the nation-wide onslaught on the Industrial Groups; and that it would be impossible for them to be certain of maintaining whatever political gains they made as long as Gair was permitted to remain as Premier. Hence Gair awaited the inevitable attack.

This came with the splitting of his government by a majority decision of the Queensland Executive in 1957. Gair believed that he would gain a significant electoral advantage in the ensuing State election if his party (which included the whole of the former Cabinet, with the exception of the Minister for Transport, Mr Duggan) presented the Queensland break as a specifically Queensland affair, arising from reasons distinct from those which had caused the pre-existing divisions in Victoria and New South Wales. It was an appeal to Queensland 'nationalism' almost twenty years before Mr Bjelke-Petersen used it with such effect against Mr Whitlam and his colleagues. Accordingly, Gair contested the election as the leader of the Queensland Labor Party. The tactical decision was originally advantageous; for although Gair could not win enough seats to save his government, the QLP, headed by Gair, won 11 seats, compared with the 21 won by the official ALP. The issue, however, was fundamentally the same as that involved in the split in the southern States. The additional votes obtained over and above those who might have voted for a Queensland branch of the DLP, through emphasis on specifically Queensland issues, lost interest and went back to one or other of the major parties. The QLP soon merged with the DLP.

By the early 1960's, therefore, the minimum organizational base needed to make feasible the DLP's strategy of attrition had been achieved. The Party had broken out of Victoria into every State, although with different degrees of strength. It had approximately 500,000 primary votes throughout the Commonwealth. The second preference votes were generally firmly disciplined, especially in Victoria, although subject to State variations. Malcolm Mackerras has estimated that from 1958 to 1969, over Australia as a whole, 81.5 per cent of all DLP preferences went against the ALP. In Victoria the percentage rose to 86.1 per cent.[2]

The DLP in addition had somewhat unexpectedly won representation in the Senate—originally in Tasmania and Victoria, but to be followed by Queensland and New South Wales. This was due to the accidental fact that elections for the Senate were conducted under a system of proportional representation. While it was the effect of the highly organized second preferences being repeatedly thrown against the ALP, and often depriving the ALP of government, which was the only finally important factor in the DLP strategy, the DLP's capacity to elect Senators was, naturally, not to be despised. It guaranteed a parliamentary voice for the Party's policies and it created a small group of publicly known political leaders. The fact that Senate elections offered the chance of actually electing DLP representatives to Parliament meant that from 1961 onwards, until the end of the decade, the DLP always attracted a better total vote for Senate than for House of Representatives elections.[3]

The advantage of being able to project well-known figures like Gair, McManus, Cole, Byrne and later Kane, compared with the relative unknowns who comprised the bulk of DLP candidates, offered particular advantages to the Party's prospects in the States which they represented. In 1970 (a year which was marked by persistent disillusionment with the Liberal Government led by Mr Gorton), McManus actually polled 19.2 per cent of the total vote in Victoria, not far short of the percentage required to elect two Senators from the one State. It was similar in Queensland, where Gair, well-known as a former Premier, polled 16.4 per cent of the vote in the same election.

Electing parliamentarians was a far more comprehensible political objective than the constant denial of office to the ALP. The latter was the one strategic objective which really mattered, but it allowed its enemies to represent the DLP as a 'nark' party.

It is traditional that on those occasions on which Senate elections are held apart from elections for the House of Representatives, voters can cast a protest vote without risking putting the Opposition into government. On these occasions it was possible for non-DLP voters to cast a protest vote for the DLP without affecting the Liberal Government's tenure of office. This was proved by the fact that when the Senate and Representatives elections came together again in the double dissolution of 1974, the DLP Senate vote fell away drastically and the DLP lost its entire parliamentary representation in one blow. The Whitlam Government's programme had completely polarized the electorate. Furthermore, a new—and numerous—voting generation had come into being which either did not understand or was no longer interested in the DLP's purposes. So the electorate voted overwhelmingly for one or other party which might conceivably become the government. The DLP Senate representation was eliminated.

Within the DLP itself, the election of DLP Senators had naturally strengthened the argument of those who held the view that the time was ripe to promote a 'third' or 'Centre' Party in Australia, and that this was the more rational objective at which to aim. It is difficult to estimate how widely or seriously this view was held. If this view had taken root, a conflict of strategies would have been inevitable. If the majority had swung to make the real aim of the DLP the creation of a 'Centre' Party which might hope to form part of a coalition, it would have been essential only to maximize the primary vote. There would, then, be occasions on which it would be sensible to allot second preferences to the ALP, whether because it was the most convenient way of marking the ballot-paper or as part of an inter-party bargain. Under these circumstances, it would be impossible to maintain a completely disciplined vote—which was indispensable if the aim was to be the different one of 'stone-walling' the ALP, until it was forced to an agreement with the DLP to re-create one anti-Marxist Labor Party.

A clear decision had therefore to be made as to the Party's essential strategy. The overwhelming majority view from the very first days of the DLP was that its aim should be success in the strategy of attrition, wearing down the ALP until it was forced to an agreement in harmony with the minimum principles of the DLP. The nature of the strategy and the success which attended its strictly limited aim were described succinctly by Reynolds:

From its first electoral contests, the party was interested in excluding the ALP from office and thereby forcing a reconciliation on DLP terms. If Labor refused to negotiate, it would face the prospect of being out of power indefinitely, and such a situation might well place intolerable strains on the party, perhaps resulting in a further split. If this occurred, the DLP could then merge with that faction which favoured a reunion, thereby facilitating the return to power of a 'renewed' ALP purged of its left-wing and pro-Communist elements. To this end, therefore, the DLP consistently allocated its preferences to the Liberal or Country Parties, with the result that the government's position was strengthened in the elections of 1958,1963 and 1966, while its defeat was averted in 1961 and 1969. Over this period, the ALP refused to consider reuniting with the DLP, despite occasional overtures from individuals on both sides, and the DLP responded by continuing to deny the ALP its second preferences.[4]

I was never under any illusions that success, in these terms, would be easily achieved. I recall explaining this strategy in two discussions with distinguished European political figures who visited Australia in the early days of the DLP experiment: the West German Foreign Minister, von Brentano, in 1957; and the British Labour politician, Anthony Crosland, in 1963. Both were strongly anti-Marxist and prepared to accept that if the DLP could hold its vote for a sufficiently long period, one day the ALP would be forced to come to terms. But I could see that neither rated the chances very highly.

As for myself, I did not believe that the alternate objective—of attempting to build the DLP into a permanent party of the Centre—was either possible or desirable. It was natural that some of the leaders among the European migrant groups—the strictly numerical importance of whose votes was never as large as commonly believed, but nevertheless was not insignificant—should think in terms of a Christian Democratic Party. For good or evil such a party was outside the Australian historical tradition, which in its political expression was completely secularist. Historical traditions are not easily changed. Furthermore, even in Italy, Germany and Holland, where Christian Democrat parties were most successful, they relied not only on a historical tradition strongly represented in public life over centuries, but on a degree of ecclesiastical assistance inconceivable at any time in Australia, but doubly so after the tumultuous events of the late fifties.

250

DLP Senators C. Byrne, F. P.
McManus, V. C. Gair, J. Little and
J. T. Kane

The most important reason of all for arguing against following that signpost was, however, that it had no relationship with the basic reason which had originally brought the Industrial Groups into existence. That reason was to keep the Australian Labour Movement, but especially the unions, free of Communist control. The only major political party traditionally associated with the trade union movement was the Labor Party. A strategy which would take the DLP in a totally different direction—even in the unlikely contingency that it won parliamentary representation in the Lower House—would have no relationship with the original and central purpose of work which had already lasted two decades.

The Party must therefore, by definition, remain within the Labor framework. While every vote was valuable in bidding up the DLP's hand, it was clear that the DLP's position within a reunified Party would depend on the proportion of its voters who were likely to follow its leadership back into the ALP.

Despite the fact that it turned its face resolutely against a concept as attractive in principle as Christian Democracy, the DLP in its perennial attempt to widen its base continued to be dogged by the sectarian weapon, which never lost its potency. In the light of Dr Evatt's own earlier relationships with the Movement, and of his attempts subsequent to the Split to open up some kind of relationship with the Catholic Bishops, the use of anti-Catholicism to damage the DLP was completely cynical. The Victorian Labor Legislative Council member, J. M. Tripovich—speaking naturally with an eye to Catholic votes—said that 'it is completely false to say that the DLP has the backing of the Catholic Church'.[5] The Sydney *Bulletin* pertinently pointed out that it was unfair to call the DLP a 'Church Party' since 'it has spent much of its time and energy helping Protestant Liberals defeat Catholic Laborites . . . Indeed, a case may be made out for the D.L.P. as an anti-clerical party, at least in N.S.W.'.[6]

Naturally, the more that the largely Catholic base of the DLP was emphasized, the less chance it had of proving attractive to voters of other persuasions. The support of the NCC was indispensable to the DLP in all States, and not merely in the field of organization. It was continually necessary to remind its supporters of their long stake in the anti-Communist struggle. This could not merely be done privately. But when the influence of the NCC in the DLP was constantly emphasized, through such lurid publications as *The Black Hand of Santamaria* (tens of thousands of copies of which were originally published and later reprinted by several Communist-led unions), some of the DLP leaders naturally felt that public association with the NCC was damaging to their constant attempt to widen their electoral appeal. This bred a certain amount of tension.

Since the myth of 'secrecy', which had been used with such great effect throughout the Split, had to be overcome, for the sake of both organizations, the NCC decided that it must use every opportunity to wear it down. The NCC determined to be as 'visible' as possible, and never to miss any opportunity of explaining itself and its policy on the media. The opportunities were few and far between, since the NCC suffered from the same media hostility as the DLP.

So it was with open arms that the NCC embraced the opportunity offered to me by Archbishop Mannix in 1960 to appear weekly on the Melbourne Catholic television session *Sunday Magazine*. The Archbishop's decision was only made after the 'Catholic Hour' Committee, which ran the television session, had run out of alternative commentators on world affairs. Previous commentators had proved unsuited to the new medium. The invitation offered an opportunity, of which the NCC was glad to avail itself, as the only means of reaching a relatively significant mass public. In this way we might attempt gradually to overcome the misleading and harmful propaganda to which both the NCC—and derivatively the DLP—had alike been subject for nearly seven years without any opportunity for an effective reply.

The problem created by the decision of the NCC to use television as the only way of refuting the charge of secrecy was that it meant giving prominence to the NCC, focussing on it nearly as much attention as on the DLP. My own regular weekly public appearances helped those who, not always innocent of the desire to cause divisions, represented me as a kind of 'grey eminence' of the DLP, playing continually on the allegedly Machiavellian connotations of an Italian name.

It was obvious that the Left had both the DLP and the NCC 'going and coming'. If the NCC did not explain and defend its position publicly, it would be effectively destroyed by the sectarian campaign, with not insignificant consequences for the DLP. If it did promote its policies publicly, it made the task of those who, by continually emphasizing the NCC's influence, sought to damage the DLP, easier than it would have been if the NCC had opted for a subterranean existence.

Accepting that there would be disadvantages and losses either way, I thought that the better course for the DLP was simply to stand by the historical record: that the DLP was the lineal descendant of the Industrial Groups, formed to carry on their fight by means of the only political strategy available after the expulsions from the ALP; that there had been a close connection between the Movement and the Industrial Groups; that the NCC had supported the DLP from the beginning and that its support was welcome. This was, in fact, the view taken and publicly expressed by the DLP Federal President, Robert Joshua, former MHR for Ballarat. He stated that NCC support of DLP objectives was 'open and undisguised', of 'inestimable value and . . . appreciated by all those who had our principles at heart'.[7]

The more thoroughly one examined the identity of the characteristic DLP voter the stronger this argument seemed.

Although I did not have the advantage of the surveys—of varying validity, some utterly fanciful—taken later to establish the profile of the characteristic DLP voter, I had little doubt of the identity of the social grouping on which it would be compelled to rely. The evidence assembled by Reynolds[8] led that writer to a twofold conclusion. He wrote:

It is grossly misleading to talk about the DLP as being based on 'the Catholic vote'. There is very little evidence to suggest that there is anything resembling a solid phalanx of Catholics who will vote *en masse* in a certain direction for reasons connected with religion. It is doubtful whether the DLP has ever had the support of a majority of Catholics in Victoria, and at no stage has the party ever had, or looked like having, the support of a majority of Catholics in other states.[9]

On the other hand, Reynolds added,

It can be inferred from this evidence that the DLP does not attract 'the Catholic vote', but does have an attraction for a specific type of Catholic voter. Mol[10] sheds further light on this special Catholic support . . . [His] information reveals the group to be orthodox and devout in their religious beliefs and practices, while further indication of their very close connection with the church was given by Mol when he showed that Catholics who had attended church schools were twice as likely to prefer the DLP as those who had gone to state schools.[11]

At no stage did I have any doubt that with all of its strengths and weaknesses, this social group was the essential electoral base of the DLP; that since it was not primarily interested in electoral success, it was the one force which really mattered in the fulfilment of the DLP's strategy; and that being what it was, it would not be held to its political loyalty merely by appeals from political leaders on purely political grounds. How to ensure the continuity of this support, in the event of the death of Archbishop Mannix, was an ever-present problem.

What could not be envisaged was the effect on the DLP vote and, indeed on the entire anti-Communist effort, of the gradual—and at first almost imperceptible—disappearance of the type of Catholic described by Reynolds and by Mol, as the result of the doctrinal turbulence within the Catholic Church in the aftermath of the Second Vatican Council. If that could have been foreseen, it would have been even more obvious that there was a strict time-limit on the possibilities of success of the DLP's campaign.

Murray correctly sums up the course and the ultimate effect of this particular problem:

Many well known names fell away from the DLP in the succeeding year or years, but sufficient remained and sufficient new blood was recruited to keep it astonishingly effective. The 'Santamaria' and 'centre party' issues recurred from time to time, but never ruinously.[12]

One question which was constantly in my mind was whether on balance it would not be better if I ceased all activity, hoping as a consequence to eliminate the constant damage to both the NCC and the DLP by their association with a name which during the Split had been given such unfavourable connotations. This would allow both the NCC and the DLP to take their own chances. The real problem in such a decision was its likely effect on the morale of the leading members of the NCC, who had suffered such bitter blows both from enemies and from former friends. To leave them would be interpreted as an act of desertion at the very moment when the future of both organizations was highly conjectural.

To this consideration, one had to add the peculiarly New South Wales factor.

If building up the strength of both organizations in New South Wales was almost a condition *sine qua non* of the effectiveness of the strategy of attrition, there was one aspect of the problem which, if it was capable of solution, could only be solved by myself. That problem was that in the eyes of those New South Wales Catholics who had previously been associated with or influenced by the Movement, and whose goodwill was important, the manifold blunders and villanies attributed to the national Movement were particularly associated with myself. After the death of Dr Mannix in November 1963, as a result of a strange combination of circumstances, Sydney became accessible to the weekly television session 'Point of View'. Perhaps by dint of continuous, persistent, personal explanation through the medium of television, in which one was personally seen and heard, New South Wales Catholics and others might be persuaded to look beyond the official propaganda line and to make up their own minds, on the basis of their personal observation and evaluation.

The opportunity came about through an expected, and therefore unsurprising, event following immediately on the death of Archbishop Mannix. My companion on the Catholic TV session 'Sunday Magazine' was Fr John Cahir, whose segment dealt with specifically spiritual subjects and with whom I was on friendly, if not close, terms. Fr Cahir was also a close friend of Archbishop Simonds, who had now succeeded Dr Mannix. We had often joked about what would take place when Dr Simonds came to power. I had told Fr Cahir that my part on 'Sunday Magazine' would not last long beyond the life of Archbishop Mannix. His reply was that I did not understand the Coadjutor-Archbishop, who was a man of great generosity of spirit and who, when he succeeded to the Archdiocese, would act with prudent deliberation. So, long before, I had bet him a pound that I would get my marching orders within twenty-four hours of Dr Mannix's funeral. As it turned out, I 'walked it in'. My dismissal from 'Sunday Magazine' came exactly sixteen hours later! Fr Cahir was an honest punter, and paid up.

This dismissal, which raised as great a furore among friends and supporters as it occasioned delight among enemies, was likely to be understood—once again!—as signifying a further withdrawal of support, without which the work of the NCC, whatever its constitution might state, could not go on. I was thus forced quickly to give a public indication of the decision I had already taken about the future of the work. To a press which was always much more ready to give space to our defeats than to any victories or even to our viewpoints, I issued the following statement:

I was officially informed yesterday that my part in Sunday Magazine had terminated as from the preceding Sunday.

Sunday Magazine is under the personal direction of the Archbishop of Melbourne.

Archbishop Simonds is completely entitled to make whatever arrangements he believes to be best in connection with this session.

I am grateful for the opportunity which this medium has afforded me for any good I was able to do through it over the past three years—and to the late Archbishop Mannix for the opportunity he gave me.

The medium of television was a valuable adjunct to my work.

The fact that these facilities are no longer available does not mean any alteration or interruption in the work of opposing Communist influences in public life.

The need has never been greater. With God's help, our response will match this need.[13]

Although I had been under no illusion that dismissal from 'Sunday Magazine' would come quickly, as the most public action the new Archbishop could take to reverse the Mannix policies, and as a clear indication of his opposition both to the NCC and to myself personally, his precipitate action in fact worked to the NCC's benefit.

It was rightly regarded by many Catholics, who were suffering a deep sense of personal loss at the death of Daniel Mannix, as an attack on the policy and memory of the dead Archbishop. It thus helped to consolidate the Mannix tradition not only among the laity, but among the overwhelming majority of the Victorian clergy (and the pro-Mannix clergy in other States).

The one immediate practical advantage gained from my summary dismissal by the new Archbishop from an obscure TV programme was both unexpected and ironic. My dismissal was to date from 10 November. The Menzies policy speech was on 12 November, with the Federal elections due on 30 November.

Some three days after my dismissal I received a phone call from Sir Frank Packer, whom I had never met, asking whether I would like to appear on Channel 9 in both Melbourne and Sydney at peak viewing time (6.30 p.m.) on the following Sunday to explain my position. I answered that such a statement would have little effect, but that if he would permit me to develop a new (but similar) session on Channel 9 for three months, I would be glad to accept his invitation. He accepted this proposal.

So I appeared on Channel 9 on the following Sunday night, 17 November. One of Mr Menzies' own election telecasts followed immediately. This might have tickled my vanity had I not understood that the political purpose of the juxtaposition was to consolidate the DLP vote, which might have been shaken and weakened by the death of the Archbishop.

The re-christened 'Point of View' thereupon appeared for the next three months. Before that period had elapsed, I succeeded in convincing Sir Frank that if he were interested in the anti-Communist struggle, and not merely in advancing the political fortunes of the Liberal Party, there was a point in continuing the session. On this basis, 'Point of View' continued to appear on a Sunday morning—when no rational individual should be watching TV. It appeared originally before a session entitled World Famous Wrestlers, and later, after Humphrey Bear! However, the Channel 9 session has ultimately spread to some twenty channels in every State of Australia, in most of which the TV time is paid for by local committees of supporters who have raised the not inconsiderable sums involved.

Although it represented a considerable expenditure of time away from other NCC duties—since there were neither research workers nor script-writers—the organization always regarded the use of television has having a twofold value.

As the well-known Australian journalist, Sam Lipski, pointed out in relation to the Melbourne *Age*, some sections of the media discriminated significantly against the DLP, compared for instance with their later treatment of Senator Chipp's Australian Democrats.[14] This naturally extended to the NCC as well. More damaging was the fact that every stupidity uttered or perpetrated by any anti-Communist, however 'way out', was described as a 'DLP attitude'. (This public image of DLP attitudes became so harmful that many years later, even a Professor Peter Wiles, having stated his own viewpoint on Australia's strategic situation in terms identical with the DLP analysis, added: 'I do not want to sound like a member of the DLP'.)[15]

'Point of View' enabled about half-a-million viewers each week to hear the NCC viewpoint, and to judge for themselves whether NCC viewpoints were as backward, reactionary, or even stupid, as the persistent caricatures of their opponents asserted them to be. In this way, because 'Point of View' came to appear weekly in every State, in all State capitals except Hobart, and to cover extensive provincial and country areas, the NCC was helped to maintain its support throughout the Commonwealth, and to withstand potentially fatal blows like the later fading of the DLP. We therefore had good reason to be grateful to Sir Frank Packer for his utterly unexpected interest at a moment when we were apparently threatened with oblivion.

This problem of legitimacy or validation was referred to, in a somewhat different way, by two writers who dealt with the question of the return of DLP voters to the ALP in the event of a satisfactory agreement between the two parties. P. J. Duffy, SJ,[16] refers to his own view and that of Peter Coleman (later leader of the New South Wales Parliamentary Liberal Party):

> Senator McManus' estimate of 70-80 per cent of D.L.P. voters returning to a reunited A.L.P. seems optimistic; even 50 per cent might be a generous estimate. Perhaps Mr Santamaria's forceful advocacy might raise the figure to 70 per cent, if and when the reunion is imminent, but only, as Mr Coleman has observed, 'if he can prove to the D.L.P. voters that they would still be voting for the D.L.P.'.[17]

The conviction which would have had to be imparted was not so much that DLP voters 'would still be voting for the DLP', as that the fundamental attitudes and principles which had led traditional ALP voters not only to vote against the ALP but to give their second preference to the Liberals were in fact being observed in both the formal terms and likely consequences of a settlement.

The 1961 Federal election saw the Menzies Government win, but only with a majority of two seats. It showed how frail was the thread by which the DLP strategy hung. In the event of a further rise in unemployment which accompanied the recession of that year, the next election would be fought under circumstances even more favourable to Mr Calwell, who might then be expected to win back some Catholic votes, as Evatt could not. Mr Menzies obviously recognized this danger, by directing his government to follow an essentially inflationary policy in order to end the recession at whatever cost.

The Australia-wide vote for the DLP's House of Representatives candidates fell from 9.4 per cent in 1958 to 8.7 per cent in 1961, although the specifically Victorian segment of the DLP vote did rise (from 14.8 per cent to 15.1 per cent), and the Australia-wide Senate vote, as distinct from that in the Lower House, rose as well.

The progressive erosion of the DLP vote in the House of Representatives continued thereafter: from 8.7 per cent in 1961 to 7.4 per cent in 1963, to 7.3 per cent in 1966, to 6 per cent in 1969, to 5.3 per cent in the year of the Whitlam victory in 1972. The Senate vote was consistently higher. After 1961 Senate elections were held separately from those for the House of Representatives, a fact which helped the DLP to gain part of a normally Liberal protest vote when the fate of the government was not at stake. Nevertheless, the line of downward development was clear. The further that events moved from the injustices of 1955, the more the memories tended to fade,

258 | especially as death progressively claimed some of the best of the first solid core on which the Party was founded.

The results of the 1963 election, which after the near-disaster of 1961 Mr Menzies won comfortably, confirmed me in the belief that the DLP vote, which had held for eight difficult years, was essentially a wasting asset. This was the very election in which the fact that the DLP existed, and that its vote was of sufficient importance to the Liberals, forced the 1963 breakthrough in the field of State Aid for independent schools.* If the section of the electorate which was primarily concerned with State Aid was sufficiently intelligent to understand what was happening, the logic of the situation was that they should add to the strength of the DLP vote, if they were not voting DLP already. This did not happen. It was the Liberal vote which benefited primarily.

After 1963, even before the new voting generation of the post-Vietnam period made its appearance and began to invalidate previous political preconceptions, I was conscious of the fact that the strategy of attrition had better win soon, or it would not win at all.

The former Federal Secretary of the ALP, who was now Senator Kennelly, apparently drew quite a different conclusion from the 1963 result. As he saw it, after the near-win of 1961, 1963 showed that Labor was as far as ever from office—and life was marching on. There was not much consolation in a possible victory in the seventies if one was not there oneself to enjoy the Treasury benches. The DLP vote was still 7.4 per cent across the nation, while the ALP and the LCP were locked together with 45.5 per cent and 46 per cent of the vote respectively. The DLP preferences were still overwhelmingly against the ALP. The DLP was obviously capable of playing a highly significant role for some years ahead. As far as Senator Kennelly was concerned the strategy of attrition was still too well on course to be ignored.

To my surprise a friend of Senator Kennelly's contacted me and said that it was time for an exploratory discussion to determine whether the regrettable differences between the parties could be ironed out. While I believed that it was urgent to test any possibilities of settlement while the DLP vote was still a major factor, to participate in such a discussion was extremely risky. I had little reason to trust anyone who had been involved in the proceedings of the mid-fifties, least of all the architect of 'the numbers', who had put his mathematical skills behind Evatt's crude sectarianism. Still, it was even more risky for him, and there was a real need to explore the ground.

The proposal was discussed with the leadership of the DLP, including Senators Gair and McManus, and the future Senator,

---

* See Ch. 29.

Kane. They thought I should proceed, so long as discussions were purely exploratory, and so long as it was made clear that I was not representing the DLP, but was simply there to see whether a sufficient measure of agreement was possible to enable more official discussions to take place. I took with me the Federal Secretary of the NCC, Norm Lauritz. We met Senators McKenna (ALP Senate Leader) and Kennelly (ALP Senate Deputy Leader) in the Yarraville home of one of Kennelly's friends.

There were half-a-dozen meetings on consecutive Saturday nights during the winter of 1965. Senator Kennelly made it clear that the reasons which had brought him to the table were purely pragmatic. He liked us no better in the mid-sixties than in the mid-fifties. He was now convinced, he said, that the DLP preferences could be 'turned on and off like a tap'. At the end of six meetings, we had hammered out a large measure of agreement both as to the policy of a re-united ALP, and as to the representation which the DLP could expect at all levels (including the parliamentary) in a re-united party, to guarantee that the policy changes would not be merely superficial. Quite miraculously, the existence and the content of the discussions were kept confidential by both sides.

The two Labor Senators were aware that any such proposals would precipitate a major convulsion and, almost certainly, another split in the ALP. For them, the risks were therefore quite substantial. They were prepared to take the risks because they believed that the 'hiving-off' of the extreme Left would not cost the new ALP many votes, while the adherence of the DLP would restore the necessary lost votes to form a government.

As with all policies, the vital question became 'How?' The two Senators thought that if the four Parliamentary Leaders of the Labor Party backed the settlement, the result could be achieved. This meant seeking the support of the Leader (A. A. Calwell) and the Deputy-Leader (E. G. Whitlam) in the House of Representatives. The other two Parliamentary leaders—the Senators—were present in the room. At the last two of our meetings, whether accurately or not, they said that they had reported their discussions to their two colleagues, that Mr Whitlam was favourable, but that Mr Calwell was passionately, indeed obsessively, opposed to any deal. So it stayed—and so the opportunity vanished.

If Mr Calwell never achieved his overwhelming ambition of becoming Prime Minister, it was thus probably as a result of his own obsessiveness. As for myself, it was fortunate that it was the ALP parties to our discussions who, to their own regret, were compelled to break them off. When I reported the final prospects to the DLP leadership—whom Lauritz and I had kept informed throughout— they indicated that they now wished to take over the discussions themselves, which was in accord with our original arrangement. I was uncertain as to whether, if the ALP leaders had persisted, a final settlement would actually have been achieved.

In the course of the two months of discussions, I came to know Senator Kennelly at least a little better. He was a professional politician, primarily concerned with the acquisition and maintenance of political power. I was surprised, however, at how far he was prepared to carry pragmatism. It was at one of these meetings that he told me what a 'bloody fool' I had been not to get him expelled from the ALP in 1953. Like most others who got to know Kennelly, I found him personally a man full of worldly wisdom, both likeable and amusing.

These abortive 1965 discussions ended any real prospect for the realization of the DLP's strategy. Mr Whitlam became leader of the Parliamentary Party after the 1966 election. For a while—during the long drama in which the Left sought to expel the Secretary of the Tasmanian Trades and Labour Council (Brian Harradine) from the ALP as a residual 'Grouper'—Whitlam pursued a right-wing policy to the point of encouraging Harradine to fight the Left. Whitlam's attack on Harradine's enemies resulted in a challenge to his ALP leadership by Dr Cairns, who pressed the issue to a vote of Labor's Parliamentary Caucus. Dr Cairns failed to unseat Whitlam by a bare six votes, recording thirty-two to Whitlam's thirty-eight. Mr Whitlam suddenly understood the facts of life, and reversed his right-wing orientation, in a much less dramatic but equally decisive way as Dr Evatt had reversed his pro-Industrial Group policy after the defection of the Petrovs. The profound swing of Labor opinion in relation to Vietnam in 1968 led Mr Whitlam to make the ritual transformation which alone would ensure his survival as leader.

# 29 The Struggle for State Aid

While the fact that the DLP vote was essentially a wasting asset led me to favour discussions with Senators McKenna and Kennelly in 1965, it was highly aggravating to find the DLP, inescapably, functioning as the main effective cause of the constant re-election of Liberal governments, without any recognition by the Liberals that they owed something in return. That virtue should be its own reward is a sound moral principle, but an extremely arid political principle. DLP preferences cost the ALP seventeen of its thirty-six seats in the 1955 Victorian election. Three years later, after the 1958 Federal election, the ALP's own spokesmen stated that the Liberal–Country Party coalition won twenty or twenty-one of its thirty-eight seats on DLP preferences. As P. J. Duffy, SJ, writes:

In the last eleven years there have been 26 federal and state lower house elections throughout Australia. The non-Labor parties have won 19 of them, the A.L.P. only 7: 3 in N.S.W., 2 in Tasmania, and one each in South Australia and West Australia. The D.L.P., with its policy of preference-distribution away from the A.L.P. and in favour of Labor's opponents, has played a major part in that sharing out of electoral prizes.[1]

The prizes unfortunately all went to the Liberals. For them the electoral strategy of the DLP and the firmness with which it was pursued were literally manna from heaven. Mr Menzies saw the situation with a perspicacity which none of his successors demonstrated.

After the near-defeat of the Liberals in 1961, I felt that something should be done to alter this rather absurd situation. Throughout 1962, the Liberals lived through the perpetual trauma that one death in their ranks would force them to the polls, in which event it was commonly believed that they would face electoral massacre. Early in 1962 I discussed the relevance of the narrow Liberal margin with Archbishop Mannix, and suggested to him that the time was ripe for him to make another approach to the Federal Government, to enquire whether they might not see the virtue of reversing their traditional opposition to State Aid.

262

He agreed with the suggestion but proposed instead that I should discuss the matter on his behalf with the Federal Treasurer (Mr Holt), with whom I had something better—though not much better—than a passing acquaintance. In the subsequent interview with Mr Holt, I was amazed at how downcast that normally equable politician was. It was obvious that, as Treasurer, he was receiving much of the blame for the financial measures which had brought the Menzies Government to near-defeat in 1961.

For nearly eighty years, the education injustice—suffered in particular by Catholic families, but more widely by all families with children in independent schools—had been the subject of countless speeches at Catholic functions. From 1913 to 1916, the attempt of the Catholic Federation to redress the grievance by electoral means had ended in failure and in the expulsion of a number of prominent Catholics from the Labor Party.

The reason for the continual record of failure was not far to seek. It was commonly understood that by far the greater proportion of the votes of Catholics was safely in Labor hands. There was therefore no need for Labor to bid for them. The Liberals, being the party of the White Anglo-Saxon Protestant ascendancy, were not only tradition- ally unsympathetic to Catholic influence, but saw no practical political purpose in seeking any of those votes for themselves. If some far-sighted leader had thought of offering State Aid in return for the votes of a majority of Catholics—and, improbably, had been able to get away with it in his own party—it would have seemed a foolish strategy since by far the greater proportion of Catholic votes were unshakeably attached to the Labor Party.

As fervent a Catholic as James Scullin, Prime Minister of Australia from October 1929 to Janury 1932, had in fact opposed the Catholic Federation campaign of 1915-16. As he saw the situa- tion, the economic gains which the working class—to which the vast majority of Catholics belonged—would obtain from a Labor Government, far outstripped anything which could be gained by State Aid, a campaign for which would threaten the unity of the Labor Party.

The interview with Mr Holt confirmed that the Government had given no consideration to tackling the State Aid question. The meagre concessions which the Federal authorities had offered to independent schools in the Australian Capital Territory were regarded as exceptions, based simply on the fact that the Federal Government had to meet the concrete problems created by the mass transfer of Commonwealth public servants from Melbourne and Sydney to Canberra.* They were not seen as a precedent. The

* The Federal Government undertook to cover interest payments on loans for construction of independent schools in the ACT, to a level of 5 per cent and of twenty years' duration.

Government's attitude was still based on the strictly legalistic position that Section 116 of the Constitution precluded the Commonwealth from providing financial assistance to religious schools.

The argument I put to Mr Holt was simple. In 1961 the DLP preferences had gone solidly against the ALP, despite the force of the economic recession which nearly took the ALP to power. Without the DLP preferences the Government would certainly have been defeated. I would not pretend that the DLP would mark its preferences in favour of the ALP in the next Federal election, quite irrespective of anything which his Government might or might not do in relation to State Aid. Whether a sufficiently high percentage of DLP voters would follow the Party ticket was, however, uncertain. There was no doubt that erosive factors were at work. These arose from the current economic stringency, coupled with the passage of time and the fading of memories since the 1955 Split. I strongly suggested that the Government should offer some 'breakthrough' in the matter of education allowances, however meagre the initiative might be, and that it should accompany this proposal with improvements in child endowment for the children of large families. Dealing first with the child endowment proposal, Mr Holt remarked that any substantial improvement would be too expensive for the Federal Budget. I answered that it was only endowment for the first and possibly the second child which demanded great sums of public money. The cost of endowment of third and later children was inconsequential. As to State Aid, he was guarded, but thought there was some merit in my suggestion and offered to discuss it with the Prime Minister. There were two other similar conversations, one later in 1962, and one towards the middle of 1963.

Whether these representations would have had any effect if the Liberals had been more comfortably placed I do not know. Their anxiety after the near-disaster of 1961 was, however, very great. The Labor Party then provided a graphic endorsement for my argument.

The 1953 Federal ALP Conference—two years before the Split— had seen the acceptance by the Labor Party of the principle of State Aid. It could hardly be disputed that this was a result of the strength of the Industrial Group forces, which was the only new factor operative in a party which had always been opposed to the principle, and which both at the parliamentary and 'machine' levels, still contained bitter opponents. At the 1957 Federal Conference—two years after the Split—the decisions reflected the total victory of the anti-Group forces at Hobart in 1955 and reverted to the pre-1953 position. By thirty-six votes to nil it declared Labor's total opposition to State Aid and confined the Party to offering scholarships for secondary pupils, expressly excluding any 'benefits of a like nature to students of primary schools'.[2]

The 1963 Federal ALP Conference, the last to be held before the 1963 Federal elections, saw the anti-DLP forces in full cry. Three important attitudes were strongly expressed by this Federal Conference other than on the education issue. The Conference rejected the proposal to establish a US Naval Communications Station at North-West Cape. It witnessed strong attacks on the American alliance. The obvious powerlessness of the Parliamentary Leader (Mr Calwell) to preserve even the appearance of autonomy for his Parliamentary Party—despite his own belief in the indispensability of the American alliance—before the massed forces of the Left, led to the cry that the Parliamentary Party was in fact a pawn in the hands of the 'thirty-six faceless men' (the thirty-six Conference delegates). This was a damaging claim, exploited with great effect in the 1963 Federal election campaign.

Turning its attention to the question of independent schools the Conference, in essence, repeated the 1957 position. Direct aid to independent schools was once again prohibited, although Labor Governments were permitted to grant undefined 'fringe benefits'.

The defence and foreign policy decisions were a clear reflection of the influence of the extreme Left within the Labour Movement, the issue around which the Bishops had divided from 1954 to 1957. The victory of the ALP's Federal President, F. E. Chamberlain, on the State Aid issue, had direct and serious implications for the financial future of the religious schools and generated a different controversy within the Church. It argued strongly against the view that, if the Church yielded ground on the Industrial Groups as it had effectively done, the influence of Catholics might be maintained within the Labor Party, and be justified by other results, particularly on the question of financial justice to independent schools. The 1963 Federal Conference indicated that yielding on one issue had no effect on the other, except to strengthen the forces of anti-Catholicism on all issues, including that of State Aid.

New South Wales Labour Catholics were obviously under considerable pressure to show results. A strong public agitation on the State Aid issue had arisen among Catholics, particularly in Victoria and New South Wales, organized through 'Parents and Friends' organizations of various types. In Goulburn (NSW) this agitation expressed itself in the spectacular Goulburn 'strike', more accurately the closure of Catholic schools for a short period to demonstrate solidarity with the education claims. The most active in these organizations tended to be non-ALP Catholics, some of whom were strong supporters of the DLP, others being Liberal or Country Party supporters. In New South Wales the claim was made that the Cardinal and his supporting Bishops, while insisting that Catholic children attend Catholic schools and that Catholic parents meet the costs, were in fact permitting the New South Wales Labor Government, in which there was still a high percentage of Catholics, to evade its responsibilities in the field of education, as well as in that of the Industrial Groups. In this situation, what justification was there for the policy which had been pursued during the Split, other than the earthy consideration of 'jobs for the boys'?

In Goulburn, the Auxiliary to Archbishop Eris O'Brien, Bishop John Cullinane, identified himself closely with the lay protest. The reaction of the Cardinal and his supporters to the resolution to close the schools is related vividly by Hogan:

From Sydney, Bishop Carroll phoned Bishop Cullinane on the day after the public meeting, advising him to have the decision reversed. 'Bishop Cullinane told him to mind his own business' reported one of the Wagga leaders. In public Cardinal Gilroy expressed guarded support but privately he shared Bishop Carroll's horror at the turn of events. Archbishop O'Brien in Canberra had given his approval, but only after Cullinane had left him no room to manoeuvre without publicly repudiating his auxiliary in his own parish.[3]

Obviously aware of the renewed danger of the alienation of the still resentful group of activists who had followed his directions to remain in the ALP in 1956, Bishop Carroll moved smoothly to bring the situation under control.

On 10 September 1962, he accompanied the Cardinal in a formal call on the New South Wales Premier (Mr Heffron) to place five claims before him, in studiously moderate language, to distinguish his approach from the violent Goulburn action. Of these it was the fifth which turned out to be politically important—that the Government should provide assistance for science laboratories and equipment in independent schools.

The motives behind this move have been described by Hogan, who acknowledges Archbishop Carroll (as he now is) as one of his main sources.[4] Hogan writes:

In the N.S.W. bishops' meeting, Bishop Henschke of Wagga and Bishop Cullinane argued for the autonomy of the lay organisations which had taken root in their dioceses. For the majority of the bishops, however, the desired role of the lay organisations was clear: to co-operate with the bishops. Since the main bishop concerned was Bishop Carroll that role could be made more explicit: to keep quiet and not to rock the boat. The infant lay movements had to be satisfied that the bishops did not condemn them or publicly dissociate themselves . . .

The civil authorities were left in no doubt that the Catholic community were the bishops, not the lay organisations. The Sydney bishops spoke for all. It was a clear move by Bishop Carroll and the Cardinal to wrest back the initiative from the lay people after the events at Goulburn and in the weeks after. A similar message was being sent, of course, to the Catholic community as well as to State authorities: not only were the bishops in charge, but they were really doing something. In this respect the move was an endeavour of Bishop Carroll to counter the charges that the Sydney bishops dealt only by 'back room deals' with Labor politicians in which the politicians always won. Nothing could have been more public, nor less of a 'back room deal' than the Cardinal's visit to the Premier.[5]

Already, in June 1962, the New South Wales State Labor Conference had passed a resolution requesting the Labor Government to provide science laboratories and science teaching facilities to poorly equipped schools. In the months between the favourable decision of the June 1962 State Conference, which was followed by the Cardinal's visit to the Premier in September 1962, and the Federal Conference in Perth in July 1963, Hogan reports that

the different sections of the Catholic lobby in N.S.W. were united with Bishop Carroll in optimism. The N.S.W. Labor Party would hardly have gone out on such a precarious limb unless it were sure of the outcome at Perth. An explanation of the Catholic confidence in a change in Labor policy need not depend on conspiracy theories of secret deals with bishops. Simple political acumen, based on the actions of the N.S.W. Labor leaders, was sufficient. However, it was those leaders themselves who had been lacking in political acumen. They had seriously under-estimated the strength and resolution of the left wing of the party, led in this issue by F. E. Chamberlain. They did not 'have the numbers' in Federal Conference, and Chamberlain did. Moreover he was quite willing to cut the limb from under the N.S.W. Labor leaders—or at least he was able to convince them that he was. This became obvious at the meeting of the Federal Executive prior to the Conference. The best deal which N.S.W. could salvage was that Conference should not ban all forms of aid (as Chamberlain's Western Australian delegation was suggesting), but should reaffirm the party's policy on scholarship assistance, payable direct to the student. The June decision of the N.S.W. Congress was left clearly in conflict with the federal policy and was thus inoperable.[6]

The controversy in Catholic ranks became heated. The opponents of the Sydney policy argued that it not only involved abdication on the issue of the Industrial Groups and of Communist influence in the unions but obviously brought no compensating advantages on the lesser, but still important, issue of independent schools.

The New South Wales State ALP Executive, sensitive to the political force of this argument, attempted to meet it in August 1963, that is, after the Federal Conference decision. It renewed its support for the general principle of aid to independent schools, and attempted to interpret the Federal Conference's permissive policy in relation to 'fringe benefits' as comprehending capital allocations for the provision of science laboratories in independent schools. If the New South Wales State Executive had been permitted to get away with this, it would not only have overridden the express intentions of the left-wing influence dominant at the Federal Conference but would have marked an important tactical victory for the Sydney policy. The grant of funds for the building of science blocks could be represented as a breakthrough into the vital field of capital grants for independent schools. Anyone who really understood the Federal President, Chamberlain's, attitude would have known that New South Wales Labor would not be permitted to breach Federal policy. Hogan continues his narrative:

Chamberlain made it clear in private that he would enforce federal policy. The N.S.W. parliamentarians, led by Heffron, and convinced by federal leader Calwell, backed down. The scheme for granting direct aid for science facilities was abandoned. It was an extremely damaging blow to the electoral prestige of the N.S.W. Labor government—publicly humiliated by the out-of-State, left wing faction of the A.L.P.

Chamberlain was not satisfied with this humiliation. The Federal Executive decided to censure the N.S.W. Executive for having grossly misled the State Party . . .[7]

The ALP Left, led by Chamberlain, had thus vented its collective spleen on the New South Wales ALP, whose partial escape from the purge of the fifties in Victoria and Queensland they bitterly resented. By the same token, Chamberlain and the Left had put their own party in a position to be publicly out-manoeuvred on the State Aid issue by the Liberals, if the latter only grasped their opportunity. Of the Liberals, only Mr Menzies, with his intellectual subtlety and developed pragmatism, was likely fully to understand the nature of the opportunity thus offered. It was, and has remained, quite rare to find a Liberal leader who understands what is going on among Catholic voters sufficiently to grasp whatever electoral opportunities their changing moods may offer.

My conversations with Mr Holt in 1962 and 1963 were largely an attempt to elucidate the political significance of the by-play going on within the ranks of the New South Wales and Federal ALP; and to persuade the Liberals, through Mr Holt, that their own political interests in the forthcoming 1963 Federal election would be served by showing up the failure of the New South Wales right-wing Executive and Government.

It is now a matter of State Aid history that the Liberals used Mr Menzies' policy speech on 12 November to make concessions on State Aid which amounted to a breakthrough.

Two or three days after Mr Calwell's policy speech was delivered, I was invited to see Mr Holt again. He asked me to assure Archbishop Mannix confidentially that Mr Menzies' policy speech on 12 November would register a real advance. I told the Archbishop at once. He said:

I have never stopped speaking about this question in all the years since I came from Ireland. But I thought I had wasted my time. I haven't wasted my time. But we do not owe it to anything that I have done. We owe it to the men who stuck to their guns.[11]

It was fortunate that I did tell Dr Mannix, since the Archbishop did not live long enough to hear the Menzies policy speech. He died on 6 November 1963. In his policy speech Mr Menzies announced that the Federal Government would make capital grants to build science blocks in independent schools. To choose the very concession which Cardinal Gilroy had tried unavailingly to obtain from the New South Wales Labor Government, and which that Government had been precluded from offering by the ALP's left-wing Federal authorities, was as politically effective as it was ironic.

In contrast to their near-defeat of 1961, the Liberals won the 1963 elections on 30 November with relative ease. They increased their vote from 42.1 per cent in 1961 to 46 per cent in 1963, while the ALP vote was reduced from 47.9 per cent to 45.5 per cent. The DLP scored 7.4 per cent of all first preference votes (in Victoria, 12.4 per cent), the Liberals winning the overwhelming majority of DLP second preferences.[8] I am sure that it was not State Aid but the combined issues of the American alliance and of the 'thirty-six faceless men'—indelibly impressed on the Australian imagination by the assassination of President Kennedy only a few days before the Australian elections—which were the major factors in the reversal of the 1961 result.

The State Aid issue, while it should not be elevated in importance to rank with the issue of the American alliance, was nevertheless quite significant.

Mr Menzies denied—with perfect accuracy—that he had had discussions with the DLP Leader, Senator Cole, on this question.[9] The matter had in fact been raised with him by Mr Holt.

In the end, the decision was obviously made by Mr Menzies himself. Smart states that McMahon's attempt to have the Cabinet adopt State Aid met with little response at the Cabinet meeting of 15 October, where the proposal to call an election on 30 November was probably discussed.[10]

While many factors were no doubt involved in the historic entry of the Federal Government into the field of capital grants, and while there were many who later sought to diminish the importance of the DLP vote, the significance of the DLP factor was widely understood at the time.

The State Aid saga continued in one form or another over another decade. I always believed that there was only one principled solution to the question. It did not lie with the making of capital grants, or of grants according to the 'needs' of independent schools, as those 'needs' would be estimated by some politician or public servant. Speaking on the final night of the Christian Social Week in September 1960, I had suggested that there was only one satisfactory principle, which I then expressed in a rather cumbersome phrase: 'equal treatment for all children from the public revenues irrespective of the school attended', or alternately, that 'each child in every type of school has an equal claim on State revenues'.[12] The form by which this principle might be put into effect could only be a per capita system of payment: in principle, that if Federal and State Governments spent $X per annum on each child in Government schools, they should spend $X per annum on each child in independent schools. If it were objected that some parents of the latter group of children were wealthier than many parents of the former group, income tax and probate tax could be used to bring about greater economic equality. The method of financing education should deal with that subject alone.

The opportunity to establish this system of per capita payments by judicious use of the DLP vote did not offer itself until the Victorian

State election in 1967. There was very little flexibility in the use of the DLP preferences. While it was committed to the strategy of compelling the ALP to cleanse itself of Communist influence through the method of denying it office, it was axiomatic that the DLP preferences could never be offered to the ALP as part of a bargain on State Aid. It was emphatically not a State Aid Party, although some did try to use it primarily for that purpose.

The 1967 Victorian elections offered an unusual opportunity both of safeguarding the major objective of keeping the pressure on the ALP, while improving the situation in relation to the minor objective, that of State Aid.

Sir Henry Bolte, the Victorian Premier, shared the Victorian Liberal conviction that to be forced into a coalition with the Country Party was a fate worse than death. Victoria was constantly regaled with the threat of 'unstable government' and further unimaginable disasters if the Liberals were ever driven into coalition with Victoria's agrarians. In 1967 it appeared that the Victorian Country Party could improve its position sufficiently to threaten the Liberal monopoly of power in that State.

Several approaches previously made to the Liberals to introduce the per capita principle in the State of Victoria had proved unavailing. The DLP preferences were regarded by the Liberals as being 'in the bag': why then bargain with the DLP? However, in the 1967 situation, it was open to the DLP to give its second preferences in country electorates to the Country Party rather than the Liberals. This would not risk the emergence of a Labor Government. It could, however, cost the Liberals several seats, and force them into disagreeable coalition with the Country Party.

Accordingly, the proposal that the DLP might actually commit the abominable crime of assisting the Country Party was leaked to the press. Sir Henry at once initiated enquiries as to whether it was seriously proposed to 'blackmail' him. He was assured that what was proposed was no different from any business dealing, the basis of which is a *quid pro quo*. Instead of simply keeping the unilateral benefit of DLP preferences without any mutuality, the Liberals should face up to their responsibilities. As soon as he was convinced that the proposal was serious, Sir Henry, no stranger to pragmatism, understood that there was really no choice. It became simply a matter of the amount of the per capita payment. What he offered was small enough but it was a precedent. What mattered was that per capita payments thus became available for the first time to every pupil in every independent school in Victoria, whether it was Catholic, Protestant, or non-religious. The Victorian precedent rapidly spread to other States. It is worth noting that at no stage did the Catholic Church enter into the proposal, directly or indirectly. Archbishop Knox, who had succeeded Archbishop Simonds, was simply informed of what was proposed by Sir Michael Chamberlin the day before Sir Michael, the Victorian Premier and I met in Sir Michael's home.

By 1967, therefore, the century-old battle for the principle of educational equality had been won, not merely for Catholic children but, with the exception of the Aborigines, for every child in Australia, regardless of race or creed or colour. While the historian may account for the change in the many apparently sociological changes in the structure and attitudes of the Australian community, including the softening of sectarian differences, I have my doubts as to whether these had any effect whatsoever. There was singularly little sign of a diminution in the uses of sectarianism in public life even in the sixties. The change, in my view, came about almost exclusively because of the change in party alignments, consequent upon the Labor split of the fifties; the size of the DLP vote and the significance of DLP preferences to the Liberals; and the fact that, in Mr Menzies, the Liberals had a leader with the intellectual capacity to grasp what this political transformation represented, the pragmatism to seize the opportunity, and the control over his own party needed to reverse a century of inherited attitudes.

The acceptance of the principle of per capita payments by State, and later Federal, governments provided an ideal financial mechanism for the change, since it related governmental expenditure to the educational needs of every child, per capita expenditure on children attending government schools being the measuring-rod. If all government payments on behalf of children attending independent schools had been made by way of voucher to the child itself, to be cashed at the school which the child attended, any direct financial relationship between Church and State, or even independent school and State could have been avoided. One consequence might have been the avoidance of any legal basis for the constitutional challenge to the system of State Aid, which was launched before the High Court during the course of the seventies.

# 30 James McAuley

When I told Archbishop Mannix in the first days of November 1963 that the Prime Minister would make his statement on State Aid in his policy speech on 12 November, the timing could not have been more providentially apt. For Daniel Mannix, having been suddenly stricken down on the late afternoon of 5 November with a complaint of long duration, died at 12.35 p.m. on the following day, in full knowledge that victory had been won on the great issue to which so large a part of his life in Australia had been devoted.

While the death of a man already in his hundredth year must, of course, have been expected at any time in the preceding three decades, I found it difficult to accept the earthly disappearance of one who in the face of so many adversities had seemed so indestructible. It was by the purest chance that my life had become so intertwined with that of a man who was already 50 when I was born; whom I did not even meet until he was 71; who had become not merely the point of reference for every major design or project, but in a sense my conscience. So it was that we had evolved an understanding. He had made it clear on more than one occasion that while he might offer advice, and that while he remained free to give or withhold his support, I should make my own decisions. On the other hand, I had asked him that if and when he believed that my presence was no longer of any positive value, perhaps even counter-productive, he would tell me and I would go.

On the afternoon after his Requiem Mass in St Patrick's Cathedral, I looked into the future and found it utterly bleak. It had been almost thirty years since at his request I had joined the National Secretariat, years which had been filled, on the one hand, with ideals and adventure, but on the other, with continual struggles, and the alienation of so many of my early friends. Some of my children were entering the most critical years of their lives; and much as I had tried to keep close to them, through constant absences I must have failed

James McAuley

them on many occasions. Was it not time to call my colleagues together, to convince them that we had done as much as could reasonably be expected, and to seek to return to normal living? What weighed with me, however, was not some great conviction as to the importance of what I was doing, which always seemed doubtful, but the fear of appearing to run away from the difficulties of a new era without the great Archbishop. It weighed equally that if the Mannix principles meant anything, they should be perpetuated.

The 'Mannix Chapter' in my life was thus concluded. It was rather a long chapter, lasting effectively twenty-eight years. There was another, almost equally long, associated with James McAuley. The two chapters intersected as it were over a period of eight years—from 1955 when I first met McAuley until November 1963 when Daniel Mannix died. It was my friendship with McAuley which enabled me to set aside the sense of isolation with which I felt myself threatened with the departure of the great Archbishop.

This friendship began in the days which followed Dr Evatt's attack in October 1954, a time when the news was undilutedly bad. The two most powerful State Executives of the ALP, New South Wales and Victoria—on which the hopes of the Industrial Groups rested—were both under direct attack and probably could not be saved. Within the Movement itself, division was already deep between the national organization and its New South Wales Branch, as the latter bent before and finally succumbed to the pressures exerted by Cardinal Gilroy and his Auxiliary.

The daily media propaganda, of which the most powerful and hostile was that of Alan Reid in the Sydney *Sun*, constituted an implacable pressure on both the mind and the will. Reid was less a journalist than a combatant, having been one of the small group who participated in the drafting of Evatt's statement.[1] His most significant piece, 'Power in the Shadow of Politics', had as its centre a photograph of myself, behind me a large crucifix hanging from the wall. It was a representation calculated to make honest Anglo-Saxons tremble for a country about to fall into the hands of a latter-day Savonarola. Accompanying Reid's intelligent and powerful propaganda pieces, there were some rather pathetic statements by a number of Catholic politicians anxious to save their endorsements by trumping every enemy epithet with a more lurid one of their own.

With support apparently ebbing through every crack in the door, and apart from that of Daniel Mannix hardly a friendly voice to be heard anywhere, a letter from a total stranger, signed 'James McAuley', appeared in the *Sydney Morning Herald* of 29 October 1954. It said everything that I would have wished to say, at a time when there was little chance of being reported at all, except unfavourably.

274 | Sir,

Without necessarily agreeing with all that has been said, many people, including many Catholics, will have appreciated the reasonable tone of your editorial comments on the present crisis in the Labour Party.

Catholics may be excused for thinking some other critics and commentators hard to please. If Catholics, seeking to join forces with others of good will in the work of the Industrial Groups, try to avoid obtruding themselves as an organised Catholic bloc, for fear of the sectarian animosities which are never far below the surface in this country, they are accused of a secret conspiracy to capture the Labour movement for dark ends.

If they give strength and striking force to the Industrial Groups by being willing to do their part in attending meetings, voting against Communists, distributing propaganda, knocking on doors, and doing all the other menial but essential tasks without which Communist control cannot be broken, they are accused of adopting illegitimate Communist methods and destroying the democratic process.

If they are willing not only to fight Communism but to try to remove the corruption and maladministration which has given Communists their chance, and also to try to apply Christian ethical principles to the development of Labour policies, they are journalistically labelled 'fanatical' and placed on the 'extreme Right wing'. Complaints are made about 'outside control', about 'a foreign movement', about 'disloyalty' to some recondite and peculiar set of 'Labour principles' of which Dr. Evatt is held to be the custodian and administrator. On the other hand, if they do not fight Communism, do not seek to remedy corruption, betray no interest in Papal social teachings, and lend themselves to the breaking up of the anti-Communist alliance, they are rewarded with the label 'devout Catholic' and are politically 'moderate'.

All this raises an issue of permanent importance. People who enter the Labour Party do so from many different backgrounds. They have prior convictions and allegiances, Catholic or Protestant or humanist or whatever. Is the Labour Party to be regarded, as some of its members seem to imply, as a supreme and total moral authority to which all other loyalties must bend or break? Does one have to check one's principles at the door, or is it permissible to take them into the party rooms? In particular, may Christians seek to develop the consequences of their Christian principles and persuade men to their views without being accused of tainting the pure milk of Australian Labourism with a Levantine ideology?

This question is the more urgent because the party is admittedly devoid of a policy today and is not likely to develop one if the only alternative to a complete cessation of all genuine discussion is cries of treason and treachery. As the *Herald* remarked editorially last Saturday, the only thinking on policy being done in the Labour Party is being done by the Catholic group now under attack, who are interested in the reform of the present industrial-capitalist order by improved labour relations, increased worker participation in ownership and management, the strengthening of the family, and the better administration of social welfare.

In this connection something might be learnt from the new constitution of the Dutch Labour Party, which explicitly recognises that people must bring their consciences into the party, and provides for Catholic, Protestant, and humanist groups to study policy in the light of their principles and seek a measure of agreement.

This may or may not work, and it is perhaps not suitable for Australian conditions where intellectual awareness is so faint; but it at least serves as a challenge to Australians to bring to an end the present disgraceful confusion of ideas.

James McAuley[2]

The commonsense observation that 'people who enter the Labour Party do so from many different backgrounds' was later to be argued powerfully, if unavailingly, by Dr Lloyd Ross, former Marxist, Secretary of the New South Wales Railways Union, and a member of the New South Wales ALP Executive. McAuley's point was obvious to any reasonably dispassionate observer. Of these there were few in a period in which reason was 'out' and passion was 'in'.

There was no reason to believe that having made his statement, McAuley, until that moment known as a poet but not as a man of political interests, would or even should have involved himself further.

By accident, I met a close friend of McAuley's early in January 1955 and asked him to convey my gratitude for his word in season.

McAuley replied at once with a note which was the beginning of a close friendship which was to last, undisturbed, until his death.

In his letter he suggested that the Catholic Bishops should devote a Social Justice Statement to New Guinea. Evidently he had not understood how rapidly my position had been eroded with one powerful section of the Catholic Bishops. His letter then added: 'Is there anything you feel I could or should be doing in relation to Catholic activity? Apart from a reading of Lelotte I have very little knowledge about the whole subject'.[3]

His offer to help with his suggested Social Justice Statement on New Guinea raised the issue of his responsibilities as a public servant. (He was then Senior Lecturer in Government at the Australian School of Pacific Administration.) His concern may seem somewhat dated in an era in which 'leaking' public documents is apparently regarded as an occupational skill required of those in high public positions. On 21 January 1955 he wrote:

You will appreciate that I am in a fairly exposed position as an obvious source of views and information, whether these be embodied in a Statement of the hierarchy or are used in some other way; and to some extent my usefulness as well as my personal prospects are dependent on not having the finger pointed too clearly at me. However, any risk of this kind that needs to be run I am perfectly willing to take.[4]

In the same letter, he asked his own questions concerning the principles on which the Movement based its methods of organization. The hostile propaganda had raised questions which demanded answers. With commendable foresight, McAuley insisted on sorting out the difficulties of association at the very beginning.

In reply I said I thought that he should not become a member of the Movement, but that we should merely keep a personal link on matters we might feel it useful to discuss with each other. I also suggested that I might introduce him to the Apostolic Delegate (Archbishop Carboni), from whom he might obtain, if not a dispassionate view of the Movement, at least an intelligent appreciation of the reasons which had led a Vatican diplomat, with a good deal to lose, to believe that he should support it.

In a letter of 3 February McAuley replied:

I have also no real doubt that I shall see a clear path for helping you in the general manner you suggest, but I'll leave the matter in suspension until I have seen the Delegate and sorted out my ideas. I'm sure you'll appreciate that it is best to raise the possible problems at the outset, so that if an association does result it can be without unnecessary reservations. It is nice of you not to resent the implication which you *could* have read into my letter that your methods of organization and consultation were morally questionable! I do not think that. But I have to know what to think, so far as it concerns me. I am simply a convert of three years standing, with a keen desire to serve the Church, but with no real knowledge of the nature and scope of your activities. Such insight as I have into them on the industrial-political side comes largely from friendship with John Kerr to whom, for all his close alliance with your work, your organization remains a mystery. (I shouldn't be surprised if this sense of walking hand in hand with a hooded figure does not eventually cause difficulties in his mind. But that is your problem; I mention it only in passing.)[5]

A quite extensive correspondence followed throughout 1955, although in fact we did not meet throughout the entire year. There was a good deal in our correspondence about New Guinea; about his concern with the Christian missions, particularly in that island and the Northern Territory; and, perhaps less than one would expect, concerning the political vicissitudes of the year 1955.

However, the latter did arise. One incident which might have seriously affected McAuley's own developing association, is referred to in his letter of 30 August 1955, which told me of the alienation of 'X'—the mutual acquaintance through whom we had first met.

You may not have heard that X has suffered some change of sentiment as far as the Movement is concerned. It arose out of the Painters Union case where, in the midst of trying to prove—in accordance with the story given him—that the opposition had 'stacked' the meeting with non-members, he discovered that the truth was the other way round. He has since understood that this tactic is a settled policy, and he doesn't like it.

I've tried to break it down for him by pointing out that those concerned are not acting in bad conscience because they accept the advice given them that the tactic is justified under the circumstances, but as far as he is concerned all it means is that everyone, from the Cardinal down, is guilty of conniving at flagrant dishonesty.

In his reaction there is, of course, an element of hurt pride because he feels that he has been given a special 'handling' by you, and others, with special attention to his moral susceptibilities.[6]

McAuley's note made it clear that the matter constituted a problem not only for X but for himself and that it should be discussed.

Some weeks passed before I was able to take up the matter. It was a year of 'all hands to the pumps'. The desperate efforts which had to be made to build up the organizational machinery of the DLP in Victoria, with a State election in May and a Federal election to come later in the year, were only one aspect of the problem.

McAuley's good opinion had even by this time become so important to me that these considerations would not have delayed my reply. What did delay it was on the one hand, persistent ill-health during 1955, and on the other, the need to investigate the allegation that the Movement had 'stacked' union meetings in New South Wales. Several similar allegations had all proved to be politically inspired and factually wrong.

So I was unable to reply for some weeks. When I did reply it was to describe what my investigations had revealed: that the 'stacking' of the Painters' Union meeting had in fact taken place; that the action was a breach of Movement policy which, as far as these practices were concerned, had been decided as far back as 1946; that we did not accept casuistic reasons to justify breaches; and that as far as the national office of the Movement retained any authority over New South Wales activities, we would do our best to ensure that there was no repetition.[7]

Twenty-five years later, with all the human villainies and tragedies of Vietnam, Cambodia, Ethiopia, of urban guerilladom in Italy and elsewhere, it all sounds curiously unimportant and even archaic. Yet these were among the small things which mattered at the time, which have not been embellished in the light of after events, and which may serve to explain both how we retained our virtue and lost the war!

(Parenthetically, X never came back: whether because he did not believe us, or because it was becoming a different kind of fight, I do not know.)

I did not meet McAuley personally until the end of January 1956. But we had come to know something of each other and our respective attitudes during 1955. His long-planned visit to Melbourne lasted two days, and took place at Belloc House, the home of the Institute of Social Order. For both of us it was a voyage of personal discovery. Throughout that short time, we did not speak to any other person, as we traversed areas of thought and experience far beyond the limits of the current political crisis, into the fields of religion, philosophy and the rest.

To that point, our acquaintance had been personal but not intimate. My view was that the limits of his assistance would be literary, that is to say in the field of dialectics and controversy. In these areas his help would in any case be invaluable, since the media, without one single exception which I can recall, were unreservedly hostile. In that colloquy at Belloc House I did not suggest that the times perhaps demanded something more, least of all that he should make common cause with those who were about to tread the road of political martyrdom. As to the future of his association, since I asked him no question, he owed me no answer. At the end of the two days he simply said that he would be in touch when his ideas had clarified. His form of 'being in touch' was the poem 'In a Late Hour', which he sent me soon after and which I reproduce in its original form (the version ultimately published differs slightly):

Though all men should desert you
My faith will not grow less,
But keep that single virtue
Of simple thankfulness.

> Despair had fallen around me,
> Dangers had pressed me low,
> You sought me and you found me,
> And I will not let you go.
>
> The hearts of men grow colder,
> The final things draw near,
> Forms vanish, Kingdoms moulder,
> The antirealm is here,
>
> Whose order is derangement
> Close-driven, yet alone,
> Men face the last estrangement:
> The sense of nature gone.
>
> Though the stars run distracted,
> And from wounds deep rancours flow,
> While the mystery is enacted
> I will not let you go.

I had not moved in circles in which men communicate through poetry. I would have liked to question him in relation to the real meaning of the lines he had sent. Did he mean what he had written in the sense of one who, himself undergoing a religious crisis, had now found a cause which would engage the whole man—mind and spirit, public and private life? That in the harsh and unpromising circumstances in which we now found ourselves, he could see a chance of asserting faith over apparently hopeless odds? Or, as has been suggested, was he simply describing my own mood, as he found it in those critical moments, one with which he could identify himself on the basis of our shared beliefs? I did not know and did not ask. What I did know was that if our two days together represented a temporary withdrawal from a world of rapidly accelerating hostility, a short period of reflection and retreat, *In a Late Hour* broke down the sense of isolation in which I could too easily have been enveloped.

I did not believe then, nor at any later time, that he was making a purely political choice. What seemed to be a political choice forced by a squalid party conflict in Australia's rather improbable environment arose from a fundamental philosophic conviction which contained two components: the necessity for unity between men of goodwill, who might differ on a multitude of non-essential issues; but the equal necessity for that unity to be founded on explicit principles. Those principles excluded accommodation with the Stalinists, or the appeasement practised by those whom Lenin had called the 'useful idiots' of the liberal Left.

Twenty years before President Carter launched his 'human rights' campaign against the Soviet Union, McAuley understood the strategic significance of the dissident movement within the Soviet Empire. His 'Reflections on Poznan' (the rising of the Polish workers in 1956) constitute a strong attack on the 'accommodationist' illusions of the liberal Left, which do not seem to me to have been fundamentally shaken even by the self-exposure of the Chinese fraud, the tragedy of the Vietnamese boat people or the Cambodian genocide. This was McAuley in 1956:

It is fitting that the Poznan rioters should have drawn attention to their feelings just at the time when George Kennan had been developing policy recommendations based on the acceptance of the Communist regimes in Eastern Europe as an irreversible fait accompli. What the Kennan policy ignores is that the surest and most numerous of the potential allies of the free West are the people of the Communist dominated countries themselves. They at least have no delusions. They do not become fuddled with draughts of Geneva spirit. They do not soar off into fantasy-fuges of peace and brotherhood every time B & K execute one of the old well-tried moves in the co-existence bluff. They do not foresee the imminent emergence out of revolutionary atheism of a cosy comfortable peace-loving democratic bourgeois-spirited non-expansive Russia satisfied to abandon the world imperium which is now almost within its grasp. They want to be liberated from the tyranny into which Western muddle-headedness and treachery helped to push them. Every time a Western statesman writes them off as lost for good; every time they see Western statesmen fawning on their masters and never raising any queries about the victims of Communism, a little more hope dies in their hearts, and a little more despair and distrust of the West takes its place.[8]

Just as Colin Clark's ideas began to flow into the social policies of the Movement soon after our meeting in the mid-forties, so now McAuley's exposition of the principles which guided his activities broadened the intellectual foundations of the organization and its members, becoming an essential part of its philosophical framework.

The ecumenical breezes had begun to blow through the corridors of Australia's largely Irish Catholicism following on the apparently new 'insights' of the Second Vatican Council. As far as one could estimate, ecumenism evoked a somewhat formal response from the practising section of Australian Catholics. This showed itself in a long-overdue explosion of good manners towards the 'separated brethren' of the various Protestant Churches, but without any weakening of the essential Catholic beliefs which were the conceptual framework of the adult generation of the late fifties. With sections of the Catholic intelligentsia, however, prone to mistake changing intellectual fashions for ultimate truths, there was a strong disposition to hold that everything in Catholic doctrine which was unacceptable to Protestants was a divisive obstacle on the road to true unity.

Movement members immediately found themselves in conflict with the new mood. Speaking primarily for himself, but also for the Movement current within Australian Catholicism, McAuley set out to establish the proper guidelines between true and false ecumenism in a lecture which he delivered at Newman College late in August 1958. He traced the wider ramifications of the relationships between the same Movement current and the Australian political community at approximately the same time in a *Sydney Morning*

*Herald* article, 'A.L.P. Crisis and Roman Catholic Church' (1 September 1958).

These two statements broadly established the position which Movement Catholics took on these issues for the first half of the sixties.

At the philosophic-theological level, he expressed not merely his own views on unity, truth and compromise in these words:

Christians are easily cast in the role of opponents of progress, anti-social elements, 'enemies of mankind', as the early Christians were called. They will not agree that 'one religion is as good as another', that 'all paths lead to the one summit'; that 'it doesn't matter what you believe so long as you do the right thing'; that 'the right answer is always a compromise'; that (Mr Truman's Point Four) 'greater production is the key to world peace'; that (Kant in 1792) 'the Human Race is continually advancing towards the Better'—or other such tranquillizers which seem to many to be the finest fruits of the enlightenment and which seem to the Christian to be mental drugs leading straight to betrayal, stultification and barbarism.

To every proposal of false unity by way of soft entanglements and persuasions the Christian answer is an uncompromising 'No'.

When tolerant words change to threats and force, as they have a way of doing, the ultimate answer is the one which is the central historical concern of St. John: the blood-witness, the testimony of martyrdom.[9]

The atmosphere which followed Vatican II was hardly favourable to ancient concepts like 'the blood-witness, the testimony of martyrdom', which recalled the now widely discredited spirit of Trent.

McAuley defended the equally unfashionable positions which the Movement had been compelled to take in the late fifties when, in his simultaneous *Sydney Morning Herald* article, he strongly criticized the division in the ranks of Catholics who had formerly been united in one Movement. For this he placed the responsibility squarely on the shoulders of those who insisted on clerical control of political action at the expense of lay autonomy. Coming in from the outside, as it were, he saw clearly that if a bishop insisted on assuming the responsibility for political policy, there could be as many policies as there were bishops. It was only if an organization was a voluntary association of laymen, who entered into relationships for a common purpose and established their own organs of authority, that nation-wide unity was possible.

The open division among the Australian bishops and the determination of a minority of them to enforce on their own diocesan branches of 'The Movement' their own view of political tactics caused turmoil and confusion in the Church. The issue became fundamentally a question of clericalism versus the rights of laymen. Knowledgeable outsiders laughed cynically at protestations that the Church does not interfere in purely political matters when it was well known that some bishops were leading a private diocesan army of laymen along a line of political tactics on the plea of 'loyalty to the bishop'.

Meanwhile, the Communists hailed with delight the division and confusion in the Catholic ranks and advised the relative encouragement of the 'Gilroy Catholics', who in their view were treading the same path as the 'regime Catholics' of Eastern Europe.[10]

I have always believed that unless the inevitable intellectual problems associated with action by small and creative minorities, are presented with rational solutions, they must soon succumb to the force of numbers, the weight of political or economic power. In a critical moment of uncertainty, McAuley's contribution was indispensable.

If the aftermath of Vatican II sent not a few of the Catholic 'progressives' who had headed the anti-Movement drive of the early fifties out of the priesthood or out of the Church, it created a problem of a different kind for McAuley himself.

He was personally affronted by the line pursued by the Catholic authorities in Sydney in relation to the Split. It disturbed him emotionally that what seemed to him a policy of betrayal should be upheld as an example of political prudence (the survival of most of the Catholic Labor forces in New South Wales being presented as its own justification) and that the fact that it was purchased by the abandonment of their colleagues in Victoria and Queensland should be ignored.

On 1 June 1960 he wrote to tell me that the final text of his epic poem 'Captain Quiros'—written between 1958 and 1960—would be ready in a few weeks and that he would send me a copy as soon as it was finished. 'You will perhaps see more in the poem in certain aspects than most people, because the experiences that I have brought to bear in interpreting the historical situation is our own experience.'[11]

It seemed to me that for him the writing of 'Captain Quiros' was as much a spiritual as a poetic adventure. Certainly after 1958 his commitment to NCC work became total. He took on the presidency of the State branch in New South Wales. When in May 1961 he went to Hobart to become Reader and later Professor of English at the University of Tasmania, he became State President both of the NCC and the DLP, although this was an identification of the two organizations which we did not normally encourage.

To all external appearances, the cause which he had espoused went from one defeat to another. He felt those defeats more than I did. Perhaps I had understood a little earlier how long the odds really were. After an early—and quite startling—success in the first New South Wales by-election in the seat of Burwood, there was a State election in which the DLP performed badly. A few days later he sent me these lines to which he had given the name 'Nocturnal':

> I walked abroad at night
> Out of the world's heat where our hopes were dying.
> Low in the northern sky, full-spanning bright,
> The Swan was flying
> Seaward, as if to quit the shore
> That heeded its design no more.

> I cried: Do not depart,
> Bright image of desire: if you forsake us,
> Dishonour in our deeds, death in our art,
> Will overtake us;
> Your wing-beats, O celestial Swan,
> Are all that makes the heart go on.
>
> It seemed that it replied:
> Do not complain if absence rules the season;
> The works of men are freighted on a tide
> Whose secret reason
> Moves also the bright signs above:
> Turn back and fight the wars of love.[12]

The long struggle wore on, punctuated like all long struggles with good news and bad, the bad always predominating unless we lesser mortals could share the spiritual vision which accepted that divine designs might perhaps be accomplished more frequently through human failure than success.

I began to understand that we were built a little differently. He could endure these harsh vicissitudes in the essentially alien arena of politics for long periods of time. Yet the sheer tawdriness of daily politics would force him into short periods of withdrawal, like a diver who, too long submerged, has to come up for air. There is evidence that some of his finest poetry of the later period, contained in 'Surprises of the Sun' and 'Collected Poems', was written in these periods of withdrawal from active engagement.

He thought that I was mistaken in not following his example, that unremitting active engagement was personally damaging. It was this sentiment which led him to send me, as a Christmas gift, the lines which he entitled 'Retreat'.

> Come into yourself a while,
> Be deaf to outer cares;
> Ask not who wins, who fall, who rages,
> Or what each doubtful sign presages,
> Or what face treachery wears.
>
> Soon you must return to tasks
> That sicken and appal:
> The calumnies will never cease,
> Look only to the sign of peace,
> The Cross upon the wall.
>
> This is that sole instrument
> That measures every chart;
> This square and level overrules
> The subtle calculus of fools
> By a celestial art.
>
> It is not said we shall succeed,
> Save as his Cross prevails:
> The good we choose and mean to do
> Prospers if he wills it to,
> And if not, then it fails.

Nor is failure our disgrace:
By ways we cannot know
He keeps the merit in his hand,
And suddenly, as no-one planned,
Behold the kingdom grow!

This aspect of McAuley's temperament—a man of action but distrustful of activism—was partly understood by the critic Robert Brissenden in his article 'The Wounded Hero', published in *Southerly*. Brissenden wrote:

This notion that McAuley is a sort of simple-minded, dogmatic and declamatory sort of poet really won't stand up if you look at what is happening precisely in those poems where this is supposed to be the story. In fact, there is a great deal of inner division and doubt and anguish.[13]

'Inner division and doubt' seem to me to describe the years 1961 to 1967. These years were years of reduced political activity, although McAuley's participation was both continuous and unequivocal. Part of the reason was no doubt his new academic responsibilities in Tasmania, where the unexpected death of Professor Murray Todd meant that within a few months of his arrival in Tasmania as Reader in the English Department of the University, McAuley was appointed to the Chair. The work of reorganizing the department and of preparing lectures would have been sufficient reason for total withdrawal from political activity.

A second reason may perhaps have been grounded in a series of unresolved problems within the DLP. In its reaction against Dr Evatt's abuse of the powers of the Federal Executive of the ALP to snuff out the autonomy of largely independent State branches, the DLP, in its Federal Constitution, had insisted on the complete autonomy of the States. Although understandable, this constitutional framework was bound to lead to difficulties, the DLP as a national party always running the risk of being handicapped by the occasional eccentricities of State branches, and of newly prominent political figures whose generosity of spirit often exceeded their political acumen. This was less a problem in the three largest eastern States, in which the leaders of the DLP were men who had occupied leadership positions in the old ALP and possessed long political experience and considerable political skill. It tended to be a problem in the smaller States, of which Tasmania was one.

This perennial if generally muted issue of whether the DLP should forget about the reformation of the ALP and become an ordinary party seeking government arose once again with the 1964 Tasmanian State election. McAuley was to chair the opening meeting of the campaign on 8 April. For some reason—probably the simple fact that the policy speech was not ready until the last moment—he was not given a text beforehand. Indirectly, McAuley heard that the speech would opt for a 'third party' view, and that it contained a number of references to university affairs which he, as chairman of the Professorial Board, believed to be partly mistaken and partly absurd.

Reluctantly but firmly McAuley refused to chair the meeting and withdrew from the campaign, explaining his action in a letter sent to the DLP's State Secretary.

A copy of the policy speech was not sent to me, but on Tuesday morning I heard indirectly that the first part of the policy speech was so framed as to present a 'permanent third party' view of the D.L.P. I regarded this as a breach of good faith, since it is well known that I am opposed to this policy—indeed, if this policy were adopted officially by the party I would leave it—and I should therefore never have been asked to chair a meeting and appear to endorse a policy which is not that of the party and which I regard as completely wrong . . .[14]

The occasional problems with some State branches of the DLP were not, however, the effective cause of the malaise which afflicted McAuley, as it afflicted most Catholics of the Movement current in this period. We were disturbed by what came about, not as a result of the healthy achievements of Vatican II, but rather of the revolutionary endeavours of those who consciously set out to use an undefined 'spirit of Vatican II' to empty Catholicism of any real content.

It was amazing, for instance, to watch the whole Catholic opposition to Marxism vanish, as a result of the vulgarization of 'liberation theology' on the one hand, and of the ultimately still-born attempts at 'dialogue' like that at Marianske Lanze on the other. Possibly neither would have had effect if, at the same moment, two Popes—John XXIII and Paul VI—had not radically altered the diplomatic posture of the Vatican *vis-à-vis* the Communist régimes of the Soviet and Eastern Europe.

While the resultant gains were conjectural, the immediate losses were clear. The Vatican was seen to have waived its practical opposition to Marxist totalitarianism, while the latter remained unchanged. The ambivalent Vatican policy had particularly grave consequences when the struggle for Vietnam reached its peak in the early seventies.

I frequently discussed both the arguments for and against the policies, as well as the consequent problems, with McAuley, and suggested that he might turn his mind and pen to a new and dangerous development. One result of these discussions was his article in the April 1970 issue of *Quadrant*:

Under John XXIII the Vatican pursued a policy of seeking an understanding with the Soviet government in respect of East European problems. In 1962 the curial bishop Willebrands was sent to Moscow to gain the participation of observers from the Russian patriarchate to the Second Vatican Council, and to secure the freedom of East European bishops to attend. He succeeded in these objectives by doing a deal: the price was an assurance that the Second Vatican Council would not denounce Communism or encourage political anti-Communism. The result was a blatant and instantly noticed silence in the Council documents, and a subsequent rapid erosion of both political and doctrinal anti-Communism in Catholic circles . . .

The difficulty of the choices confronting the Church authorities deserves sympathetic respect. One notes, all the same, that the Polish Cardinal Wyszynski has been unhappy with the Vatican line, which was in conflict with the views of the Polish episcopate. 'If anything offends us, it is above all lack of faith in us . . .' he told the Pope in 1965. Whether or not Wyszynski and the Poles are right, the fact remains that, after not hesitating to promote political anti-Communism backed by firm doctrinal and moral directives for a century, the Vatican now *seems* to be treating the committed forces which it evoked as an expendable inconvenience at a time of changing opportunity. It is very doubtful to me whether the opportunist gains will outweigh the loss.[15]

I was indebted to McAuley for this particular contribution to a very real problem. It was one thing for Catholics to face up to the disapproval and outright opposition of a section of the Australian Hierarchy, because of their insistence on taking the Communist problem seriously. It was quite another when the Vatican itself seemed to have relegated it to the realm of the insignificant—except on those subsequent occasions when the Communists asserted themselves in Italy and when the Vatican's own political influence in that country consequently declined, as it did with the legalization of divorce and abortion!

By the time this article was published, McAuley's period of withdrawal was at an end, and in the struggle within the Universities, one of the results of the Vietnam War, we were both once again to be fully engaged in an organizational rather than a purely literary sense.

James McAuley died on 16 October 1976, after a long struggle with a cancer which had already reduced him to a physical shadow of the man whom I had known for twenty-one years. In that single personality I had enjoyed the poet transcribing poetic sensibility into language of limpid clarity; the man of affairs, deeply involved in the political struggles of the day, in which the essential issues appeared to him to be simple and ultimately uncomplicated; and the unwavering friend who, having committed himself to the responsibilities of friendship more than twenty years before, never changed his mind—as I did not concerning him.

The last verses, written in the immediate aftermath of the final verdict on the disease which he now knew would soon consume his physical existence, combined within themselves the final small rebellion against physical extinction with the deeper acceptance of entry into a world unseen and uncertain. It was the epitome of a religious faith unlike that of Pasteur's utterly certain Breton peasant, but close to Daniel Mannix's 'faith clinging firmly to the edge of a precipice'.

> So the word has come at last:
> The argument of arms is past.
> Fully tested I've been found
> Fit to join the underground.

No worse age has ever been—
Murderous, lying, and obscene;
Devils worked while gods connived:
Somehow the human has survived.

Why these horrors must be so
I never could pretend to know:
It isn't I, dear Lord, who can
Justify your ways to man.

Soon I'll understand it all,
Or cease to wonder: so my small
Spark will blaze intensely bright,
Or go out in an endless night.

Welcome now to bread and wine:
Creature comfort, heavenly sign.
Winter will grow dark and cold
Before the wattle turns to gold.[16]

# 31 The Unions: From Monk to Hawke

Until 1967-68, the ALP was the scene of constant conflict between the extreme Left, based on the Communist-led unions, and the more moderate forces based on unions led by the former New South Wales Industrial Groupers, the great majority of whom had remained within the ALP. Except for the New South Wales Branch of the ALP itself, whose leaders were concerned primarily with State matters and, so long as they were left alone, content to leave Federal control of the Party to the Left, victories within the machine were almost invariably being won by the latter. Mr Calwell's continued capitulation to the extreme Left enabled him to retain the leadership of the Parliamentary Party until after his overwhelming defeat in the 1966 election.

At the time of the 1966 election, the Vietnam commitment was still popular in Australia. Mr Harold Holt, who had succeeded Mr Menzies as Prime Minister, capitalized on the issue through the visit to Australia of President Lyndon Johnson. Mr Holt's shrewd 'All the way with LBJ' paid handsome dividends in 1966, giving him a record voting majority of thirty-nine seats (forty counting the Northern Territory's single electorate). What made Mr Calwell tolerable to the left-wing leadership of the Labor machine—acceptance without public protest of the domination of the extreme Left—finally rendered him anathema to the electorate. Mr Whitlam, who had been within an inch of expulsion from the Party because he had sought to repudiate the Party policy against State Aid, and who accompanied this show of independence with an attack on the 'twelve witless men' of the Federal Executive[1], succeeded to the Party leadership after the 1966 electoral disaster. Mr Whitlam thus commended himself to the swinging vote which would not swing towards a visibly Communist-influenced Labor Party.

Apart from hanging on to their New South Wales positions, the anti-Communist union leaders were at a discount in the Labor

Party's federal machine, their colleagues in general having either been expelled or having resigned in all other States. The anti-Communist force nevertheless maintained considerable strength within the trade union movement, as distinct from the Labor Party, despite the attempts of the Communists and their allies to isolate them industrially as they had successfully isolated them politically.

This was due in large part to the policy of Mr Albert Monk as President of the ACTU. Our own union forces were not greatly enamoured of Mr Monk's policy, although that policy was understandable from his viewpoint. He was essentially a moderate, theoretically opposed to the existence of legal sanctions in the Arbitration Act, but prepared to use the threat they represented to maintain discipline within the union movement. Like the former ACTU President Percy Clarey MHR, he had been inconspicuous during the 1954-55 split, being one of the more moderate elements associated with the Evatt forces. He was quite determined, however, that the Split should not be carried into the ACTU, and that 'Grouper' unions like the Ironworkers, Clerks, and Shop Assistants should not either be expelled or encouraged voluntarily to depart. However, that was the limit of his concern for the large anti-Communist unions.

Mr Monk's rationale was that the trade union movement was an amalgam of Communist, anti-Communist and 'centre' forces. To those who represented to him that Communist union leadership had proved itself to be a security risk and still was, his answer was that it was not for him as President of the ACTU to become a crusading leader against either of the inveterate opponents, since the ACTU must willy-nilly reflect all forces within the union movement. This view was no doubt sincerely held. Nevertheless it was also convenient to hold it, since it prevented the disaffiliations which might lead to the weakening of the always-frail financial base of the ACTU.

However, side-by-side with this financial factor, which led him to oppose the Communist aim to institute a pogrom against the 'Grouper' unions, Monk built up an informal power structure which, in fact, operated against the anti-Communists. He had developed a close relationship with Mr Harold Holt, who was Minister of Labour and National Service before he became, successively, Federal Treasurer and Prime Minister; and through Mr Holt, with the Liberal Government. On the other side, he also had close links with the ablest of the Communist union leaders, Jim Healy, Federal Secretary of the Waterside Workers' Federation, who could speak for the entire Communist union force, and who if antagonized could cause Mr Monk a great deal of trouble. Through his association with the Government, Mr Monk disposed of a good deal of patronage, particularly in the form of overseas trips. Through Healy's association with Monk, the Communist leader was not without influence even with a Liberal Government. The anti-Communist union leadership paid the penalty of those disposed normally to be loyal to the constitutional order. They did not have to be cultivated, and so got few if any rewards.

The one issue which disturbed the tacit co-existence between Monk and his ACTU 'centre' group on the one hand, and the former Industrial Group forces within the ACTU on the other, was the invitation given by the ACTU to the Chinese Communist 'trade union' movement to send a delegation of three of the latter's officials to Australia. To add insult to injury the ACTU Executive imposed a levy on all affiliated unions to finance the visit.

Since the breakdown of the World Federation of Trade Unions (WFTU) as the single umbrella body covering both the free trade unions of the Western world and the so-called 'unions' of Communist countries, the International Confederation of Free Trade Unions (ICFTU) had always been deeply concerned about what were known as reciprocal visits. To Communist Governments, these visits gave international union recognition to their State-controlled organizations as genuine trade unions. Hence, despite the rulings of the ICFTU, the policy of reciprocal visits was persistently pursued by the Soviet Union, China and other Communist States. They could be assured that Communist-controlled affiliates of free union organizations like the ACTU (the Australian Seamen's Union and Waterside Workers' Federation being specific examples) would always work for these visits to Western countries.

The ICFTU position, which should have been followed by Monk and the ACTU, was contained in a resolution of its Executive Board, which was passed in December 1955 and reaffirmed in March 1958:

NOTING the increasing efforts of the communist countries to secure an exchange of labour delegations with free lands;
 REALISING that the communist dictatorships seek such delegation exchanges for the purpose of
1  winning moral respectability and legitimacy for their State company unions;
2  misleading the workers of the free world into accepting these organisations, run by the Communist Party, as bona fide free trade unions;
3  facilitating communist infiltration and subversion in the free world; and
4  promoting the expansionist interests of Soviet imperialism . . .
 URGES all affiliates to inform the General Secretary of the ICFTU about any invitation for such visits received by the affiliate from any dictatorship country, so that they may be fully appraised of the aims and consequences of this communist drive and that the ICFTU may be enabled to work all the more effectively in defeating this communist strategy of confusion and disruption of the free world labour movement.[2]

This resolution was reaffirmed by the subcommittee meeting in March 1958, which added a rider urging 'that the ICFTU be consulted before an invitation is accepted or sent by any organisation affiliated with the ICFTU or by any member of such an organisation'.[3]

290   Despite the known situation, Monk, Clarey (and to my personal
disappointment, my own associate in the days before the Split, Jim
Kenny, Secretary of the Labour Council of New South Wales), had
compromised themselves by accepting trips to Communist China.
They were therefore naturally bound to support proposals for a
return visit to Australia.

Hence, despite strong opposition offered by a number of unions
headed by the Ironworkers, the Clerks, the Hospital Employees and
others, 1960 became the year for a return visit by Liu Chang Sheng,
the Vice-President of the All-China Federation of Trade Unions,
and Chen Yu, the Director of its International Department.

Presumably neither Monk nor his supporters knew much about
Liu Chang Sheng, who was in fact one of the most unreconstructed
Stalinists in the senior hierarchy of Chinese Communist officialdom.
At the Eleventh Meeting of the General Council of the WFTU,
which met in Peking during 1960, Liu had made a ferociously
intransigent speech on 8 June, entitled 'On the Question of War and
Peace'. Published in the *Peking Review* of 14 June, its fundamental
propositions were that:

1  Communist Revolutionary wars are just wars.
2  The Trade Union Movement must 'stand for and uphold just
   revolutionary wars'.
3  War between the Communist and non-Communist worlds is
   inevitable. 'It is entirely wrong to believe that war can be eliminated forever while imperialism still exists.'
4  Nothing should be done to settle the war situation in Indo-China,
   Algeria, Cuba, etc. 'The belief that wars of the above-mentioned
   types can be averted is entirely wrong and contrary to fact. Such
   views will deprive the oppressed peoples of their fighting spirit.'
5  Communist disarmament proposals were openly declared to be
   only a subterfuge. 'The purpose of putting forward such proposals
   is to arouse the people throughout the world to unite and oppose
   the imperialists' (i.e. United States, Britain, France, Australia,
   etc.).
6  Communists must 'continuously expand the revolutionary forces
   of the people within the imperialist countries'.[4]

This was the amiable character to whom Australian trade unionists were urged to give a comradely welcome, during October 1960.

The Ironworkers and other anti-Communist unions, having
unavailingly sought the cancellation of the visit through normal
ACTU channels, initiated one or two protest marches against their
presence in Australia, of which the Melbourne march was the
largest. The Communist union leadership in that city then proved its
devotion to the cause of free expression by organizing groups of
hoodlums, headed by a former Australian heavyweight champion,
to break up the march. One or two young Melbourne University

students who belonged to the NCC were badly beaten up. In Morwell, the heart of the Gippsland brown coalfield, the Victorian State Government associated itself with the welcome to the Chinese officials. It was, to say the least, incongruous to see seven carloads of 'strong-arm men' attach themselves to the official party, and when a protest demonstration took place, systematically beat up a number of respectable Gippsland citizens. The procedure shed a rather lurid light on Monk's claim, made during a television interview on TCN 9, that their visit to Australia might actually cause the Chinese Communist officials to 'open their eyes' to the real situation in the free world.[5]

The declaration of a number of dissentient unions that they would not pay levies to finance such visits, and that if the ACTU Executive insisted on excluding them from an ACTU Congress as a result of such a refusal, they still would not pay, brought Monk to a realization of the position in which he was placing himself. Without the presence of delegations from anti-Communist unions at an ACTU Congress, the elections to the ACTU Executive would become increasingly subject to the electoral pressure of the Communist unions. So he moved to defuse the issue and thus retain the affiliation to the ACTU of several of its largest large unions.

The 1960 visit was the last such visit from Communist China. Ironically, the All-China Federation of Trade Unions was one of the many agencies of the Peking Government which vanished in the upheavals associated with the Cultural Revolution. Liu Chang Sheng, its Vice-President, vanished with Liu Ning-I, its President. Whether they have since been 'rehabilitated'—either posthumously or otherwise—with the present 'rehabilitation' of the cadres who were condemned with Liu Shao-chi, I have not been able to discover.

Until two years before Monk's retirement as President of the ACTU in 1969, the strength of the combination of Communists and fellow-travellers within the ACTU had generally been contained, even though Communist power in several key unions and total Communist strength at an ACTU Congress remained undisturbed. Despite the Split, unions in which NCC members were influential retained a considerable number of delegates at an ACTU Congress. They remained influential in the Melbourne Trades Hall Council.

There, 'Mick' Jordan, who had succeeded Stout as Secretary and who had accommodated himself to the Evatt forces at the time of the Split, was now in danger of defeat from the extreme Left. He began to cultivate those whom he had previously opposed. In the Tasmanian Trades and Labour Council, Harradine, strongly anti-Communist, was becoming a force, and was supported strongly by NCC delegates. In New South Wales the Labour Council was held by former

Industrial Groupers. In brief, the entire anti-Communist force within the unions was in a far stronger position than anyone could have anticipated ten years after the withdrawal of ALP endorsement from the Industrial Groups and the consequent division within the Movement's own ranks. While the Communists had succeeded first in isolating and then in destroying the nation-wide alliance of anti-Communists within the ALP, as far as the trade union movement as a whole was concerned they had partly failed in their objective. They had succeeded in winning back a number of key unions (like the AEU) which they had lost in the great days of the Industrial Groups. But they had not eliminated the anti-Communist force from the unions, as they had from the ALP.

A new and significant factor was beginning to emerge in the mid-sixties, as a result of the divisions which opened up within the ranks of the CPA in the aftermath of the Sino-Soviet split. While these divisions soon became public and were obvious to those whose business it was to understand developments within the CPA itself, it was a long time before practical results manifested themselves within the trade union movement.

It was in fact only at the 1973 ACTU Congress that Pat Clancy, Federal Secretary of the Building Workers' Industrial Union, and the leader of the pro-Soviet forces among the Australian Communists, was actually opposed for his position on the ACTU Executive by another Communist. This was Norm Gallagher of the Builders Labourers' Federation, who presented himself as a member of the small pro-Chinese Party. Thereafter, however, the division in Communist ranks did become a factor within the trade union movement proper: not so much in that it led to inter-party contests over ACTU or similar positions, or over policy resolutions at ACTU Congresses, or in daily trade union activities, as that the discouragements consequent on division tended to lead to resignations from the Communist Parties and greater difficulties in recruitment.

It soon became noticeable that the pro-Soviet elements under Clancy which ultimately formed the Socialist Party of Australia (SPA), tended to dissociate themselves from the often vicious eccentricities of the widely touted 'youth revolt' of the late sixties. On the other hand, the Australian Communist Party conducted its recruitment among the 'liberationist' elements, primarily concerned with abortion, homosexuality, lesbianism and similar causes.

It is conceivable that this weakening of the Communist forces within the community could have resulted in a perceptible diminution of Communist union strength if the anti-Communists and their non-Communist associates could have extended their growing unity of action. That the developments turned out to be quite different was largely due to the decision of the Industrial Advocate of the ACTU (R. J. Hawke) to seek the presidency of the ACTU when Albert

Monk retired in 1969. Hawke's alternative would have been to defer his candidature for a further five years. This was what would have been involved in allowing the Secretary, Souter, to become president according to the normal principle of seniority. Souter could have had only five years as president before reaching retirement age.

The anti-Communist forces and the moderates generally had decided to back Souter, whom they trusted and who, on the normal basis of seniority, was entitled to expect the presidency. Thus when Hawke decided to seek the presidency in 1969, he had no alternative but to base his campaign on a coalition of all the left-wing forces.

Mr Hawke possessed much more than organizing skill. He demonstrated little short of genius in manipulating the media to his own purposes. In fact he would not have won the presidency without unprecedented media support. His prolonged campaign of cultivating the political correspondents, the industrial reporters and TV journalists paid off handsomely. Their support was maintained undiminished until his retirement from the ACTU presidency for a seat in the Federal Parliament in 1980.

It was a rare day when the originally pugnacious, aggressive tones of the new Messiah did not disturb the quiet of family living-rooms. Ten years later, the rough proletarian signalized his projected entry into the Federal Parliament, through which he had already cast himself as Prime Minister, by presenting himself altogether more respectably in a blue pin-striped suit, making strong appeals for consensus and national unity. It says a good deal about television and its viewers that in 1979-80, the polls indicated that it all worked out as anticipated and that Australia's most gifted television performer was actually the most widely supported candidate for the prime ministership.

His original abrasive television manner, coupled with his reliance on a high proportion of Communist votes at the 1969 Congress which elected him to the presidency, led a number of ordinary citizens to believe that Mr Hawke was a man of the extreme Left. This was, of course, nothing of the kind. He lived in a very comfortable suburb and his children went to the best public schools. His association with the Left was no more than a marriage of convenience, neither more nor less cynical in intent than the designs of most politicians resolved to use any available stepping-stone to the prime ministership.

In 1967, however, all this lay ahead. To meet the support of the Right and Centre for Mr Souter, Mr Hawke's tactical objective had to be to weld the Left Coalition into a united force to support his candidature two years hence, on Mr Monk's anticipated retirement in 1969. It was therefore inevitable that he would be beholden to the Left, that if he succeeded the Left would be greatly strengthened, and the moderates weakened, within the structures of the ACTU.

It would not have been difficult for a former Rhodes scholar accurately to analyse the figures. The 1967 Congress would have about 650 delegates. Of these the Communist Party could normally control roughly 200-220 votes, comprising its own members and fellow-travellers. There was an additional number of that type of left-wing member of the ALP who, although not classifiable as a 'fellow-traveller', is ready to co-operate with the Communists in the interests of what he considers industrial militancy.

Mr Hawke himself must have organized approximately another eighty 'Centre-Left' votes on a personal basis. These disparate forces he welded into a strong voting alliance.

Non-Communists, like Mr Petrie of the Storemen and Packers' Union, were offered more distinguished official positions within the ACTU hierarchy, with Left support. The Communists were persuaded to give their support, the prize being an increase in their own influence on the Interstate Executive of the ACTU. The result of the operation was a total transformation of the ACTU position.

Before the 1967 Congress, the Monk bloc on the ACTU Executive (which, granted the inadequacy of labels, might be defined as 'moderate', 'non-Communist' and, on some issues, even vaguely anti-Communist) totalled fourteen members. There were only two Executive members who could always be relied upon to oppose the majority in the pro-Communist interest. As a result of Mr Hawke's reorganization of forces, the position on the ACTU Executive, after the 1967 ACTU Congress, was radically re-shaped. The Monk bloc was reduced to nine votes. The Hawke bloc numbered eight, one new position, representing the Australian Workers' Union, increasing the size of the Executive from sixteen to seventeen. Numbered among Mr Hawke's eight there were new Executive members, but three who had previously supported Mr Monk switched sides.

At this stage death took a hand, and favoured Mr. Hawke. Vice-President Jim Kenny died in October 1967, reducing the Monk support to eight. The Executive was thereupon stalemated at eight-all, and it became impossible to fill the vice-presidency until the 1969 Congress. The anti-Communist Secretary of the South Australian Trades and Labour Council, Brown, died exactly a year later, in October 1968. He was replaced as Secretary by Shannon, the Left nominee, who thereafter represented South Australia on the ACTU Executive. This gave the Hawke forces nine votes to seven. Jordan's death in June 1969 led to his replacement by Stone, but this change did not affect the balance of power.

By the time of the 1969 ACTU Congress, Mr Hawke's Left Coalition was a smoothly working political machine. Mr Monk retired. Mr Hawke won the presidency by 399 votes to 350. The price which Mr Hawke had to pay for Left support could be divined

from two changes in the policy pursued by the ACTU Executive after his victory at the 1969 Congress:
1 The attitude of the ACTU to explicitly political stoppages;
2 The attitude of the ACTU to open confrontation with Australia's traditional system of compulsory arbitration, which included enforceable legal sanctions for breaches of Arbitration Commission awards.

The removal of all legal restraints against strike action, especially the sanctions provisions of the Arbitration Act, was a primary objective of Communist policy. Without the removal of these restraints, it would be impossible to develop the 'revolutionary character of the politicalised [sic] strike movement'.[6]

While Mr Monk preferred to base his power in the ACTU on the maintenance of a careful balance between Left and Right (labels which, in many senses, are quite misleading), there were two issues on which the character of his policy and his view of the nature of the trade union movement clearly emerged. He kept the ACTU resolutely clear of explicitly political strikes, in the belief that in so far as the unions sought political objectives, they should seek them through the ALP. He guided the ACTU away from final confrontations with the Government, clearly accepting the fundamental proposition that in a parliamentary system of responsible, representative government, the unions must in the last analysis abide by the constitutional order.

The 1969 ACTU Congress, which saw the consolidation of Mr Hawke's Left Coalition and his consequent election as president, followed upon the carefully stage-managed O'Shea case, which ended in the imprisonment of the Maoist Secretary of the Victorian Tramways Union as a result of a refusal to pay fines imposed on the union. The 1969 Congress set the stage for the attempt to eliminate court sanctions, not by parliamentary action through the ALP, but by confrontation with the law—refusal to pay the fines backed up by threats of mass strike action if any attempt was made to collect them.

The O'Shea case came to a head in May 1969, some months before the ACTU Congress. But Aarons, the General Secretary of the CPA, had already made it clear that his party had understood the opportunities which now offered as a result of the radical change in the complexion of the ACTU Executive since 1967. He wrote:

The time has come for determined militant confrontation of this system of legalised repression. Right-wing influences at top trade union levels, in the ACTU and some Labor Councils, has always obstructed united action against the penal powers, even when criticising them in resolutions and statements . . .

Workers are looking for a new policy *now that the deadlock is broken on the ACTU Executive* [my emphasis]. If a firm stand is taken now, when a new tide of industrial action is on the flood, the government's bluff can be called . . .

A new stage of industrial struggle may emerge in which the arbitration system itself is challenged.[7]

296

That there was a clear issue between the democratic and the Communist views of unionism was indicated by Mr Monk when, as President of the ACTU, at the Melbourne Labour Day Dinner (8 March 1969) he said:

> Penal legislation in this, or other countries, cannot be removed by the use of strike action. What is placed on the Statute Book of a punitive character, can only be removed by legislative action.
>
> There is need for more responsibility by a section of unionists and unions— particularly some of the more powerful organisations and their members.
>
> . . . Instances have occurred recently where unions themselves have not attempted to guide workers on the job in a number of work establishments as to the irresponsible action that is taken which leads to the organization being involved in penal applications before the Commonwealth Industrial Court.[8]

The Aarons and the Monk statements represented the classic Communist and Labor positions respectively. The classic Labor position had always favoured arbitration; had considered sanctions essential to such a system; and had always asserted that if the 'penal clauses' were to be removed from the Arbitration Acts it must be by legislative action, rather than strike action. As J. Palmada of the National Committee of the Communist Party wrote: 'They ["unions and militant workers"] have not all forgotten that it was a Federal Labor Government which introduced the origins of the present penal provisions into the Commonweath Conciliation and Arbitration Acts'.[9]

The replacement of the classic Labor principle by the classic Communist principle in the official policy of the ACTU, thus began with the changes on the ACTU Executive in 1967. The new ACTU Executive backed direct action in the O'Shea incident in May 1969. The transformation of ACTU policy was consolidated by the ACTU Congress in August 1969, the decisions being reached in an atmosphere of hysteria carefully manufactured out of the O'Shea incident.

From that day onwards, although legal sanctions have formally remained part of the various Commonwealth and States Arbitration Acts, it has been impossible to enforce them. The disappearance of the arbitration system as an effective method of ordering industrial relations was all but completed within two years. The factors involved in the disappearance of the system were many. They included the increasing technological complexity and capital-intensiveness of industry, which greatly increased the power of small minorities to inflict damage on the community; and the concomitant of growth of the doctrine that the object of arbitration was the purely pragmatic resolution of industrial disputes rather than the application of a certain, but abstract system of law. These factors however would not have become as powerful as they did and would not have prevailed so rapidly without the successful defiance of the arbitration system in the O'Shea case, in which the Communist position of changing the law by industrial confrontation was for the first time supported by the 'new model' ACTU Executive.

The ACTU Interstate Executive's endorsement of specifically political strike action followed: over the Vietnam Moratorium (8 May 1970), the Budget (25 August 1970), Social Services (21 July 1971).

What has been gained and what lost as a result of Mr Hawke's alteration of the political complexion of the ACTU Executive? The real losses were to the Australian economy as a whole. How long the sanctions provisions of the Arbitration Act might otherwise have been maintained, granted the enormous growth in the power of small groups of unionists through the rapidly increasing capital-intensiveness and technological complexity of industry, must inevitably be subject to debate. Nevertheless the legal restraints on union power which Labor Governments had never been willing to remove have disappeared *de facto*. Had these legal restraints been maintained and enforced, it is possible that they might have diminished the force of the wage explosion of the early seventies, with its impact on the rate of inflation in Australia, especially in 1973-74.

The weakness of Liberal Governments in permitting the law relating to sanctions to be changed *de facto* if not *de jure*, not by Parliament but by industrial threats was another major contributing factor. The result, however, was that with the elimination of the legal restraints which had been exerted on the excesses of unionism, the distinctive difference between the Australian and the British systems disappeared. By the mid-seventies, industrial power was almost as much abused by non-Communist as by Communist union leaders, most of them now being willing to use the opportunities for direct action which henceforth could be exercised with legal immunity.

In 1967—the year which saw Mr Hawke's first move towards the ACTU presidency—the number of workdays lost through strikes was only 705,315. In 1975, after six years of non-enforcement of the legal sanctions in the Arbitration Act, the figure had risen to 3,509,900 days. This development occurred despite the restraining influence of the new high levels of unemployment.

Politically, in Mr Hawke's home State of Victoria, the Hawke forces helped Mr Whitlam in what was seen as a purge of the Victorian ALP in 1970. This charade improved Mr Whitlam's public image of moderation and thus helped him to win the 1972 Federal election.

How illusory Mr Whitlam's purge of the Victorian Branch of the ALP was could be divined from the fact that ten years later, in 1980, the control of the Victorian ALP was in exactly the same Socialist Left hands as it had been before Mr Whitlam's spectacular intervention in 1970—with Mr Hawke himself, now favouring a moderate position, promising to lead another assault on the same citadel!

On the other hand, there has been no weakening in the grass-roots position of the anti-Communist force in any of the major unions. The AWU, the Ironworkers, the Australian Society of Engineers, the Federated Clerks' Union, the Shop Distributive and Allied Industries Employees' Association—with a total of over 600,000 members—remain solidly anti-Communist. So do the NSW Labour Council and the Victorian and Tasmanian Trades and Labour Councils. The anti-Communist numbers at an ACTU Congress are relatively as strong as they have been over the last twenty years, although the position of the Left has been strengthened on the ACTU Executive by the special representation offered by Mr Hawke to white-collar unions, as the price of their affiliation. That the anti-Communist position remains relatively as strong as it is, despite the realignment of forces during the Labor split of the fifties, owes little to chance and everything to organized resistance.

# 32 Foreign Policy: from Tutelage to Independence?

Sir Robert Menzies retired from the office of prime minister of Australia, which he had held without interruption since mid-December 1949, on 20 January 1966. Among the deserved tributes which marked the occasion, the *Sydney Morning Herald* reflected on the relationship between the former Prime Minister and the DLP.

. . . Sir Robert has made his alliance with the DLP yield much more than their office-giving first preferences. No party has been more responsible than the DLP for focusing public attention on matters of foreign policy and defence. No one has been more successful than Menzies in making it appear that the Liberals have been the movers and not the moved on these issues. He has utilised the enforced togetherness of his tandem campaigns with the DLP to make concern for defence and foreign affairs appear as important individuating characteristics of the Liberal Party and essential for the preservation of its soul in the 'me-tooism' of politics in the affluent society. He has given the form, but failed lamentably in achieving the substance . . . [1]

The performance of Australian governments in the matter of defence has become immeasurably worse with every passing year from 1966, although the governments which followed the Menzies Administration had infinitely less excuse. With the outbreak of major hostilities in Indo-China between the brutal Vietnamese Communist régime and the genocidal 'government' of Pol Pot; the Chinese attack on Vietnam; the establishment of Soviet 'facilities' at Cam Ranh Bay, Da Nang and Ho Chi Minh City as a result of the Soviet-Vietnamese military alliance; and a general recognition that the US cannot be depended on to assist Australia in a moment of emergency, it borders on criminal irresponsibility to continue the habitual neglect of defence. To 'solve' the problem by proposing to fill the vacuum not with Australia's own strength, but with US bases is to move from a colonial mentality to colonial status.

The long prime ministership of Sir Robert Menzies covered a distinct period. The man who was popularly regarded as the most successful prime minister in Australian history had presided over the destinies of Australia during the Indian summer of Anglo-American world supremacy. The Cuban crisis of October 1962 was the last visible exercise in American supremacy. The murder of President Diem, one year later, for which President Kennedy could not entirely disavow responsibility, followed by Kennedy's own assassination only three weeks later, was the beginning of the rapid American decline. Sir Robert Menzies knew that Australian security had long depended on the US rather than on Britain. But his deeper emotional ties were with Britain, the Commonwealth, and the Monarchy, which was the centre of his affections. As long as the Commonwealth stood, and American military power, resting on the supreme sanction of the atom bomb, was obviously overwhelmingly superior to that of the USSR, the Prime Minister might justify his government's neglect of defence. Recalling the post-Korean economic crisis and his own near-defeat in the 1961 election, he might be excused for believing that Australian defence was primarily a function of the American alliance, with Australia's responsibility limited to providing a largely symbolic contribution.

For what it was worth, my own view over a period of years had been quite different. If the *Sydney Morning Herald* judgement was correct, that 'no party [had] been more responsible than the DLP for focusing public attention on matters of foreign policy and defence', this happened to be the area of DLP policy in the formulation of which I was best able to help.

Two factors, totally disregarded by politicians and people alike, were of overwhelming importance. The first was the factor of 'lead-time': that it took a minimum of ten to twelve years of intense preparation to acquire an adequate military structure to confront serious defence contingencies. The second was the nature of the contingencies against which one should plan. These were by definition the worst reasonably foreseeable contingencies. They were already beginning to become manifest.

The decade of the forties had witnessed two major events which represented a complete revolution in the strategic situation of the eastern hemisphere. The first was the Japanese attack on Southeast Asia, which accompanied the assault on Pearl Harbour on 7 December 1941. Although the Japanese were finally defeated, they had totally destroyed the structures of European colonial power in Southeast Asia on which the defence of Australia had depended for more than a century and a half. The Communist victory on the mainland of China, completed before the end of the decade, ensured that the most populous nation in the world would be under the control of a totalitarian dictatorship, then allied with the Soviet Union, which would attempt to extend its power throughout Southeast Asia. Because it was Chinese, it would seek to manipulate ethnic minorities; because it was Communist, it would support the Chinese factor with the habitual techniques of subversion and of 'wars of national liberation'. It was obvious that regardless of whence the challenge might come, Australia's entire strategic situation was completely transformed. To raise the question of Australia's physical survival—as a nation of European background and broadly Christian culture—as a practical issue which would have to be resolved before the end of the century, was derided as an infantile aberration, as seeing Communists under every bed. Yet there were also intelligent voices which expressed the same view.

This question had been the central issue raised in the discussion I had with the West German Foreign Minister (Dr Heinrich von Brentano) in the course of his visit to Australia in March 1957.* He had only recently returned from talks which he and the German Chancellor Adenauer had conducted in Moscow with Khrushchev and other Soviet leaders. He was profoundly pessimistic about the future after his encounter with men whom he regarded as little better than 'thugs and criminals'. He was not even sure that the US would finally face its obligations under NATO in Europe. The factor of distance made Australia's prospect of receiving timely aid even more doubtful. 'Although West Germany is directly confronted by Soviet arms in Central Germany', he said, 'I feel that in the long run our position may be relatively safer than yours'.

Von Brentano was not the only person expressing this view. On 7 March 1953 Barbara Ward had contributed a supplement on Australia to the *Economist*. She had written:

Australia's position is unique. There are other areas of the world where resources are still to be developed and a higher population can be maintained—Canada for instance or Brazil or parts of Africa. But none of these areas lies so close to Asia. None of them has the densest of the world's overcrowding on the very doorstep. The chance of exploration that, a century and a half ago, began to bring a European population to the largest—and the last—of the under-populated areas of South East Asia has its fateful consequences today as the Asiatic islands fill up and the time of saturation coincides with a strong upsurge of Asiatic nationalism.

. . . It needs no prophetic gift to see that, should the pressures stoked by the Asiatic birthrate reach a dangerous intensity, Australia would be able to call on the unequivocal and wholehearted support of the United States and of the Commonwealth only if meanwhile it had done all in its power to people its land, make the fullest use of its resources and maintain itself as a major supplier of foodstuffs in peace and as an efficient, versatile, hardworking main base for military activities, should war come.[2]

The question was, whether there was any commonsense reason for raising the ultimate question of national survival so many decades before it would become visible and actual. The cost of doing so would be to be accused of seeing 'crises' where none existed, and of imparting a 'crisis mentality' to those who might be influenced. My own answer to this challenge was that if one were listened to at all,

---

* See p. 249.

302

the continuing illusion that British and American power still existed, coupled with the prevailing hedonism, meant that it would take more than twenty years before the seed germinated. Thereupon, to mix the metaphor, the struggling shoot would only just survive in the competition for budgetary allocations with pressure groups which had more tangible, shorter-term interests to promote. After that, even if political acceptance of the need for a serious defence programme had been won, the factor of 'lead-time' meant that another decade would pass before any substantial results could begin to emerge. Unless you began to implant the seed in the early fifties, it was mathematically impossible in the Australian environment to achieve a result in the eighties. Hence it was better to be ridiculed than to be silent.

The cost, even among those competent to evaluate the arguments, was considerable. When he reviewed my *Defence of Australia*, Professor Hedley Bull wrote:

Where Mr Santamaria continues to swim against the tide is in proposing that the period of relative security we probably have in the next few years should be used to achieve defence self-reliance as a matter of urgency. He would like us to spend $6\frac{1}{2}$-7 per cent of GNP on defence, to embrace 'the Swedish prototype', especially by switching to home production of most of our defence material, to develop a carrier force strong enough to neutralise the Soviet fleet in the Indian Ocean, to develop our own military aircraft, to introduce universal military service, and to maintain an army of 150,000.

The conventional wisdom is to say that goals such as these are beyond us. I think Mr Santamaria is right in his view that we could achieve them, or something like them (despite our technological inferiority to the Swedes), if we had the will. Clearly, we do not have the will: predictions of possible dangers will not prod Australia into efforts of this kind: only actual dangers will.

But should we have the will? Most of us find Mr Santamaria too single-minded in his pursuit of military strength, too oblivious of the need to seek to prevent external threats rather than simply prepare to meet them, too Cartesian and doctrinaire in his manner of argument (it is this, not his Italian background, that really makes him an outsider).[3]

It was the founding of the Chinese (Communist) People's Republic on 1 October 1949, and the outbreak of the Korean War which followed not long after, which was the source of the Movement's renewed emphasis on foreign policy and defence. This concern was heightened by the fall of Dien Bien Phu on 6 May 1954, when it was clear that the defeat of the French by the Vietminh could not have been accomplished if the Chinese had not supplied the artillery with which the French fort was mercilessly bombarded from the surrounding hills.

Foreign policy was a not insignificant factor in the ideological aspect of the conflict which led to the Labor split. The Communists and extreme Left concentrated on supporting the Soviet Union and Communist China. The moderate Left took their lead from Chifley in supporting the attitudes of Nehru and of a general neutralism. The

Movement was strongly opposed to the diplomatic recognition of the Peking Government, a policy which became more rational only when China and the Soviet Union split and began their historic conflict. The question of whether or not to accord diplomatic recognition was a matter of means, and less important than the achievement of a realistic appreciation of the potential power and ultimate policy of the rulers of Communist China. On the issue of recognition, a sinologist like Professor C. P. FitzGerald might disagree with the views which the Movement expressed, but his view of the ultimate policy of the Chinese People's Republic was apparently the same. He wrote:

The Chinese sphere of power which they are at present re-establishing was established 2,000 years ago and, if that was an appropriate range of power in those days of the horse and cart, one must assume that with modern weapons the present range is multiplied many times over.

It would seem likely that the Pacific region is now considered by the Chinese as a part in which they are acutely interested and where they have a full right of consultation. That means Japan, South-East Asia, Australia and New Zealand. Probably they would not be indifferent to anything in the Indian Ocean as far as the coast of Africa.[4]

It might indeed be a 'natural distribution of power', as Professor FitzGerald suggested, but whether such a distribution of power—or the alternative establishment of Soviet or Japanese power in Southeast Asia to counter the Chinese—should be regarded with equanimity by Australia was a quite different question.

It was, however, only after the Labor split, and with the establishment of the DLP as a distinctive party, that the work of developing a more or less systematic foreign and defence policy acquired a high degree of priority. In this development, the attitudes to be taken towards Communist China, the Soviet Union, Japan and Indonesia were no more than aspects of one co-ordinated policy. Murray remarks that:

Santamaria's view of Asian relations, which in a more developed way became the powerful concern of his middle years represented something of a pioneering approach to Australian foreign relations. While the Liberals and the Country Party, particularly Menzies, saw events very much in terms of relations with Britain, America and the European colonial powers, and Labor was dominated either by isolationism or by a pacifistic view, the Movement's contribution was a distinctively Australian approach to armed and allied preparedness—a subject European countries had had to concern themselves with for centuries.[5]

Granted that the departure of Britain from Southeast Asia was inevitable in view of the drain of two world wars on Britain's financial power which removed her from the ranks of the Great Powers, what was to be thought of the reliability of the United States, granted the smallness and remoteness of Australia?

In a series of articles which ran from 1958, I attempted to develop an Australian defence and foreign policy. A brief selection of the more significant statements is shown on pp. 369–70.

304

The intellectual formation imparted to National Civic Council members, largely through these publications, emphasized two themes: the approaching defence crisis of the Western world as a whole; and the specific strategic problems of the Eastern hemisphere, with their direct consequence on the security of Australia. As to the former, the clearest exposition was perhaps that given in an address delivered at the Eighteenth National Convention of the National Catholic Rural Movement in Albury (15 April 1958), and published as *Peace or War: The Global Strategy of World Communism.*

The issue at stake is the future of 250 million people of Western Europe and the vast economy of that whole area, which one day we might hope would be united in a Federation of Western Europe . . .

The Communists propose to operate not through Western Europe at all, but through the Middle East, from Turkey to Persia. Lenin is supposed to have said, 'The road to Paris lies through Peking'. Zinoviev certainly said that the road to world revolution lies more easily through the East than the West. Obviously the Russian plan today is based on the aphorism, 'The road to London lies through Cairo'.

How can that be explained? The economy of the whole of Western Europe is largely an industrial (or factory) economy with the people being mainly employed in those factories . . .

What is needed to make those factories operate and produce today? The answer is: Oil . . .

The oil of Western Europe is obtained almost entirely from the Middle East. Middle Eastern wells provide 90 per cent of Europe's, and most of Australia's, oil . . .

The Russian strategy is very simple. They propose in one way or another to turn off the tap of Middle Eastern oil, to stop that oil flowing to Britain, France, Italy and elsewhere.

This the Communists propose to do through political warfare, by using the tremendous weapon of Arab nationalism which, today, is sweeping the whole of the Middle East. Arab nationalism finds its epitome in the Government of Nasser . . .

His government, being an Arab nationalist government, while it may be even anti-Communist internally, is overwhelmingly and powerfully anti-Western. Arab nationalism is a reaction, not against Communist Russia, which they do not know, but against Britain and France, which they do know. They were the colonial powers which used their people and resources, ruled them, and, in the eyes of the Arab nationalist at least, exploited them for more than a century. Arab nationalism is a reaction against that past. In the effort to get rid of every trace of European influence, the Arab nationalist is ready to bite off his nose to spite his face . . .

The whole purpose of Russian strategy is not to bring about Communist régimes in the Middle East (because that might easily inflame Arab nationalism against the Communists). It is to throw out the old type rulers like King Saud of Saudi-Arabia, and the present Premier of Iraq (who are used to dealing with the West), and to bring to power the type of popular demagogue epitomized in Nasser, in the hope that ultimately they will break the relationships of the entire Arab world with the West.[6]

This was said four years before the Cuban crisis, when the US was at the height of its power. One can hardly blame those who dismissed it all as a case of lunacy.

As directly important for Australia itself was the need to drive home two complementary principles. On the one hand, it was necessary to fight hard to defeat the ALP Left who set out to destroy the American alliance. The anti-American factor was predominant in the resolution of the 1963 ALP Federal Conference that a Labor Government should deny to the US the facilities of the Naval Communications Station at North-West Cape. On the other, it was equally necessary to destroy the illusion that, whatever the provisions of ANZUS, the US would come to the aid of Australia in any serious defence contingency, or that, in situations short of war, it would support Australian policy on ordinary issues of strategic importance to this country.

The point was made in March 1959, after the signature of an Agreement between the Menzies Government and the Indonesian Administration, in which Australia undertook not to oppose any arrangements over West New Guinea which Holland and Indonesia might reach, so long as they were arrived at 'by peaceful processes and in accordance with internationally accepted principles'. The hand of the US Adminstration was evident in the Agreement, its aim being to seal off a potentially serious conflict between the ally to whom it was bound by ANZUS, and a still-unsatisfied Sukarno Government ruling the immensely rich and strategically important Indonesian island chain. It was equally obvious that the US had decided that West New Guinea should go to Indonesia, and that it was placing heavy pressure on both Holland and Australia to accept that situation.

In *New Guinea: The Price of Weakness*, a short article published in March 1959, I argued that from the overall strategic viewpoint, no one could dispute the wisdom of US policy in seeking to maintain links with Indonesia as it had sought—with limited success—to prevent India falling into the Soviet orbit. Nevertheless the sheer secondariness of Australia's legitimate concerns to the US should not be ignored.

This view was challenged by the journalist Alan Reid in a rather heated interview on the Sydney session 'Meet the Press' in November 1959.

*Question* . . . Earlier this year you wrote a pamphlet about New Guinea, in which you said that the United States had already decided that the Indonesians should get West New Guinea in what you described as a 'tidy and logical bargain', and that this was part of the United States' general aim of building up Indonesia as an anti-communist country? Did you have any evidence for saying that?

*Answer:* No. I made a series of deductions.

*Question:* But in December 1959 do you still believe that is true?

*Answer:* I believe that this is true. If the United States felt that you could get a strong anti-communist government in Indonesia by fortifying that government with the gift of West New Guinea, that the United States, in its own best interests, would not stand in the way.

*Question:* You also said in this pamphlet, 'in the same way the United States would support a Japanese claim to East New Guinea'. Do you still believe that?

*Answer:* I believe that that is far longer-range. The central point I was making is this: that the United States is building its immediate defensive interests in the Pacific on great nations like Japan and Indonesia, and not on nations like Australia.

*Question:* Do you think it is more important that anti-communist nations should be built up than that Australia should hang on the mainland and East New Guinea?

*Answer:* I don't believe in the dilemma. I believe that whether Australia holds her own territory to begin with—which is the most important thing—depends on what she does with herself by way of the immigration programme and the development programme. If we could do enough in the next fifteen years, then Australia would have no need to fear that type of American policy.

*Question:* You suggest that this is in America's best interests. Do you view the plan as also being in Australia's best interests?

*Answer:* Not at all. That was the point I emphasised in that pamphlet.

*Question:* In the pamphlet you suggested that it was already cut and dried. I gather you have changed your mind a bit about that, about West New Guinea?

*Answer:* No. Without debating what was said in the pamphlet, what I said was that if America feels that in the end she can get an anti-communist Indonesia by the gift of West New Guinea, she will use her pressures in that direction. That's what I said then and that's what I believe now.[7]

Up to 1963, my belief that the US would not necessarily sustain Australia's vital policy interests was based on the view that there was no necessary identity of interests between the US, with the responsibilities of a Great Power, and Australia, with purely local and regional problems. After 1963, and especially after the obvious US involvement in the overthrow and assassination of its own ally, President Diem of South Vietnam, I became increasingly concerned with a far more basic problem inherent in the alliance—the national cohesion and political 'will' of the US to sustain any serious obligation whatsoever. It was no longer a matter of differing strategic interests—which must be accepted. Nor was it a matter of US military capability—which, then, was not in doubt. It was a matter of political 'will': whether, because of its internal weakening, the US could in fact use its undoubted military power even for essential strategic purposes, which Australia's safety certainly was not.

This unease continued to grow throughout the sixties as Vietnam became a 'quagmire' for the US, not primarily because of a mistaken political–military strategy, but because of the all-but-total misreading of the internal situation of the US by its own Administrations. This was witnessed not merely in the widely publicized and extremely effective Vietnam 'dissent' movement, but also in the drug problem which riddled the US forces in Vietnam. It was also evident in President Johnson's mistaken attempt to finance military operations in Vietnam—which in the end were costing $30,000 million a year—by printing dollar notes.

During May 1971, I was present at an international seminar on the future of Southeast Asia, which was held near Washington. Lord Casey had been insistent that I call on his former associate, Dean Acheson, who was then in official retirement but still active in the upper reaches of the foreign affairs establishment. Only on the previous day, he and other former US Secretaries of State had lined up publicly to support the continued presence of US forces in Europe. I emerged from that discussion profoundly depressed not merely as to the permanence of a 'forward' US policy in Asia (which he obviously regarded as of purely transient importance), but of its possibilities of intervening effectively in Europe and the Middle East in conditions short of the disaster of total war.

With the acquisition of West New Guinea by Indonesia in 1962, it was apparent that the US intended to rely on diplomatic influence with Indonesia rather than direct military power in Southeast Asia. Vietnam was an accidental though progressively escalating involvement rather than a calculated design; not so different from the American involvement in Korea after Acheson had indicated that Korea was outside the American defensive perimeter in Asia. If the American alliance was therefore to become both limited and uncertain in its implications, and if Britain was on the way out both of Southeast Asia and the Middle East, it ought to have been the responsibility of the Department of External Affairs to formulate some alternative strategic concept which the political leadership might propose to the electorate.

At least as far as the public record is concerned, the Department appeared to be wedded to a much less urgent evaluation of the situation. I had little confidence in the effectiveness of the SEATO Pact and wrote accordingly in the *Bulletin* on 16 February 1963:

Britain and France, both in the twilight of Empire, regard the Orient as a region in which they no longer have any real interest . . . [for them] any war in the Pacific—whatever has to be sacrificed to avoid it—is the 'wrong war in the wrong place' for Powers whose interests are overwhelmingly European.[8]

The criticism of my view made as late as 1967 by Sir Alan Watt, a former Permanent Head of the Department of External Affairs, known for his balanced and responsible statements, was:

This criticism, though illustrative of an attitude of mind in a section of Australian opinion, is clearly exaggerated. For instance, it underestimates the importance of British interests in Hong Kong and Malaysia, the continuance of British bases and military forces there, and British readiness to use such forces in certain circumstances, despite the financial and military burden involved: for example, in support of Malaysia against Indonesian confrontation. An important development since Santamaria wrote has been the public recognition by the British Labour Government that 'it is in the Far East and Southern Asia that the greatest danger to peace may be in the next decade, and some of our partners in the Commonwealth may be directly threatened. We believe that it is right that Britain should continue to maintain a military presence in this area'.[9]

Sir Alan Watt, however, acknowledged that

nevertheless, there [was] an important element of truth in Santamaria's view that South-East Asia must, for European countries, be an area of at least secondary importance. It could be argued that the eventual readiness of Great Britain and France to join in creating SEATO reflected less a desire to make it a positive, effective body

B. A. Santamaria and President
Thieu of South Vietnam, 1973

than a decision, while maintaining prestige as world powers, to prevent SEATO from taking any action which might lead to a war likely, in their opinion to escalate in due course into an atomic war in Europe.[10]

That, precisely, was my fear, and the reason why I attempted to formulate an alternative strategic design for East and Southeast Asia and the Indian Ocean. It would rest on the foundation of American naval power centred on Subic Bay. It would bring Japan into a more organic relationship with the weaker nations of Southeast Asia. It would exclude the Europeans, who could not be blamed for pursuing their own interests in Asia, who were not really concerned with the security of the non-Communist nations of that region and were prepared to sacrifice them if it became necessary.

Accordingly, at the Christian Social Week in September 1963 I expanded the notion of a proposed Pacific Community, which I had originally outlined in *Quadrant* of Summer 1962:

The central problem of the Pacific Region is therefore to discover a principle of order which is neither communist nor militarist; and which offers the people of the region a better alternative than the Oriental despotisms which have prevailed as the characteristic order of the East for as many centuries as history records.[11]

In brief, the proposal—on the roughest of analogies with the European Common Market—was that Australia should pursue an active diplomacy to bring about the closest economic, political and *de facto* military relationships with Japan (and her 'subordinate' economies in Taiwan and South Korea), India, and what are today known as the ASEAN nations. The exception at that time was necessarily Indonesia, then under the control of Sukarno, although once he was replaced by Suharto in 1965-66, Indonesia was to become a considerable accretion of strength.

The proposal was aimed at the containment of China, which in the post-Bandung period was closely associated with the Sukarnoist forces in Indonesia through the political influence of Aidit and the PKI. The latter was still in alliance with the Soviet Union, and was continuing to pursue an active revolutionary course in providing assistance to the various liberation forces in other Southeast Asian countries.

These nations [i.e., Japan, South Korea, Formosa and the present ASEAN group] have a total population as great as that of Communist China. In terms of economic power, the presence of Japan gives them a modern industrial economy, today far stronger than that of contemporary China. They have the population base to provide as many foot soldiers as China. Their economies are technically sufficiently developed to enable them to produce the most sophisticated modern weapons.

Strategically, they are so placed as to hold China at three points—on the east through Japan, on the west through India, and in the south through Australia and New Zealand. Should the time come—and it has not yet come—when one could be certain that the Soviet would not assist China militarily, China's strategic position in relation to this combination would not be good.

If at a particular moment of history—after President Sukarno had passed from the scene—political forces in Indonesia permitted Indonesia's accession to this Confederation, the country would be a valuable addition to the common pool. It must not be overlooked that events can act for us as well as against us.[12]

A number of significant changes have taken place within the region since that time. Indonesia, under Suharto, has closely associated itself with Western interests, and has proved itself to be the pivot of ASEAN. The Soviet Union and Communist China have had their fateful division. India, to seek protection from China and to eliminate Pakistan so as to re-unify the sub-continent, has opted for the Soviet Union as a more reliable ally than the US.

What remains valid in the concept is an association between Japan and her subordinate economies; Indonesia and her ASEAN partners; Australia and New Zealand. This provides the framework of a naval alliance which would ensure a continuous link between Japan and the Persian Gulf, thus safeguarding the maritime routes through which Japan's oil supplies from the Persian Gulf must necessarily pass. The uncertainties are manifest: the future policy of Peking, which must inevitably be influenced by the internal power struggle; the establishment of Soviet naval and air power in Indo-China; the military power of Communist Vietnam; the political future of the Suharto regime in Indonesia. What is indispensable is a concept which keeps Japan's primary alignment with the West rather than with China and which keeps open the Malacca and the Lombok Straits.

The response from Australian government circles was precisely nil. It was an ironic and amusing consolation that the idea was noted in the Soviet Union. The Soviet foreign affairs periodical *Za Rubezhom* actually welcomed the concept as proposing the type of neutralist international organization which would exclude the United States from Asia!*

Sir Robert Menzies retired at the beginning of 1966, making way for Mr Harold Holt. On the eve of Mr Holt's accession to office, the British Labour Government sent its Minister for Defence (Denis Healey) to Australia, to seek an Australian financial contribution towards the maintenance of British naval and air power in the Indian Ocean and Southeast Asia. The figure unofficially mentioned was

---

*An interesting by-product came about some time later. Lord Casey made an appointment for a Soviet scientist, Dr Kapitsa, son of the great Soviet nuclear scientist, to see me in my office. A pleasant, highly intelligent man, he congratulated me on my 'realism' in relation to the Chinese, but suggested that the only security for Australia lay in alliance with the Soviet Union. The United States, he added, was in a state of decline, so that the American alliance could not be of any use to Australia, while it might actually create serious dangers. He concluded by expressing surprise that I, as a Catholic, could favour alliance with an American nation riddled by drugs and promiscuity—an interesting essay in quasi-theology from a professed atheist! As far as an alliance with the Soviet Union was concerned, I had to say that some remedies were worse than the disease.

approximately $120 million a year. Mr Holt, then still Federal Treasurer, used the occasion of the Sixteenth Annual Citizenship Convention to announce that Australia could not afford to assist, because 'any increase in defence expenditure would be at the expense of the present growth rate'; and that 'Australia had a balance of activities, including development and defence, which could not readily be altered without creating new problems'.[13]

When Mr Healey returned to Britain, he was reported to have declared: 'If I had been the Australian Government, I would have taken Britain's hand, and slapped it so hard on the meat hook that we would have had trouble in getting it off'.[14]

The incident furnished a classic example of the seemingly permanent Australian policy of relying on 'great and powerful friends' at a time when the latter were being forced to reassess their military responsibilities towards Southeast Asia and were discovering that Australia was not of great importance. It could hardly be expected that the electorate would be more aware of the significance of the new situation than the Government. Irresponsibility received an undeserved reward in the election held at the end of 1966, when Mr Holt capitalized on the euphoria occasioned by the visit of President Johnson and, coining the magic phrase 'All the way with LBJ', won an overwhelming majority of thirty-nine seats, a defeat which spelt the end of Mr Calwell's ambitions.

Mr Holt's tragic death on 17 December 1967 should have opened the way for Australia's External Affairs Minister Mr (later Sir) Paul Hasluck. The latter, although strongly supported by Sir Robert Menzies, was opposed to campaigning for himself. This allowed Mr (later Sir) John Gorton to become Australian Prime Minister, by the barest of majorities, at the beginning of 1968.

Within the month, the Tet offensive in South Vietnam pointed to the possibility of ultimate American defeat. Mr Gorton, who had held various Ministries in both the Menzies and Holt Cabinets, and was Minister for Defence for some months in the McMahon Cabinet, and who had been regarded as a spokesman for a pro-American, pro-Taiwan and generally anti-Communist foreign policy, underwent a strange metamorphosis.

He left for the US on 23 May 1968, on a mission whose central purpose was to discuss defence and foreign policy with President Johnson. As a result of a conversation I had had with the new Prime Minister, at his request, at the beginning of April, there was reason for concern at the attitude Mr Gorton might adopt.

Grounds for concern had developed as far back as July–August 1967, while Mr Holt was still Prime Minister. It was during this period that Clark Clifford, who was to become US Secretary of Defence, visited America's allies in Southeast Asia. He was accompanied by General Maxwell Taylor and a high-level entourage. His

312 | purpose was to obtain a—largely symbolic—increase in their respective defence commitment to South Vietnam, not primarily for any military purpose, but to prevent the erosion of US domestic support. He visited Canberra on 30 July. There he found that partly because of the basic domestic uncertainties of the US itself, Mr Holt was already hedging on the pledge implicit in 'All the way with LBJ'. It was known that Clifford returned to Washington greatly disappointed with his reception everywhere in Southeast Asia, not excluding Australia. In fact it was the Australian and New Zealand reactions which disappointed him most. 'If the nations living in the shadow of Vietnam', he was later to write, 'were not now persuaded by the domino theory, perhaps it was time to take another look'.[15]

The significance of Australia's reluctance was far more substantial than might appear. The *Australian* declared: 'The point of Mr Clifford's article is that the gap between what Australia professed to believe and what she was prepared to do was so enormous that it compelled a basic reappraisal of the US position'.[16] This was the atmosphere in the US Administration at the time of the psychological shock of the Tet offensive.

On 31 March 1968 President Johnson announced that he would not run for the presidency at the end of the year and that he would partially suspend the bombing of North Vietnam while he sought peace talks. It was apparent that American policy was about to change, with significant consequences for the future of any US commitment to the region.

At the beginning of April, Mr Gorton suggested a general talk in his office. In this interview he appeared mainly interested in discussing industrial affairs and the question of State Aid to independent schools. I indicated that although I was naturally interested in both, it was the Australian relationship with the US which had priority. Mr Gorton's attitude was extremely disquieting. His concern with Australia's defences could apparently be summed up in the proposition that Australia faced only two major contingencies. The first was that in the event of a cataclysmic conflict between the US and China, Australia would merely have to render small token assistance in order to symbolize the fact that it was a good ally of the US.

The second contingency—over a much longer period—concerned Indonesia. It was conceivable that Indonesia might become a modern industrialized State, with the military power which would flow from that fact, and that it might again become an enemy of Australia. In the event of hostilities, we would have to have sufficient military strength to hold out for six months until the Americans came to our aid.

'And what if the Americans do not come to our aid?' I asked. 'In that eventuality', he replied, 'there is nothing that we can do'.[17] This was a long way from the attitude I had hoped to find in a Prime

Minister whom the media had represented as likely to emphasize Australia's national identity rather than the previous habitual reliance on great and powerful friends. Such a philosophy demanded a high degree of self-reliance in defence, resting on a foreign policy of close association with, but not dependence on, the US. Mr Gorton apparently had no more interest in this than his predecessors—or successors.

Mr Gorton's first electoral test came in October 1969. A man of independent spirit, he became increasingly resentful of the dependence which his party had had on DLP preferences in almost every election since 1955. There were plenty of Liberals to advise the Party's policy-makers that they had no need to concern themselves with the DLP's importunities. The DLP, they held, had nowhere to go but to support the Liberals. So why worry about them? It paid the ALP and its friends in the media to encourage the thought in order to split the Liberal–DLP alliance. More than once, I tried to warn different Liberal leaders that it was a mistake to take the DLP for granted; that about three-quarters of the DLP votes had originally been Labor, and that in the event of a conflict, half of that proportion would return to the ALP, and that there were many signs that the children of some of the original DLP voters, now reaching maturity, might not have the same political priorities as their parents. It would have been too much to expect the new breed of post-Menzies Liberals to understand the reason for this judgement, or to look beyond the next election. Nor did they. Mr Gorton, and a later Liberal leader, Mr Snedden, both shared the strengthening Liberal view that it was unnecessary to worry about the DLP.

A serious clash between the Gorton Government and the DLP on the eve of the 1969 Federal election arose in this climate. The issue at stake was, however, far more important than the atmosphere in which it erupted. What was proposed by the Department of External Affairs, and clearly accepted by both the Prime Minister and the Minister for External Affairs (Mr Freeth), was that Australia should enter into some kind of informal relationship with the Soviet Union—now that the US was proving itself a breaking, if not broken, reed—in order to contain China. This revolutionary concept was evolved as an alternative to the sacrifices needed to attain defence self-reliance. The problems created for the whole of Southeast Asia by the development of Soviet influence, and its acquisition of military facilities in South Vietnam at the end of the seventies, illustrate why the Freeth suggestions had to be fought and were fought a decade before.

In May 1969, Matveyev, the leading foreign affairs commentator in *Pravda* (and obviously the chief non-official exponent of Soviet foreign policy) first publicly suggested the wisdom of a Collective Security Pact for Asia. He said that the withdrawal of British and

American forces 'should pave the way for the laying of the foundations of collective security, in which case the countries that have gained freedom would, by pooling efforts, consolidate peace and repulse all machinations of imperialist expansionist forces'.[18]

On 7 June, Brezhnev addressed the Conference of World Communist Parties and formally emphasized the importance of a 'Collective Security System' for Asia:

The burning problems of the current international situation do not conceal from our view the longer-term tasks, namely the creation of a system of collective security in areas of the globe where the danger of another world war, of armed conflicts is concentrated.

Such a system is the best replacement for the existing military/political groupings. We are of the opinion that the course of events is also bringing to the fore the need to create a collective security system in Asia.[19]

Outlining these facts to the August 1969 State Convention of the NCC, I suggested that Brezhnev's statement was worth detailed study from the viewpoint of its implications for Australia's security which, in default of defence self-reliance, depended on a number of existing alliances:

—It was a proposal for a collective security system, by which phrase the Soviet envisaged the ultimate development of military arrangements like the Warsaw Pact.

—The Soviet was not proposing that this end should be achieved by itself joining any of the existing regional alliances which included the United States or any of the Western Powers.

The Brezhnev statement described the proposed system as 'the best *replacement* for the existing military/political groups'. The 'military/political groups' to be replaced were clearly those which existed—the US–Japan Security Pact, SEATO, ANZUS, the Commonwealth Defence Arrangements, ASPAC and ASEAN.

It was pointed out that several of these regional pacts drew their strength from US membership, but that others did not and were therefore genuinely regional. The Soviet proposal was that *all* should be swept aside as expressive of America power, which should be excluded and replaced by pacts based on Soviet power.

During Mrs Gandhi's visit to Japan in June 1969, a strong Soviet propaganda campaign was launched against ASPAC and ASEAN.

Quite separately, it became clear that, apart altogether from the question of alliances, the Soviet was not prepared to tolerate viable but strongly anti-communist States in Asia. On 5 April 1969, Moscow Radio had declared that 'the reactionary and terroristic régime in Indonesia can be overthrown only by armed struggle'. The theoretical journal *Kommunist*, in November 1968, speaking also of Indonesia, had said that 'the task has been set of providing practical training for armed struggle against the Suharto Government'[20] (with which, ironically, the Russians were cultivating trade, aid and general diplomacy).

It was not surprising that on 17 June 1969, ten days after Brezhnev's speech of 7 June, the semi-official Indonesian paper, *Nusantara*, condemned 'the expansion of Soviet influence in this part of the world'.[21]

The Soviet support of North Vietnam had at all stages remained firm, and both the US and Australian Governments testified that there was no sign of any Soviet attempt to bring North Vietnam to the conference table. Mr Freeth stated this fact in specific terms in his *Bulletin* interview on 19 August 1969.

From all of these facts, only one deduction could be drawn: the Soviet was proposing what was meant ultimately to be a military alliance for Southeast Asia, which would exclude any American participation; which would condemn any authentically regional alliances, even those in which the Americans did not participate; which would be based upon Soviet military power; and which would be accompanied by attempts to overthrow anti-Communist Southeast Asian Governments, like the Indonesian Government, by all methods, including 'armed struggle'.

This was the background and substance of the proposal for which the Soviet was engaged in making soundings throughout Asia—and Australia.

Brezhnev's speech of 7 June made it explicitly clear that his collective security system for Asia was not a modification of Soviet ideology rendered necessary by the need to contain China, but that it was in fact an expression of Leninist ideology. His proposal was one isolated sentence in a general Leninist dissertation that imperialism remains the chief adversary and that communists must unite to destroy their opponents.

When the *Bulletin*'s political commentator, Peter Samuel, put this aspect of the matter to Mr Freeth in his interview of 19 August, the Minister replied in effect that Brezhnev's ideological utterance was merely a form of politician's talk. Mr Freeth said: 'Brezhnev was talking to the Communist Parties. Now I suppose, just as when we talk to our political parties, you have got to make allowances for the particular emphasis'.

On 7 July, exactly one month after Brezhnev's proposal was made, Mr Fairhall, Minister for Defence, warned publicly against the expansion of Soviet military and naval power in the Indian Ocean. Five weeks after Mr Fairhall's warning, Mr Freeth admitted—in his statement on international affairs of 14 August—that discussions had been under way between Canberra and Moscow. It was clear that the Defence Minister knew nothing at all about the existence or content of the discussions. In fact, Mr Fairhall confirmed this.

316

On 10 July, three days after Mr Fairhall's warning had been given in Australia, Gromyko, the Soviet Foreign Minister, gave a review of the international situation to the Supreme Soviet. In it, he stated that 'the pre-requisite and potential for an improvement of our relations with Australia exist'.[22] That he should mention Australia at all was remarkable. So was the fact that at a conference of all Soviet Ambassadors in Asian countries, the Ambassador to Australia was included for the first time. It was therefore clear, even before Freeth's statement, that discussions of some type had been going on between Australia and the Soviet Union.

On 14 August, Mr Freeth presented his statement on international affairs to the House of Representatives.[23]

Mr Freeth's statement admitted that 'the Australian and USSR Governments have also been in contact, both in Canberra and in Moscow, on matters of bilateral interest, and *also in discussing wider issues*' (my emphasis).

Mr Freeth's statement drew attention to a Soviet proposal for a system of collective security in Asia, and added: 'Australia has to be watchful, but need not panic whenever a Russian appears. It has to avoid both facile gullibility and *automatic rejection of opportunities for co-operation*' (my emphasis).

The statement also justified the appearance of the Soviet Union in our vicinity: 'In principle, it is natural that a world power such as the Soviet Union should seek to promote a presence and a national influence in important regions of the world such as the Indian Ocean area'.

The statement acknowledged that at this stage the Soviet Union was feeling its way and looking for friendly reactions: 'It appears that at this stage the Soviet Union itself is exploring reactions of other countries before trying to convert the idea into any firm or detailed proposal'.

Soviet feelers had, to this point, met with almost universal coldness. As already indicated, the semi-official Indonesian newspaper, *Nusantara* (17 June 1969), had condemned 'the expansion of Soviet influence in this part of the world'. India had stated that it wanted the Indian Ocean neutralized and all great powers excluded from it. Mrs Gandhi was to repeat this on September 14. Japan had coldly refused to consider any arrangement which might involve it in the Soviet's conflict with China. *In fact, the Australian suggestion that the Soviet proposals should be explored was the first sign of welcome to come from any country in the region.*

There has been a little bit of competition between Russia and China as to who would have the predominating influence, but now there seems to be this change in emphasis on the Russian part to a desire to prevent Chinese communism expanding into South-East Asia and we read into that, as following on that, a Russian desire to prevent South-East Asia going communist, because if it goes communist it will be dominated by Chinese communism. So to that extent we have some common ground.

Now I don't put it any stronger than that, and I've drawn attention I thought pretty carefully in my speech to all the limiting factors: that you've got to be aware of the Russians and the things they've done in Europe, the dreadful things they've done in other parts of the world. But the plain fact is that China is not a member of the international community in the same sense that Russia is.[24]

That was Mr Freeth's remarkable justification.

That Mr Freeth could seriously believe that the Soviet Union had become an anti-communist force in Asia could only mean that he did not understand the meaning attached by the Soviet Union to its collective security system for Asia, nor the Leninist perspective in which the proposal was first formulated by Brezhnev as a weapon against imperialism.

On 29 August, the Leader of the DLP (Senator Gair) stated:

The Freeth response is wrong for many reasons.

It is a naive acceptance of Soviet language. When we speak of collective security we surely mean something very different from the Russians, whose model must be their only existing such treaty, the Warsaw Pact. This is used to keep Eastern Europe in a state of Russian subjugation.

It is wrong for Australia to welcome the Soviet move because the countries of South-East Asia have, without exception, expressed either scepticism or hostility to the Brezhnev proposal. Flirting with the Russians will only reinforce Australia's image in Asia as feckless and rudderless. It will make us look like servile colonials always looking for a great and powerful mother country. Finally, it will make us look like racialists, looking for another white supporter when the British and the Americans are running out.

It is sure to weaken what diplomatic strength we have after Mr Gorton's sabotage of Australia's relations with Singapore and Malaysia.[25]

On the following day Mr Gorton gave a TV interview, in which he stated that he would not submit himself to 'blackmail' by the DLP. If the DLP were a party of principle, it had to support him on the basis that his defence and foreign policy, however much open to criticism, was at least better than the ALP's.[26]

The turmoil continued unabated almost to the eve of the election. On 9 September Mr Gorton gave a studied answer to a question in the House of Representatives. The *Age* reported:

The Prime Minister [Mr Gorton] yesterday rejected suggestions that the Russian naval presence in the Indian Ocean was part of an 'encircling movement'.

He said Russian influence in the sphere could not be regarded as against Australia's interests as long as it was exercised in accordance with Australia's objectives.

Mr Gorton was replying in the House of Representatives to Mr Irwin (Liberal, New South Wales) who asked if the presence of Russian warships in the Indian Ocean was an encircling movement.

In a lengthy answer, Mr Gorton deliberately faced his own back-benchers and was obviously trying to placate those of his party who see a danger to Australia from the increased Russian activity in the Indian Ocean.

'Does he view with concern the infiltration of Russian influence east and south of Suez?' Mr Irwin asked.

Mr Gorton said that on information available from defence and other sources, it would be wrong to regard the presence of some ships as being in any way an encircling movement.

318

'There is no evidence available for this judgement at all', Mr Gorton said. 'In regard to influence in the areas of the ocean, I can only say it would depend in which direction such influence is excercised whether it should be regarded as inimical to our interests or not.

'If such influence is exercised for helping relieve the international debt burden of such countries as Indonesia or other countries to build up their economic strength, I cannot regard such action as inimical to our interests at all', he said.[27]

On 15 September, however, the Prime Minister issued a 'definitive' statement which represented an almost complete change of front. He said:

'We should feel, as we have made it clear that we always would feel, that our ultimate security in Australia would be threatened by the establishment of any Russian naval or military bases anywhere in our own region.

'We feel that any military alliance between Russia and a country in our own region would pose a threat to ourselves.'

Mr Gorton continued: 'We cannot forget Czechoslovakia, and Hungary, and the Berlin airlift, and all the sorry chapters of the past.

'We have no intention, nor have we ever considered as the remotest possibility any military understanding between ourselves and the Soviet Union, or any active military involvement by Soviet Russia in collective security arrangement among the countries to our north.

'For we think that would be dangerous for us. That should be made clear. I hope it has now been made clear.'[28]

The reason for the almost total change was the fact that Federal elections were by now scheduled for 25 October; that despite his original statement that he would not submit to DLP 'blackmail', the Prime Minister now understood that there were ways in which the DLP could in fact effectively express its opposition to his foreign policy by what it called the 'selective witholding of preferences'; and that this method was provoking serious dissatisfaction with his policy among his own back-benchers, some of whom were likely, if it were enforced, to lose their seats.

The DLP leader (Senator Gair) made it clear that while the DLP would not risk victory by the Labor Party under its new leader (Mr Whitlam), it would nevertheless refuse to give its preferences to the Liberals in every seat, as the DLP had given them in the past. The prospect for the Liberal/Country Party coalition was thus a further reduction in its anticipated majority which, granted the results of the public opinion polls, was likely to be substantially reduced in any case. The DLP's terms were that the Government should oppose Soviet participation in any security pact in Southeast Asia; that it should commit itself to the building of a naval base at Cockburn Sound; to the retention of land, sea and air forces in the vicinity of Singapore (whether the British decided to remain or not); to seek an effective regional alliance in place of SEATO; to maintain a naval presence in the Indian Ocean; and generally to increase defence expenditure. When the Prime Minister delivered his policy speech on Wednesday 8 October, he publicly re-stated these commitments, which he had given privately on the previous Sunday.

Mr Gorton won the elections, but his majority was drastically reduced—to nine seats. The most important comment on the elections came not from any Australian newspaper, but from *Izvestia*, organ of the Communist Party of the Soviet Union. Its Canberra correspondent understood how disoriented Australian perceptions of foreign policy had become now that the proximate American defeat in Vietnam invalidated the conclusions Australians had uncritically drawn from the American rescue of Australia during the Pacific War.

Referring to the recovery in the ALP vote, *Izvestia* claimed that Australia's internal and external policies were now in a state of acute crisis. It claimed that a large section of the Australian public saw Australia's future in a cardinal change of foreign policy. This meant 'the withdrawal of Australian troops from Vietnam, Malaysia and Singapore, the liquidation of U.S. bases in Australia, pulling out of aggressive military blocs and following an independent, peace-loving foreign policy'.[29]

*Izvestia* went on to claim that although there were still incon-sistencies in the ALP programme, Whitlam's call for a pull-back of Australian troops from the war and an end to conscription was supported by Australians.

The 1969 result was a moral defeat for Mr Gorton from which he did not recover. In dealing with that election in 'Point of View' on 12 October, I attempted to capitalize on the commitment which Mr Gorton had given in his policy speech. I put forward a proposal which related to the future defence of the Indian Ocean.

On 1 October, Admiral of the Fleet, Lord Mountbatten of Burma, publicly attacked the continuing determination of the British Government to scrap Britain's three aircraft carriers in two years' time. He was backed up by Lord Montgomery, who pointed out that command of the seas ultimately prevails over all kinds of continental power, including the Soviet and the Chinese.

Lord Mountbatten pointed out that the *Eagle*, the *Hermes*, and the *Ark Royal* had all undergone recent extensive refittings. The London *Times* naval correspondent stated that as a result they have twelve to fifteen years active life in front of them. Their Phantom aircraft are brand new, just arrived. They are fully manned with trained carrier crews. The inability to recruit carrier crews was held to be the most fatal objection to my earlier suggestion concerning the leasing of American aircraft carriers. Well, the crews are on these ships already.

The British proposal is to scrap the carriers, despite their modernization, within two years; to disband the carrier crews, which are unprocurable in Australia; to transfer the Phantoms to land bases. Thus a superb weapons system is to be destroyed by virtue of the political decision taken by the British Government three and a half years ago, one of its underlying reasons being that Australia would not contribute to the cost.

That naval system which, until recently, largely operated in the Indian Ocean, should not be permitted to be destroyed. It has carriers, escorts, carrier crews and planes—in short, everything. It is capable of effective functioning over the next ten years while we build the lighter ships equipped with helicopters and vertical take-off

320 | planes, which the Navy will ultimately want. The greater part of it should operate in the Indian Ocean where it has operated in the past . . .

Accordingly I made the suggestion that the next Australian Government should openly request the British Government to defer the decision to scrap the carriers; that it should offer to pay the operational and maintenance costs for the greater part of the fleet if it were located in the Indian Ocean, the money coming from Mr Gorton's promised expanded defence vote. I estimated that with suitable destroyer escorts, two aircraft carriers might cost up to $120 million a year. Pending the building of Cockburn Sound, the fleet could have been serviced in Singapore. The status of the fleet, the flag it sailed under, the respective financial obligations, could be determined by negotiation between the two governments. Several objections had been made to my earlier suggestion concerning the leasing of the American carriers. Whatever their validity, none of them applied to this proposal. 'Point of View' concluded:

All analogies are, of course, imperfect. But it is an interesting reflection that the Australian community spends more than $1500 million annually on cigarettes, tobacco, and liquor. For one-twelfth of that, it could restore the position in the Indian Ocean and stabilize the situation in South-East Asia.[30]

Unusually, the media showed considerable interest in the proposal that Australia should offer to foot the bill for the maintenance of the British aircraft carriers in the Indian Ocean. The proposal was outlined in some detail in the Melbourne *Sun* and *Age*, in the *Canberra Times* and the *Sydney Morning Herald*. The proposal was immediately denounced as 'unworkable' by the Minister for Defence. My estimate of running costs—$120 million a year, which was based on a breakdown of costs contained in the 1969 British Statement on the Defence Estimates—were described by the Minister as 'bloody ridiculous', although allowing for the rise in prices, they were somewhat more generous than the subvention requested by the British Defence Minister (Denis Healey) on his visit to Australia less than four years previously. The Minister's long letter criticizing the proposal, and assuring Australians that the whole matter of Australia's naval defences was under constant consideration by the Government, was published in the *Sydney Morning Herald* on 24 October. *Inter alia*, he said:

The place of carriers in our defence forces in future is already exercising the minds of our defence planners and it is common knowledge that discussion on the same subject is by no means confined to Australia. All of this is very good reason why we should not be committing ourselves to a course of action that could compromise decisions that must be reached in the next few years. Since the *Melbourne* itself will reach the end of its life about 1978, we must ourselves have taken decisions on the role of carriers in our own defence forces by 1971.[31]

The *Sydney Morning Herald*, while stating—surprisingly, in view of its editorial conclusion—that 'Mr Fairhall was right to reject as unworkable Mr Santamaria's suggestion that Australia should take over the running costs of the three British aircraft-carriers due to be scrapped by 1972 provided they were stationed in the Indian Ocean', went on to say 'that some of the arguments the Defence Minister advanced were quite astonishing'. It concluded:

> Three British carriers, which have just been modernised and have up to 15 years' life in them, will be going begging. The Government has already unwisely rejected the offer of the Hermes. Why not reverse this decision and acquire one of the R.N. carriers for the R.A.N.?[32]

Despite the total official discouragement, the plan maintained a tenuous existence until August 1970. The London *Economist* (22 August 1970) referred to the proposal I had made, and added: 'The idea won't catch on in Australia unless the British Government is willing to consider it seriously. Should it?' It answered its own question:

> On the surface, at least, it does seem better than condemning Britain's carriers to mothballs or the scrapyard. And, because of the Australians' problem in manning another carrier, it might well be easier to persuade them to hire a carrier than to buy one outright. The British budget would be relieved of the cost of keeping the carrier in service and, with British crews and planes, the Royal Navy would keep in practice with fixed-wing flying until Britain builds its own through-deck cruisers with jump-jets flying off them . . .

It concluded: 'If it boils down to a choice between no British fleet carriers at all, and hiring one out to the Australians, Mr Santamaria's proposal should be followed up'.[33]

It is interesting to reflect that Mr Fairhall's decisions concerning the rôle of carriers in our defence forces which 'we must have taken . . . by 1971' have not been taken by 1980, and that the aircraft-carrier *Melbourne*, which was to have reached 'the end of its life about 1978', will evidently still be sailing the seas in 1988. It might also have been more comfortable if, after the Soviet invasion of Afghanistan, when it was decided to build up Western naval power in the vicinity of the Persian Gulf, the presence of two British aircraft-carriers had avoided the necessity of calling on two US carriers, one of which had to be taken from the Eastern Mediterranean, the other from the Western Pacific, straining US naval resources in both seas to the utmost. But then, if the opposite policy had been followed with the British aircraft-carriers in 1969, the build-up of Soviet power at the mouth of the Red Sea and close to the Straits of Hormuz might never have taken place at all.

# PART V

# A Cultural Revolution

# 33 The Youth Revolt

There was probably no more important phenomenon at the end of the sixties than the sapping of the political 'will' of the United States. That loss of political 'will' is the main operative cause of the repeated successful challenges of the Soviet Union to American power. It is apparent that as the conflict moves from peripheral countries like Angola to utterly critical regions like the Middle East; the world of the eighties will be fortunate to escape a cataclysm.

It was the disastrous effectiveness of Western universities in sapping the political morale of the Western democracies, particularly during the Vietnam conflict, which concentrated attention on this novel phenomenon. The Australian universities experienced the Vietnam syndrome in common with all the others. It was Vietnam which led the NCC to extend its activities to the developing struggle on the campus. This work was undertaken largely at the instance of James McAuley. Believing as he did that—on balance—Western support for the anti-Communist cause in South Vietnam was justified and necessary, he saw in the mobilization of the universities against that commitment a major support to Soviet Union foreign policy positions, and in their politicization, a challenge to the intrinsic nature of universities themselves.

Late in 1967 the Bulletin of the Soviet Embassy in Canberra announced the publication in Moscow of an anthology of Australian poetry, edited by Yevgenia Dombrovskaya. She wrote that although she recognized James McAuley as a 'good poet', his works were excluded because he had to give heed to 'civic and political considerations'. Because of these 'considerations', which included 'his extreme position in support of the U.S. war in Vietnam . . . we deliberately decided not to include his poems'.[1]

Having replied drily that he regarded his exclusion as 'a splendid testimonial to the literary worth of my poetry', McAuley went over to the offensive:

326 | With carefree, naked arrogance the Soviet chose to make this announcement in Australia. Does the Soviet Union think it can come into this country and hand out censure and reprimand to someone who lets it be known he supports our Government's commitment to Vietnam?[2]

Although McAuley's defence of the cause of non-Communist South Vietnam was a matter of public record, he was even more deeply concerned with the challenge to Australia's main educational institutions created by the leaders of the Vietnam dissent movement.[3] The university campaign, which began with the twofold demand for the abolition of conscription and the withdrawal of Australian forces in Vietnam, rapidly developed other and quite different objectives. Of these, the most far-reaching was the attempt to use the universities, the academic community and the teaching profession as the organizational centres of the politics of confrontation against the politics of parliamentary democracy. Some academics claimed to be influenced not by Marx but by Marcuse. The nature of the Marcusian alternative to the democratic order was never made clear.

The Paris 'May Days', and the campaigns of civil dissidence in the USA were physically centred in the universities. The claim that the universities were privileged sanctuaries, beyond the reach of civil and criminal law (the police being 'pigs'), was based on the romantic view that universities, having traditionally been centres of radical thought and action, might now serve as fortresses of insurrection. That movement, which reached its fullest development in Europe and the USA, had its parallel in Australia, although the Australian experience was not of the same magnitude as either the American or the French. Nevertheless, the numbers of those participating in the various Vietnam Moratoriums and similar demonstrations were proportionately larger in Australia than in the USA and Western Europe. Perhaps the reason why university dissidence in Australia was more effectively contained was that an effective resistance was mounted from the beginning.

In mid-1968 McAuley first broached the question whether we might not engage in some restorative action within Australian universities. It was not a particularly suitable moment. The attempt to end the political conflict with the ALP by reaching agreement through Senators McKenna and Kennelly had failed. The problem of maintaining the DLP vote was likely to become more acute with the resignation of Mr Calwell and his substitution by Mr Whitlam. Although the latter was at that time pursuing a Right-wing strategy, there was nothing much in his career to suggest that he would be consistent. In the trade unions, Mr Hawke was beginning his run for the presidency of the ACTU which, since the Right would back Mr Souter, must be based on the Communists and their left-wing allies. There were complications everywhere.

The problem of university dissidence was clearly a symptom of a deeper malaise, of which Vietnam was merely the catalyst. While primary and secondary education were apparently marked by a deepening illiteracy, the universities were sporadically afflicted by the use of violence to curb intellectual freedom which placed a premium on the irrational. It was not primarily an educational problem. It was a reflection of more profound social and economic changes in Australian and the whole of Western society. The most important of these changes was the disintegration of the family. It was not remarkable that children, deeply affected by the absence of so many mothers from the home, due to their increasing absorption into the workforce, should create major problems even for responsible educationists; not surprising that when their own parents, the first natural source of authority, seemed to be so little interested in them, they should listen sympathetically to the growing demand that authority of every kind should be defied and if possible overthrown.

Another powerful factor in the much-lauded 'youth revolution' was obviously economic. How many market research projects had been prepared to convince investors that the post-war population bulge, coupled with relative shortages of labour brought about by post-war reconstruction, would result in an explosion of youth wages and incomes? And that young people should be encouraged to develop an attitude of independence from, and even contempt for, parental restraints, the more easily to part the young from their money? Madison Avenue, and its pedestrian imitators among Australian advertising agencies, took the Leninist implications out of the word 'revolution' and transformed it into a gimmick to sell their jeans, transistors, cars and even milk-cartons. How far the aim of separating the young from their money was responsible for the spread of the idea that all authority—especially parental authority—should be despised as an outdated restraint is a subject which deserves its own research project.

The university revolt was thus concerned with wider issues than Vietnam. It raised the issue of whether the university was primarily a centre of learning or alternatively a privileged sanctuary for revolutionary politics.

Between the years 1967 and 1971, the Vietnam demonstrations, which kept growing both in size and political significance, threatened to make the method of confrontation rather than the method of parliamentary action, the normal method whereby major political decisions on defence and foreign policy were made, with masses of tertiary and, increasingly, secondary students being 'radicalized' in the European tradition. Simultaneously, within the trade union movement the campaign against the sanctions provisions of the Arbitration Act, which was to achieve its objective with the O'Shea affair in 1969, was at last releasing the force of unionism from the restraints of law. If both factors—confrontationist violence centred in the universities and political strike action undertaken by unions—were permitted to mature and then to coalesce, the political and social stability of the Australian continent, until that time comparatively free of major political violence, would be brought into serious jeopardy. It was not fortuitous that what began with Vietnam was to be applied in the next decade with the uranium, the Aborigines, land rights and a plethora of trendy left-wing causes.

So a resistance was mounted both at the academic and at the undergraduate level. A number of Australian academics, among whom McAuley was the moving spirit, established the organization 'Peace With Freedom'. It was a joint enterprise combining the efforts of two groups in a highly informal manner. One group was the Australian Association for Cultural Freedom, which included academics of notable courage in standing out against the fashionable intellectual orthodoxies of the anti-Vietnam movement. The other was the NCC, which was able ultimately to build undergraduate groups in almost all major and minor universities throughout Australia, long before the Liberal Clubs entered the scene, to do battle against what was later to become the Australian Union of Students (AUS).

Although since the early fifties I had been on terms of friendship with Richard Krygier, the Secretary of the Australian Association for Cultural Freedom, McAuley, as editor of its magazine *Quadrant* and also as a member of the NCC, was the figure common to both organizations. It was a two-way alliance. If the NCC was able to attract young undergraduates and through its discussion groups educate them in the real nature of the issues arising on the university campus, this association enabled me to introduce to the NCC a range of new ideas and new interpretations distinct from the familiar issues of union and political life.

At the level of organization, two results soon became apparent. As far as I can recall there was no single Vietnam 'teach-in' of any significance in which the pro-Vietnam cause was not competently represented. To say that it was represented is not to claim that it was allowed to be heard. It would be an exaggeration to say that, whatever the intellectual level of the case, it had much effect on the vast mass of Australian undergraduates. These were as effectively 'brainwashed' as were their counterparts in Europe and the USA. The anti-Vietnam syndrome had succeeded in Australian, as in other Western universities, in establishing itself as a secular religion. Its certitudes were held with a blind, unquestioning conviction by the mass of its devotees, who in general were singularly deficient in knowledge of history, geography, politics or strategy. If manifested by Christians in relation to their religious beliefs, it would have been derided as superstition. I can remember attending more than one university graduation ceremony during this period in which the occasional orator called on the newly graduated to question all accepted values. The only accepted value which they were not entitled to question was the anti-Vietnam passion.

Fuelled by Communist, Trotskyite, anarchist, feminist and other 'liberationist' forces, AUS became the focal point of university dissidence. Two factors distinguished this new development from the adolescent radicalism familiar to universities throughout the whole of their long history. AUS was a nationwide organization capable of exerting a national rather than a series of purely localized influences. At the peak of its strength, that national organization had a revenue of $750,000 a year, as a result of the affiliation of university student unions to which every student was compelled to belong. A student was not permitted by university administrations to 'sever' that part of the membership fee he was compelled to pay to his student union, which that union thereupon remitted to AUS as an affiliation fee. Thus a refusal to pay the affiliation fee to AUS was, in fact, punished by ineligibility to sit for examinations and therefore to qualify for a university degree.

Left-wing policies were further enforced by the use of systematic violence, as a result of which not merely were pro-Vietnam speakers often denied a hearing but, at a later stage, even a psychologist of international repute like Professor H. J. Eysenck was to be forced to leave Australia almost unheard. Of the performance of most university administrations in defending free speech or protecting the oft-lauded critical function of the university—by disciplining the adolescent fascists who substituted violence for argument—the less said the better.

Since the problem did not come to an end with the Communist victory in Vietnam, 'Peace With Freedom' was transformed into a permanent undergraduate organization, which continued after the Vietnam period, for which the NCC generally provided the members and the organizational back-up, and of which McAuley was the effective 'moderator'.

The first objective was to fight the Marxist domination of AUS in the interests of the restoration of the university as an arena of free debate. Once the contest was effectively joined, other groups of diverse political orientation—Liberal, ALP, Jewish among them—also entered the fray. The common aim was to reduce the financial and organizational power of AUS, which since its inception had been nothing other than the university arm of the extreme Left. A second aim was to seek the abandonment of compulsory unionism on the campus. Surprisingly, many university administrations stood out against the latter, although it was in its nature an essentially liberal reform.

State governments, by amending the relevant University Acts, could have limited the financial resources of AUS by making student membership voluntary rather than compulsory. With the exception of the Court Government in Western Australia, they proved as unwilling to do this as university administrations had proved unwilling to defend the university against violence by disciplining its practitioners.

The second objective was to play some part in rescuing the universities from systematic propagation of the 'counter-culture', the major impetus for which undoubtedly came from dozens of academics associated in most cases with the various Humanities Departments.

In the course of an address on 'Politics and the Counter-Culture', which he presented to an audience of over 5,000 NCC members and supporters at Festival Hall, Melbourne, on 14 March 1972, James McAuley defined the approach of the NCC to this question.

Pointing out that fully twenty years earlier he had expressed his own reservations about the direction taken by modern industrialism, McAuley added:

Dissent from prevailing views is not always wrong. Radical—truly radical—doubt and criticism is a necessary part of the process. But let us see what happens to the 'quality of life' and the 'conservation and pollution' issues when the Communists seize them.

They use the issue only for a one-sided attack upon our own Western democratic free-enterprise society. According to them, it is only under capitalism that the soul of man withers; it is only private corporate business that rapes the soil or pollutes the rivers and the sea. To hear them tell it, the soul of man doesn't wither under totalitarian despotism; state enterprise in the Soviet Union has never destroyed forests, degraded the soil, polluted the lakes and rivers. For anyone who knows even a little of the facts this one-sidedness is laughable—or would be laughable if it were not a sin against the truth.

But why is the issue thus perverted? Because the Communist professionals care nothing about the quality of life or conservation or pollution in Australia. They care only for two things: that a popular issue should be turned into an attack on democratic government and private business, and that people who feel keenly about the issue should be drawn into the Communist Party's magnetic field, function within organizations manipulated by Communists, and feel increasingly alienated and hostile towards the system of their own country.

My first observation therefore is that we must not react merely with impatience and hostility to people who express discontent and dissent with aspects of our present society. But also we must not let the real issues be taken out of our hands and perverted by the operators.[4]

Some five or six years after the most violent expressions of campus politics seem to have died away, the question which arises is whether the dissidents achieved anything. Or was it all ephemeral? I share the views of the first leader of SDS (Students for a Democratic Society) in the USA, Tom Hayden, today perhaps better known as the husband of Jane Fonda; and of Sam Brown, the organizer of the Vietnam Moratorium movement in the USA.

By 1975 Hayden was thirty-five years of age. With the decline of fashionable campus radicalism, he announced his candidature for the 1976 American Senate election. Asked to justify his switch in joining 'the system' instead of campaigning violently for its overthrow, he stated that only his tactics were different. He said:

The situation has changed. It calls for new tactics. Everyone is polite and people are willing to listen to us. What we said in the past was outlandish to these people, and now they realize it was true.[5]

His campaign slogan was: 'The Radicalism of the 1960's is Becoming the Common Sense of the 1970's'.[6]

Two years later he was, however, to make this remarkable statement:

Sometimes it seems to me that the country can't be governed right now by anybody because there's no consensus.

We had stable presidencies roughly from 1900 to 1960, but no one under 18 remembers (or more accurately, has lived in) a normal presidency. For a long time, the country had a roughly bipartisan consensus—the New Deal at home and the cold war abroad. But that fell apart in the 1960's, with the civil rights movement, the women's movement, and the war in Vietnam . . .

With that consensus in shreds, it becomes harder to be President. I think Carter and all of them recognize that, but they approach it as a public relations problem . . .

Well, you don't chop a sense of purpose out of the typewriter simply because you need it. It's either there or it's not there, and right now, it's not there . . .

I used to be absolutely sure I knew where things were going, but now I don't know. I only know the stalemate is for real . . .[7]

Looking back on the confrontationist techniques of the preceding decade, Sam Brown, the founder of the Moratorium movement, now an official in the Carter Administration, also had second thoughts: 'I'm not sure it was a mistake in the 1960's, but it's a pattern you can't afford to continue'.[8]

Unfortunately, once the horse has bolted, it is too late to close the stable door, as the American hostages in Teheran, who have succeeded the sailors on the *Pueblo* as the most spectacular victims of American impotence, might ruefully have contemplated.

By the end of the seventies it was apparent that the violence associated with the universities at its beginning had subsided. It might or might not recur. The deeper problem, however, remained. The life of the universities would not revert to the pre-Vietnam normality because the stability and prosperity of Western society had disappeared. It had foundered in the inflation which had pushed the index figure of the value of the pound sterling from 100 in 1910, to 301 in 1956, to 500 in 1970, and to over 1,000 by the end of the decade. Side by side with the de-stabilization of the economic and political structures went—cause or effect?—the extraordinary outbreak of sexual promiscuity, largely through the popularization of the Pill, the trivialization of marriage, and the progressive disintegration of the family. In this situation it was inevitable that the universities would once again emerge as specifically political problem centres for democratic communities. For after all, they now educated the entire leadership echelons of modern societies—their politicians, bureaucrats, academics, teachers, media personalities, even their religious leaders. They rather than the unions were the key to the eighties. Whether the universities were the victims of the breakdown of the Christian consensus on which Western civilization had been built, or whether they were the chief carriers of the destructive virus might be debated. What was beyond debate in 1980 was that universities were essential arenas of conflict, even if the purely political struggles of the sixties and seventies must be replaced by the battle of ideas.

# 34 The Impact of Vatican II

While the difficult, but indispensable, effort to broaden the denominational base of the NCC was put in train, in practical terms it was clear that that particular road would be hard and long. For a long time ahead, both for practical workers, and for moral and financial support, we should have to rely largely on the Catholic section of the population. Yet as the consequences of the Second Vatican Council began to manifest themselves in Australia, it was obvious that even apart from local troubles, this support could no longer be simply assumed. It may not be entirely irrelevant, therefore, to discuss the effects of the period following Vatican II on the content of Australian Catholicism, effects which were as distressing to many Catholics as they were mystifying to those non-Catholics who had believed that, for good or evil, Catholicism was monolithic.

The disintegration of the Catholic community—evidenced in the fields of doctrine, morals, discipline and organization—was somewhat less obvious in Australia than in Holland, France and the United States. To those who accepted the primacy of supernatural values over the purely mundane values of politics and economics, the strictly religious consequences of the period of anarchy which followed the Second Vatican Council were the more important. Nevertheless, the political consequences were also real. Just as the loss of basic religious conviction by large numbers of Catholics proved itself to be destructive for vocations to the priesthood and to the religious orders, so it also greatly reduced the number and lowered the level of motivation of those Catholics who, without the spur of a political career, were willing to sacrifice time and energy to play their part in trade unions or similar organizations.

The many Catholics who expressed their concern about this new climate of opinion were almost universally damned as traditionalist, obscurantist and reactionary. Whatever was 'traditionalist' became archaic: whatever was new was given instant, automatic welcome.

The innovators flourished in the approval of the media, which continued to find it sensational when prominent Catholics attacked their own Church—even when such attacks became frequent and commonplace. There were promises and prizes for everybody: the prospect of the pill for the laity, the end of celibacy for the clergy, and intellectual woolly blankets to comfort consciences all round. No wonder there was a wholesale exodus of priests, brothers and nuns from their ministries, not a few of them leaving the Church as well. No wonder public opinion polls began to disclose that a significant proportion of younger Catholics no longer believed in the Church's teachings on contraception or in its teachings on premarital sex or divorce. A philosophic reconciliation between sexual freedom and an undisturbed conscience was naturally an attractive prospect.

The chaos and anarchy in the Church was not the result of Vatican II, whose conclusions were completely in accord with the Catholic tradition. It was initially the result of the concerted activities of a powerful group of theologians-turned-propagandists, who used Vatican II to 'revolutionize' the Church from within. Their work of 'de-mythologization' could end in nothing else but to empty Catholicism of any supernatural content. In this particular task the original organizing impetus came from an organization with the acronym IDO-C (International Centre of Information and Documentation concerning the Conciliar Church). This group acquired much influence during Vatican II itself, by setting itself up as an organized reference centre for the world media, whose one-sided 'documentation' left no doubt as to its ultimate objective. Jacques Maritain, who with Daniélou, De Lubac, Congar and Courtenay Murray, belonged to the small group of Catholic philosophers whose ideas had prepared the way for Vatican II, finally rebelled against the rush from an orthodoxy which he had always sought to defend in modern terms, but never to destroy. His last work, *The Peasant of the Garonne*, was in a sense the *cri de coeur* of one who had seen his endeavours betrayed.

As the theologian Hans Küng saw quite early, the entire enterprise depended for its success on the disintegration of the concept of authority within the Church itself, central to which was the 'magisterium' or the defining authority of the Papacy.

No single factor was more important in the realization of this objective than the massive campaign which was launched against the Encyclical Letter *Humanae Vitae*, promulgated by Paul VI on 25 July 1968. In this Encyclical Letter the Pope simply re-stated the Church's traditional teaching on contraception. The long delay of five years between the appointment of a mixed Commission to report on contemporary aspects of the question and the publication of the Encyclical was as effective in eroding Papal authority as the equally long period taken by the Papacy to determine the standing of Henry VIII's marriage to Catherine of Aragon.

What made the campaign against the authority of the Papacy unique was that it was led by a large number of professional Catholic theologians, with the tacit support of more than one national Hierarchy. It was obvious that what was essentially in issue was not contraception, but the authority of the Papacy within the Catholic Church in the definition of its religious doctrine, and of its moral principles; that the repudiation of that authority which would begin with contraception would quickly extend from the field of moral to that of doctrinal teaching, not excluding the Divinity of Christ.

Since what was at stake was clear even then, I attempted to explain that issue in a booklet *Contraception: Reflections on the Pope's Ruling*, which was written just after the publication of the Encyclical and published in September 1968, two months after its promulgation.[1] It sold some 30,000 copies. It pointed out that the question raised by the Encyclical was one which related to Catholics. Non-Catholics, by definition, did not accept the claims of the Catholic Church to speak with authority and so were not involved in the issue of authority. As far as Catholics were concerned, the primary issue involved in *Humanae Vitae* was not the question of contraception at all, but the question of authority and, therefore, of the nature of the Church.

The Protestant Reformation had established the fundamental distinction between the Protestant and the Catholic positions. The Protestant took his stand on the ultimate sovereignty of the Bible and, subject to that, the finality of the private judgement of the individual conscience on matters of both faith and morality. The Catholic position was that, when either Pope or Council spoke 'authoritatively' on matters of faith or morals, the content of those declarations was binding on the conscience of the Catholic. If a Catholic believed that such definitions were outrageously wrong then he must come logically to the conclusion that the Church which promulgated them could not be guaranteed in the rightness of its declarations by God Himself. It was difficult to see what point there was in belonging to a Church whose basic claim had thus been falsified in the event. If, however, the Catholic believed that the fundamental basis of divine guidance on this quite restricted list of subject-matters was established, he was clearly bound by what was thus guaranteed.

There are strong arguments for both Protestant and Catholic positions, both of which have been held by strong intellects animated by high principles. But they are basically opposed positions.

Accordingly, I wrote:

The binding force of this external authority is the exact difference between the Catholic and the Protestant positions. It is in fact what the Reformation was all about. It is why Thomas More and John Fisher went to execution.[2]

Paul Johnson, then editor of the *New Statesman*, who was totally opposed to the traditional Catholic teaching on contraception, and who supported the majority Report of the Papal Commission dealing with the birth control issue (which Paul VI rejected), saw the issue clearly:

The Report . . . goes very much further and says it's not the Church's business to lay down detailed guides for living the Christian life, but merely to state general principles and leave the rest to the individual's conscience. This was precisely the central issue of the Reformation. The Roman Catholic Church has finally turned Protestant.[3]

Hans Küng had no trouble in solving the problem. Against those who were attempting to establish that the exact content of the Church's teaching on contraception was a matter of doubt, he asserted that as a matter of history it had, in fact, been propounded authoritatively by the Church throughout the whole of its existence; that the teaching was quite obviously wrong; and that what these two facts, taken in conjunction, proved was that neither the Pope, nor even the Church, could be regarded as infallible. Catholic couples, who had governed their marital relationship by the Church's principles—often at great sacrifice to themselves—precisely because they believed those principles to be divinely guaranteed, could hardly be expected to be as cheerful about Küng's conclusion as the professional theologian.

The issue was extremely clear to James McAuley, who saw the question from the view of one born an Anglican, who had become an agnostic, and ultimately a Catholic, basically because he was persuaded of the rationality of the Church's claim to ultimate authority in matters of faith and morals. In his review of Russell Kirk's *Enemies of the Permanent Things*, he referred to 'this strange episode' by expressing his puzzlement at

. . . the years of delay which occurred before the present Pope reaffirmed the traditional teaching on contraception in a document defending marriage from its improvers. As in other matters, his *ultimate* determination to maintain orthodoxy is admirable, and it seems that he never had any intention of changing the Church's position. But his apparent hesitation and prolonged silence opened a wide gap, through which conscientious bishops, priests and laymen poured in large numbers, in the belief that the traditional teaching could and would be changed. Many still believe that it can and will be changed in the end; I doubt it, but have no immovable opinion.
What interests me is the . . . damage done to the structure of religious authority, and in consequence to the . . . unwavering personal self-discipline of vast numbers of people whose morale was closely dependent on religious authority . . .
The Pope by his silence *appeared* to be saying for several years that he could not tell the difference between right or wrong in a matter of vital human concern . . . The Catholics of this generation will not cease to experience the earth-tremors radiating from this strange episode. It was in this period that clerical voices were heard discovering that marriage might after all be dissoluble, that abortion might after all be justified, that after all there was a case for homosexuality and masturbation, and that, at least in North America, pre-marital intercourse was all right if it was a nice boy and you loved him . . . There is really no limit to 'new insights'. By the time the Australian bishops tried to speak recently against abortion legislation, no one was listening.[4]

That 'no one was listening' reflected a substantial weakening of Australian Catholicism. The number of those who could be expected to undertake the responsibilities of public activities for a spiritual motive and purpose was greatly reduced. This was so particularly among those who attended Catholic schools from the late sixties onwards. To an extent which seemed inconceivable and which still defies rational explanation, the systematic teaching of the doctrines of the Catholic Faith largely disappeared from Catholic schools. In place of systematic teaching, which was publicly derided by a mass of university-trained teachers of religion as 'indoctrination' and 'brain-washing', there were substituted a number of trendy educational methods, of which the 'discovery method' and the 'life situation' method for a while had the greatest vogue. The result was doctrinal confusion, moral relativism, and a widespread loss of faith among those subjected to them.

In the Riddell Memorial Lectures which he delivered at the University of Newcastle-upon-Tyne in December 1974, Bryan Wilson defined the entire development as part of the general process of secularization, a process which he also believed, incorrectly one hopes, to be irreversible. 'Religions', he concluded, 'are always dying. In the modern world it is not clear that they have any prospect of re-birth'.[5]

Wilson placed the general revolt in the Catholic Church within the context of 'a militant youth culture and . . . the serious disruption in the universities that occurred throughout the western world at that time . . .'[6]

He added:

What many of those involved were discovering, often painfully, was that they could in fact challenge the Church, could threaten the Church, and eventually could live without the Church. For some, this reinterpretation of their position ultimately led to agnostic or political conclusions. Having been in the Church for so long, some priests found that they had to express even their incipient anti-religious dispositions in terms relevant to the religious organization to which they belonged. Only after some years has it become apparent to many of them that their specific struggles for 'change within' were in fact merely the symptomatic sickening for the eventual decision to get out.[7]

The trivialities and inanities of the trendy clergy could not disguise the fact that Christianity was witnessing the transference to the field of religion of the principles of the Romantic revolution. Stemming from the Renaissance, it had established the foundations of mass democracy through the agency of the French Revolution. It had then revolutionized art, literature, thought, in an explosion of self-assertion, often extending to self-idolatry. As far back as 1925, Ortega y Gasset had written that the detestation of the orthodox in traditional art would be carried through to an assault on the entire social order. 'It goes hand in hand', he wrote, 'with hatred of science, hatred of State, hatred, in sum, of civilization as a whole'.[8] 'Such modern phenomena as Existentialism, Situational Ethics, and the Theatre of the Absurd', observed Duncan Williams, 'are only intelligible in the context of this loss of faith in an external and eternal God'.[9] From philosophy, through politics, art, science, and once again through politics, Romanticism now set about destroying Christianity, in general, through the activity, the self-doubt, or the negligence of those who often held the commanding heights of office within official Catholic institutions.

In one of the more ironic manifestations of the general mood, St Thomas More was invoked as authority for the dubious proposition that the private conscience was the supreme arbiter of a Catholic's religious and moral beliefs: that so long as it was done in good conscience the obligation of Sunday Mass could be set aside (if the ceremony 'did you no good'), or that pre-marital sex was permissible (so long as the couple genuinely loved each other).

Some five centuries too late, one began to feel a little sorry for the martyred Chancellor. It was bad enough to be beheaded in the sixteenth century. It was much worse to become a cult figure in the twentieth. Because of the dramatic brilliance of Robert Bolt's *A Man for All Seasons*[10], he came to be regarded as the patron saint of 'protest', in the name of individual conscience against external authority: a kind of sixteenth-century Jane Fonda.

Although it was difficult, since serious history was as much in danger of dying out as serious religion, it became necessary to point out that Thomas More was nothing of the kind. His carefully framed last words—'the King's good servant, but God's first'—indicated the opposite.

On the five hundredth anniversary of the birth of Thomas More, I thought it opportune to point out what the death of Robert Bolt's hero (in *A Man for All Seasons*) really signified:

It is now claimed, with increasing emphasis, that Thomas is not only, in Bolt's words, a 'man for all seasons', but the common property of all Christian religious persuasions. For, it is said, he died for conscience, and this is the only thing which really matters. For this reason, Thomas More is sacred to all Christians, regardless of denomination, just as are Latimer and the Anglican martyrs, who also died, equally and undoubtedly, for conscience.

In our own age, we have seen Marxists, anarchists, Serbs, Croats, Macedonians, all die bravely for conscience. Like all brave men who die for ultimate conviction, they are worthy of our admiration, however one may judge their principles.

But it is a very different thing to imply either that the principles for which men die are all equally valid, because heroic men have died for all of them; or equally unimportant, since what matters is not the principles but the tribute of conscience, regardless of the principle, in the martyr's final testimony.

Such a view seems to make a nonsense of their decision to die at all. Why die violently, when what you think you are dying for is not of ultimate worth at all?

If the Christian denominations permit themselves to be deluded by this subjectivist doctrine of conscience, they are, obviously and logically, preparing the way for their own extinction. It may require superhuman effort to discover what is true and what is false. Indeed, we may never discover it, beyond substantial doubt.

But unless the Christian denominations seek to build their unity on the basis of what they come to agree to be objectively true, ecumenism will succeed only in excluding from the Christian profession those who believe that faith must be validated by reason.[11]

It is at least conceivable that when the Western world's current obsession with sex wanes, Pope Paul VI's greatest achievement may be seen to be what were regarded as his most unpopular measures: the promulgation of the Encyclical *Humanae Vitae* in July 1968, complemented by the *Declaration on Sexual Ethics* in January 1976. Their reasoned assertion of the necessary link between human love, permanent marriage, and procreation, may one day be all that stands between the human person, in all his fallible but free humanity, and the beast conditioned by climate and season.

The Religious Affairs correspondent of the London *Times*, Clifford Longley, whose views on these matters are different from mine, nevertheless grasped the same point when he wrote that if the Pope had spoken differently, it would inevitably have led to 'the collapse of any generally accepted and precise philosophy of sexual ethics'. Longley went on to say: 'There is more than a hint in *Humanae Vitae* that Pope Paul saw the point clearly, more clearly perhaps than any non-Roman Catholic church or lay authority'.[12]

This collapse, of course, has since occurred. The difference between the view of the London *Times* Religious Affairs correspondent and my own is that he apparently believes that the wholesale change should be accepted as part and parcel of twentieth-century Christianity.

Since 1968, the retrogression has been total: the rise—and fall—of the Pill; then, as a substitute, sterilization, which began by being voluntary and ended in India by becoming compulsory; the epidemic of abortion which, while raising different moral issues from contraception, clearly came to be used as a back-up method when contraceptive methods failed; the use of the organs of aborted foetuses for transplantation: the (rather limited) prospect of the substitution of the 'test-tube' baby for children who in the pre-abortion era were available for adoption; the further promise of 'banks' of ova and spermatozoa, from which parents might choose their favoured type of offspring. The list is almost infinite. We have not yet seen the end of the process whereby the human person is reduced to a computerized specimen for scientific experimentation.

My booklet *Contraception: Reflections on the Pope's Ruling* was primarily directed to the central issue which was in contention within the Catholic Church during that decade, namely the teaching authority of the Papacy. It did not concern itself, except parenthetically, with medical, biological or other scientific aspects of contraception. However, it did add:

It is quite possible that the day will come in which the Pope's decision—given on

*Top:* Mother Teresa and B. A. Santamaria at the Myer Music Bowl, Melbourne. 40th International Eucharistic Conference, February 1973

*Bottom:* B. A. Santamaria looks on as his daughter Bernadette meets Pope Paul VI at the Vatican, 1971

moral and *not* on medical grounds—will be vindicated even on medical grounds. On the evidence available, it would be a gross exaggeration to talk of another thalidomide scandal in relation to the contraceptive 'pill'. But the most recent medical reports as to the relationship between the 'pill' or 'pills' and thromboembolic (or 'clotting') diseases in previously healthy women, would indicate caution rather than enthusiasm in their use, moral considerations apart.[13]

Paul VI's Encyclical was less an act of sheer personal courage than the acceptance of a responsibility inevitably associated with his office. This, in the view of Catholics, is to teach with Christ's authority, whether the teaching is acceptable to the mass of men or, as was Christ Himself, is repudiated by them and ends in the crucifixion of the teacher. The call for personal courage came, however, when several influential national assemblies of Catholic bishops, following the example of their English predecessors at the time of Henry VIII, used remarkable casuistry, in theory to uphold but in practice to destroy, the traditional position which his Encyclical merely re-stated.

A quite different issue was raised, however, by the diplomatic policy pursued by Paul VI in his dealings with the Soviet Union and the other Communist powers. This occasioned major difficulties, even in Australia.

The year of *Humanae Vitae*—1968—was also the year of the Tet offensive, of the retirement of Lyndon B. Johnson, and of the beginning of the US withdrawal from Vietnam. In the mood induced by the anti-Vietnam campaigns, Communism ceased to be a threat, the 'domino theory' was nonsense, in the view of the 'revisionists' the Cold War had been caused by the United States rather than by the Soviet Union.

When in 1969 Dr Kissinger opened up the new channel to Peking, and his exploratory journey was followed in February 1972 by President Nixon's official visit to Mao, it was obvious that there were good, as well as bad, Communisms. In the new atmosphere Maoist China was represented in the West—as uncritically as the Soviet Union had been represented in the thirties—as a Utopian paradise; the Cultural Revolution (which apart from taking the lives of three million Chinese, destroyed China's entire educational system) as being authentically about culture; while the policy of détente was based on the proposition that the Soviet lion was about to lie down with the American lamb.

In this climate any organization whose existence was based on the proposition that Marxism should be resisted internally and externally hardly accorded with the popular mood. To intensify the difficulties, the Vatican had decided to adapt the policy of détente to its own diplomatic purposes.

The nature of the new Vatican strategy had become clear from the quite disgraceful methods used at the Vatican Council to stifle

342 debate on a petition signed, before 3 December 1963, by 200 bishops from forty-six countries. This petition requested that 'Catholic social doctrine would be set forth with great clarity and the errors of Marxism, socialism and communism would be refuted on philosophical, sociological and economic grounds'.[14] This proposal literally got nowhere. It was never even presented to the Council for rejection. By October 1965, the number of bishops demanding a discussion of the question had risen to 450. The Joint Commission responsible for the Schema on the Church in the Modern World, made no mention of Communism in its text, nor did it even refer to the request of the 450 bishops, even though their 'intervention' had been lodged within the specified time with the General Secretariat of the Council. It emerged that the official who had actually received the document in time, but claimed that it arrived too late to be considered, was Monsignor Achille Glorieux, who was Joint Secretary of the Commission responsible for the Schema, as well as Secretary of the Commission dealing with 'The Apostolate of the Laity'.

When the attention of Paul VI was drawn to the somewhat unorthodox conduct of this prominent writer on theological subjects, the Pope directed that the Church's existing teaching on Communism be inserted as a footnote in the Schema. As Archbishop Sigaud of Diamantina, Brazil, a main force behind the submission, wryly remarked in relation to the footnote: 'There is a difference between carrying a hat in your pocket, and wearing it on your head'.[15]

This series of events was extraordinary enough. No less amazing was the assertion by the heroic exile, Cardinal Beran of Prague, that he had received a press report from Communist Czechoslovakia which 'boasted that communists had succeeded in infiltrating every commission at the Vatican Council'.[16]

This policy was inherited by Paul VI from his predecessor, John XXIII. There is no doubt, however, that it was a policy with which Paul found himself in intuitive agreement. It was the ecclesiastical aspect of the diplomatic policy of détente.

The Pope would have been encouraged in this policy by both American and French influences, the latter strong within the Vatican. The basis of the Pope's predilection would however have gone back to much earlier days, to his own formative years in the thirties, the time of the Spanish Civil War. The future Pope had been greatly influenced in his intellectual formation by Jacques Maritain, for whom Paul VI retained a deep personal affection to the very end. In international affairs, and particularly in relation to Spain, the general run of the French Catholic intelligentsia would have been regarded as broadly to the left of the generally accepted Catholic position of the time. This group had a strong influence over the mind of the future Pope.

The policy pursued by both John XXIII and Paul VI in relation to the Communist powers referred back, however, to a much more ancient tradition and purpose in Vatican diplomacy. It has been said that the Vatican has only one ultimate foreign policy objective—to place the Church in every country in the best possible position to give the Last Sacraments to every one of its children. If this means coming to terms even with infamous governments, even those with a long record of persecution, then the Church should—prudently—be prepared to do so. It should be prepared to deal with any government with which it is possible to have dealings, regardless of ideology. It is a rational position, which should not be dismissed too cavalierly by those who have suffered from its particular expressions. For, in the last analysis, the Church ought not to be about politics. It ought to be about opening the gates of Heaven to those who perhaps may have closed them against themselves.

The argument for accommodation with Communist States rested on the necessity for a resumption of ordered religious life within Communist countries, if it could possibly be negotiated. The policy of intransigent opposition to Communism associated with the Pontificate of Pius XI and Pius XII had not prevented the consolidation of Communist régimes in the Soviet Union, Eastern Europe and China. Since that fact had to be accepted it was necessary to protect the religious faith of those condemned to live under them and, if possible, to relieve them from harsh persecution.

What was understandable in theory, however, had difficult consequences in practice. Just as a finely tuned intellect can understand the real meaning of, and the 'linkages' involved in, the policy of détente, so such an intellect would not be confused by the attempt to establish limited accommodation between the Church and a Communist State, without prejudice to a policy of principled and resolute opposition to Communism as an ideology. Unfortunately, the distinction, while tenable in principle, is not always comprehensible to the masses and can have quite catastrophic consequences in practice.

The Vatican policy of political accommodation with Communist States, while maintaining organized resistance to Communism as an ideology, has had similar results as the policy of détente in the field of international affairs. There have been only marginal improvements in the condition of Catholic communities in Iron Curtain countries, except in Poland where, under the leadership of Cardinal Wyszynski, the Church has won a large area of freedom for itself. It was won, however, not by accommodation, but by resistance. On the other hand, the removal of Cardinal Mindszenty from his office as Primate of Hungary illustrated the costs of such a policy and occasioned widespread disapproval. The policy of the 'open hand' pursued towards the Russian Orthodox Church had succeeded in alienating the Ukrainian Catholics, and not only the Ukrainians.

In the Western world, the policy of accommodation has caused a considerable weakening of Catholic political influence, not least in Italy itself, evidenced in the massive defeats sustained by the Italian Church on the issues of divorce and abortion. Nevertheless the remaining Christian Democratic vote, although for many reasons reduced, remains the bulwark of the anti-Communist resistance, unaffected by offers of dialogue, the propaganda of détente or the ecclesiastical diplomacy of accommodation.

Nobody will ever know how far John Paul I, the gentle and engaging successor of Paul VI, would have varied the policy of his predecessor. The former Cardinal Luciani, Patriarch of Venice, was strongly anti-Communist, but he survived his election for only one month. On his death, the Catholic Church and the world experienced the extraordinary phenomenon of a Polish Cardinal succeeding to the See of Peter. For the first time since the late fifties, it appeared that, in the formidable character of Karol Wojtyla, there was a Pope who, realizing that the enforcement of norms was as important as their promulgation, might end the religious anarchy, face the Communist world without illusions or fear, while resolutely proclaiming the Church's doctrine of human rights and social justice.

Behind the immense mass successes of the visits to Poland, Latin America, Ireland and the USA, the strategy of the new Pontificate gradually became clear.

Within eighteen months, the decisive positions had been taken: insistence on the binding force of the teaching authority of the Church, the Papacy and the Council; reassertion of the necessity for the systematic teaching of Catholic beliefs within the framework of the Catholic school system; reiteration of the entire Catholic system of sexual ethics; disavowal of the liturgical exaggerations which, since the disappearance of the Latin Mass, had cheapened Christian worship with practices more fitting to a discotheque; repudiation of the politicization of religion and of a political rôle for the clergy; insistence on the need for a firm doctrinal formation in the seminaries for the education of priests. That the new Pope did not intend to content himself with statements which were not enforced was indicated in the firm but careful handling of both Hans Küng and of the Dutch Church.

On the basis of his own practical experience of Marxism in Poland, the new Pope turned his face against the Marcusian aberrations of liberation theology, and against the intellectual nonsense of dialogue between Catholicism and Communism, which he described as 'two concepts of the world diametrically opposed'. The new Pope's policy thus reflects a total absence of illusions concerning either Marxism, or the possibilities of any deal with the Marxists, or of any policy other than that of facing the political and military

strength of Communism with the moral strength of Christianity.
A little more than a year after his election as Pope, John Paul II
moved to repair the damage created by the Vatican's earlier insensi-
tive handling of the Ukrainian Bishops, as it pursued its policy of
seeking an accommodation with the Russian Orthodox Church,
which in its highest, as distinct from its lower, levels, is little more
than an arm of the Soviet Government. He called a Synod of the
Ukrainian Bishops; consecrated a coadjutor with the right of succes-
sion to Cardinal Slipyi; and in nominating him as archbishop of
Lvov, clearly indicated that he did not accept what Paul VI had not
been prepared to dispute—the absorption of the Catholic Uniate
Church by the Russian Orthodox Church.

The approach of the new Pope to the Communist question is not a
reversion to a more traditional diplomacy prepared to come to terms
even with totalitarian régimes if they were willing to guarantee the
religious liberties of Catholics. John Paul II looks at the totalitarian
challenge in much the same way as does his fellow Pole, the former
Marxist and exiled Professor of Philosophy of Warsaw University
Leszek Kolakowski, now a Fellow of All Souls, Oxford, who
describes himself as not a Christian but 'a friend of Christianity as I
understand it'.

The essential evil of Marxism, wrote Kolakowski, lies not in the
fact that it is by definition atheistic, but in the fact that it is in essence
totalitarian.

Totalitarian States, whether Communist or Nazi, he added, perse-
cute religion not primarily because Marxism is intrinsically
atheistic—the official neutrality of democratic States is barely
different—but because it is the essence of totalitarianism that no
nook or cranny of human society, whether it is the family, the
community or education system, the trade union, politics, or the
Church, can be permitted any independence or escape from the
official ideology of the State.

In the encounter with totalitarian, as distinct from merely authoritarian systems, wrote Kolakowski, no Christian church should
accept offers or favours for itself—like freedom of religious practice
or of Christian schools—while at the same time the government in
question uses legal sanctions to deny 'the inalienable right of every
person to a free choice of his own form of spiritual life', whether he is
Protestant, Moslem, Orthodox, Catholic, Jew, or nothing at all.[17]

In that statement, Kolakowski seems to me to reflect the exact
position of the new Pope.

John Paul II has, furthermore, shown himself to be equally devoid
of illusions concerning the validity of the Western political and
economic system. Poland, he has pointed out, had long since chosen
the side of the West. The Western system of parliamentary
democracy does not use the methods of the Police State, and is

346 | thereby overwhelmingly preferable to Marxist totalitarian governments. Nevertheless, John Paul obviously does not believe that the Western system will necessarily prevail over its Marxist rival. His reasons are twofold. In the spiritual order, the West is obviously a decaying post-Christian society, in which the most basic obligations which have held society together, even the bonds of marriage and family, are being permitted to wither away. Like any reasonable man, he asks how States founded on such abdications can last. In his view, there is a chain of connection between moral and spiritual decline, and economic and political decay.

In his first Encyclical Letter *Redemptor Hominis*—which the Pope wrote by hand in his native Polish language only a month after his election—he called into question 'the financial, monetary, production and commercial mechanisms which, resting on various political pressures, support the world economy'.[18]

But it is for ethical, much more than for material, reasons that the patterns of social thought to which John Paul II will in future refer are unlikely to come from the consumer societies of the West.

Like Solzhenitsyn, John Paul is essentially a Slav. As Solzhenitsyn has emphasized, despite their industrialization, the strength of the Slav societies of Eastern Europe resides still in the sometimes primitive but nevertheless hardy and independent peasantry, which, whether in Poland, the Ukraine, the Soviet Union (or even China), has fought and at least partly won the battle for survival against the Commissar.

It is on that world—more closely linked with the poorer communities of Asia, Africa and Latin America than are the consumer societies of the West—that John Paul II bases his hopes for the reassertion of the strength of Christianity.

For the first time since Vatican II, I believe that there is a firm Christian philosophical base for activity in the political and social order, and that the re-discovery of sound foundations will have its effect in daily practice.

# 35 From Whitlam to Fraser

The three years from 2 December 1972 to 11 November 1975 have gone down in Australian history as the Whitlam years. They provided Australia's closest approach to what are loosely called the 'new' politics. Taken in conjunction with the five years of the two Fraser Governments which followed, they illustrated the near-impossibility of solving problems like inflation and unemployment by purely political means, since the problems are only apparently economic but are in reality social and structural. For the NCC they also illustrated the problems involved in adapting a movement created to meet the challenge to constitutional power by Communist-led unions to a situation in which unionism itself, rather than Communism within unions, apparently challenged the authority of an increasingly bureaucratic State.

Alan Renouf, who worked under Mr Whitlam as Secretary of the Foreign Affairs Department, summed up the contribution of the first Labor Prime Minister since 1949 in these words:

... In my opinion, Whitlam's good qualities far outweighed his bad ones. He was intelligent, hard-working, patriotic, decisive, zealous to reform, and was driven by the national interest rather than by personal ambition. He saw that after 23 years of conservative, status quo governments there were many things that had to be done in Australia. In foreign affairs, Whitlam was more than anything else a modernizer. He realized that the world political and economic situation had changed drastically since Spender had in 1950 drawn up the foreign policy which conservative governments in Australia had followed faithfully ever since and that Australia's policy had to be adjusted accordingly.[1]

Yet by 1975, the majority of Australians were thoroughly sick of the Whitlam style for which they had opted in 1972. The majority of fifty-five seats in the House of Representatives—the largest in the history of Federation—which they gave to Mr Fraser three years later was proof of the intensity of their reaction. Although the new Prime Minister was not a 'glad-hander' and although the Canberra

Press Gallery was against him almost unanimously in the 1977 elections, the people gave him the second largest majority in the history of the Commonwealth—forty-eight seats. In the 1980 election this was, not unexpectedly, greatly reduced, but Mr Fraser was still left with a majority of twenty-three seats.

The 1972 election campaign epitomized the method of the 'new' politics as an American plant grown in Australian soil. They were described in a *National Times* article (23-28 July 1973) inspiringly entitled 'The Marketing of the ALP: How the "It's Time" machine put pizazz in the policy':

The selling of the ALP and Gough Whitlam, his wife Margaret, and the Labor team introduced to Australia the tactics and methods of the advertising world on a scale which never before had been used in a political campaign.

The article described Mr 'Sim' Rubensohn's PR campaign as 'possibly the most significant marketing exercise since World War II'.

The description of the technique was enlightening.

By deliberately likening the ALP to any other marketing problem it set out to find a solution. In particular the agency pointed to lessons from the very successful campaign run in Australia by Johnny Walker scotch whisky.

For example, Johnny Walker sells half the scotch whisky sold in Australia. One hundred and two brands of scotch compete for the market, and on taste tests people can't tell one from the other. However, most people believe Johnny Walker to be superior, because it is perceived to be the best . . . what they really perceive is not the whisky in the bottle, but what is imagined to be in the bottle.

It then set out to put into the bottle a whole new image of the ALP.[2]

It is an interesting reflection on a sophisticated western community, which spends over 8 per cent of its GDP on what is charitably called education, that it permits its choice of Prime Minister not merely to be influenced by the advertising techniques developed to sell a bottle of whisky, but even to be deceived as to the contents of the bottle. However, the triumph of the new science of public relations in the running of election campaigns was not a phenomenon confined either to Mr Whitlam or to Australia.

Behind all of the trendy nonsense associated with the 'It's Time' theme, there was in fact a carefully calculated strategy. The political strategy had been prepared even before Mr Whitlam succeeded to the parliamentary leadership of the ALP after Mr Calwell's disastrous defeat in 1966.

The first necessity facing the new leader in his quest for the ultimate acquisition of power was to win and retain control of the Labor Party. The second was to lead that party to electoral victory. Mr Whitlam, being extremely intelligent, understood that the same formula would suffice for both. The moderates in the machine and the blue-collar workers in the electorate could be relied on unconditionally. What was necessary was to associate the Communist-based Left in the unions and the new middle classes in the suburbs.

The so-called moderate—but essentially careerist—forces in the ALP, based on the New South Wales Executive, had no alternative to Mr Whitlam; so they could be taken for granted.

Like the careerist moderates in the Labor machine, over 40 per cent of the electorate could be regarded as safe for any Labor leader, regardless of policies and attitudes. As far as social attitudes went, the blue-collar manual workers were a rather conservative group, but they were used to voting Labor: this, regardless of the fact that 'their' party was beginning to become the vehicle of highly-salaried young professionals whose minds were conditioned by the fashionable shibboleths of the Left picked up during their university studies in the great days of the Vietnam teach-ins.

Even if the blue-collar workers were likely to be temporarily upset by some of Mr Whitlam's disciples, they were safely locked into overwhelmingly Labor electorates. Even if a high proportion were to change their votes, these seats would remain safe.

The McGovernite forces, composed largely of the trendy well-heeled professional classes, steeled in the symbolic fires of the anti-Vietnam demonstrations, took over the US Democratic machine during 1972. The same 'new class' established itself in control of the ALP in Australia at almost exactly the same time. Mr Whitlam's Education Minister (Mr Kim Beazley) was one Labor man who was not impressed with this development. He was quoted as saying that when he first went as a young man to ALP forums those present were the cream of the working class, while now those there in many cases represented the dregs of the middle class.[3]

The trendy middle class lived in the outer metropolitan suburbs of Sydney and Melbourne, or in the inner suburbs of Carlton and Paddington, from which the poor were excluded as the affluent newcomers pushed up the price of land and houses. This was the class which Mr Whitlam set out to capture to create his new electoral alliance.

The economic basis of the alliance was Mr Cameron's encouragement to the Public Service to act as pacemakers in claims for higher salaries and better conditions, in the full knowledge that the 'flow on' principle would draw in the entire white-collar electorate. It was ironic that Mr. Cameron, at heart an old-style left-wing Labor man, should give a major impetus to the economic advancement of the new middle classes, only later to denounce those whom he had encouraged to enrich themselves as 'fat cats'.

It was not difficult to provide an ideological basis as well as an economic interest for the policy of attracting the new class. Mr. Whitlam was evidently a believer in the causes associated with the arts, the environment, censorship, easier divorce, abortion, and all of the excesses of Women's Lib—until the last became grossly counter-productive in mid-1975.

The Communist-based Left in the unions was primarily interested in ensuring that a Labor Government would finally abandon the 'penal clauses' in the Arbitration Act, thus freeing union power from legal restraints which might be imposed on political strikes. They were also seriously interested in foreign policy. The violent anti-Americanism of some of Mr Whitlam's senior ministers, in their statements following the bombing of Hanoi, was not an essay in cynicism. It was heartfelt. It delighted the Communists and their allies. It was followed by the 'raid' on the headquarters of ASIO (the Australian Security Intelligence Organization) by his Attorney-General, the then Senator Murphy; the persecution of the Croatian minority which, wittingly or unwittingly, was calculated to intimidate every central and east European ethnic minority in the country; the total withdrawal from Singapore, and the consequent destruction of ANZUK, despite the original Whitlam compromise that 600 troops would be left; the withdrawal of military aid from South Vietnam and Cambodia, and the welcome given to representatives of the Provisional Revolutionary Government immediately afterwards; the precipitate withdrawal of diplomatic recognition from Taiwan on terms far more unfavourable than those Peking was perfectly prepared to concede to the United States, Canada and Japan, as the price of a new relationship.

There was also Mr Whitlam's criticism of the continued presence of American troops in Thailand, which led to the *Bangkok Post* telling him to 'mind his own bloody business' and which added to the isolationist mood in the US; the recognition of the Soviet occupation of the Baltic States; the attack on US proposals to build a base at Diego Garcia in the Indian Ocean; the sending of 'humanitarian aid' to the various guerilla forces in Africa; the application for observer status at the conference of the non-aligned nations, as a symbol of Australia's 'third world' orientation; the less-than-even-handed policy towards Israel; all of these—and other forgotten gestures—were part of the revolution of symbols in which the Canberra Press Gallery delighted as an assertion of Australian independence, while the Left saw in it the weakening of the relationship with the US, which was the central purpose of its policy.

The abolition of conscription—introduced during the Vietnam War—by administrative decree, which followed immediately on Mr Whitlam's accession to office, was the symbolic coping-stone of the new policy, which in the view of the Left marked the abandonment of the 'sterile' Cold War policies of previous Governments.

The Whitlam commitment to the new foreign policy and the new industrial policy thus served to consolidate Mr Whitlam in the leadership—which was very different from the control—of the Labor Party. This achieved, his attachments to the causes dear to the new class served to forge alliances with sufficient numbers of white-collar workers to win two elections—in 1972 and 1974.

With the power of government in his hands, there was little doubt that Mr Whitlam had the native ability to provide effective political leadership, had he been prepared to turn his mind to it. The practical work to be done for Australia by a new government was quite clear, even if it meant a gradual modification of his pre-electoral promises. In an increasingly dangerous international environment, what was imperative was the strengthening of Australia's defences, and a clear-cut foreign policy, without any illusions about the reliability of the USA, seeking close association with ASEAN and Japan.

An economy in which the fires of inflation had already been lit by the McMahon Government needed restraint rather than extravagance. The poor deserved substantial improvements in their condition. These improvements were basically to be measured in family income. They were profoundly different from the programme which was actually adopted, a programme of social 'innovations' grandiloquently aimed at providing universal cover for the rich, the middle-income groups and the poor alike, which could result only in the creation of vast bureaucratic structures, and the consequent advantage of those who occupied the newly established positions of administrative power.

The election of 1974 gave Mr Whitlam pause. The rate of inflation approached 20 per cent and statistical unemployment 4.5 per cent. With Mr Hayden in the Treasury and Senator James McClelland as Minister for Labour, he set out to reverse some of his earlier economic policies.

In supporting the policy of wage indexation against the opposition of Mr Carmichael, President of the Communist Party of Australia, who acted through the AMWSU, Mr Whitlam now turned against the main economic policy objective of the extreme Left. For the first time the elements of a real conflict between the Whitlam Government and extreme Left were present.

Unfortunately the matter was never put to the test. Mr Fraser pulled the rug from under Mr Whitlam's feet before it could be determined whether Mr Whitlam would really have backed Senator James McClelland in his challenge to Mr Carmichael during the threatened national metal trades strike in September 1975.

Australia's rather threadbare version of Camelot finally collapsed on 11 November 1975. It would be consoling to believe that it collapsed because the rate of inflation bred by the public expenditure it required—rising from approximately $10 billion to $22 billion in three budgets—ultimately reached a level almost unequalled in the Western industrial world; consoling to believe that even the new class, which benefited most, finally had the decency and social compassion to rebel against the injustice which inflation inflicted on young couples on lower incomes who could not buy homes, and on the elderly, whose assets were simply stolen by the depreciation of the currency.

It would also be consoling to believe that this reaction came from a belated realization of what Mr Whitlam's trumpeted independence in foreign policy really meant: a ludicrous situation in which Australia recognized what was at the time a non-existent Provisional Revolutionary Government in Saigon and a non-existent Sihanouk Government in Cambodia; the impotence displayed over Timor, and the consequent souring of relations with Indonesia.

Even in the moment of Mr Whitlam's defeat, I had my doubts that the real reason was much more than a sense of insecurity felt by a small proportion of his allies, occasioned by endless rising prices.

The subsequent Fraser years were to reveal that Australia's problems, like those of the West in general, were far more deep-seated than the Whitlam style of government; and that without a complete change in popular expectations and assumptions it was impossible to solve Australia's basic problems.

When Mr Fraser came to power at the end of 1975, he promised in good faith what Mrs Thatcher was to offer, in equally good faith, when she came to power in May 1979. He promised drastically to reduce government expenditure, to balance the Budget, to reduce taxation, to increase the disposable income of individuals and businesses, to conquer inflation, to allow business profitability to revive, and so absorb the unemployed.

As I now write, it can be claimed that, under Mr Fraser's administration, the economy has become far more predictable. But if Federal Budgetary expenditure roughly represents a Federal Government's choice of priorities, one can only note how little has changed. Perhaps the 1978-79 Federal Budget, the last before the crude oil levy began to make its large impact on public finances, illustrates the apparently permanent nature of the problem.

The 1977-78 Budget deficit was approximately $3,000 million. So was the anticipated Budget deficit for 1978-79. In the former year, Federal Budget income was 26 per cent and expenditure 29.7 per cent of the GDP; in the latter year, the anticipated proportions were 26 per cent and 29 per cent respectively: that is, to all intents and purposes, unchanged.

In the former years 8.9 per cent of Federal outlays went to defence. These remained at 8.7 per cent in 1978-79. Social security, health, education and welfare took 46.7 per cent in the former year, and were estimated to be identical in the latter. Economic services moved from 6.0 per cent to 6.1 per cent. General public services were 6.7 per cent in both years. Payments to the States were to rise marginally from 22.1 per cent to 22.7 per cent. Interest on the public debt was scheduled to rise from 6.1 per cent to 6.6 per cent.

Thus Mr Fraser's professed social and economic philosophy might be utterly different from Mr Whitlam's thriftless trendyism. It was hard to find it reflected in any radical change in their respective Budgets.

In May 1980 it was announced that despite the several revolutions in Medibank, Australia's health bill was now running at $8,000 million annually. Yet the life-expectancy of a 40-year-old Australian has scarcely increased since the turn of the century, and—in mid-1980—the Bureau of Census and Statistics turned out the surprising announcement that 50 per cent of Australians are suffering from chronic diseases.

It is comforting to know that every section of the health industry, as it is now sometimes called, is being more adequately remunerated; that far more sophisticated medical equipment exists; that nurses may soon all have tertiary degrees, which will elevate their status closer to that of doctors, while the actual nursing is performed by nursing aides. But the end-product of the whole expensive effort is hardly startling.

The statistics revealed a wholesale change in social attitudes from a community in which people intuitively believed that the care of the young, the sick, and the old was primarily the responsibility of the family, to a community in which the path of wisdom was for the family to divest itself of its assets so that even the relatively wealthy would finish their lives on a pension paid by those much poorer than themselves. From 1970 to 1980, the total number of recipients of pensions and benefits had more than doubled—from 1,048,560 to 2,336,000. The cost grew from $780 million in the 1968-69 Budget (or 11.8 per cent of Commonwealth outlays) to $6,442 million (or 22.2 per cent of Commonwealth outlays) in 1978-79.[4]

The Sydney *Bulletin* correspondent, Peter Samuel, commented:

Take just one item, the age pension, costing $3.4 billion this year in total or $560 annually per worker, more than $10 a week out of the average paypacket. It now goes to over 80 per cent of men over 65 and women over 60. Perhaps 10 per cent or even 20 per cent might have been unable to provide for their retirement by savings, but it is a scandalous perversion of welfarism that we should have arrived at a situation where four-fifths of old people live off the taxpayers.

Since the means test was abolished, only income (no longer wealth) is used to limit pensions (and over 70 they are even given to millionaires) and struggling workers have been asked to supplement the incomes of the affluent old.[5]

At the end of four years of Fraser Government, the inflation rate is 10 per cent, the prime interest rate is above that figure, public expenditure is taking a marginally higher proportion of the GDP than it did during the Whitlam reign, the Budget deficit would be far greater than Mr Whitlam's if Mr Fraser had not fed the crude oil levy into it, as Mrs Thatcher has fed the profits from the North Sea oil. In both cases a depletion allowance, which ought to be treated as capital, is being diverted to finance current expenditure.

So what is wrong?

There is no difference between Australian trends and those in Britain, the US, and other Western European countries in which the

354 | unparalleled increase in the volume of money simply indicates that almost all governments have lost control of the financial system. The explosion in government expenditure has been accompanied by an even greater explosion in private spending. This extraordinary increase in both public and private spending has arisen as a result of the wholesale revolution in material expectations over the past thirty years. To pander to those expectations was the road to political advancement. To warn against them was to be rejected as a Cassandra.

As Colin Clark has written:

Buying votes out of social service money is . . . one of the lowest forms of political corruption. 'The corrupt politicians of the 18th century', said Evelyn Waugh, 'did at least use their own money to bribe the electors.' A political order which depends on such buying of votes will end in uncontrollable inflation.[6]

This revolution in material expectations came about in three waves. The initial post-war expectations were apparently modest: Lord Beveridge's Welfare State and Lord Keynes' Full Employment. The State would guarantee health and jobs. Fair enough!

The second wave came with the fifties, which was the high-noon of consumer capitalism. Technology and its handmaiden, mass advertising, showed how, in addition to health and jobs, we could all command cars, TV sets, washing machines, refrigerators, overseas holidays. So—why not?

The realization of these expectations could, of course, only be financed by the various forms of hire purchase or consumer credit at what had until then been regarded as usurious rates of interest. Together with back-breaking repayments on the family home, built on metropolitan land at prices inflated by the excessive concentration of population in capital cities and secondarily by the general rise in all prices, the neatly presented system meant that the family needed two incomes, so that the wife and mother must go out to work. So, together with womenkind in most western societies, between 40 per cent and 50 per cent of them did so, some because they wanted to, but the vast majority as a result of economic or psychological compulsions.

Inevitably, the third stage in the social revolution followed. Neglected children and neglected sick and old people set up enormous demands for creches, schools, and hospitals. Although families tended to solve the first-named set of problems by not having more than one or two children, the escalation in the cost of pensions, hospitals, schools and the rest, was apparently unstoppable.

As Christopher Booker has written,

The real problem lies in the way our whole society has become dependent, through the revolution of rising expectations on a kind of amalgam of State and Consumer Capitalism—to provide a material standard of living which almost certainly cannot survive the rest of this century, and should probably begin reducing long before that if anything is to be saved at all.[7]

It is not without irony that the Australian Senate Standing Committee on Social Welfare, at the end of three years of investigation, reported that Australia's health and welfare services were completely 'out of control'.

With neither rhyme nor reason, the sacred 'system' nevertheless provides the excuse for the existence of a vast, all-powerful bureaucracy.

The only remedy the Standing Committee could propose is another tier of bureaucrats to evaluate the performance of those already there. But who will evaluate the evaluators?

The quasi-Hayekian or quasi-Friedmanite approach naturally evokes sympathy among business interests which would like to see company tax and income tax rates reduced. It is, however, far from the whole of the story. The difficulty of controlling the issue of money is due not merely to the explosion in public expenditure. The other equally important part of the modern inflation is the régime of 'managed' prices and wages in which, in key industries, major corporations and their counterparts in the union movement come to terms which, thereupon, as often as not, are legally validated by Arbitration and Trade Practices Commissions. What is happening is, on the one hand, the development of an increasingly onerous Welfare State and, on the other, the gradual substitution of the Corporate State for the parliamentary system.

The political aspect of the social revolution was described, perhaps unwittingly, by the former British Prime Minister, Mr Callaghan, when he declared that political parties required vested interests as their basis, organized industry and commerce for the Conservatives, and the trade unions for Labor.[8]

All that this can mean is that skilled workers, or even the relatively unskilled in industries which can paralyse public activity, can expect constantly increasing wages and shorter hours, while the number of those living below a realistically estimated poverty line will continue to increase. The battle-lines of a different class-war are thus drawn, the antagonists being an alliance of the rich, the skilled and the leaders of the powerful unions, against the unskilled, the larger families and the weaker unions.

The problem is therefore neither budgetary nor even financial. Its roots lie deep within the basic assumptions of the social and economic system itself.

Hence the only solution to what is a fundamental problem lies in a modification of the system itself, although this is apparently regarded as impossible and unthinkable. That modification needs to begin at the most basic level. As the French have finally discovered (and, in the Communist world, the Hungarians), it requires legal,

356 | financial and taxation reforms which will counter the continual erosion of the family unit, so that this delicate but highly durable mechanism can once again fulfil the specific purposes for which it was devised by either God or Nature—the primary care of the young, the sick and the old. For this simple mechanism, bureaucrats, teachers, social workers, hospitals, crêches, are an expensive and inefficient substitute.

Side-by-side with that primary principle, there is the equally necessary restoration of the small and medium unit in business, government and administration. As Karl Mannheim has pointed out, there is no alternative other than social disintegration to a return to a system of limited size which allows everyone to understand what is required of him and what to expect from the group.[9]

Unless those things can at least be attempted, neither Mr Fraser nor Mrs Thatcher will be able to achieve anything more than the temporary stabilization of a largely monopolistic economy which, in constitutional theory, will be governed by the canons of parliamentary democracy, but, in administrative practice, by an Anglo-Saxon version of Mussolini's Corporate State.

# Epilogue

Because they must face elections every three years, the political parties are inherently unlikely to provide national leadership, on issues of public policy which are of long-term importance but not of immediate urgency, to an electorate whose interests are ephemeral. A systematic re-education of public opinion needs therefore to be undertaken to draw the new parameters of ideas within which governments, political parties and pressure groups, in their own ultimate self-interest, will find it necessary to act. More important than the battle for the control of institutions and organizations is the battle of ideas, without which the former is directionless and sterile. One needs to act in the hope that Keynes was right when he wrote: 'The power of vested interests is vastly exaggerated compared with the gradual encroachment of ideas'.[1]

His observation is certainly true in relation to the emergence of the Welfare State. The concept of the Welfare State first conquered public opinion and thereby prescribed the ambit within which governments, radical or conservative, have been compelled to work within the past two decades, whatever Prime Ministers and Cabinets, with their knowledge of the facts of the economy and of the danger of inflation, might have prescribed. A similar task must be accomplished in the interests of national defence, decentralism, the family.

To the solution of these deep problems of our national life, which is the product of a Western cultural inheritence installed in a vast but undeveloped and unpopulated continent on the southern rim of Asia, forty years of effort by the small but creative minority with which I have been associated has made only a small contribution. Nevertheless, as a result of this small effort, it is no exaggeration to claim that up to 100,000 persons who have passed through the ranks of the Movement, the NCC and the DLP have been significantly influenced by the play of these ideas. Of these there are some 20,000

358 | Australians politically well informed; with practical experience through activities in unions, university associations and political parties; motivated by a sense of spiritual responsibility towards their fellows; seriously intent on solving the problems of Australia's national existence regardless of personal political advantage. There are no doubt many others as well.

Hence, however meagre the result may appear to be, however remote a turn in the tide may seem, I still believe it worth the effort to turn the energies of these Australians to work in their political parties; to hold and expand the base in the trade union movement; to work in the universities; to provide backing and help to bodies like the Australian Defence Association and the Australian Family Association, so that the ideas proposed in these memoirs may continue to do their work in what, rightly or wrongly, I regard as the interest of Australia.

# Notes

## 2 The *Catholic Worker*

1 James G. Murtagh, *Australia: The Catholic Chapter*, Sheed & Ward, New York, 1946, p. 215.
2 *Catholic Worker*, 1 February 1936, p. 1.

## 3 The Mannix Tradition

1 Rt. Rev. Dean Mulcahy, 'Reminiscences', *Irish Ecclesiastical Record*, September 1945, p. 163.
2 Letter from Monsignor O'Riordan to Dr Mannix, 9 July 1912.
3 Archbishop Mannix, at Geelong, August 1917. Cited by Frank Murphy in the prefatory quotation to *Daniel Mannix*, The Advocate Press, Melbourne, 1948.
4 Shane Leslie, *Cardinal Manning*, Clonmore & Reynolds, Dublin, 1953, Ch. XIII.
5 E. R. Norman, *The Catholic Church and Ireland in the Age of Rebellion 1859-1873*, Longmans, Green & Co., London, 1965, p. 133.
6 Dr J. G. Hurley, cited in *Laurels*, Christmas 1965, p. 5.
7 H. V. Evatt, *Australian Labour Leader*, Angus & Robertson, Sydney, 1940, p. 410.
8 Walter Lippmann, *The Public Philosophy*, Mentor, New York, 1958, p. 27.
9 *Argus*, 29 March 1913.

## 4 The Spanish War

1 W. H. Auden, *Modern Canterbury Pilgrims*, edited by the Dean of New York, Mowbray, London, 1966, p. 41.
2 Samuel Hynes, *The Auden Generation: Literature and Politics in England in the 1930s*, Bodley Head, London, 1976, p. 242.
3 W. H. Auden, in 'Spilling the Spanish Beans', *New English Weekly*, 29 July 1937, citing George Orwell, *Selected Essays*, vol. 1, p. 269.
4 A. J. P. Taylor, *English History 1914-1945*, Oxford University Press, 1965, pp. 394-5.
5 C. M. H. Clark, in Notes for a Talk at Graduation Ceremony, University of Melbourne, 21 December 1974.

# 5 Apprenticeship

1 *Argus*, 29 May 1939.
2 ibid.
3 ibid.
4 *Socialisation*, Social Justice Statement, 1948, Renown Press, Carnegie, Victoria, p.17.
5 Pope Pius XI, Encyclical Letter *Quadragesimo Anno*, 15 May 1931, Australian Catholic Truth Society publication, 15 July 1931, p. 21.
6 T. R. Luscombe, *Builders and Crusaders*, Lansdowne Press, Melbourne, 1967, pp. 193-4.
7 W. E. Hocking, 'The Social Values of Farm Life', 1942 Year Book of the US Department of Agriculture, cited in *The Earth Our Mother*, Araluen Publishing Co., Melbourne, 1945, as Appendix A, p. 164.
8 ibid., p. 165.
9 Robert Murray, *The Split: Labour in the Fifties*, F. W. Cheshire Publishing, 1970, p. 115.

# 6 The Climate of the Times

1 Dean Acheson, *Present at the Creation*, Hamish Hamilton, London, 1970, p. 195.
2 Sidney Hook, 'David Caute's Fable of "Fear and Terror"', *Encounter*, January 1979, p. 559.
3 Anthony Boyle, *The Climate of Treason*, Hutchinson, London, 1979.
4 William Manchester, *American Caesar: Douglas MacArthur, 1880-1964*, Little Brown, Boston, 1978, p. 579.
5 Sidney Hook, op. cit., p. 58.
6 David Caute, *The Fellow-Travellers*, Weidenfeld & Nicolson, London, 1973.
7 Acheson, op. cit., pp. 473-4.
8 J. N. Rawling, *Newcastle Morning Herald & Miners' Advocate*, 30 January 1940.
9 George Orwell, Introduction to *Animal Farm*. Written in 1945 but not printed. Published as 'The Freedom of the Press' in *New York Times*, 8 October 1972.
10 Transcript, Australian Broadcasting Commission, Radio Drama and Features Department, 'The Making of an Australian Communist': Rupert Lockwood Interviewed by Tim Bowden, 16 September 1973, pp. 17-18.
11 ibid., p. 12.
12 ibid., pp. 13-14.
13 John Sendy, *Comrades Come Rally!*, Nelson, West Melbourne, 1978, p. 12.

# 7 Communist Penetration

1 Letter from Archbishop Mannix to E. J. Hogan, 28 February 1933.
2 Reply from E. J. Hogan to above letter.
3 J. N. Rawling, 'The Communist Party of Australia to 1930', Work in Progress Seminar, Australian National University, 4 May 1962, p. 6.
4 Victorian ALP Conference 1936, Executive Report (1935-36), p. 2.
5 Victorian ALP Conference 1936, Agenda Paper, Items 54-62, 64-5.
6 Brian Fitzpatrick, *A Short History of the Australian Labor Movement*, Rawson, Melbourne, 1955, pp. 212-13.
7 Victorian ALP Conference, 1939, Agenda Item 155, C.E./V-R Item 21.

# 8 The Movement: Its Origins

1 Frank McManus, *The Tumult and the Shouting*, Rigby, Adelaide, 1977, p. 25.
2 Murray, *The Split*, p. 7.

3 See evidence given by V. Stout in Oct. 1960, in the Victorian Supreme Court,
*R. A. Cameron* v. *Australian Labor Trust Society Ltd.*, F. P. McManus and others,
pp. 499-503.
4 McManus, op. cit., p. 24.
5 Brian Fitzpatrick, *A Short History of the Australian Labor Movement*, p. 213.
6 McManus, op. cit., p. 25.
7 L. F. Crisp, *Ben Chifley: A Biography*, Longmans, Melbourne, 1960, p. 354.
8 Commonwealth Labor Report No. 35.
9 C. Sharpley, *The Great Delusion*, Heinemann, London, 1952, p. 67.

# 9 Building a National Organization

1 Minutes, Extraordinary Meeting of Australian Bishops, 19-20 September 1945.
2 P. J. Duffy, SJ, 'Catholic Judgments on the Origins and Growth of the Australian
Labor Party Dispute 1954-1961', Thesis submitted for the degree of Master of Arts
in the University of Melbourne, 8 December 1967, pp. 33-4, 36.
3 Letter from Archbishop Mannix to Australian Bishops, 19 November 1945.
4 Murray, *The Split*, p. 51.
5 ibid., p. 51.
6 ibid., p. 51.
7 'Constitution of the Catholic Social Studies Movement', 1946, Article 2.
8 'Catholic Resistance to Communism', Australian Bishops' Report to Rome,
1950, p. 3.

# 10 The Sectarian Dilemma

1 George Watson, *Politics and Literature in Modern Britain*, Macmillan, 1978,
cited in review by W. W. Robson, *Times Literary Supplement*, 21 July 1978.
2 ibid.
3 L. F. Crisp, *Ben Chifley*, p. 357.
4 John Kerr, *Matters for Judgment*, Macmillan, Australia, 1978, p. 143.
5 H. V. Evatt, *Australian Labour Leader*, Angus & Robertson, Sydney, 1945, p.
410.
6 Frank McManus, *The Tumult and the Shouting*, p. 24.
7 ibid., p. 38.
8 G. F. Walsh, 'The Origins of the Clerical Workers' ALP Industrial Group',
Thesis submitted in partial fulfilment of the requirements for the degree of Master of
Arts in the Politics Department School of Social Sciences, La Trobe University,
Bundoora, Victoria, August 1978, p. 64.
9 W. J. McKell, cited in *ALP Industrial Groups Handbook*, issued by the ALP on
behalf of the ALP Industrial Groups, Sydney, 1946, p. 5.
10 J. A. Ferguson, cited in *ALP Industrial Groups Handbook*, p. 15.
11 A. B. Davidson, *The Communist Party of Australia: A Short History*, Hoover
Institution Press, Stanford University, California, 1969, p. 131, citing C. Sharpley,
*The Great Delusion*, Heinemann, London, 1952, pp. 40-1.
12 Cited by G. Piera (State Organizer, Industrial Groups of Victoria) in *Trade
Unions and the Labor Party*, p. 3.
13 *Freedom*, 12 December 1945.
14 B. A. Santamaria, 'The Split', *Australian Quarterly*, June 1971, p. 101.
15 E. F. Hill, *Tribune*, 12 December 1951.
16 C. Sharpley, Melbourne *Herald*, 4 June 1949.
17 R. Dixon, *Tribune*, 12 December 1951.

## 11 Labor's Reply to Communism

1 C. Sharpley, *I was a Communist Leader*, Melbourne Herald publication, 1949, p. 8.
2 Melbourne *Argus*, 13 December 1945.
3 Sharpley, op. cit., p. 14.
4 ibid., pp. 7, 14.
5 B. Chifley, *Sydney Morning Herald*, 4 July 1949.
6 *Second Annual Report of the Joint Coal Board (1948-49)*, Sydney, 1950, p. 35.
7 J. McPhillips, 'ACTU Congress Decisions', *Communist Review*, no. 167, November 1955, p. 344.
8 *Laurence Short* v. *Federated Ironworkers' Association of Australia, Industrial Information Bulletin* (Department of Labour and National Service), 6(12) December 1951, p. 994.
9 Sharpley, op. cit., p. 10.
10 Sharpley, *The Great Delusion*, p. 80.
11 Daphne Gollan, 'The Memoirs of "Cleopatra Sweatfigure"', Paper delivered at Women and Labour Conference, May 1978.
12 Approved Defence Projects Protection Act, 1947: Appendix to H. V. Evatt, *Hands off the Nation's Defences*, Federal Capital Press, Canberra, 1947.
13 Evatt, *Hands off the Nation's Defences*, pp. 6-7.
14 *Catholic Worker*, August 1949.
15 *News Weekly*, 19 August 1949.
16 Edgar Ross, *The Socialist*, 16 March 1977, p. 5.
17 ibid.
18 J. D. Pringle, *Australian Accent*, Chatto & Windus, London, 1958, p. 78.

## 12 The Menzies Challenge

1 Alan Watt, *The Evolution of Australian Foreign Policy 1938-1965*, Cambridge University Press, paperback edition, 1968, pp. 240 ff.
2 Victor Purcell, *The Chinese in South-East Asia*, Oxford University Press, 1951, p. 400.
3 C. Sharpley, *The Great Delusion*, p. 111.
4 Melbourne *Herald*, 5 January 1977.
5 John Gittings, *The World and China 1922-1972*, Eyre Methuen, London, 1974, p. 151.
6 ibid., p. 151.
7 *News Weekly*, 11 January 1950.
8 Letter from Archbishop Mannix to H. Holt, 7 January 1950.
9 Memorandum from B. A. Santamaria to H. Holt, 7 January 1950.
10 ibid.
11 Murray, p. 81.
12 Murray, p. 79.
13 H. P. Breen, Former Permanent Head of Department of Defence Production, 'Make our Defence the Keystone of all Policy', *Australian Quarterly*, December 1959, p. 22.
14 Murray, p. 88.

## 13 High Noon

1 Sydney *Sun*, 17 November 1952.
2 H. V. Evatt, Address to Industrial Groups Rally, Sydney Town Hall, 30 March 1952.
3 Judah Waten, *Labor History*, May 1980, p. 96.

# 14 Asian Interlude

1 Statement by Catholic Bishops' Conference of India, Calcutta *Herald*, 15 January 1956.
2 Letter from B. A. Santamaria to A. Mehta, 18 May 1959.

# 15 To the Labor Split

1 Murray, p. 43.
2 R. Dixon, *Tribune*, 12 December 1951.
3 L. L. Sharkey, *Communist Review*, July 1954, p. 197.
4 Melbourne *Age*, 12 November 1953.
5 *Hansard*, House of Representatives, 6 April 1954, p. 31.
6 e.g., Murray, pp. 147-8.
7 Murray, p. 147.
8 Melbourne *Age*, 26 June 1980.
9 J. B. Paul, 'The Petrov Affair: Let's bury the Legend', *Bulletin*, 17 June 1980, p. 41.
10 ibid.
11 Michael Thwaites, *Truth Will Out: ASIO and the Petrovs*, Collins, Sydney, 1980, p. 55.
12 Paul, op. cit.
13 Murray, p. 177.
14 Alan Reid, Sydney *Sun*, 5 October 1954.
15 Mr Justice Owen, cited by Murray, p. 158.
16 *Age*, 16 August 1954.
17 Murray's *The Split* is the best available account.
18 Allan Dalziel, *Evatt The Enigma*, Lansdowne Press, Melbourne, 1967, pp. 168-70.

# 16 The Two Camps

1 Murray, *The Split*, p. 190.
2 J. Cain, cited by Murray, op. cit., p. 251.
3 H. V. Evatt, Victorian Labor Hour, 15 May 1955.
4 Murray, p. 179.
5 General de Gaulle, War Memoirs, *Unity 1942-1944*, Weidenfeld and Nicolson, London, 1959, p. 184.

# 17 Beginnings of Conflict

1 Murray, *The Split*, p. 129.
2 P. J. Duffy, S J, 'Catholic Judgements on the Origins and Growth of the A.L.P. Dispute 1954-61', Thesis submitted for the degree of Master of Arts in the University of Melbourne, 8 December 1967, p. 306.
3 See M. Charlesworth, *Catholic Worker*, December 1956, and my reply, Melbourne *Advocate*, 6 December 1956.

# 18 The Movement Divides

1 Letter from B. A. Santamaria to Bishop Lyons, 16 May 1951.
2 J. T. Kane, Personal Notes, 'Events in the NSW Branch of the ALP, 1953-56'.
3 Murray, *The Split*, p. 130.
4 Letter from Bishop Carroll to B. A. Santamaria, 4 August 1954.

## 364    19   The Movement Unwinds

1 Letter from Bishop Carroll to B. A. Santamaria, 27 October 1954.
2 Letter from Bishop Carroll to B. A. Santamaria, 28 November 1955.
3 ibid.
4 Letter from B. A. Santamaria to Bishop Carroll, 7 December 1955.

## 20   The Principles at Stake

1 See P. J. Duffy Thesis, op. cit., for the most complete compilation of memoranda, correspondence, etc., in which the two sides explained their respective positions.
2 Letter from Cardinal Gilroy to Australian Bishops, 2 August 1956.
3 Duffy, op. cit., p. 171.

## 21   The Plan of Campaign

1 Kane Notes, op. cit., pp. 15-16.
2 Joint Pastoral of Australian Bishops, 27 April 1955.
3 *Sydney Morning Herald*, 1 May 1955.

## 22   The Assault on New South Wales

1 J. T. Kane, Report re ALP Federal Executive, p. 18.
2 *Catholic Weekly*, 19 and 26 April 1956, 10 May 1956.
3 Letter to Movement Organizers, 20 June 1956.
4 Murray, *The Split*, p. 302.
5 J. T. Kane Notes, Events in NSW Branch of ALP 1953-1956, pp. 21-2.
6 ibid., p. 22.
7 ibid., p. 24.
8 ibid., p. 26.
9 Murray, p. 303.
10 *Sydney Morning Herald*, 12 and 13 June 1959.
11 Michael Carroll letter, *Sydney Morning Herald*, 24 June 1959 (supported by affidavit sworn on 25 October 1959).
12 Archbishop Romolo Carboni, *An Apostolic Delegate Speaks*, St Anthony's Guild, Paterson, New Jersey, 1961, p. 239.
13 T. Truman, *Catholic Action and Politics*, revised edition, Georgian House, Melbourne, 1960, p. 199.

## 23   Rome has its say

1 Letter of resignation of Movement officials to Bishops, 18 July 1956.
2 B. A. Santamaria, 'Religion and Politics', *Twentieth Century*, Winter 1960, pp. 368-9.

## 24   The 'Conscience' Issue

1 H. V. Evatt, Address in Wollongong, 24 March 1955.
2 Kane Notes, pp. 15-16.
3 Murray, p. 276.
4 Decree of the Congregation of the Holy Office, 13 July 1949.

5 *Age*, 14 August 1958.
6 *Sydney Morning Herald*, 15 November 1958.
7 Melbourne *Herald*, 19 November 1958.
8 Sydney *Daily Telegraph*, 21 November 1958.
9 Melbourne *Sun*, 21 November 1958.
10 ibid.
11 *Age*, 24 November 1958.
12 Letter from James McAuley to Archbishop Enrici, 23 March 1964.
13 Letter from Archbishop Enrici to James McAuley, 2 April 1964.
14 Letter from James McAuley to Archbishop Enrici, April 1964.

## 25   In Retrospect

1 e.g., P. L. Reynolds, *The Democratic Labor Party*, Jacaranda Press, Brisbane, 1974.

## 27   The National Civil Council

1 Murray, *The Split*, p. 351.

## 28   The Democratic Labor Party

1 P. L. Reynolds, *The Democratic Labor Party*, Jacaranda Press, Brisbane, 1974, p. 23.
2 M. Mackerras, 'DLP Preference Distribution', Table V, p. 11, cited in Reynolds, op. cit., p. 49.
3 Reynolds, op. cit., p. 53.
4 ibid., p. 49.
5 J. M. Tripovich, cited in DLP Column, Melbourne *Sun*, 22 January 1960.
6 *Bulletin*, 19 December 1964, p. 13.
7 R. Joshua, Presidential Address to Third Commonwealth Conference of DLP, in 'Speakers Notes', 1961 Elections, p. 28.
8 Reynolds, op. cit., pp. 58-9.
9 ibid., p. 59.
10 J. J. Mol, 'Church Schools and Religious Belief', *Australian and New Zealand Journal of Sociology* 4, no. 1, April 1968.
11 Reynolds, op. cit., p. 59.
12 Murray, *The Split*, p. 354.
13 Melbourne *Age*, 15 November 1963.
14 S. Lipski, ABC radio interview, 19 October 1979.
15 Professor Peter Wiles, 'The Need to know more about Vietnam', *Quadrant*, December 1979, p. 34.
16 P. J. Duffy, SJ, 'The Democratic Labor Party', in *Australian Politics: A Reader*, ed. Henry Mayer, Cheshire, Melbourne, 1966, p. 358.
17 P. Coleman, *Bulletin*, 15 February 1964, p. 20.

## 29   The Struggle for State Aid

1 Duffy, 'The Democratic Labor Party', p. 343.
2 ALP Official Report of Proceedings of 22nd Commonwealth Conference, Brisbane, March 1957, Resolution 136, p. 75.

366 3 M. C. Hogan, *The Catholic Campaign for State Aid*, published by Catholic Theological Faculty, St Patrick's College, Manly, NSW, printed by Catholic Truth Society, Hong Kong, 1978. p. 71.
4 Hogan, op. cit., p. vii.
5 ibid., pp. 74, 75-6.
6 ibid., p. 79.
7 ibid., p. 80.
8 Reynolds, *The Democratic Labor Party*, p. 50.
9 Hogan, op. cit., p. 85.
10 Don Smart, *Federal Aid to Australian Schools*, University of Queensland Press, St Lucia, 1978, p. 71.
11 B. A. Santamaria, *Archbishop Mannix: His Contribution to the Art of Public Leadership in Australia*, Melbourne University Press, 1978, p. 34.
12 B. A. Santamaria, 'Equality in Education', in *The Price of Freedom* (Second Edition), Hawthorn Press, Melbourne, 1966, p. 197.

## 30  James McAuley

1 Murray, *The Split*, p. 179.
2 McAuley, *Sydney Morning Herald*, 29 October 1954.
3 McAuley to Santamaria, 11 January 1955.
4 McAuley to Santamaria, 21 January 1955.
5 McAuley to Santamaria, 3 February 1955.
6 McAuley to Santamaria, 30 August 1955.
7 Santamaria to McAuley, 2 November 1955.
8 McAuley, 'Reflections on Poznan', vol. II, *Free Spirit*, no. 11, July 1956, pp. 1-2.
9 McAuley, Newman College Lecture, August 1958.
10 McAuley, *Sydney Morning Herald*, 1 September 1958.
11 McAuley to Santamaria, 1 June 1960.
12 James McAuley, *Collected Poems*, Angus & Robertson Paperback edition 1973, pp. 104-05.
13 R. Brissenden, 'The Wounded Hero: James McAuley's *Collected Poems*', *Southerly*, vol. 32, no. 4, 1972, pp. 267-77.
14 McAuley to Miss M. Lane, 13 April 1964.
15 McAuley, *Quadrant*, April 1970, p. 41.
16 McAuley, *Quadrant*, December 1976, p. 5.

## 31  The Unions: from Monk to Hawke

1 E. G. Whitlam, *Sydney Morning Herald*, 16 February 1966.
2 *Free Labor World*, May 1959.
3 ibid.
4 Liu Chang Sheng, *Peking Review*, 14 June 1960, pp. 13-14.
5 *Observer*, 15 October 1960, p. 3.
6 L. L. Sharkey, *The Trade Unions*, Current Book Distributors, Sydney, revised edition, 1961, see pp. 9-14.
7 L. Aarons, *Tribune*, 29 January 1969.
8 A. E. Monk, Address at Labour Day Dinner, 8 March 1969.
9 J. Palmada, *Tribune*, 28 April 1971.

## 32  Foreign Policy: from Tutelage to Independence

1 *Sydney Morning Herald*, 21 January 1966.
2 Barbara Ward, *Economist*, 7 March 1953, p. 683.

3 Hedley Bull, *Canberra Times*, 25 April 1970.
4 C. P. FitzGerald, *West Australian*, 22 January 1960.
5 Murray, *The Split*, p. 57.
6 *Peace or War? The Global Strategy of World Communism*, Renown Press, Carnegie, Vic., 1958, pp. 10-11.
7 'Meet the Press', Channel 9 TCN, Sydney, November 1959, in *Spotlight on Santamaria*, Hawthorn Press, Melbourne, 1960, pp. 64-6.
8 *Bulletin*, 16 February 1963, p. 30.
9 Alan Watt, *The Evolution of Australian Foreign Policy 1938-1965*, Cambridge University Press, 1968, p. 160.
10 ibid.
11 'The Idea of a Pacific Confederation', in *A Pacific Confederation?*, Proceedings of the Eighth Christian Social Week, Melbourne, 1-8 September 1963, printed by the Advocate Press for the Institute of Social Order, p. 11.
12 ibid., p. 18.
13 H. Holt, *Age*, 19 January 1966.
14 *News Weekly*, 26 January 1966.
15 Clark Clifford, *Foreign Affairs*, June 1969.
16 *Australian*, 19 June 1969.
17 *Social Survey*, November 1969, p. 316.
18 *Pravda*, 29 May 1969.
19 *Pravda*, 8 June 1969.
20 *Kommunist*, November 1968.
21 *Nusantara*, 17 June 1969.
22 Singapore *Mirror*, 25 August 1969.
23 *Hansard*, House of Representatives, 14 August 1969.
24 G. Freeth, interviewed by P. Samuel, *The Bulletin*, 22 August 1969.
25 Senator Gair, Address to S.A. State Conference of the DLP, 29 August 1969.
26 J. G. Gorton, interview in 'Four Corners', 30 August 1969.
27 J. G. Gorton, *Age*, 10 September 1969.
28 J. G. Gorton, *Age*, 16 September 1969.
29 *Izvestia*, cited by Hobart *Mercury*, 30 October 1969.
30 'Point of View' television commentary, 12 October 1969.
31 A. Fairhall, *Sydney Morning Herald*, 24 October 1969.
32 *Sydney Morning Herald*, 15 October 1969.
33 *Economist*, 22 August 1970.

## 33  The Youth Revolt

1 *Soviet News Bulletin*, 10 September 1967, p. 4.
2 James McAuley *Sydney Morning Herald*, 17 October 1967.
3 McAuley, *Advance Australia*, September 1966, pp. 3-4.
4 McAuley, 'Politics and the Counter-Culture', 14 March 1972.
5 Tom Hayden, *Australian*, 22 September 1975.
6 ibid.
7 Hayden, *International Herald Tribune*, 19 July 1978.
8 Sam Brown, *International Herald Tribune*, 19 July 1978.

## 34  The Impact of Vatican II

1 B. A. Santamaria, *Contraception: Reflections on the Pope's Ruling*, Freedom Publishing Co., Melbourne, 1968.
2 ibid., p. 6.
3 Paul Johnson, *New Statesman*, 28 April 1967.

368 | 4 James McAuley, Review of Russell Kirk's *Enemies of the Permanent Things*, *Quadrant*, April 1970, pp. 41-2.
5 Bryan Wilson, *Contemporary Transformations of Religion*, Oxford University Press, London, 1976, p. 116.
6 ibid., p. 28.
7 ibid., p. 29.
8 José Ortega y Gasset, *The Dehumanisation of Art*, Princeton University Press, Princeton, N.J., 1968, p. 45.
9 Duncan Williams, *Trousered Apes*, Arlington House, New York, 1971, pp. 62-3.
10 Robert Bolt, *A Man for All Seasons*, Heinemann Educational Books, London, 1960.
11 B. A. Santamaria, 'Point of View' Television Commentary, published in *News Weekly*, 22 March 1978.
12 Clifford Longley, London, *Age*, 9 August 1978, p. 9.
13 *Contraception*, p. 20.
14 For a general discussion of this episode see Ralph M. Wiltgen SVD, *The Rhine flows into the Tiber*, First British Edition, Augustine Publishing Co., Devon, 1978, pp. 272-8.
15 ibid., p. 278.
16 ibid., p. 273.
17 Leszek Kolakowski, 'God, Caesar and the Catholic Church', *Quadrant*, July 1979, pp. 39-42, *passim*.
18 Pope John Paul, Encyclical Letter *Redemptor Hominis*, 4 March 1979, p. 54.

## 35    From Whitlam to Fraser

1 *Canberra Times*, 29 June 1980.
2 *National Times*, 23-28 July 1973.
3 *Bulletin*, 2 October 1979, p. 40.
4 Daryl Dixon, Policy co-ordinator, Commonwealth Social Welfare Policy Secretariat, Address to Australian Pharmaceutical Manufacturers Association, 27 August 1979.
5 Peter Samuel, *Bulletin*, 5 June 1979, p. 107.
6 Colin Clark, 'Tax: Let the Poor Choose', Melbourne *Herald*, 27 May 1980.
7 Christopher Booker, 'The Unmentionable Issue', *Spectator*, 28 April 1979, pp. 12-13.
8 London *Tablet*, 14 June 1980, p. 572.
9 Karl Mannheim, 'The Great Society and the Loss of Self-Regulation', in *Private Life and Public Order: The Context of Modern Public Policy*, ed. T. J. Lowi, Norton & Co., New York, 1968, p. 85.

## Epilogue

1 Lord Keynes, *General Theory of Employment, Interest and Money*, Macmillan & Co., London, 1936, p. 378.

1958    *Peace or War? The Global Strategy of World Communism*, Address to Eighteenth National Convention of NCRM, April 1958

'China's Plans', *Observer*, 12 July 1958

'Migration and Australia's Future', Address to Christian Social Week, Melbourne, September 1958, published in *The Price of Freedom*

1959    *New Guinea: The Price of Weakness*, March 1959

1962    'The Under-Developed Nations in the Light of *Mater et Magistra*', Address to Eucharistic Congress in Manila, February 1962, published in *The Price of Freedom*

'Principles of National Defence Policy', Address to Christian Social Week, August 1962, published in *The Price of Freedom*

1963    'Realities of Power in Asia', originally published in abridged version as 'Why SEATO is Useless' in the *Bulletin*, 16 February 1963; and later in *The Price of Freedom*

'The Idea of a Pacific Confederation', published in *A Pacific Confederation?*, Proceedings of the Eighth Christian Social Week, September 1963

1966    *Determined to Survive*

1967    'The Holt Stereotype', *Quadrant*, July-August 1967, the text of an address given to the Victorian Branch of the Australian Institute of International Affairs, 18 April 1967

1969    'Russia Moves South and East', *Social Survey*, August 1969

'Soviet Advances and Australian Policy'. *Social Survey*, November 1969

'Australia's Strategic Situation', *Pacific Community*, No. 2, Spring 1969

1970    *The Defence of Australia*

1974    Address to Australian Institute of International Affairs, 23 October 1974

1975    'Australia's Commitment to Vietnam: We Had No Choice',
        *National Times*, 2-7 June 1975

1976    '1976', *Quadrant*, November 1976

1978    'The International Situation', *News Weekly*, 22 March 1978

1979    'An Australian View', *A.N.Z.U.S. in the Eighties*, published
        by Victorian Branch of Australian Defence Association

        In addition, there were numerous commentaries in the
        weekly television session 'Point of View', and in *News
        Weekly*; and many addresses, not published, given to various
        bodies, such as the Joint Staff Services College and RAAF
        Staff College in Canberra, and other organizations.

# Index

# INDEX